AESTHETICS
IN
FEMINIST
PERSPECTIVE

AESTHETICS IN FEMINIST PERSPECTIVE

Edited by
Hilde Hein and Carolyn Korsmeyer

INDIANA
UNIVERSITY
PRESS
Bloomington and Indianapolis

The paper used in this publication meets the minimum requirements of American
National Standards for Information Sciences—Permanence of Paper for Printed
Library Materials, ANSI Z39.48-1984.

 ™

Manufactured in the United States of America

Library of Congress Cataloging-in-Publication Data
Aesthetics in feminist perspective / edited by Hilde Hein and Carolyn Korsmeyer.
      p.   cm.
Includes bibliographical references and index.
ISBN 0-253-32861-6 (cloth : alk. paper). — ISBN 0-253- 20774-6 (paper : alk. paper)
   1. Aesthetics.   2. Feminist theory.   3. Feminism and the arts.   I. Hein, Hilde S., date.
II. Korsmeyer, Carolyn.
  HQ1219.A38 1993
  305.42'01—dc20

                                                                    92-23948

1 2 3 4 5   97 96 95 94 93

CONTENTS ✧✧✧

Philosophy, Aesthetics, and Feminist Scholarship

CAROLYN KORSMEYER

Feminism describes not only political movements but also intellectual perspectives informing scholarly investigation. After more than two decades of feminist scholarship, there is now hardly an academic discipline unchallenged by reflections on the operations of gender in research and theory. This has prompted widespread examination of disciplinary assumptions and methods, new understandings of the histories of fields and their classic texts, and refinement of awareness of how scholarship retains gender bias. Despite all the feminist analyses of art, literature, and philosophy that have appeared in the course of the last twenty-five years, philosophical aesthetics has remained relatively untouched until recently.[1] This late entry into feminist debates is an oddity, given developments in related fields, and may indicate just how much is at stake in feminist challenges to traditions in this area of study.

Virtually all feminist scholarship begins with a challenge to the assumption that disciplinary inquiry is gender-neutral. In no field is this more subversive than philosophy, which traditionally is typified by the aspiration to universality, that is, to the formulation of theories that pertain to all situations, all human beings, at all times. Within this discourse gender is presumed to disappear, taking its place among all the other accidental traits of human beings that are considered irrelevant to matters of philosophical scope. Thus in philosophy a gender-neutral stance is particularly tenacious because of the requirements of philosophical theory as it usually has been understood.

Feminism poses a deep challenge to this stance, since it probes for the presence of gender in virtually all conceptual schemes, however masked they may be by claims to generality and universality. In addressing questions about art, audience, perception, and interpretation from feminist points of view, the authors of the essays in this volume depart from several presumptions about aesthetic theory that have largely defined the field in the past. To see how feminist perspectives are developing within philosophical aesthetics we need to situate analyses of gender in relation to the traditions and history of this discipline and to discover how the mask of universality and gender-neutrality has operated in the field of aesthetics.

The modern traditions of aesthetics originate in eighteenth-century Europe, during which time analyses of beauty and pleasure focused attention on the characteristics of a particular variety of perception. Discussions of the nature of aesthetic pleasure from their beginnings through much of the twentieth century have been virtually uniform in their claim that apprehension of aesthetic qualities transcends personal interests and concentrates one's attention on the object of appreciation itself. Thus pure aesthetic attention is conceived to be incompatible with interest in other values, including moral and social values and cognitive concerns for truth and falsity. Preoccupation with one's own particular situation or interest is a standard mark of nonaesthetic attention. Because awareness of gender necessarily directs one's attention not only to the act of perception but also to the perceiver and her or his position within a social and political context, one of the revisions that feminism implies is the abandonment of the doctrine that a disinterested state of contemplative attention characterizes aesthetic appreciation and appropriate apprehension of art.

Some nonfeminist theories of the perception of aesthetic quality have also recently moved away from ideas about disinterested attention, concentrating instead on the role that convention and the perceiver's cultural fluency with the language of art play in defining appreciation and validity of critical interpretation.[2] While this move is more congenial to feminist approaches than its predecessors, these theories also by and large treat audiences as a uniform group, the taste of whose members (potentially and ideally) converges in similar judgments of taste and meaning. Feminist perspectives often challenge the idea of a generic perceiver altogether, and so the questions addressed in this book represent major changes in the way philosophical issues have been posed in aesthetics. Gone is the idea that we can speak of "the" act of appreciation and perception, and in its place is a complex model of readers and beholders whose particular genders, histories, and other "differences" such as race and cultural situation frame interpretation and the ascription of value. In this volume one finds no attempt to characterize the nature of appreciation and attention to art in any way that is general or universally binding. Rather, different modes of interpretation and perception and their abilities to disclose gendered meaning are the focus of inquiry. Gone as well is the idea that matters of "aesthetic" quality can be isolated from their traditional contraries: practical or instrumental value, moral significance, the exercise of political power. The answers to the questions posed from feminist perspectives are far from settled, but the framework within which they are formulated has altered the landscape of inquiry.

Debates over the general concept of art and the formulability of a definition that captures the essential qualities of art have also been a long-standing project of philosophical aesthetics. Feminist perspectives on this subject have reoriented inquiry to include consideration of the notable absence of women from among the canonical practitioners of the arts. Examination of the reasons for this have led to explorations of masculine bias as an integral structural element of the historic concepts of creativity, excellence, and artistic purpose.[3] In addition to criticizing gender bias in the basic concepts of art and aesthetic theory, feminists have centered attention on the artifacts women have produced, whether or not they have been counted among "art" objects. For example, while the authors of the essays in this volume consider work by women that is conventionally identified as fine art, they also extend their nets to include examination of fashion, political cartoons, and ritual dance, which normally are not accorded that status. Because standard quests for a definition of art do not yield answers in response to feminist questions, these questions illuminate the limits of the historic concept of art and prompt speculation about alternative concepts.

Let us now consider what marks the presence of feminist *philosophical* perspectives within theories of art and aesthetics broadly construed: What distinguishes philosophical feminist aesthetics from the many other theoretical studies that have advanced our understanding of gender in areas such as literature, film studies, and art history? The word "aesthetics" itself permits a number of different connotations. This term was coined for academic discourse and does not have a strong history in vernacular usage.[4] Philosophers usually speak of the "aesthetic" with reference to theories of perception of beauty and aesthetic quality, and especially to aesthetic qualities illustrated in critical discourse about the arts.[5] A number of different meanings have become attached to the term as well, including a general sense of style or the style of a particular artist or movement. Under this usage the boundary between criticism and philosophy becomes blurry.

Answers to this question are further complicated by the fact that feminist research tends to be interdisciplinary. This is deliberate, for many feminist scholars discovered early in their work that their own disciplines not only ignored gender but also lacked adequate disciplinary tools to revise their fields suitably to cope with issues of women's experience and gender differences. Few feminists give high priority to disciplinary purity, and eclectic studies have replaced narrower research methods. Just as feminist philosophy has benefited by the use of strategies of textual, representational, and psychological analyses, so too feminist scholars of literature and art have profited by employing philosophical views to illuminate their own studies.

It is therefore difficult to separate neatly the work of philosophers from that of other scholars in aesthetics, and indeed it would be pointless to do so. Nonetheless "interdisciplinary" does not describe a single style or method. Feminist studies, like any that draw upon the tools of several fields, are usually marked by some choice of method or approach. Though all of the essays in this collection address philosophical issues, not all are by philosophers, and the reader will notice that the different methodological orientations represented here to an extent mark the disciplines of the authors. Ten of the essays are by philosophers, and most of these contributions emerge from the analytic traditions that characterize anglophone philosophy in the twentieth century. (The authors come from the United States, Australia, and New Zealand.) The essays by Barwell and Robinson and Ross, for example, have evident roots in this methodological tradition. Nineteenth- and twentieth-century European philosophy is the point of reference of other philosophers such as Newman. A European orientation has been especially influential in recent literary studies, and this is evident in the essays by Henderson and Donovan. In addition to philosophy and English literature, the authors of the essays gathered here include scholars from music, psychology, and African American studies.

Philosophy, musicology, literature, film, and visual arts all provide substance for the explorations of these essays. While they exhibit no single theme or perspective, many of the authors share an interest in examining the supposition that there might be a distinctively "feminine" or "female" or "woman's" domain within art and conceptual schemes related to art. Some of the authors are inclined to defend a distinct area of "female" cultural artifacts, while others regard that claim with skepticism. Topics discussed range through the history of philosophy, cross-cultural studies of music, the work of modern women artists, literary texts, suffragist cartoons, movies, and fashion. Many of the authors are interested in clarifying such concepts as *feminine, female,* and *feminist* and in explicating their suitability as descriptors for cultural objects produced by women. In addition, whatever their respective positions regarding the presence of feminine styles and themes in art, most contributors are on guard against essentialism and the implication that women's nature is fixed in some enduring feminine essence.

The opening essay, "Refining Feminist Theory: Lessons from Aesthetics," by Hilde Hein, is a rumination on traditional philosophical methods developed to cope with the diversities of art and on their potential usefulness for feminist theories struggling with issues of pluralism. Feminist challenges to traditional research have often begun with the disclosure of masculine bias in the "universal" voice of generalization, and thus incursions of feminism into scholarship have resulted in a certain splitting, even fragmenting, of inquiry along gender lines and other marks of identity. This pluralization is regarded as salutary, although conceptual unity and the ability to generalize may seem to be threatened. Aesthetics has a long-standing respect for diversity while remaining committed to the discovery of unity within it. Because aesthetics has always dealt with multiplicity in considering various art forms and individual artworks, its methodology, once freed of the burden of universal laws of perception and interpretation, clears the way for the development of feminist theories of art and experience, and for feminist theory generally. Hein places feminism and aesthetic theory in stride with one another, orienting feminist aesthetic theory as a model for feminist philosophy and ultimately for philosophical theory as a whole.

The following essays are grouped according to theme. As they are arranged, the contributions to each section move from general theoretical explorations to more particular illustrative treatments of specific art forms or artists. The latter thereby serve as models and invitations to continue similar analyses.

Part II, "The Nature of Art: Some Feminist Alternatives" includes essays that consider the dominant concepts of art in the recent Western philosophical tradition, speculating upon alternative feminist conceptual schemes that take women's projects as their origin and inspiration. Estella Lauter examines the works of a variety of contemporary women artists in "Re-enfranchising Art: Feminist Interventions in the Theory of Art." She notes ways in which feminist views of art raise new questions for traditional aesthetic theory, which she characterizes as "formalist." She argues that feminist art, with its emphasis on connection with social and community concerns and its rejection of the isolation of the aesthetic from all other values, has the potential to reestablish art as a central force in society. Lauter is also persuaded that there are shared stylistic features that distinguish women's art, and thus her essay on visual art concurs with the essay that follows.

Renée Lorraine shifts our attention to music in her advocacy of "A Gynecentric Aesthetic." She identifies several features of certain traditional forms of music that are signs of its connection with woman-centered traditions, including participation by all members of a group (rather than performance by an individual or small group for a passive audience), a mingling of aesthetic and erotic elements, and a sense of art as one of the aesthetic instruments of daily life. Ancient European and traditional African music are compared, using the tools of anthropological surmise, feminist theory, and musicology. Lorraine concludes with the hypothesis that despite cultural differences, there are important musical features shared cross-culturally that can be identified as "gynecentric" and that may serve as a model for ideal feminist artistic expression.

Josephine Donovan explores a feminist concept of art in terms of a "nondominative" aesthetic. In "Everyday Use and Moments of Being: Toward a Nondominative Aesthetic," she draws attention to an aspect of creativity prevailing in such influential theories as Kant's, by which the artist distances and subdues or masters his subject in the act of creativity. This drive to master, she argues, is inimical to the approach espoused and manifest in the work of such writers as Virginia Woolf, Willa Cather, and Alice Walker, who develop the idea of art in everyday domestic crafts and activities. Donovan ties these values with Adorno's notion of art as a "negative critique" of a world where objects are viewed principally in terms of commodity exchange. She melds recent Marxist ideas and the work of these authors to formulate an alternative, nondominative aesthetic congenial to feminism.

Artistic creativity and audience participation are the subjects that frame a statement of purpose by Marilyn French, who asks "Is there a feminist aesthetic?" from the dual point of view of a literary scholar and novelist. A feminist perspective, she observes, "endorses" female experience in such a way as to reveal inadequacies of the moral and social dimensions of patriarchy. She sets out certain principles of feminist art, including its accessibility to widely diverse female audiences. At the same time, she acknowledges the difficulties that must be confronted in order to forge a new, untraditional language of feeling appropriate to capture female experience. The politics that surface with such endeavors are clear in French's piece, which also confronts the choices that feminist artists have to make in crafting their projects. Here we see that theory and practical engagement are inextricably linked.

As a specific type of practical engagement, cartoons published in the service of the woman suffrage movement constitute a particular genre of feminist art. These are the subject for Alice Sheppard's "Suffrage Art and Feminism." She observes an interesting twist in these cartoons, for they both confirm and perpetuate the traditional view of women as virtuous and caring, but they also challenge the social roles assigned to women and demand specific political change. Thus, for example, though feminist cartoonists represent women with stereotypic maternal qualities, these are portrayed in terms of public political strength rather than as merely domestic virtues. Sheppard sketches out a typology of female styles of cartoons and the imagery they employ, noting that what counts as "feminine" in style often reflects particular cultural attitudes.

The essays in Part III, "Interpretation and Point of View," address the complexities that arise when art is ascribed feminine or female points of view. The first three entries in this section take literature as their focus.

Ismay Barwell in "Feminine Perspectives and Narrative Points of View" offers a painstaking critique and defense of the idea that there can be a distinctively feminine voice that appears in texts so diverse that they seem to defy such generalization. She argues that the project of finding a *universal* feminine voice is fruitless, for the voices of women are also the voices of people of different back-grounds living in different cultures, different times, and different social conditions. However, with the construction of an analytical scheme that identifies narrative points of view within specific texts, one can make sense of the "organization of texts" from feminine points of view, thereby vindicating the idea that there is such a thing as a "feminine aesthetic."

In "Women, Morality, and Fiction," Jenefer Robinson and Stephanie Ross argue a skeptical position regarding the proposition that there is a discernible feminine or female voice to be found in literature. They put together the psychological research on moral reflection of Carol Gilligan, who argues for a gendered "different voice," with Martha Nussbaum's advocacy on behalf of a moral philosophy to be found in the novels of Henry James. Robinson and Ross examine the claim that feminine attitudes are distinctively caring, particular, and attentive to detail, arguing that, at best, this affirmation echoes stereotypes of the female rather than disclosing characteristically feminine properties. They conclude by exploring what features might distinguish a reader response that is distinctly *feminist*.

In "Speaking in Tongues: Dialogics, Dialectics, and the Black Woman Writer's Literary Tradition," Mae Gwendolyn Henderson uses Gadamer and Bakhtin as authors of contrapuntal theories that jointly illuminate the complex position of black female subjects in literature. Bakhtin's dialogic approach is adversarial and aptly describes the difference between the subject and others that she experiences as a result of her position at a point where multiple social forces converge. Gadamer's dialectic foregrounds the experience of fusion and of continuous fellow-ship within a community. Henderson argues that black female subjects in novels illustrate both "glossolalia"—the scriptural speaking in tongues that is not under-stood by those outside the fellowship of the inspired—and "heteroglossia"—the ability to speak multiple languages from multiple positions. She illustrates this theoretical point with analyses of novels by Zora Neale Hurston, Sherley Anne Williams, and Toni Morrison.

Some of the most powerful theories of perception, methods of identifying the male gaze, and analyses of women as objects of that gaze have arisen within studies of film. Laurie Shrage's "Feminist Film Aesthetics: A Contextual Approach" critically explores several trends in feminist film criticism, offering in place of psychoanalytic and semiotic schemes of analysis a method that is more sensitive to the cultural formation of viewers' sensibilities. Using the film *Christopher Strong* as a focus for study, Shrage argues for the presence of a feminist dimension to films that her contextual approach is able to disclose. This essay, like Robinson and Ross's "Women, Morality, and Fiction," strives to isolate the dimensions of interpretation and meaning that can be described as feminist.

Painter Georgia O'Keeffe was an artist who—in spite of her protests—was lauded for expressing female sexuality when her work became acclaimed in the early twentieth century. In "A Woman on Paper," San MacColl compares this early interpretation of sexuality in O'Keeffe's work with later feminist adoption of O'Keeffe as a feminist progenitor in the 1970s, noting how the artist herself resisted both categories. MacColl explores various meanings of "feminine" and "female" that were attributed to O'Keeffe's work and how such critical approaches necessarily reflect a climate of understanding of sexuality and society, as well as appreciation of the artworks themselves. As with Sheppard's piece, the historically shifting terrain of "the feminine" is explored in this essay.

Part IV, "Philosophical and Critical Legacies," introduces the reader to selected aspects of the history of philosophy and critical traditions and feminist readings of that history. The section opens with two essays on one of the most influential philosophers in the Western tradition, Immanuel Kant. In "Beautiful Exiles," Mary Bittner Wiseman considers the process of reading philosophy when one is female and the "displacements" that occur with the awareness that the investigatory voice of philosophical texts is invariably male. Her treatment includes not only Kant's *Observations on the Beautiful and Sublime* but also texts from Plato, Aristotle, and Descartes. Traditionally women read such texts as men, she observes, identifying with the investigatory "we" of philosophical analysis. But it is possible for women to read *as* women, thereby bringing to the foreground apparently peripheral observations about gender. Wiseman uses Kant's text to demonstrate how women readers, while initially excluded, can reenter the text with the awareness of gender differences invoked as a ground of contrast, as between the feminine/beautiful and the masculine/sublime. Wiseman demonstrates how consciousness of one's "displaced" position can give the aware female reader additional insight into the meaning of a text and its governing concepts.

Jane Kneller's "Discipline and Silence: Women and Imagination in Kant's Theory of Taste" looks closely at the concepts of taste and femininity in Kant's later writings, particularly the *Critique of Judgment* and *Anthropology from a Pragmatic Point of View*. Women and the faculty of imagination function in parallel ways, according to Kant's analysis. The imagination must be bound by the strict governance of the understanding in the development of taste, just as women must be governed by their husbands for purposes of morality and familial and social order. This hierarchy, Kneller argues, impoverishes Kant's grasp of both taste and morals. She outlines the possibilities for transforming Kant's insights to serve feminist philosophy, correcting his masculine bias and adjusting his perspective on the nature and power of the imagination. These two essays on Kant present different perspectives on the criticism and reclamation of a major theorist, and the methods they employ invite similar analyses of other philosophical texts.

Amy Newman's "Aestheticism, Feminism, and the Dynamics of Reversal" offers a slant on the postmodern movement and its suitability for feminist inquiry by looking at the precursor theories of Nietzsche and the nineteenth-century European "aestheticist" movement. She locates in both the older theories and their contemporary offspring a dangerous masculine bias that she thinks feminists need beware. This caution is directed particularly at the postmodern idea of the fragmented "subject" or self, which she argues subverts feminist efforts to locate, explore, and strengthen understandings of female perspectives and experiences.

Another slant on postmodernism is presented by Michele Wallace in "Modernism, Postmodernism, and the Problem of the Visual in Afro-American Culture." Wallace begins with consideration of the tensions present in visual perception of beauty among children who grew up in segregated America, as it was studied by sociologists in the 1950s. Unlike music and even literature, the visual art of Afro-Americans has remained largely invisible, Wallace argues. While modernist painting was significantly influenced by African art, that art was labeled "primitive" and kept at a distance from the modernist movement. These separate categories have obscured the participation of black artists in the development of modernism, a problem that continues with postmodernism. Moreover, in both these movements the black female subject frequently is still allotted the status of the exotic or the primitive, losing subjectivity of her own. Like Henderson, Wallace views the confluence of race and gender in art as one of the critical points of attention for feminist criticism and cultural understanding.

The text of Samuel Beckett's *Molloy* fuses the reading of literature and philosophy in "Analogy as Destiny: Cartesian Man and the Woman Reader." Carol H. Cantrell examines Beckett's novel and its Cartesian exploration of "the" self, a self that, she argues, is in fact markedly masculine. This specific text is the vehicle for a critique of the idea that "the human condition" is a unitary experience that overrides gender differences. It is thus an argument against the idea that the apparently universal claims of philosophy are really gender-free and unbiased. By situating Cartesian metaphysics in the framework of literature, Cantrell reveals masculine biases that might go unnoticed in the more abstract language of the philosophical text. This essay is a particular example of discovering "points of view" in a literary text, and it can be seen as a continuation of the exploration of strategies of reading philosophy advanced by Wiseman in "Beautiful Exiles."

From this general perspective we move to a specific and rather unusual topic for aesthetics, fashion. Karen Hanson expands the role of the aesthetic beyond conventionally defined art in her defense of beautiful clothing in "Dressing Down Dressing Up: The Philosophic Fear of Fashion." She finds in traditional philosophy not only the male-female dualisms widely noted in feminist theory (and explored in Cantrell's "Analogy as Destiny" as well) but a related emphasis on the value of the mind over the body. This, she believes, has contributed to misplaced sobriety and bad humor when philosophers consider dress, and she advises feminists to challenge this disposition in evaluating their own positions and visions for the future.

The six essays in Part IV, of course, represent only a small sampling of the possible adaptation of feminist analyses to philosophical and aesthetic theories. They are intended to orient the reader to the problematics of reading for gender within the philosophical and critical traditions that have shaped our consciousnesses. They alert us to the possibilities for transforming traditions to reduce masculine biases in the experience and assessment of art. This section, like the preceding two, closes with an implicit invitation to the reader to venture beyond the studies given and pursue similar questions with additional art and art forms in mind.

It will be clear from this summary that the essays collected here speak with each other in more than one way, and that their arrangement under four categories represents but one of several combinatory possibilities. The history of philosophies of art is examined for gender bias and for reclamatory potential; theories of art and interpretation are investigated to discover whether there is anything distinctive about artifacts created by women; and the parameters of female or feminist perspectives as expressed in art, music, film, and literature are explored. As interpretive theories of art are examined for gender bias, the history of aesthetic theory is shown to require reexamination as well. These feminist enterprises pose questions that are new to philosophical aesthetics and proffer answers that, taken together, invite further and deeper examination of gender and cultural life.

Notes

1. *Hypatia* 5: 2 (Spring 1990), the special issue upon which this collection is based, was the first philosophy journal issue in English devoted to feminist perspectives in aesthetics.

2. See, for examples, Arthur Danto, *The Transfiguration of the Commonplace* (Princeton: Princeton University Press, 1980); George Dickie, *Art and the Aesthetic* (Ithaca: Cornell University Press, 1974) and *Evaluating Art* (Philadelphia: Temple University Press, 1988); and Joseph Margolis, *Art and Philosophy* (Atlantic Highlands, 1978). John Dewey's *Art as Experience* (New York: Milton, Balch, 1934) is an early and important exception to the tradition here discussed.

3. A recent examination of the masculine concept of artistic genius, for example, is to be found in Christine Battersby, *Gender and Genuis: Towards a Feminist Aesthetics* (Bloomington: Indiana University Press, 1989). See also Parker and Pollack, *Old Mistresses* (London: Routledge and Kegan Paul, 1981), and Linda Nochlin, "Why Have There Been No Great Women Artists?" in *Art and Sexual Politics*, T. Hess and E. Baker, eds. (New York: Macmillan, 1973).

4. Alexander Baumgarten introduced the term in his *Aesthetica* of 1750; he used it to refer to the sort of inferior, nonrational cognition that one attains through beautiful objects and art. In the course of the work, Baumgarten shifted the connotation of the original Greek term, which meant sense perception, to refer to a general study of a sense of beauty or taste. This usage was later adopted by Kant in the *Critique of Judgment*. Ever since its introduction into modern languages, philosophers have alternately been at pains to specify its meaning and complained about its vagueness.

5. Some standard treatments of this theme include Frank Sibley, "Aesthetic Concepts," *Philosophical Review* LXVII (1959), 421-50; J. O. Urmson, "What Makes a Situation Aesthetic?" *Proceedings of the Aristotelian Society* 31 (1957-58), 75-92; and Monroe Beardsley, "The Aesthetic Point of View," in *Contemporary Philosophic Thought*, Howard E. Kiefer and Milton K. Munitz, eds. (Albany: State University of New York Press, 1970), 219-37.

PART ONE

Aesthetics, Feminism, and Methodology

ONE

Refining Feminist Theory
Lessons from Aesthetics

HILDE HEIN

Because it embraces a domain that is invincibly pluralistic and dynamic, aesthetic theory can serve as a model for feminist theory. Feminist theory, which takes gender as a constituted point of departure, pluralizes theory, thereby challenging its unicity. This anomalous approach to theory is also implicit in conventional aesthetics, which has for that reason been spurned by centrist philosophy. While aesthetics therefore merits attention from feminists, there is reason to be wary of such classic aesthetic doctrines as the thesis that art is "autonomous" and properly perceived "disinterestedly." That belief has roots in somatophobic dualism which ultimately leads to consequences as negative for art and the aesthetic as for women. Feminists rightly join with other critics of traditional dominative dualisms; yet they can learn from the expansive tendency in aesthetics toward openness and self-reflexive innovation.

WHY THEORY?

Controversy persists over the need that feminism has for theory. I am a partisan of theory although I acknowledge the defects identified by its detractors. Properly used, without reverence but with respect, theory can take us beyond anecdote to experience that is enriched and enlightened. I believe that feminist practice stands to benefit from well-developed theory, but we need to reconceptualize what theory is and does. I will argue here that feminist theory can learn from the theoretical discipline of aesthetics. I do not have in mind a feminist aesthetics, i.e., an aesthetic theory conceived by feminists for the elaboration of a feminist ideology.[1] Such an aesthetics is certainly desirable, and some of my colleagues in this volume are working to produce one, but I will discuss something much more conventional, namely a discourse drawn from the typically male-identified claims of aesthetic theory and meant to illuminate those experiences, objects, and concepts classically associated with beauty and with art and its cognates. To be sure, such discourse put to the use of feminism may eventually affect aesthetic theory as well, a consequence dearly to be hoped for, if not yet foreseen. My chief point here, however, is that conventional aesthetic theory has unique relevance for feminism in view not only of the issues it addresses but, more importantly, of the manner in which they are addressed. Aesthetic theory, though motivated by the same drive to bring about order and unity that dominates all conventional theorizing, is bound by the peculiarities of the domain it covers to be uniquely open-ended and to preserve the diverse and disorderly. Indeed, it is obliged to cherish such "defects" in the world. Aesthetics can no more transcend the perversely fluid messiness of the ordinary and commonplace than ignore the extraordinary and irreproducible. Its very identity is rooted in such contradictions.

Science has given us the working paradigm of theory that assigns to it the task of simplification and reduction. Given the bewildering profusion of experience, men have sought, as long as history records, to make that complex manifold intelligible in terms of some principle, author, primeval stuff, or reified relation— and thereby to diminish its terror. The pattern tends to reproduce itself. Once in place, it dictates the character of future understanding. It limits the what as well as the how of experience, displacing more fundamental encounters with its own articulation. Theory overflows into interpretation, becoming not only a filter of reality but the standard of what is real. Theory provides the terms in which reality is conceivable, controlling the means of its expression and the language of its legitimization. With the aid of theory experiences can be described, understood, ranked, and submitted to a semblance of control; without theory, we live, mutely, in a tower of Babel. Surely theory—or the capacity to produce it—is a boon to humanity.

In the realm of the senses, however, and more broadly in the domain that I provisionally call the experiential, there is a certain resistance. That superfluity we sometimes identify with the aesthetic and memorialize through such acts of imagination as art creation does not readily succumb to simplification. While refusing to be discounted as private hallucination or rant, it will not be reduced to a common core and flees the formulaic. Anyone who dares to contrive a theory of the aesthetic is challenged not just to accommodate plurality, as any theory must, or to tolerate diversity, as liberal social theories profess to do, but to embrace that very ground of confusion—indeed to increase and intensify it. Moreover, the recognition of aesthetic diversity entails appreciating that the various objects met with modify one another and are variably modified, perhaps even to the point of mutual annihilation. The pursuit of the aesthetic leads at last to the embrace of the nonaesthetic and the antiaesthetic, as these are drawn into the aura of aesthetic valuation (Binkley 1977). Even the most ponderously unifying of aesthetic theories, those most intent upon discovering and replicating an overarching order, divine or rational, in the chaos of the given, nevertheless resort in the face of that complexity to metaphors of organic dynamism, holistic interactivity, and innovation—to generative myths of order-in-variety and unity-in-diversity, or to symbolisms of multilayered, ambiguous meaning and/or structures. They cannot otherwise countenance the constant reconfigurations whose presence they both justify and deplore. Aesthetic theory is inherently grounded in paradox and has been so recognized by all major aesthetic theorists from Plato to the present.

I shall argue that because aesthetics has never entirely betrayed or abandoned its openness to all kinds and grades of experience, has never denied its association with transient pleasure or yielded to the impulse to conflate that with something more permanent and austerely abstract, it remains, however deficient, a model for feminist theorizing. Aesthetic theory has always appreciated the unique and singular individual—even while yearning for the universal. No aesthetic theory is simply reductionist.[2] The things that win aesthetic attention are irreducibly unique, singular, and discoverable only through intimate acquaintance.[3] Yet, miraculously, we share and communicate our experiences of them, although they cannot be predicted and no single explanation will suffice to make them intelligible to all perceivers at all times. One does not step twice into the same aesthetic stream; each encounter is new and transformative.

Feminist theorists have been struggling with similar dilemmas of diversity and singularity. Lately come to the discovery of plurality and difference among themselves and to an appreciation of its significance, many feminists now repudiate as a relic of an ideology of oppression the belief in a single feminine nature or essence that is transcendent of class, race, history, or culture. Although dubious of such universalism and essentialism, and therefore mistrustful of the traditional metaphysics and epistemology that endorse them, some feminists nevertheless see a need for theory. Some are attracted to postmodernism's assault on traditional foundationalism, agreeing with its celebration of difference and the contextualization of judgment that it sanctions (Harding, 1986a, 1986b; Fraser 1989). Postmodernism appears, oddly, to offer a way-station between the new need for immediate activism and the old demand for a comforting discipline. Other feminists, wary of postmodernist relativism and nihilism, are seeking different theoretical answers to the problems inherited from traditional philosophy (Hawkesworth 1989); Herrnstein-Smith 1988). I believe, along with other critics of postmodernism, that its exuberant posture disguises a position ultimately born of desperation. (That attribution would not, of course, be sufficient reason for declaring it mistaken, though I think it is.) Pushed to the renunciation of objective standards of truth and validity, postmodernism (in some of its formulations) declares all judgments to be equally nonrational and contingent. But, as the critic Barbara Herrnstein-Smith points out (1988), that conclusion is strictly a *non sequitur*: It does not follow from the failure of objectivism that there are no other parameters by which judgments may be measured. Why should we believe that order and meaning are achieved only in conformity with a single canon of principles established by a self-appointed cohort of authorities? The privilege of declaring meaning, once reserved to an arguably rational God and now democratized, is so proliferated in the delegation that no one signification ostensibly carries more weight than any other. While some read in this situation an invitation to the use of force, others exult in their liberation from it. Those decrying authority dispossessed are in effect making the arrogant claim that if I am not right, there is no right; if the truth is not mine to decree, then there is no truth. While appearing to renounce all theory, they are reaffirming by negation the very theory they renounce, namely their own conviction that one and only one confirmatory system is valid.[4] The question is—whose? One cannot abdicate power one has not held. Women have not been in a position to confer meaning and reality. Having never been the arbiters of the right, the true, and the beautiful, women have no stake in losing that status (Harding 1986b). Women's rebellion against the monolithic claims of conventional theorizing, therefore, does not represent the same sacrifice of privilege that it does for men, and it does not automatically link women to postmodernist nominalism (Alcoff 1988). It is, I believe, an error to interpret a superficially similar attraction to diversity as reflecting political unanimity with postmodernism or even conceptual congruence with it.

Is there, then, an alternative way to theorize? Some feminists advocate a new definition of theory that decenters, displaces, and foregrounds the inessential and that does not flee from experience but "muses at its edges" (Young-Bruehl 1987). If the essence of theory is to unify, and if gender entails a binary order (at least), then genderized theory is a contradiction, yet one that we can hardly avoid. Feminism has no choice but to recast theory; yet in so doing, it makes apparent nonsense of the very concept of theory. Or at least it suggests yet another turn from the one to the many.

The reconceptualization of theory began with reflection upon the theory of gender but was quickly driven to a general reassessment of thinking and so to the audacious conclusion that theoretical thought is genderized.[5] Once gender ceases to be represented as an object of study and is seen as a relation of power, a reshuffling of the comparative status of subject and object necessarily elevates the former object of study to a state of subjectivity. The thinking being suffers no loss of gender, since gender modifies its thought. Feminist theorists are committed to the legitimacy of a genderized cast of thought and to dethroning a view of theory that would discredit it.

GENDER THEORY: FROM THE THEORY OF GENDER
TO THE GENDER OF THEORY

Typically feminist theory has had to do with gender. In the eyes of most of the world that is what feminism is all about. The distinction made between the biological polarity of reproductive sex, male and female, and the social attribute of gender, masculine and feminine, was an important constatation, and feminists have been much occupied with exploring implications that might follow from gender. Following De Beauvoir's observation that one is not born a woman but becomes one, feminists have also found that one does so differently depending on whether one is rich or poor, Moslem, Jewish, Christian, white, black, French, Chinese, American, lesbian, heterosexual, urban, rural, etc., etc. The ways of being a woman do seem infinite in their variety; but they are clearly discernible from the equally infinite variety of ways of being a man.[6] In fact, gender seems not to be a category at all, but rather a way of qualifying *adverbially* the many things we do and are, these becoming appropriated as we are normally acculturated in our overlapping social identities. Gender, while apparently not reducible to either ontology or epistemology, is also not quite voluntary. One may not be born a woman, but once identified by gender, one learns rather rapidly, and almost without conscious effort, how to think consistently like one.

It is quite possible that all or most experience is gendered, implying that one's activities are adverbially genderized. On this view gender is not an antecedently bifurcated ground of being, upon which other features are fused, but a qualifier of how (not who) we are (Le Doeuff 1981).[7]

Might it not be that gender comes into being through and as a result of practice rather than prior to it? Some people, indeed, do strive to evade an appointed gender identity by exhibiting behavior considered atypical, eccentric, odd, or pathological, while others strive, perhaps unconsciously, to realize a stereotypic model of gender identity.[8] The former way of being is no less adaptive to a historic reification of gender than the latter. Both ways affirm the basic duality of gender.

Genderized thinking is not confined, however, to thinking about gender. Woman-ly (man-ly) thinking is not thinking *about* women (men); it is simply thinking *as* a woman (man). The adverbial quality of gendered thinking (behavior, etc.) applies to whatever one does or thinks about. One goes through life learning how to do it according to the conventions of one's society, and, of course, one can flout those conventions—but only after having learned them.

The gender equivocity of certain thoughts and actions is puzzling and elusive. Though performed by both sexes, walking, talking, eating, sitting are not done in the same way. They are gender-specific as well as culture-specific. A Japanese woman does not walk like a Japanese man, and neither walks like an American man or woman. Woman-ly heroism is not the same anywhere as its man-ly counterpart. (Typically it has more to do with endurance than with agency.) There really is such a thing as "throwing like a girl"—in part a function of anatomy, I maintain, but Iris Young has a more complex analysis (Young 1988). It seems that even reading and writing, not to mention seeing, hearing, and especially listening, are adverbially modified by gender. Moreover, gender identity is generally thought to include certain attitudes toward the "opposite sex," thereby constituting bipolar sexuality, if not heterosexuality, within the very concept of gender (Rich 1980). If that is the case, then not only gender but its concomitant polarity and therewith the inevitability of otherness are inescapable. Knowing oneself as woman is to know oneself as the other (De Beauvoir 1972). Thus theorizing gender brings us face to face with the ineluctable paradox of difference; and where there is difference there is the possibility that things might be other than they are.

Feminism, unlike gender, is a matter of choice. One can choose not to be a feminist, or by not choosing not become one. The default mode remains nonfeminist. One is definitely not born a feminist; nor does one become a feminist *par hasard* or simply in consequence of being gendered female.[9] To be a feminist is to be a self-designated other, and this choice entails acknowledging the determinative role of gender. It does not follow that all feminists hold a theory of gender, although some have undertaken to formulate such a theory in the interest of advancing feminism. These theorists may be motivated by an interest in thought as well as in gender, and this is where traditional aesthetics can be of use.[10]

AESTHETIC THEORY AS A MODEL
FOR FEMINIST THEORY

Aesthetic theory has a long and discontinuous history that changes with its object. Scientific theory changes too; but not on the supposition that its object changes.

It is commonly assumed only that its object has been imperfectly understood, and that theory will change as that object becomes better known. (The idea that the object itself should have any part in this understanding is almost unheard of.) Dissenters following Popper, Kuhn, Feyerabend, and Lakatos may disagree on what drives theoretical change in science, but few would argue that the instability of the universe is the cause, since the uniformity of nature is the major presupposition that makes science and its theory possible.[11]

Aesthetic theory, by contrast, thrives on the inconstancy and inconsistency of its domain, that being defined in accordance with a "discourse of reasons," itself a matter of controversy.[12] The "artworld" is unstable by choice, the more so since its existence is contingent upon an ever-changing pool of private sensibilities.

Aesthetic experience, like gender, is quintessentially qualifying, or adverbial. The manner of experiencing—not the object—is modified. It is commonly held that anything can be experienced aesthetically—or not—at one and the same moment, by the same or different persons. Moreover, we invite others to share our perceptions aesthetically by taking them with us to experience what we experience and to talk about that experience together. (Do you see that. . . ? Try squinting when you look at it . . . stand over here. Have you thought of it in this light. . . ? In relation to . . . compared with. . . ?) The dispensation of information or abstract principles has a place in such conversations, but it is incidental to communicative sharing of the experience itself.[13] What then is communicated or shared?

Philosophical aestheticians have long been troubled by certain paradoxes, not the least of which is the reliability of our aesthetic judgments, grounded as they are in the shifting sands of personal experience. It is mystifying that an experience so intensely private as one's response to a work of art should command assent from others. Most human affections do not carry such authority. I do not expect the world to love my lover or to find my children and grandchildren as adorable as I do. Aesthetic rightness or fitness has an insistent imperative quality reminiscent of the categorical (thou must) that issues from neither rule nor principle (Mothersill 1984). The very identification of the aesthetic, let alone what is a "work of art," defies logic.[14] Moreover, the sources of aesthetic delight are multifarious and obscure. We are capable of deriving intense aesthetic pleasure from things we know to be horrible, sometimes finding this very enjoyment a cause for ethical anguish—a state which, in its own turn, can yield a redoubled, doubly disturbing second-order aesthetic gratification.[15] Aesthetic pleasure delights in its own delight and so is endlessly convoluted. The aesthetic dimension, in a manner of speaking, rides "piggy back" *ad infinitum* on all our experiences, thoughts, and feelings. We can divert our attention away to consider things refracted otherwise, but the aesthetic is a presence accessible to, if not directly before, consciousness. It haunts the edges of being, sometimes lightly (with apologies to Milàn Kundera), sometimes comically, sometimes sweetly or tragically or surreally, sometimes lucidly and sometimes salvifically; but unless we are asleep or anesthetized, it is there always as a gloss upon experience undergone.

Sometimes we yield ourselves wholly to the aesthetic having of an experience. Nothing is beyond credibility or incapable of acceptance if rendered aesthetically convincing—a tribute to the mysterious force of aesthetic persuasion that can be alarming ethically or unsettling of one's commitment to rationality. But this is not a matter of meeting standard truth conditions or complying with practical norms. Indeed it invites aestheticians to formulate new patterns of assent that complement ordinary logic.[16]

Cognitive and ethical theories identify warrantability with the capacity to ground the particular in the general or to make intellectually elegant hypothetical derivations. Aesthetic theory finds no comfort in such reductions but multiplies the puzzles it is given and intensifies complexity to achieve an aesthetic parallel to confirmation. Conventional aesthetic theory has by no means abandoned all its claims to universal assent; but it is regularly driven to discard the usual means of obtaining it. Where science consolidates, making once "breakthrough" discoveries into routine assumptions and methodologies of future procedures, aesthetic theory gives new meaning to the past, transforming it to meet present sensibilities that leave the future uncertain as ever. It is precisely the non-normativeness of present *seeming* that aesthetics attends to. Drawn to the logic of appearances, aesthetic theory reclaims the superficial and subverts what science has reified as substance. Aesthetics magnifies what science neglects, the inessential objects whose place in history is indeterminate. Where scientific theory illuminates by creating order, aesthetic theory, like art, augments confusion under cover of heightened experience.

Foundationalist philosophers undoubtedly intended their aesthetic reflections to conform to the same rigorous standards that constrained their other theorizing. However, their success has been mixed. The field of aesthetics seems to tolerate a degree of incoherence and tentativeness that in other areas is debunked as obfuscation. Despite the best efforts to bring it into line, there appears to be *de facto* agreement that aesthetics dances to its own tune. The legitimacy of doing aesthetic theory, however, does not seem in doubt—regardless of its outcome. That being the case, feminist theoreticians may as well make selective appropriations from it.

LIMITS OF THE MODEL

For the purpose of this argument, I have focused upon the pluralism of conventional aesthetics, noting that aspects of its logic support a multivalence that other theory discourages. I do not mean to suggest, however, that aesthetic theory is uninfluenced by traditional philosophy or adaptable wholesale to a feminist theoretical strategy. On the contrary, some of the most formative and central doctrines of classical aesthetics are not at all compatible with feminism and have been inimical to women. Feminist critics of the aesthetic tradition find themselves in accord with other philosophers who propose revision from the perspectives of Marxism, phenomenology, pragmatism, environmentalism, and the history of technology and, above all, from the vantage point of a radically changed world of art. Some of these have made common cause with feminists in identifying their antagonists, though not necessarily with full comprehension of the feminist reasons for their selection.[17]

The present erosion of some canons of aesthetic theory that are unsympathetic to feminism is, of course, good news to feminists and relieves us of the burden of undermining them alone. It is heartening that other thoughtful people, motivated by independent objectives, are discovering the same defects that have turned feminists away from those classical ideas that we have all been taught to respect and that we nevertheless find wanting.

However, since feminists are frequently challenged to respond to traditional aestheticians and to explain our "defection," I think it important to develop here arguments that show how the concepts we reject are not just passé or irrelevant to feminism but are deeply implicated with a system of gender theory that is dysfunctional and repressive of women.

The doctrine of aesthetic disinterestedness is a case in point. Contemporary theoreticians disagree on the current viability of that doctrine, and the vehemence of their dispute varies with their interpretation of the meaning and scope of "disinterestedness." In principle, the term might sanction tolerance to the wildest experimentalism and pose no bars to pluralism. That representation of the doctrine makes it offensive to people who expect a close relation between art and morality and who find the indifference of aestheticism an abdication of moral responsibility. Others, by contrast, see a moral challenge in the laissez-faire availability of uncommitted vicarious experience. Each position seems to accept uncritically the epistemological claim that the experiencing self can remain apart from that which is experienced and thereby place itself optimally to judge. This (voyeuristic) presumption privileges certain judging persons and judgmental activities, while it diminishes and degrades others. Women are typically ranked among the latter.

The doctrine of "disinterestedness," closely associated with the notion of "autonomy" of the aesthetic, is generally held to emerge in Western thought in the eighteenth century. Kant's *Critique of Judgment* (1790), hailed by Hegel as the "first rational word on aesthetics,"[18] is taken to be its canonic statement. It expresses the view that aesthetic judgment, properly addressed to objects perceived by the senses and without cognitive reference, is grounded in pleasure that is immediately felt but serves no practical (moral) or utilitarian interest, does not evoke desire, but commands universal agreement necessarily. Works of fine art are commonly taken to be the prime source of aesthetic satisfaction, although that is not what Kant said, and they are thought to be produced by artists, men of unique and transcendent genius.

This doctrine has its roots in the Cartesian opposition of mind and matter and in the still more ancient antagonism of body and soul (Spelman 1982). The primary relation affirmed between mind and matter is *knowing*, whereby the former appropriates the latter. This aggressive act is performed by an agent, or subject, upon a passive object or subject-objectified. In knowing it, the subject exercises power over the object, demonstrating the capacity to control and bend it to the knower's will. Intellect masters nature, binding her to him in what Francis Bacon called a "chaste and lawful marriage."[19] The highest form of knowledge is that in which the knower remains unmoved, aloof, and untouched by the object it cognizes. Pure and dispassionate theoretical knowledge is self-contemplative and has no object beyond itself. It does not descend into the maelstrom of desire and has no practical ends. Modeled upon a conception of the Divine as pure subject, wholly self-sufficient, omnipotent, and omniscient—mind, unencumbered by bodily needs or passions, is wholly free. It is therefore eminently detached. Pure knowledge remains distant from its object at the same time that it takes possession of it. All other human activities, including both the ethical and the aesthetic, are viewed as subordinate to and derivative from this model of pure knowing, to which they all aspire.

Aesthetic enjoyment is excluded from achieving that exalted state because of its inherent preoccupation with embodiment. Aesthetics, we recall, has to do with perception by means of the senses and derivatively with feeling—with taste. Aesthetic enjoyment approaches divine detachment only by analogy, by being disinterested and autotelic, or self-contained. The post-Kantian doctrine of the "autonomy" of art is linked to the view that works of art are designed to elicit nonconsummatory, idealized aesthetic indifference. Possession of works of art thus indirectly testifies to the spiritual superiority, not merely the worldly wealth, of whoever possesses them. The spectator/speculator is elevated by the goods that he controls, and these are reverentially placed in temples which celebrate the owner as well as the objects. Visitors approach them piously (disinterestedly), setting aside the concerns of ordinary living for temporary relief and contemplation.[20]

Pursuing the epistemological quest for certainty, aestheticians have tried to vindicate aesthetic judgment by detaching it from its base. How can an experience of private pleasure in a particular object generate conclusions that are not partisan and limited? The parallel question posed to empirical knowledge is troubling, but there are conventional answers. Objective standards of truth as well as reliable discovery techniques have been agreed upon, a security absent in aesthetics. Ultimately the cognitive standards depend upon the immateriality of the ideal knowledge situation—its mathematical abstractness—and this is no refuge for the aesthetic experience.[21]

Seeking comparable rectitude, traditional aestheticians as well as ethicists have certified fictional "ideal observers" and agents, authorizing them as qualified to judge since they are, by definition, free of private interest or partisan bias. The same incentive has licensed such hypothetical constructs as the "sense of beauty" and the "moral sentiment," faculties, or dispositions attributed to ordinary persons rather than to an elite guard of critics. To make ethically sound or aesthetically valid assessments, a person must exercise such a purified faculty, or, in a more recent vein, by volitional self-voidance dissociate herself from personal, "interested" associations with the object or situation experienced.[22]

Various theoretical devices and fictions work to highlight the abstract quality of the aesthetic experience and assimilate it to the exalted condition of pure knowledge. Among these are Coleridge's "suspension of disbelief," Keats's "negative capacity," and Edward Bullough's quasi-ethical exhortation to assume "optimal psychic distance" with respect to a work of art.[23] All of these expressions refer to a dialectical impasse or state of vacuity. The perceiving subject is liberated from any personal ties or investments and lifted to a state of "aesthetic ekstasis" (literally a standing apart from self). The divestment of interest—personal, practical, partisan, possessive—described by Kant as indifference even to the existence of the object that evokes an aesthetic response leads at last to full spiritualization. The respect paid to art at that peak moment of contemplation is pseudo-religious.

Though still grounded in material stimuli, the aesthetic object, properly apprehended, escapes clear of earthy confinement and, as soul to body, achieves transcendence. He who makes the dissociative move, renouncing personal self, is born again as universal (knowing) self. This is the lesson of Cartesian mind/body dualism and the legacy of somatophobia recurrently identified in feminist gender theory (Spelman 1982).

Its longevity notwithstanding, the doctrine of aesthetic disinterestedness has parented a strange line of descent. It has fostered the view that to be art, something must be cut off from the reality from whence it sprang. It must not be useful or personally significant. The pleasure that it evokes derives from a "cold hedonism" only distantly related to the "cozy foothills of humanity."[24] It follows, moreover, that an object with any function other than disinterested contemplation is aesthetically suspect; that anyone who produces useful objects, whatever their additional appeal, is not an artist; that the value of an object as art is unrelated and yet superior to whatever other value that same object might possess. Strictly speaking, the value of an object as art should not be measured in the same currency (money) as other value that it possesses; but so far the art market has failed to mint a more spiritual coin. The autonomy theory also implies that proper appreciation of art should occur in an environment free of other encumbrances, e.g., a museum or concert hall, and that certain (professional) producers and connoisseurs of art are the only persons properly qualified to make aesthetic judgments. Other persons are advised to defer to the experts, thereby creating a hierarchy of the "cultured" and the "masses." These consequences in their turn have such real and theoretical spinoffs as the "artworld" and its denizens, the "Canon of Preferred Art," the dichotomy of art and craft, the discrimination against non-Western traditional, folk, and popular art, and the commercialization of aestheticism.

Feminists join with other critics of Cartesianism in denouncing the political and interest-driven strategies of dualism. The link between the metaphysics and epistemology of the Enlightenment and the socio-political oppressions of the modern state have been described elsewhere.[25] Here I stress the less well-documented axiological constructs: the "ideal observer," "l'homme moyen sensuel," and that infamous fiction of the law courts, "the rational man," who, provided with all available evidence, may be relied upon to sift through it impartially and to tote up the overwhelming probabilities "to a moral certainty." There is good reason to question the possibility of existence of such paragons of nonpartisanship and even greater reason to doubt that it would be desirable. Leaving aside ethical indifference, the divorce of the aesthetic from ordinary experience would serve only to trivialize and render it irrelevant. We can see all too clearly that the effect of aesthetic autonomy is not to exalt art but to fetishize and make of it a plaything of privilege.

Albeit some women are among the privileged, women are not well served by the "disinterestedness" thesis. Feminists do have a special mission to expose its somatophobic and misogynist bias. Figuring all too frequently as the matter displayed and transcended in art, women's subjectivity toward art is nullified by that theory. A feminist theory that would rectify this wrong is surely desirable. Notwithstanding that reservation, I have argued in this essay that there is redeeming value in conventional aesthetic theory and that feminists can learn from studying it. Its merit lies in its reflexivity, its constant reference to experience, and its refusal to suppress the multiple and the marginal for the sake of simplicity and order.

CONCLUSION: AESTHETICS AND FEMINIST THEORY

In 1956, Morris Weitz ventured the bold hypothesis that aesthetic theories do not generate real definitions of art but actually make critical recommendations. He did not say this in a spirit of condemnation of theory as covertly partisan. Weitz, a Wittgensteinian, meant to reaffirm the open texture of art and to warn against foreclosure through theory of the very conditions of creativity in the arts. Other theorists have been similarly skeptical of general definitions of art and have advocated attention to genre, to style, to art practice and performance as constitutive of art's identity. Emphasizing particularism and change within the arts, these theorists risk the charge of nominalism and are sometimes vilified for their anarchism and obscurantism. But, like the upstart dissenters to an internalist, logic-driven history of science (Kuhn, Feyerabend, Lakatos), aestheticians who are sensitive to the impact of social change upon the arts recognize that the end is not in the beginning.[26]

All those aesthetic enquiries that explore the indiscernibility of art and nonart, whether from the perspective of a Deweyan convergence of experience with "an aesthetic experience" (1934) or from that of a Dantoesque concern with stylistic liminalities (1990), confront the battle of essentialism and *a priorism*. These struggles are currently being waged within the galleries and alternative spaces of the artworld. Earthworks, installations, vernacular architecture, the banalization of dance, and the personal intrusiveness of some performance art all testify to indiscernibilities that have been denied or ignored for at least a century. By their very being these art forms trespass the lines of demarcation. We are forced to reconsider their indelibility. Why were we so gullible in the first place as to believe that a cathedral is art but a house or tepee is not? Why have we been so slow to recognize jazz as an art form? And why, come to think of it, did we fail to see that quilts are art? Could it be that those lines of demarcation marked frontiers that sheltered interests beyond aesthetic disinterest? Could it be that they are not sacrosanct?

The institutional theory of art, though far from satisfactory as either a theory of art or an analysis of institutions, must be taken seriously as an attempt to come to terms with radically new art forms. Its chief weakness is its inability to stretch beyond the present limits of the artworld. As Dickie contends, arthood is conferred upon a candidate by representatives of the artworld; but that excludes precisely those who are invisible to the artworld. More recent historicist aesthetic theories are also seeking to accommodate novelty while retaining some continuity with the aesthetic as understood in the past. Some would go so far as to permit a plurivalent logic that grants simultaneous truth of contrary interpretations of a work and even the unfixing of past truth without thereby sacrificing the identity of that which the truth affirms (Margolis 1991). Many feminists would certainly be content with such proliferation of truth, even where they might take issue with any given version of it.

Whether or not one is impressed by these uses of theory to fortify diversity, the effort on the part of the aestheticians to confront the ever-changing reality of art and aesthetic sensibility warrants respect. My aim here, however, is not to deliver moral felicitations to those who risk ridicule for the sake of existential integrity. Aesthetic theory has more than inspirational value. It is useful especially at those junctures where the imperative to reassess theory is compelled by discontinuities in creative imagination. We cannot fail to hear the clamor of voices seeking alternative expression. These challenges and the manner in which they are taken up are instructive for feminist theory, for we too are answerable to those who claim exclusion and demand attention. We too must yield to the compulsion of discontinuity. In our struggle to welcome plurality with grace and imagination we have the model of aesthetic theory, which has gone much of the route before.[27]

Notes

1. I use the expression "feminist aesthetics," as distinct from the singular "a feminist aesthetic." The latter is often used to refer to a stylistic quality or characteristic mode of expression ascribed to women artists. Much of the current literature of feminist criticism aims to identify differences, both in production and reception of art, that are to be found between women and men. The question of gender in voice and authorship, as well as gendered "readership," has greatly complicated and multiplied the issue of the identity of works of art. A correlative concern is the historic preference awarded to the so-called male style of production and appreciation, that preference conveyed through the politics and practices of artworld and realworld institutions. While I am not wholly convinced that there are gender-based distinctions in artistic expression that are fundamental, I do not rule out that possibility. It seems, in any event, that contingent differences exist, presumably the result of systematically different experiences which are gender related. It also seems clear that social arrangements in most if not all cultures give priority to the male-identified forms of expression and tend to devalue the female forms. It follows from this contingent fact alone that women who aspire to artistic prominence have in the past been forced, as much as they are able, to conform to the male-identified canons. It is now possible to challenge that requirement and to propose that alternative, non-canonic modes of expression, including the so-called female, be equally valorized. The exploration of those alternative modes is therefore a worthwhile project and I endorse it wholeheartedly, but it is not the subject of this essay. In the present context, the term "feminist aesthetics" does not apply to artistic production, but designates a theoretical undertaking. My task is neither art historical nor critical but philosophical. It aims to reconceptualize theory, indeed to engender a theory of theory that will be adequate to what feminists believe must be explained.

2. Within the literature of aesthetics there is a large component of exploration that seeks to characterize the logic of the work of art. Is it as universal to particular, as type to token, as class to member? None of these models fits adequately and their imperfections become increasingly apparent as technology and imagination expand the variety of art forms. (Wolterstorff 1975; Wollheim 1968).

3. This is true even of conceptual art, where direct perceptual acquaintance is not absolutely necessary. One can know the work by description alone; however, such knowledge depends upon the presence of a unique gestalt of prior information, some of which entails memories that are perceptual. (See Binkley 1977.)

4. Jane Roland Martin argues that the denunciation of essentialism by feminists has not only produced a chilling atmosphere in which theoretical reflection is difficult but has also generated a new "methodological essentialism": "Paradoxically, our acts of unmasking and reveling in the differences among women have become occasions for imposing a false unity on our research. Condemning essence talk in connection with our bodies and ourselves, we have come dangerously close to adopting it in relation to our methodologies" (1991, 4).

5. Genderizing thought, Young-Bruehl refers to "minds as conversations," having their importance relationally and rejecting hierarchy in favor of radically democratic interaction. Thinking, on her view, is not a matter of subordinating (as in a debate) but of "unsilencing of suppressed voices and the break-up of inhibiting monistic formations" (1987, 219).

6. Julia Kristeva (1981) refers to a "diagonal relationship" (that may or may not be distinctive of gender) which cuts a path linking certain sociocultural formations crosswise traversing other group identifications.

7. Michele Le Doeuff (1987), beginning from a different philosophical point of departure, lays the invidious duality between the masculine and the feminine at the feet of an outmoded and simplistic belief in substances, each characterized by specific and mutually exclusive attributes. From that perspective, the notion that real persons might mix and match capacities in order to achieve some human or social wholeness comes down to alchemy—an archaic doctrine, unworthy of philosophy itself.

8. Some of the more controversial examples of this are found among transsexuals such as Jan Morris, whose characterization of "her" new femininity strikes feminists as a caricature of women, reflecting a male's eye view of gender pushed to extremity.

9. College administrators should take note that one is not a feminist by virtue of one's gender, nor is one competent to teach courses in feminist theory or women's studies simply because one is a woman. Neither is it self-evident that one is utterly incapable of doing so simply because one is not. Such competencies are, like most skills, acquired through a combination of natural talent, inclination, hard work, and experience.

10. The will to improve upon the theory of theory may precede an interest in feminism. The two are logically independent. Some authors, scientists, artists, and thinkers have been claimed by feminists as foremothers because their explicit or implicit approach to theory has been illuminating or at least compatible with feminism; yet some of these people have repudiated feminism as such, e.g., Barbara McClintock, Georgia O'Keeffe (Keller 1983; MacColl 1990).

11. Externalists in the Kuhnian tradition or proliferationists like Feyerabend do maintain that *social* instabilities affect theoretical change. "Big" science as a result of war-related collaborations and "secret" science as a result of censorship and constraint must have consequences in how science pursues its ends and ultimately in its very nature, but that is not to say that the nature that science studies (except for the social sciences) is inconstant. This is exactly what aesthetics does confront.

12. The expression, used by Arthur Danto, in an evasive move that bypasses metaphysics, relates to the illocutions and perlocutions that confer (or withhold) art status upon candidates contingently arising within history (Cohen 1973).

13. Arnold Isenberg describes this sharing in "Critical Communication" (1949). Such communication is often misunderstood and confused with the pronouncements of "experts." The jurors on the Mapplethorpe trial who acquitted the director of the Cincinnati Art Museum of the charge of displaying pornography evidently believed that museum officials have the authority to determine what is art. They were deferring their own aesthetic judgment, understandably, in a context where politics overwhelmed the perceptual conditions of aesthetic judgment.

14. The relation of aesthetic properties to the physical properties upon which they are supervenient and of aesthetic concepts to empirically descriptive statements was a major preoccupation of analytic philosophers in the 1950s and '60s (see Sibley 1959, 1965; Hungerland 1963, 1968). The identification of "work of art" has its own history of essentialism, anti-essentialism, and various strategies of compromise that continue to

animate aesthetic controversy (see Beardsley 1961; Weitz 1956; Dickie 1969; Danto 1964, 1981).

15. One may, for example, be troubled by one's own fascination with violence or perversity yet find that very fascination curiously interesting. The excellently made film *Blue Velvet* seems to capitalize on just that narcissistic ambiguity in its audience reaction.

16. Aristotle credits poetry with greater plausibility than history, and there is a veritable industry of vindicative strategies among analytic philosophers seeking to justify or at least to make sense of the way in which fiction, metaphor, and make-believe can be "accurate," "right," or otherwise correct. Such strategies are sometimes obliquely expressed as fables or analogies, just as Plato is held to have cast some of his more uncertain reflections in figurative language (MacDonald 1954; Hospers 1960; Walton 1973).

17. Arnold Berleant (1991) presents an argument against classical theory based on an aesthetic of continuity and integration of the "aesthetic field." He argues in favor of a proper response as engagement with rather than distance from art. In doing so he claims an affinity with feminism among other movements. By and large, however, this is circumstantial, since his position does not arise out of a fundamental critique of dualism and hierarchy, nor from a political analysis, but from an examination of the current state of the arts. Joseph Margolis (1990) begins with a more radical critique of legitimization as such and ends by holding forth a dialectical, self-monitoring (post-analytic) form of justification that he thinks feminists *ought* to adopt.

18. Cited in Osborne (1968, 171).

19. Francis Bacon in "The Refutation of Philosophies" (quoted in Leiss 1972) expresses this manipulative view of knowledge more explicitly than Descartes does, but both the empiricist and the rationalist traditions give the same pride of place to the knower as against the known and to the active principle over the passive object.

20. Museum architecture and the social organization of museums reinforce the same philosophical conviction. One knows that they are hallowed ground and that eating, noisemaking, or other disrespectful behavior except in permitted spaces is out of order. One tries to banish venal thoughts from one's mind in order to be worthy of the experience to which one aspires.

21. This is not the place to make it, but I think a case might be made for the thesis that the rise of "dematerialized," conceptual, and minimalist art represents an endeavor to rid art of its dependency upon the particularizing aesthetic. The move to disembodiment transfers to the art form the impulse to transcendence which was formerly attributed to the spectator. The appreciative burden of disinterestedness, to approach the object with a proper aesthetic attitude (detachedly), is now partially relieved by denying to the object any features that might elicit a partisan or personal reaction.

22. Some aestheticians refer to a trait or sentiment that is positively responsible for an aesthetic (or ethical) judgment; others call for the negation or suppression of interests that would impede the making of an aesthetic judgment purely *in vacuo*.

23. All these devices represent states of suspended animation, in which the agent yields maximally to the inclination to act upon a stimulus without actually moving. An affective parallel to that state is the "aesthetic attitude" reverentially assumed as one enters the museum or concert hall. Like those other states, it is a condition of maximal receptivity combined with minimal release. It has been roundly denounced by George Dickie ("Myth of the Aesthetic Attitude") who conflates it with ordinary intensified attention that one might give to any task or object in which one is deeply absorbed.

24. Clement Greenberg's reference to Matisse's hedonism in "The School of Paris: 1946" was cited in a brochure for the exhibition of the Cone Sisters' Collection at the Boston Museum of Fine Arts, November 1991. It complements Clive Bell's disparagement of the associative concertgoer.

25. Attacks on Cartesianism have, of course, been recurrent throughout the history of philosophy since the Enlightenment. Gilbert Ryle's ridicule of "the ghost in the machine" is a notable instance from the recent past. But there is something new in the current assaults, namely a recognition of the ideological character of the doctrine. This is the ground of the

objection to the subject/object distinction and its correlated hierarchy as understood both by feminism and by a number of other politically driven philosophies. It is important to bear in mind that while acknowledging their own political objectives, these theories are drawing attention to the fact that Cartesianism is not politically innocent but is also driven by interested motives and that it has far-reaching political consequences that are disguised as natural or metaphysical necessities (Flax 1983; Bordo 1987).

26. Arthur Danto does incline toward the view that the end of art is imminent (1981). Despite his Hegelian tone, however, this finality appears not to be the outcome of an inevitable logic but rather a product of a particular history. Danto distinguishes between coming to an end and coming to a stop (1990). People will not stop producing artworks even though a particular art history has come to an end. In effect, he is arguing for a philosophical liberation, finding in the end of art the freedom to generate new beginnings. And who knows what next will be identified as art?

27. I am grateful to Carolyn Korsmeyer for repeatedly reading and criticizing this and other papers, forcing me to think more clearly and write more honestly.

References

Alcoff, Linda. 1988. Cultural feminism versus post-structuralism: The identity crisis in feminist theory. *Signs* 13, no. 3.

Beardsley, Monroe. 1961. The definition of the arts. *Journal of Aesthetics and Art Criticism* 20: 175-87.

Beauvoir, Simone de. 1960. *The second sex.* H. M. Parshly, trans. New York: Bantam.

Bell, Clive. 1914. *Art.* London, Chatto and Windus.

Berleant, Arnold. 1991. *Art as engagement.* Philadelphia: Temple University Press.

Binkley, Timothy. 1977. Piece: Contra aesthetics. *Journal of Aesthetics and Art Criticism* 35: 265-77.

Bordo, Susan. 1987. *The flight to objectivity: Essays on Cartesianism and culture.* Albany, SUNY Press.

Bullough, Edward. 1912. "Psychical distance" as a factor in art and an aesthetic principle. Reprinted in G. Dickie and R. Sclafani, *Aesthetics: A critical anthology,* 1977, New York: St. Martin's Press.

Cohen, Ted. 1973. The possibility of art: Remarks on a Proposal by Dickie. *Philosophical Review* 82: 69-82.

Danto, Arthur. 1964. The artworld. *Journal of Philosophy* 61: 571-84.

Danto, Arthur. 1981. *The transfiguration of the commonplace.* Cambridge: Cambridge University Press.

Danto, Arthur. 1990. *Encounters and reflections.* New York: Farrar Strauss and Giroux.

Dickie, George. 1964. All aesthetic attitude theories fail: The myth of the aesthetic attitude. *American Philosophical Quarterly* I, no. 1: 56-66.

Dickie, George. 1969. Defining art. *American Philosophical Quarterly* 6: 253-56.

Eisenstein, Hester. 1983. *Contemporary feminist thought.* Boston: G. K. Hall & Co.

Elton, William. 1954. *Aesthetics and language.* Oxford: Oxford University Press.

Feyerabend, Paul. 1975. *Against method.* New York: Schocken Books.

Flax, Jane. 1983. Political philosophy and the patriarchal unconscious: A psychoanalytic perspective on epistemology and metaphysics. In *Discovering Reality.* S. Harding and M. Hintikka, eds. Dordrecht: D. Reidel.

Fraser, Nancy. 1989. *Unruly practices.* Minneapolis: Minnesota University Press.

Harding, Sandra. 1986a. *The science question in feminism.* Ithaca: Cornell University Press.

Harding, Sandra. 1986b. The instability of the analytical categories of feminist theory. *Signs* 11, no. 4.

Hawkesworth, Mary. 1989. Knowers, knowing, known: Feminist theory and claims of truth. *Signs* 14, no. 3.

Herrnstein-Smith, Barbara. 1988. *Contingencies of value: perspectives for critical thinking.* Cambridge, MA: Harvard University Press.

Hospers, John. 1960. Implied truths in literature. *Journal of Aesthetics and Art Criticism* 19: 37-46.

Hume, David. 1757. Of the standard of taste. In Dickie and Sclafani.

Hungerland, Isabel Creed. 1963. The logic of aesthetic concepts. Proceedings of the APA, vol. 40 (1963).

Hungerland, Isabel Creed. 1968. Once again, aesthetic and non-aesthetic. *Journal of Aesthetics and Art Criticism* 26: 285-95.

Isenberg, Arnold. 1949. Critical communication. In Elton (1954).

Keller, Evelyn. 1983. *A feeling for the organism: The life and work of Barbara McClintock.* New York: Freeman.

Kristeva, Julia. 1981. Women's time (Le Temps des femmes). In *Feminist Theory: A Critique of Ideology.* Alice Jardine and Harry Blake, trans. Keohane, Rosaldo, and Gelpi, eds. Chicago: University of Chicago Press.

Kuhn, Thomas. 1970. *The structure of scientific revolutions.* 2nd. ed. Chicago: University of Chicago Press.

Lakatos, Imre. 1970. *Criticism and the growth of knowledge* (with A. Musgrave). Cambridge: Cambridge University Press.

Le Doeuff, Michele. Women in/and philosophy. Reprinted (and translated) in Toril Moi, *French feminist thought.* Oxford: Blackwell.

Leiss, William. 1972. *The domination of nature.* New York: George Braziller.

MacColl, San. 1990. Universality and difference: O'Keeffe and McClintock. *Hypatia* 5, no. 2.

MacDonald, Margaret. 1954. "The Language of Fiction." Reprinted in J. Margolis, *Philosophy Looks at the Arts: Contemporary Readings in Aesthetics,* 1962, New York: Charles Scribner's Sons.

Margolis, Joseph. 1990. Reconciling analytic and feminist philosophy and aesthetics. *Journal of Aesthetics and Art Criticism* 48, no. 4.

Margolis, Joseph. 1991. Historicism and the arts. Unpublished lecture.

Martin, Jane Roland. 1991. Methodological essentialism, false difference, and other dangerous traps. Unpublished ms.

Mothersill, Mary. 1984. *Beauty restored.* London: Oxford University Press.

Osborne, Harold. 1970. *Aesthetics and art history: An historical introduction.* New York: E. P. Dutton.

Rich, Adrienne. 1980. Compulsory heterosexuality and lesbian existence. *Signs* 5, no. 4.

Sibley, Frank. 1959. Aesthetic concepts. *Philosophical Review* 67: 421-50.

Sibley, Frank. 1965. Aesthetic and non-aesthetic. *Philosophical Review* 74: 135-59.

Spelman, Elizabeth V. 1982. Woman as body: Ancient and contemporary views. *Feminist Studies* 8, no. 1.

Walton, Kendall. 1973. Pictures and make-believe. *Philosophical Review* vol. 82.

Weitz, Morris. 1956. The role of theory in aesthetics. *Journal of Aesthetics and Art Criticism* 15: 27-35.

Wollheim, Richard. 1968. *Art and its objects.* New York: Harper and Row.

Wolterstorff, Nicholas. 1975. Toward an ontology of artworks. *Noûs* 9: 115-42.

Young, Iris. 1988. *Throwing like a girl and other essays in feminist philosophy and social theory.* Bloomington: Indiana University Press.

Young-Bruehl, Elizabeth. 1987. The education of women and philosophers. *Signs* 12, no. 2.

Ziff, Paul. 1953. The task of defining a work of art. *Philosophical Review* 63: 68-78.

PART TWO

✧ ✧ ✧

The Nature of Art:
Some Feminist Alternatives

T W O

Re-enfranchising Art
Feminist Interventions in the Theory of Art

ESTELLA LAUTER

Feminist analyses of the roles gender has played in art lead to an alternative theory that emphasizes art's complex interactions with cultures rather than the autonomy within culture claimed for it by formalism. Focusing on the visual arts, I extrapolate the new theory from feminist research and compare it with formalist precepts. Sharing Arthur Danto's concern that art has been disenfranchised in the twentieth century by its preoccupation with theory, I claim that feminist thought re-enfranchises art by revisioning its relationship to its contexts.

At the center of aesthetics in the twentieth century has been the project of defining art, and despite current confusion, the "master" theory governing this project has been remarkably stable. This theory, which I call "formalist" for convenience, even though it includes other approaches, has conceptualized art as consisting of separate works or objects. "Whether in definition, ontology, or criticism," says philosopher Arnold Berleant, "the same tendency prevails to give exclusive consideration to the art object" (1986, 105). The second feature of the dominant theory is the belief that art claims a certain autonomy within culture—a conviction "given physical expression in Western societies by the sequestering of art objects in museums, cultural centres, and other such hallowed halls" (106). The third key feature of the theory is "the eighteenth-century notion of disinterestedness . . . [which] has reappeared under various guises" (106). Works of art require identification, interpretation, and evaluation by members of an art world who are trained to assume "a special attitude . . . peculiar to the contemplation of art" (106). I would add that such training comes through the study of sanctioned art objects, thus creating a cultural tautology by rendering the "expert" incapable of appreciating non-canonical work.

To Berleant's characterization of the dominant theory, I would also add the idea that art expresses the consciousness of a single artist who "sees" differently from his fellow men. Arthur Danto claims expressivity as modernism's central challenge to art history's doctrine that art progresses from lower to higher forms, since one can scarcely argue that mankind's expressive concerns have *developed* over time (1986, 104). Still, this expressive element was incorporated into formalist theory, perhaps because no better explanation of art's reason for being was available at the turn of the century to replace an outmoded notion of art as an imitation of reality. It came trailing the Kantian idea of "genius" and the possibility that art could *transcend* life. It might have led to internecine battles more serious than those waged over the "intentional fallacy" or the "affective fallacy" in literary criticism,[1] if expressive theory had been able to differentiate art from nonart on other than formal grounds. Even in the postmodern era, expressivity and formalism remain interconnected.

Formalist theory has not gone unchallenged. Signs of unrest have been evident throughout the century in realms that seem at first glance to have little to do with each other: in the practices of Dada and the plethora of experiments related to it (happenings, chance art, performance art, environmental art, conceptual art); in the work of Bauhaus theorists who valued the practical functions of art; in the argument among philosophers since the fifties over whether or not art can be defined in terms of necessary and sufficient conditions, or whether any such thing as aesthetic experience exists; in economic analyses of art offered by Marxists; and most productively, I think, in pressures from women, African-Americans, Native Americans, and representatives of non-Western artmaking traditions for recognition of alternative conceptions of art.

Nonetheless, if we may believe Arthur Danto, we have reached a state in the West where art and theory have become conflated:

> The art of our recent past . . . depends more and more upon theory for its existence as art . . . so that virtually all there is at the end *is* theory, art having finally become vaporized in a dazzle of pure thought about itself. . . . (1986, 111)

Philosophy, Danto claims, has dis-enfranchised art by absorbing it into thought.

Feminist theory, on the other hand, through its attention to the difference that gender makes and has always made in the creation, reception, and evaluation of art, not only permits us to understand many perplexities of art and the art world as interpreted by previous theories, giving artist status to women in the bargain, but it also re-enfranchises art by revisioning its complex relationships to cultures.

GENDER IN ART

Feminist research (by artists, historians, critics, and theorists across the arts) on the effects of gender on art has driven a decisive wedge into the dominant coalition of theories under formalism. I draw my examples here from the visual arts because the rather sudden discovery in the seventies of women's visual achievements forced a dramatic response,[2] but similar effects have been traced in all media. Since Linda Nochlin suggested in her provocative essay "Why Have There Been No Great Women Artists?" (1971) that the status of women in art had more to do with opportunity than with talent, a spate of articles and books has provided factual documentation of the systematic differences women experienced in *preparation* and *production* that affected their mastery of technique, their opportunities to be original, and their achievement of expressiveness. Through its analysis of the operation of gender throughout the Western artworld over four centuries, feminist practice has established that regardless of individual artists' occasional successes, art registers discriminatory cultural practices. Idealism aside, art *is* gendered.

Moreover, powerful circumstantial evidence exists that gender has mattered in the *reception* of art. Take, for example, those works once ascribed to "masters" that lost their *aesthetic* value when they were reascribed to women. The *Portrait of Mlle. Charlotte du Val d'Ognes* is the classic example. When it was ascribed to David, critics praised its colors as subtle and singular and found its content (its "merciless" view of "an intelligent, homely woman") unforgettable. When it was reascribed to Constance Marie Charpentier (1767-1849), critics suddenly discovered weaknesses in its execution, attributable to the artist's use of literary rather than plastic values. Where before the painting had been unified by a single attitude, it became an "ensemble made up from a thousand subtle attitudes" which all seemed to reveal the "feminine spirit" (Fine 1978, 54; Pollock 1987, 4).

The reception of quilts provides endlessly fascinating evidence of how gender has mattered. It is hard to look at quilts now in the wake of feminist research without asking how they came to be devalued by a dominant *formalist* aesthetic theory, since they (and their sisters, the woven coverlet or blanket) are often so obviously excellent in design, anticipating by half a century or more the principles of collage, of geometric abstraction, and even of art based on optical illusion. Nonetheless, quilts and their sisters in the larger category of needlework failed to qualify as art in formalist theory because it was assumed that they were intended to be used and so were not sufficiently separate from "life." They also failed to qualify because it was assumed that they did not express a unique point of view of a single creator.

Feminists have learned, however, that these assumptions were false in many cases; quilts and coverlets were made for many purposes, including display, and they were sometimes made by a single creator to express not only a particular feeling but a worldview. Harriet Powers's visionary Bible quilt is a case in point.[3] After her emancipation from slavery, Powers used her knowledge of the Bible to focus her scathing gaze on the Reconstruction in appliqued blocks containing scenes and figures that symbolized her vision. Why would a work like this be excluded from the category of art?

Let's examine the kind of reasoning usually offered, beginning with the notion of her intent. Suppose she did intend her quilt to be used. Since formalist theory pioneered the idea that the "intent" of a work should *not* count, why should it matter here? If intent should not count in expression (so that the work can be said to transcend the artist's life), why should it count *negatively* in social function? Cannot a work transcend its social function? Is it really true that most works of art are "useless"? Don't they serve a variety of social functions? Why is the function of covering a bed less honorable than the function of providing status to a wealthy investor? By this logic, shouldn't we value works by Michelangelo created for the church less highly than we value Duchamp's urinal?

The defender of established practice would argue that Powers was not a professionally trained artist. The feminist might respond that neither was Rousseau.

The argument would continue: he was a "genius." Nonsense: some of his works accorded with the fantasies of his audience. At least we know that his work was created by his own hand. But Powers also designed her own work and probably executed it by herself; besides, according to this principle, why would one accept Andy Warhol's work and not hers? What's more, if the work's form were effective and meaningful, why should it matter how many people created it? The formalist might complain that techniques and materials of needlework are crude by comparison with those of the fine arts. The feminist might ask why sewing on cloth with thread is less honorable for aesthetic purposes than pasting newspaper in collage.

Under the pressure of such questions, the logic of formalist theory looks far less coherent than it once did, and its practices are seen to contain elements not accounted for in theory. Quilts may not always be good art, but why would one want to exclude a whole category of potential art objects before one had looked at them to see whether or not they exhibited formal significance or expressive genius? Finally, exactly what do the criteria used to exclude quilts from art have to do with the creation of a significant form? To whom must the form be significant in order to count as art? Isn't the word "art" in the conventional usage more often a normative rather than a descriptive term? In these cases and many other similar ones, the failure of formalist aesthetic theory to recognize the *aesthetic* value of the piece in question indicates both its lack of internal consistency and its inability to provide a sufficiently comprehensive theory of art—one that explains art's many uses.

Questions such as these suggest that formalist condemnation of the utilitarian may follow from rather than dictate the rejection of women's art. To explain the exclusion of quilts from art, feminist historians, critics, and theorists have described a long and complicated historical process beginning in the late Middle Ages whereby the materials of cloth and the techniques of needlework were designated "women's work," and women, despite the occasional success of individual artists, were denied creativity (Parker and Pollock 1981, ch. 2). The appositeness of this analysis may be seen in the catalogue for a 1971 exhibit of pieced quilts (the ones most like twentieth-century abstractions) cited by Patricia Mainardi. There the curator claimed that quilts "mirror" instead of precede modern abstractions, discounted the rich expressiveness of appliqued quilts (like Powers's) as "decorative," and denied quilts the status of art because the women who made them did not think of themselves as "artists" (Mainardi 1973, 343-44).

The genre of quilts has been gendered in a straightforward way. The traces of "femininity" appear in the materials, techniques, and production of objects and form the likely basis for their categorical exclusion from candidacy for appreciation as works of art. That is, in probing why supposedly "extra-aesthetic" issues about quilts arise, feminist critics repeatedly find the traces of gender (along with traces of race and class, which are no less evident or important).

But exactly what do we mean by "gender"? The answer has changed in the last decade. Most feminists believe that "feminine" characteristics associated with women are not mandated by biology but are instead constructed by cultures. Thus, "gender" refers to the effects of acculturation as expressed in behavior and attitude. In the explosion of knowledge called women's studies, however, we have learned that cultures affect individuals to differing degrees, so that predicted marks of gender do not always appear in works by women, and when they do, they do not represent *all* women.

Beyond this general wisdom, feminist researchers often find that even when traces of gender are not apparent *in* works of art, they operate as *invisible* elements. Their evidence parallels Arthur Danto's now classic discovery that one cannot necessarily tell a work of art by looking at it; its status as art depends on factors that exist outside of it in the theories members of the "artworld" have about it (1964). Just as a bed by Rauschenberg is a work of art if seen through the artworld's filter, so work by women that seems identical in value to work by men may *not* be art (or good art) when the artworld's filters contain social biases about women along with precepts about art. In addition, to complicate the issue even further, items taken to signify feminine gender may not embody the condition or views of women at all, but instead may represent men's fantasies.

The case of Sonia Delaunay shows how gender worked invisibly (outside the work of art) to detract from the value of work that met formalist standards. Sonia Terk was an artist in her own right before she married Robert Delaunay. Throughout the early years of their marriage, she worked with Robert on the theory that became known as Orphism. They were equals in every respect. At the height of their achievement, their works were as much alike as those of Picasso and Braque during the formation of cubism. Sonia Delaunay's paintings were never denied the status of art, but they were ignored by art history. Why?

Clare Rendell explains that the artist's favorable attitude toward design, characteristic of her Russian background, threatened the idea of art as separate from life. Thus, when Sonia Delaunay turned her artistic energy to theater and fashion design in order to support her husband, she forfeited the approval of the artworld (Rendell 1983, 35-38). An earlier essay by Marsden Hartley, however, indicates that another stumbling block to proper valuing of her paintings was Sonia Delaunay's social role as wife. Note his language. Hartley began by saying that when he last saw the work of "Madame Delaunay Terck" (*sic*) she was "running her husband a very close second for distinction in painting and intelligence of expression" (1921, 113-14). In fact, Hartley thought her work was *more* "virile" and "vigorous" than Robert's, but he was aware that his judgment could be understood as a "private personal attack," and so he accounted for Sonia's power by attributing it to the "average Russian woman" (114). Despite her equal mastery of the conception and execution of the idea they created together, Hartley was sure that "Whatever there is of originality in the idea of Orphisme shall be credited to [Robert] Delaunay as the inventor" (113). Hartley's uneasiness about gender is palpable and revealing, despite his desire to support the artist. His essay offers an important clue as to how gender has operated outside the works to befuddle the formalist assessment of Delaunay's substantial body of painting.

The case of Paula Modersohn-Becker, whose art in the years 1902-1907 is uncontestably powerful and original, is even more disturbing. What could account for the silence about such work for almost three-quarters of a century? Surely nothing in its technique, design, or form, for all its moves were either present or anticipated in pieces by Gauguin, Picasso, or Matisse. Because it differed substan-

tially from the landscapes of the men in the Worpswede colony where she lived
with her husband Otto Modersohn, it might have been rejected as *too* original by
some members of the colony, but Modersohn had visited his wife Paula in Paris, as
had the poet Rainer Maria Rilke; both men must have seen that it was in the
mainstream of the avant-garde work in progress there. Perhaps she received less
than her due because of her early death. But then why has Seurat done so well in
art history with only six fully executed paintings to his credit when Modersohn-
Becker produced more than 400 paintings and some 800 drawings and etchings?

The only plausible explanation of this anomaly I can muster is that the nature
of Modersohn-Becker's content (subject matter shaped by form) blocked fair
reception of her work. A passage from Otto Modersohn's diary contains a world of
information:

> Paula hates to be conventional and is now falling prey to the error of preferring to
> make everything angular, ugly, bizarre, wooden. Her colors are wonderful—but the
> form? The expression! Hands like spoons, noses like cobs, mouths like wounds, faces
> like cretins. She overloads things . . . and children at that! It is difficult to give her
> advice, as usual. (Busch and von Reinken 1983, 324)

After reading the diaries, one can hear in Modersohn's angry tone his fear of what
he took to be a projection of his wife's independent aspirations into her artistic
form. Her innovations were inappropriate to his idea of women's place and
children's nature.

Thus, one of the traces of gender may be the shape the artist gives to her subject
matter through her attitude. But in this case a curious question arises: whose gender?
Modersohn-Becker's presentation of the power of "woman" was perhaps taken to
be more dangerous than it was. Ironically, the distortions of human form that so
disturbed Modersohn may have been an expression of the artist's vulnerability
rather than her defiance—of the unresolved conflict between her expressive ability
and the ideological and economic restrictions that kept her married rather than a
declaration of independence. The telling mark of feminine gender (woman over-
reaching her fate) that may have determined the assessment of her content was
probably in the fears of male beholders.

Through many such analyses, feminist critics have concluded that gender has
always been a factor in judging art when art is explicitly or implicitly associated
with women, even when women artists have met criteria of excellence set by men.

A DEVELOPING FEMINIST THEORY OF ART

The theoretical implications of these findings that gender has mattered even
though formalist theory claimed it did not have not seemed as clear as one might
suppose. Women artists have been understandably reluctant to take the new road
opened up by feminist research. As an ideal, the statement that art has no gender
seemed beneficial; perhaps the problem lay in the prejudices of individuals who
applied the theory and not in the theory itself. After all, *some* women have

succeeded within the framework of the dominant theory, apparently on the stated grounds: the formal excellence of individual works of art.

Another significant deterrent to the development of a feminist theory of art has been the fact that no single specific distinction between men's and women's art can be identified. The culture, however, remains preoccupied with difference understood as a constant boundary between males and females and as an indicator of *in*equality. Thus the development of a feminist aesthetics seemed to depend upon the impossible task of locating *the* "difference" with the unproductive result of creating a ghetto for women.

A third difficulty has been the lack of uniformity in women's art. All women do *not* paint alike, and the jury will be out on the question of difference in women's aesthetic sensibilities until interdisciplinary and cross-cultural studies are completed in the decades ahead. Nor do the ideas, images, and techniques found in art by some women represent *all* women. How, then, can a feminist theory of art address the issues raised by the study of gender without trapping women in a category called "woman" that is too narrowly defined?

A further complication arises in the multiplication of feminisms (cultural, materialist, black, French), so that little agreement exists among them about art or anything else. My project differs from others before me because I do not claim that feminists should agree or that women's art is definable as a separate category. Instead I argue that, despite diversity, feminist practices lead now to an alternative theory of art. I call it a "feminist" theory to credit its origins in feminist research, not to argue its uniqueness. If others wish to identify it with other cultural movements, I have no objections, so long as women's contributions to it are not lost in the process.

I find at least four reasons to articulate the conceptual results of feminist practice into an alternative theory of art. First, the ramifications of gender we have seen are unpredictable; we may solve the problem of including quilts in art only to find that gender matters in some unforeseen way. Second, women can be individually successful without making a permanent mark; feminist art history is full of such cases. Even the compilers of the latest and most optimistic history of women in art, *Making Their Mark*, which details the inroads made by women artists from 1970 to 1985 under postmodernism, concede that the artworld's turn in the mid-eighties toward neo-expressionist art by European males indicates the difficulty of securing women's place there. Third, the problem with formalism lies not so much in the fact of prejudice (which is ubiquitous) as in the theory's inability to acknowledge and explain the complex interactions of art and cultures. Finally, even if formalism did offer an adequate description of art, its exclusionary ideals and practices are no longer viable in a society whose major challenges are *in*clusionary.

To admit that gender *does* count in art (along with race, class, and many other contextual factors) is to make what has been covert and negative in formalist aesthetics the starting point for another theory altogether. Art is not produced in a rarefied atmosphere that transcends gender identification. We create as men and women who are influenced by biological and imaginative mothers and fathers. Far from being a set of discrete, autonomous art objects, art is deeply contextual. The primary function of a new theory is to *identify* art, not by proscriptive definition, but by sorting out its multiple relationships to its contexts.

Once we admit that art is inevitably related to its social context, not just as a device for proving an artist's "genius" or innovative edge, but as a means of constructing its nature as art, then formalist efforts to maintain art's separateness by definition become meaningless. Thus distinctions between art and craft or high and low art fall away along with hierarchies based upon media, materials, techniques, or subject matter (painting over printmaking, technological materials over fiber, abstraction over representation, nonpolitical over political topics). Art does not depend for its identity on absolute distinctions between itself and work that is useful, decorative, or integrally related as ritual or model to the life of a social group. Feminist practice thus expands the range of things we consider to be art.

The opposition of art to craft has been one of the first principles to give way to feminist pressure, and the (still partial) legitimation of fiber arts in the seventies is one of the most promising results of dissolving those rigid distinctions. Miriam Schapiro's work is a case in point. Her formulation of the term "femmage" and her articulate defense of "decorative" art have opened up new space for others whose work had not been recognized. As Norma Broude has said, Schapiro does not "treat her sources as borrowings to be transformed. . . . Rather, she *reveals* them—perhaps fully for the first time—as objects of aesthetic value and expressive significance" (1980, 35). If we can accept her paintings of kimonos as art, Schapiro seems to ask, why can we not accept the kimonos themselves? If we can accept her "decorative" works in femmage, why can we not accept the needlework that inspired them? If we can accept their feminine beauty, why do we continue to denigrate it elsewhere? Thus, one effect of the theory I advocate here is to open up the artworld to artists and aesthetic values previously regarded as "other."

Another achievement of recent feminist practice with far-reaching theoretical implications has been to revalue the exploration of subjectivity as a legitimate purpose of art against the grain of formalist theory, which demands that the artist individual transcend subjectivity to achieve universality. More often than not, "universality" turns out to be a code word for the preference of a dominant group. Feminist analysis of gender has proved that art is not "objective" either in its production or reception. In its frequent objectification of women, it represented a subjective point of view identified with men in a culture governed by men. Since art history has been largely a revelation of men's subjectivities, then, feminist historians and critics seek to augment subjectivity to include women.

Feminist theory affirms that art can reveal important aspects of women's thought that may not be apparent in the languages of cultures. Art will not provide knowledge of women's "essence" (which is impossible to discover, even if it exists, since we use the lens of a culture to seek it). But it is a vital means of discovering and exploring one's subjectivity, one's difference, one's distinctive place in a culture or in the physical world.

The work of Frida Kahlo consists of searing self-explorations which are nonetheless meaningful to many who have never experienced the specific traumas of her life: a double identity as European and Mexican, an accident that shattered her pelvis, repeated miscarriages, a stormy marriage to a world-famous artist and political radical. *The Broken Column* (1944), for example, represents a woman whose spinal column is damaged, and it expresses through the symbolism of the nails that stick in her flesh the pain she feels as a result (Herrera 1983, Plate XXVIII). One is free to see the work at a distance from the painter and oneself if necessary, or as a revision of art about Christ's transcendence of pain on the cross. The experience of viewing this work, however, is enriched by understanding its roots in Kahlo's life, by empathizing with the artist on the basis of experiences one shares with her, by knowing the ways it symbolizes the pain other women have felt from being broken in other ways, and by acting to reduce the pain of women's lives. From this perspective, art is a place where anything may be revealed, including the emotions of anger and grief we once thought it (and human beings) should transcend.

Another more broadly shared phase of theoretical revolt against objectivity involves refusing the idea that art must be an object presented for appreciation. Women have played an active part in extending the reference of art to include such things as performance art and environmental art. As Josephine Withers has argued, it would be specious to say that earthworks by women, for example, were radically different from those by men; still, women, as a group, have

> redirected the initial mainstream, away from the emphatically artificial construct and towards a more cooperative, organic, and process-oriented modeling. As the aesthetic effect became more integrated, even "invisible," the artwork became in and *of* the world, rather than a description of our experience *about* the world. . . . (1983, 325-26)

Feminist theory valorizes such experiments, allowing new aesthetic values to emerge, as in the integration of art with the physical world or with politics.

A corollary of this de-objectification of art is an insistence by feminist theorists on the affective value of art. With increased awareness of the ways art has always served political systems, feminists have been willing to break the taboo against overtly political art. Not all the art made by feminists is overtly political, of course, but the power to effect a response through some formal means is an identifying feature of art in the emerging feminist theory as well as a sign of its quality.

Thus, the emerging theory stimulates criticism of obsolete aesthetic standards and validates new ones, allowing us to see acts such as Suzanne Lacy's *Three Weeks in May* (1977) as art,[4] even though they may have none of the qualities of form or expression that have been required in formalist theory. That event took place in the Los Angeles City Mall Plaza, where Lacy installed two twenty-five foot maps of the city. She and her colleagues (other performance artists and invited members of the public) then documented each of the ninety rapes that occurred in those three weeks by placing a large stencil of the word "rape" on one map at the scene of the crime as soon as they received news of it. A mourning ritual followed the performance. The piece could not help but affect all who saw it. No one hoped that the audience then or those who hear about it now would maintain aesthetic distance from it. At the very least, its effect was disturbing; at best, cathartic. Perhaps it even worked for some to sponsor political activism against sexual violence. If art is not autonomous, then neither is the perceiver of art.

Consideration of Lacy's work raises the issue of who creates or controls the creation of art. One of the most distinctive elements of feminist practice is its tendency to valorize art produced cooperatively, collaboratively, or collectively—a move which has the potential to dislodge the romantic notion of the work of art as the product of genius.[5] For centuries, sculptors have had assistants in their studios who did the supposedly "noncreative" work of casting works from plaster into bronze, but feminist artists from the seventies on have gone much further in their explorations of "co-creation,"[6] particularly in murals and performance art, but also in more permanent forms.

However imperfectly Judy Chicago may have modeled the idea of co-creation in *The Dinner Party* (1975-1980) or *The Birth Project* (1980-1985), she established in the public arena the idea that artists might enlist and credit the aid of others in media they have not "mastered," to execute their own or even collective ideas. Although Chicago worked within a formalist aesthetic in many ways, she held consciousness-raising sessions with women for inspiration; she altered her designs in response to feedback from the artists with whom she worked; she made her works into events as well as objects; she incorporated other materials into the exhibit space to acknowledge her co-creators in fact and spirit.

In the same vein, feminist practice supports more active responses to art. Others who did not contribute to Chicago's works have celebrated, extended, and criticized them by producing their own pieces in response. In Frankfurt, for example, 300 women gathered in the spring of 1986 to honor Chicago's work by performing their own pieces based on the lives of historically important women. Mary Beth Edelson and Betsy Damon have regularly asked viewers for their own stories and images, making these new materials part of their art in a variety of ways. All this begins to threaten the museum mentality of formalist theory, not only by bringing ordinary objects into the museum or by creating impermanent pieces, which had been done, but by making artistry harder to separate from acts that had been considered merely supportive.

Whereas under the influence of formalism we have imagined art as a set of discrete works arranged in the shape of a pyramid that reaches ever higher (and more narrowly) toward purification of elements that do not belong to it, feminist theory asks us to envision art as more like the web Virginia Woolf used in *A Room of One's Own* to describe fiction:

Fiction is like a spider's web, attached ever so lightly perhaps, but still attached to life at all four corners. Often the attachment is scarcely perceptible. . . . But when the web is pulled askew, hooked up at the edge, torn in the middle, one remembers that these webs are not spun in midair by incorporeal creatures, but are the work of suffering human beings, and are attached to grossly material things, like health and money and the houses we live in. (1928, 43)

What is true for fiction may be true for all the arts to varying degrees. We may need more than one model for something so complex as art; even if we accept the web as model, we may want to extend it to include related images to capture nuances of different media. Yet the notion of art as *attached* to life is critical. The kind of form a spider's web has is also critical: sometimes, depending on the light, it is nearly invisible as form, and yet it serves as a scaffold for the spider.

It will not do to notice the form without granting its functions. The purpose of the spider, to catch her prey, highlights the potential value of art as a means of survival. It also reminds us that encounters with art have their dangers. Individual acts of art can trap us. We, in turn, can spoil acts of great complexity and beauty by insensitive responses. In our interactions with art, we take risks of being changed and of changing it—and these experiences, as well as those embodied in the webs, may help us learn to live our lives with greater sensitivity. In this model, art is embedded in cultures, not autonomous from their moral and political concerns.

FORMALIST AND FEMINIST THEORIES COMPARED

Thus far, the theoretical shift I am describing has taken place primarily in the form of altered feminist behavior in the established artworld and alternative structures. Nonetheless, the progress toward an alternative theory of art has been substantial. Even though the need to choose may not be pressing for some years to come, since a research program can support more than one theory to explain different aspects of its subject, and feminist theory may use formalist insight into artistic form while rethinking the doctrine of art's separateness, eventually we will need to choose which theory best explains the features of art over time.

Toward that end, I begin here a speculative process of comparison designed to clarify the difference such a choice would make in our decision making about art. That difference can be seen by direct comparison of precepts drawn from existing theory with those extrapolated from feminist practice in relation to ideas of art, artistic production, and aesthetic reception.

Formalism defines art in terms of formal properties, qualities, and principles and arranges those elements in a hierarchical order to privilege those least useful to daily life. Art consists of a recognized series of discrete objects. It develops progressively in reference to itself. Good art meets standards of excellence established by trained tastemakers. Its status depends on its formal transcendence of nature and culture, on the artist's genius, and on the critic's disinterested interpretation. Aesthetic meaning exists apart from moral and intellectual concerns.

Feminist theory describes art as everexpanding and seeks to identify it through exemplars and models instead of trying to define it. Art is a continuum of objects, enactments, concepts, and environments. It concerns life, but neither "art" nor "life"[7] can be discussed as totalities; boundaries between art and culture or art and nature are identifiable but shifting. Its status depends on its effectiveness in making life sensible to an audience for which it is produced or by which it is received. Good art reaches beyond its society of origin to suggest alternative ways of being. Its aesthetic value arises in relationship to moral and cognitive values.

According to formalist theory of artistic production, the artist is a maker of forms equivalent to or more important than nature and autonomous within culture. "He" learns the specific techniques of one or more closely related media through formal education and apprenticeship with at least one "master." He becomes a member of the artworld and works with full consciousness of it to produce something new. He develops an individual "signature," so that his technique, form, or preoccupations are immediately distinguishable from others, but he takes care to disguise relationships between his art and his personal life in order to make his view seem "universal." He rises to the top through competitions and is championed by someone in the artworld, preferably in a large center of art such as New York. The artist is most to be admired who inspires others to adopt his style and eventually to change it, thereby advancing the history of art.

In feminist theory, the artist is a co-creator of structures in an interactive system which includes both nature and cultures. The artist learns her/his techniques in any of several ways—through formal education if she is lucky, but also through a craft tradition or self-education. Although "she" sometimes achieves status through competitions, she often finds her direction through membership in alternative groups for which her art serves a purpose; her "gallery" may be alternative, collective, or even communitarian. She may in fact create with others. Her effort is to produce something that seems authentic to herself or to her audience. Thus form is important for its potential to shape subject matter into content or to disrupt the system of representation, but not so often as a thing in itself. Her art may even have a group rather than an individual signature. It may be as personal as necessary to accomplish its ends, but paradoxically, her ego is not as much on the line as in the formalist paradigm, since her art is assumed to reflect and interact with the values of a particular culture, which in turn interacts with others in weblike relation. The artist is most to be admired who best shows art's centrality to its contexts.

From the vantage point of formalism, the percipient's task is to appreciate the work of art as a thing in itself. "He" accomplishes this task by ascertaining that it fits his definition of art and by establishing the category to which it belongs. He learns how to respond appropriately through formal education (during which he is exposed to key works in accepted categories and to accepted interpretations of those works). He sets time aside from daily life to perceive art and to cultivate a separate mode of response (called psychical distance or disinterestedness) that will allow a momentary release from life's pressures. The professional has additional responsibilities to compare works, arrange them according to a hierarchy of values (with newness or uniqueness at the top), and to evaluate them according to their relative success or failure as expressive or significant forms. When he speaks or writes about the work, his likes or dislikes must be put aside in favor of the objective language of aesthetic values.

In feminist reception theory, the percipient seeks to understand art's relationships to its cultures rather than to define it or place it in categories. Optimal response involves political, social, religious, economic, *and* aesthetic sensitivity, which may come from formal education or from experience. The professional has additional responsibilities to describe and interpret the interpenetrations of art and other structures in language that will make them understandable to those who do not belong to the artist's community of origin. "She" evaluates art according to its potential to empower people to live more effective, moral, and satisfying lives in a world increasingly characterized by differences. The critic's likes and dislikes are foregrounded as stumbling blocks or starting points for the process of increasing understanding.

RE-ENFRANCHISING ART

If disenfranchisement is the consequence of formalism, then feminist theory returns art to its social contexts and reinvigorates it so that it becomes a source of power to a wide variety of people. Feminist theory enhances our experience of art by accounting for it more accurately. It expands the range of what we consider to be art and prepares the way to legitimate new art forms; opens the community of artists; revalues subjectivity in art and augments it to include women's experiences; allows us to reconnect aesthetic values with political activity; stimulates criticism of obsolete aesthetic standards and validates new ones; valorizes new modes of production; and supports more active response.

Much theoretical work remains to be done to clarify the factors that count in art's identification and valuation. In particular, feminist theorists need to construct measures of affective value and to explore interrelationships among aesthetic, moral, and political values within and across cultures. Members of the art world have argued long enough about the interpretation of works as if they were autonomous objects. Let us now study how art embodies, enacts, and changes cultures.

Notes

I am indebted to William Wainwright, Philosophy, UW-Milwaukee, and to Hilde Hein, Philosophy, Holy Cross, for many helpful suggestions.

1. See Wimsatt and Beardsley (1946, 3-18), for a classic articulation of expressive fallacies according to formalist doctrine.

2. See Broude and Garrard (1982), Parker and Pollock (1981), and Rosen, et al. (1989) for an overview of the art historical revolution to which I refer.

3. The quilt is pictured and described in Powers's own words in Bank (1979, 118-19). The quilt is apocalyptic in its condemnation of Southern slaveholders.

4. Part of Lacy's piece is illustrated in Rosen (1989, 16).

5. See Perkins (1981) for a compelling argument that creativity is not a matter of genius.

6. The concept of co-creation is modeled in creation myths from several Native American culture groups including the Iroquois, Algonquian, and Siouan, when the first creator requires assistance from other first beings, often in the form of animals or natural elements, to complete the world.

7. Quotation marks used in this section indicate a challenge to any universal construction of the term enclosed.

References

Bank, Mirra. 1979. *Anonymous was a woman*. New York: St. Martin's Press.

Berleant, Arnold. 1986. The historicity of aesthetics I. *British Journal of Aesthetics* 26(2): 101-11.

Broude, Norma. 1980. Miriam Schapiro and "femmage": Reflections on the conflict between decoration and abstraction in twentieth century art. In *Miriam Schapiro: A retrospective 1953-1980*. Wooster, OH: College of Wooster.

Broude, Norma, and Mary D. Garrard. 1982. *Feminism and art history: Questioning the litany*. New York: Harper and Row.

Busch, Guenter, and Liselotte von Reinken, eds. 1983. *Paula Modersohn-Becker: The letters and journals*. Arthur S. Wensinger and Carole Clew Hoey, trans. New York: Taplinger.

Comini, Alessandra. 1977. Gender or genius? The women artists of German expressionism. In *Feminism and art history*. See Broude and Garrard (1982).

Danto, Arthur C. 1964. The artworld. *The Journal of Philosophy* 61: 571-84.

Danto, Arthur C. 1986. *The philosophical disenfranchisement of art*. New York: Columbia University Press.

Fine, Elsa Honig. 1978. *Women and art*. Montclair, NJ: Allanheld and Schram.

Hartley, Marsden. [1921] 1972. *Adventures in the arts*. New York: Boni and Liveright. Reprint. New York: Hacker Art Books.

Herrera, Hayden. 1983. *Frida: a biography of Frida Kahlo*. New York: Harper and Row.

Mainardi, Patricia. 1973. Quilts: The great American art. In *Feminism and art history*. See Broude and Garrard (1982).

Nochlin, Linda. 1971. Why have there been no great women artists? In *Art and sexual politics*. Thomas B. Hess and Elizabeth C. Baker, eds. New York: Collier Books.

Parker, Roszika, and Griselda Pollock. 1981. *Old mistresses: Women, art and ideology*. New York: Pantheon Books.

Perkins, David. 1981. *The mind's best work*. Cambridge, MA: Harvard University Press.

Petersen, Karen. 1981. *American women artists: The nineteenth century*. Hagerstown, MD.: Harper and Row Audiovisuals.

Pollock, Griselda. 1987. Women, art and ideology: Questions for art historians. *Women's Studies Quarterly* 15(1&2): 2-9.

Rendell, Clare. 1983. Sonia Delaunay and the expanding definition of women's art. *Woman's Art Journal* 4(1): 35-38.

Rosen, Randy, et al. 1989. *Making their mark: Women artists move into the mainstream, 1970-85*. New York: Abbeville Press.

Wimsatt, W. K., and Monroe C. Beardsley. [1946] 1954. *The verbal icon*. Reprint. Lexington, KY: University of Kentucky Press.

Withers, Josephine. 1983. In the world: An art essay. *Feminist Studies* 9(2): 325-26.

Woolf, Virginia. [1928] 1945. *A room of one's own*. Reprint. Harmondsworth, Middlesex, England: Penguin.

THREE

A Gynecentric Aesthetic

RENÉE LORRAINE

In the proposed gynecentric aesthetic, which follows the work of Heide Göttner-Abendroth and Alan Lomax, aesthetic activity would function to integrate the individual and society. Intellect, emotion, and action would combine to achieve a synthesis of body and spirit. Song and dance would involve the equal expressions of all participants, and aesthetic structures would reflect this egalitarianism. The erotic would be expressed as a vital, positive force, divorced from repression and pornography. The emphasis would be off aesthetic objects to be coveted, hoarded, and contemplated, and on dynamic process, fully engaging and socially significant.

As the aesthetic expressions of women become more plentiful and authentic, art and culture will be transformed. I wish to suggest a possible shape that a gynecentric aesthetic could take. My proposal will be based on a "matriarchal" aesthetic offered by philosopher Heide Göttner-Abendroth and on a theory of anthropologist Alan Lomax on the aesthetic activity of African foragers. Although the aesthetic Göttner-Abendroth proposes is a vision based on her knowledge of ancient myth and art, while Lomax's theory is the result of a statistical study of the relationships of social structures and song and dance styles in contemporary societies, their conclusions are remarkably similar. These similarities are significant in that both of the aesthetics are attributed to the high status of women.

Both Göttner-Abendroth and Lomax are inclined to synthesize, to seek commonalities among cultures and historical periods. Göttner-Abendroth generalizes about certain ancient societies, Lomax about foraging societies, and both generalize about the influence that women or the feminine could have on art and aesthetics. There are problems involved in making transcultural and ahistorical comparisons of this type; a concentration on the similarities of different groups can make us less attentive to important distinctions among them, to particular and unique aspects of them. Yet both the analytic tendency to focus on particulars and the synthetic tendency to focus on commonalities can be of considerable value, and the two approaches can strengthen and refine one another. Speaking for the analytic end of the continuum, Sandra Harding is persuasive in contending that there "is no

Hypatia vol. 5, no. 2 (Summer 1990) © by Renée Cox

'*woman*' to whose social experience the feminist empiricist . . . strategies can appeal; there are, instead *women*: chicanas and latinas, black and white, the 'offshore' women in the electronics factories in Korea and those in the Caribbean sex industry" (1986, 192). In light of this, generalizing a feminine or gynecentric aesthetic for ancient or foraging cultures seems risky at best, especially when knowledge of these societies is relatively limited. Yet from a more synthetic point of view, there are characteristics that are common and peculiar to (biological) women in all cultures throughout history, and at least some of these might give rise to similar social and cultural behaviors. Women have X chromosomes (OX, XX, or XXX) and a predominance of estrogens. We tend to be smaller than men, store more fat in our bodies, and have relatively larger breasts and hips. We menstruate and experience menopause and can and most often do get pregnant, give birth, and nurse our babies, giving of our bodies to nurture others. Our sexual organs and orgasms are internal, and in sexual relationships with men we envelop rather than penetrate. Because we need not develop a gender identity different than that of our mothers, we can retain an identification with our mother longer than can sons (Chodorow 1978). Women in virtually all cultures have been responsible for domestic activities, nearly all have been subjugated, and most have been economically and emotionally dependent on men. To the extent that some of these factors may influence (not determine) women's contributions to culture, different types of behaviors and contributions will arise in response to different cultural contexts. Any tendency to nurture, for example, would manifest itself more prominently in contexts in which motherhood is valued highly than in contexts in which women are encouraged to be high achievers in the world outside the home. And it may be that behavior patterns of women that seem "natural" could be entirely eradicated by cultural factors. But when similar behavior patterns among women in different cultures and historical periods seem to appear—in our case, when cultures considered gynecentric have similar aesthetic activities and social structures—the commonalities should be noted and examined.

Göttner-Abendroth presents her vision of artistic activity in women-centered cultures in "Nine Principles of a Matriarchal Aesthetic" (1986, 81-94). Of the nine principles, the first is that reality is changed by magic through the use of symbols. Our ancient ancestors were able to forecast the weather through careful examination of the sky and of animal and plant behavior, and to fight disease through the knowledge and use of herbs. But they believed that technical knowledge was insufficient to influence nature or to heal the sick; powerful emotion was necessary as well. This powerful emotion was cultivated in the symbolic activity of the dance, and was thought to be magical. The goal of the dance was the health and unity of the individual and of society. In the dance, erotic and aggressive drives could be expressed but were contained within a social context. Action, intellect, and emotion merged to make the individual whole, and individuals were united as a society and as part of the natural world (1986, 81, 84-86).

The second principle is that the framework of matriarchal art is the structure of matriarchal mythology. Based on her study of myth, Göttner-Abendroth considers this structure, which is derived from basic stages of life such as birth, initiation, marriage, death, and return, to be fundamental to all mythologies, and to have influenced religions that developed from them (1982, 71-79). It is a fundamental category of the human imagination and has been passed down to us through fairy tales, folklore, legends, and festivals. Although this structure is universal, each matriarchal society gave it a different reality. Matriarchal art is, therefore, "diversity in unity, in which the unity is not dogmatic, the diversity not subjective" (1986, 81-82, 86-88).

Third, matriarchal art transcends the traditional artistic mode of communication which consists of maker/product/perceiver. It is a process in which virtually everyone in a society participates collectively to give the matriarchal structure external expression through the ritual of dance. Fourth, matriarchal art demands total commitment of all participants. Participants "operate simultaneously on the levels of emotional identification, theoretical reflection and symbolic action," a synthesis that results in ecstasy. Fifth, matriarchal art is dynamic process rather than product. It cannot be objectified, sold as a commodity, stored in an archive or museum, or evaluated or interpreted by outsiders. Sixth, this art cannot be divided into genres and breaks down the division between art and theory, art and life. Music, song, dance, poetry, movement, decoration, symbol, comedy, and tragedy are united in the ritual of the dance. Ancient matriarchal art merged with astronomy and mythology; modern matriarchal art merges with philosophy, the humanities, and the natural and social sciences. In matriarchal culture, the ritual dance could last for days or weeks, and the daily functions of life—eating, rest, discussion, meditation—were necessarily involved. Seventh, the value system of matriarchal art is based on life and love. The erotic is the dominant force, not work, discipline, renunciation. "The continuation of life as a cycle of rebirths is its primary principle, and not war or heroic death for abstract, inhuman ideals. A sense of community, motherliness and sisterly love are the basic rules . . . and not paternal authority. . . ." Eighth, matriarchal art precludes any divisions in the aesthetic sphere and is the culture's most important social activity. Patriarchal divisions of aesthetics into "a formalist, elitist, socially effective art on one hand and a popular, widespread but socially vilified and outcast art on the other" would be overcome. Finally, matriarchal art is not "art" in the patriarchal sense. Patriarchal art concerns the fictional and has existed only since the aesthetic sphere was separated from the rest of life. It is thus artificial and denatured. Matriarchal art is "the ability to shape life and so change it; it is itself energy, life, a drive toward the aestheticization of society" (1986, 82-84, 88-92).

To speak of "matriarchy" and of nature, magic, emotion, love, and the erotic in the same context may seem to some as dangerously close to sexist essentialism. It has been popular among some feminists to view women as more receptive, loving, gentle, nurturing, adaptive, and closer to nature than men. Because such "feminine" qualities have traditionally been undervalued in patriarchal culture, these feminists seek to empower women by empowering these qualities, and to feminize culture by advancing these qualities. Feminist critics of this school of thought are not so much averse to advancing the characteristics as they are to considering them essentially female. Their imposition on women, it is thought, is unnecessarily restrictive and unrealistically demanding, tends to make women subject to domination, and has made it difficult for women to deal with their own

feelings of anger and aggression. Whatever Göttner-Abendroth's position on essentialism, it should be noted that she does not envision matriarchal culture as
composed exclusively of characteristics traditionally considered feminine but as an
integration of nature and culture, emotion and intellect, the magical and technical.
And in the culture she envisions women would not be subject to domination, could
not be overpowered. For although matriarchal art, which does not allow itself to
be domesticated either formally or socially, will be fought by patriarchal societies,
"the battle will not be an exchange of hostilities but an incessant ebb and
flow/advance and retreat, an ungraspable symbolization, the creation of a completely new web of connections in the centre of this fragmented, atomized world."
In a patriarchal society, the beauty of matriarchal art is the prime opposition. "And
what weapons can be used," Göttner-Abendroth asks, "against withdrawing and
opposing, opposing and withdrawing beauty?" (1986, 93-94).

What does it mean to say that the ancient past was matriarchal? Proponents of
an ancient matriarchate, many of whom are theologians or art historians, are
concerned with relationships of art, artifacts, temples, burials, and religious and
cultural practices of various prehistoric cultures to the status of women in those
cultures (Bachofen 1973; Stone 1978, 1980; Spretnak 1982; Sjöö and Mor, 1987).
That the status of women was high in at least some of these cultures is inferred,
among other things, from the elaborate burials prepared for them, and the fact that
four times as many female as male figurines have been discovered in various areas
from paleolithic and neolithic periods. It is believed that prehistoric peoples, who
may not have understood the relationship of coitus and childbirth, reacted to
female sexuality with awe. The figurines, which are often called "Venus" goddesses
and have prominent vulvas, breasts, and bellies, are believed to have represented
the power of procreation. And the red ochre covering sacred objects and entrances
to caves where sacred rituals took place may have been representative of menstrual
blood.

Women also held a prominent position in much ancient mythology (Harrison
1922; Eisler 1987; Gimbutas 1982, 1989; Göttner-Abendroth 1980; Neumann
1963; Graves 1948; Spretnak 1978; Olson 1988). The myths of some peoples
describe a primordial time when women ruled. There are world-creator goddesses
in Sumer, Babylon, Egypt, Africa, Australia, and China. In some cultures, goddesses
are credited with providing important cultural gifts such as the alphabet, language,
writing, agriculture, or medicine. The similar names and characteristics of goddesses
from different regions of the world have suggested to some researchers that the
names may be variations of one name, or various aspects of a single Great Goddess
(Gimbutas 1989). But whether the belief is in one Goddess or many, it is held that
women once held an exalted position and power that was subsequently lost.

The idea of an ancient matriarchy is appealing in that it entails that male
domination of women is not inevitable, and that there are models for a culture in
which women would have power and autonomy. Yet anthropologists, including
feminist anthropologists, are nearly unanimous in their dismissal of a universal
matriarchy as "pure conjecture," and many deny that there is evidence of any
matriarchy at all (Bamberger 1974; Binford 1982; Rosaldo 1974; Rubin 1975). They
point out that early research on matriarchy, such as that of J. J. Bachofen (1973),

has been largely discredited. They warn against the assumption that matrilineal or matrilocal cultures are also matriarchal; there are numerous examples of such cultures in which women are dominated. They note that neither a fascination with the female form, such as that represented by the Venus figures, nor the existence in a culture of myths with powerful goddesses is any guarantee that the women of that culture will hold any power. And they find the myths and theories describing a time when women ruled less than encouraging in that the myths often assert or imply that women lost their power due to incompetence or to the natural superiority of males.

Matriarchy is most often interpreted to mean "mother rule," and it is the idea that women have ever ruled or dominated men that is regarded as being without foundation. In some conceptions of matriarchy, however, power is described as nonauthoritarian. Margot Adler, in "Meanings of Matriarchy," reports that matriarchies are often described as realms "where female things are valued and power is exerted in nonpossessive, noncontrolling and organic ways that are harmonious with nature" (1982, 132). (The existence and influence of power of this kind may have been easy for researchers with patriarchal perspectives to miss.) The evidence that cultures such as these have existed is more persuasive, and to call such cultures "matriarchal" may not be entirely perverse etymologically. The root "arch" denotes not only "rule" but something main, principal, or original; "matriarchy" could thus be interpreted as a culture in which women or mothers have the principal power and influence, in which a maternal "ethic of care" pervades the entire society. Because the term matriarchy is, in fact, often construed as an upside-down patriarchy, however, some scholars prefer to refer to ancient cultures as "matristic," "matrifocal," "gynecentric," or "gylanic," a word coined by Riane Eisler and formed by combining parts of "gyne" (woman), "andros" (man), and the Greek "lyein" (to resolve or set free) (1987, 105). Perhaps Göttner-Abendroth prefers "matriarchal" for its stronger connotations of female power.

Whatever it is labeled, Göttner-Abendroth considers her aesthetic to be characteristic of a nonauthoritarian culture where the status of women is high. Notably, there is anthropological evidence to suggest that foraging or hunter-gatherer cultures also are nonauthoritarian or egalitarian and tend to value rather than disparage women and female things. According to the work in cantometrics and choreometrics of anthropologist Alan Lomax, the aesthetic activity of these foraging societies is indicative of their egalitarian tendencies, and of the high status of women. Though Lomax refers to the relations among the sexes in these societies as "complementary" while Göttner-Abendroth theorizes that ancient societies were matriarchal, it is significant that both the social structures and aesthetics of the cultures described by the two authors are quite similar.

As defined by Lomax, cantometrics is a study of the relationships of song style and social structure, and choreometrics, of dance and social structure (Lomax et al. 1968; Lomax and Berkowitz 1972; Lomax 1976). Lomax believes that cantometrics shows, for example, that polyphonic music with independent voices or parts is reflective of a pluralistic, multi-voiced society, and that hierarchical, authoritarian societies tend to give rise to music in which some musical elements are subordinate to others. Lomax and his staff have correlated the dance and song styles evident in approximately 700 films and 400 recordings to the economic, social, and political features of corresponding societies listed in George P. Murdock's *Ethnographic Atlas*, resulting in cantometric or choreometric profiles of over 400 cultures (Murdock 1967). Statistical controls were introduced at many stages of the project, and a factor analysis was used to produce valid correlations. One of the most notable aspects of Lomax's study for our purposes is his conviction, quite apart from any explicit interest in feminism or any mention of matriarchies, that the status of women was considerably higher in ancient, preagricultural societies. Based on his research, he identifies African and Australian gatherer types as representative of the earliest and most generally distributed culture types of which we have a living record (1972, 234).[1] Hunting is a valued source of food for these groups, but the gathering of fruits, nuts, seeds, honey, grubs, and the like provided the greatest proportion of the subsistence, and gathering is the province of women. Lomax found that in societies where women are responsible for at least 50 percent of the subsistence, they also are likely to take initiative in other sectors of the society, and hence, relatively unlikely to be dominated by men (1968, 164; 1972, 238).[2]

Certain contemporary African cultures such as those of the !Kung San and the Mbuti Pygmies, where foraging or gathering is the principle source of food supply, are characterized by Lomax as egalitarian, complementary in terms of sexual relationships, adaptive, cohesive, and integrated. Fertility is regarded as a social value, and sexual standards are permissive. There is an absence of social controls and an emphasis on social solidarity. Leadership is not so much weak as irrelevant. Cantometric and choreometric analyses showed that of all the cultures Lomax studied, it is these gathering ones that have the most "integrated and cohesive" singing and dance styles. Everyone in the social group engages in dancing and singing, although the men and women may dance separately, and one sex (usually the women) may sing, clap, and play drums while the other sex dances. The singing in these societies is described as "interlocked" or "varied synchrony," a contrapuntal unity in which everyone sings together yet independently, and there is no dominant part. The vocalizing is natural, relaxed, and open-throated. The dance style is described as flowing, curved, successive, highly synchronous, and erotic, with multipart trunk action and accentuated hip, pelvis, and breast movements. What is remarkable about this is that all of these characteristics are positively correlated with the significant social participation of women. The multipart and polyrhythmic singing of varied synchrony increases as levels of female production increase. Relaxed vocalizing is correlated with permissive sexual standards, particularly for women. And the dance style is considered by Lomax to be symbolic of the feminine and the sexual, and to be prominent where "the feminine aesthetic is dominant" (1968, 164-69; 1972, 234-39).

According to Lomax, there are five factors that tend to reduce varied or "gross" synchrony of dance and song, all clustered around male predominance: "masculine aggressiveness, diffuse organization, rigid stratification, masculine dominance of production, and repressive control of feminine sexual freedom" (1968, 202). In societies which emphasize hunting or fishing instead of gathering, or in intensive, slash-and-burn agricultural societies, males are responsible for the bulk of subsistence, and there is authoritarian male rule, stratified social relationships, and sexual repression. Correspondingly, singing and dancing tend to be the province of men. Unison, solo, or highly diffuse singing is the norm, and vocalization is noisy, tense, narrow, and nasal. In contrast to the "erotic, feminine, in-gathering" dancing of gatherers, dance in these societies is more "differentiating or manipulative," and movement tends to be single-trunk, "peripheral, varied, three-dimensional, and light." (Good examples are traditional European ballet and the elaborate handplay of Oriental dance.) Some of these societies are preagricultural, but nonetheless, ones in which males are responsible for the bulk of subsistence. Australian Aborigines, for example, are a predominantly hunting and fishing society in which elder male clan heads control the economic, sexual, and ritual life. Aboriginal song is relatively incohesive, vocalization is tense, and intervals used are narrow; a one-unit body attitude is predominant in dance, and any dance synchrony arises from restriction and control. Eskimo men provide nearly all the subsistence for their society, and the status of women is very low. Male dominance is symbolized by the importance of male solo performances and male choruses singing in rough unison, and by a dance style described as angular, linear, fast, strong, and direct (1967, 222-39; 1972, 234-36).[3]

Just how egalitarian are the sexual relationships in gathering societies? The men and women generally have separate activities, and as in virtually all known societies, the women are responsible for the domestic sphere. But anthropologist Elsie B. Begler indicates that a number of anthropologists believe that certain gathering societies are "truly egalitarian in all aspects, including the relations between the sexes" (Begler 1978, 572).[4] Recent ethnographies on the !Kung San and Mbuti Pygmies bear this out. Pygmies have no chiefs or any formal council of elders, and problems and disputes are settled by general discussion. While one or two people may rise to prominence in a tribe for practical reasons, they may be female as well as male (Turnbull 1961, 110). Ethnographer Colin Turnbull reports that the Pygmy woman "is not discriminated against in BaMbuti society as she is in some African societies. She has a full and important role to play. There is relatively little specialization according to sex. Even the hunt is a joint effort. A man is not ashamed to pick mushrooms and nuts if he finds them, or to wash and clean a baby" (1961, 154). In fact, gender is significant only at the adult stages of life; Pygmy children or the elderly are referred to without differentiation of gender (1983b, 205). Pygmies are generally monogamous, but sexually permissive (1961, 125). Girls generally get married in their own time and in their own way (1961, 202). Women give birth easily (they may rejoin the hunt later in the same day), and with the assistance of female friends with whom there are strong and lifelong bonds. Education and discipline of children is shared with the group (although there is very little discipline of children under the age of three) (1983b, 211-12). Pygmy huts are built by women and considered their property. Wives who do not get their way have been known to go through the process of dismantling their huts until their husbands are willing to reach a compromise (1961, 132). There is considerable tension between the sexes for adult Pygmies; this is reflected in transvestite dances in which one sex ridicules the other (1983b, 215-16). Pygmies are not warlike, but disputes within the band can result in physical fights. Turnbull once witnessed a fight between two men in which one said he was not a woman to be ordered around. A woman then beat the man, saying that "women do not get ordered around, only children, and that is why nobody will marry him" (1965, 212). Pygmies have strong moral values and serious crimes are very rare (1961, 110). Turnbull indicates that each Pygmy is willing to share and support every other Pygmy in any way she or he is able. He once made a crutch for a lame Pygmy girl who was embarrassed to use it. All the other Pygmies reacted by making crutches for themselves, and used them for days until the girl no longer felt different (recounted Lomax 1968, 203).

!Kung San ethnographer Richard B. Lee, after a careful consideration of the relationships of the sexes, concludes that "the evidence shows a relatively equal role in society for the two sexes, and the !Kung data certainly do not support a view of woman in 'the state of nature' as oppressed or dominated by men or as subject to exploitation at the hands of males" (1979, 454).[5] San society is polygynous, but women have considerable leverage in marriages and are even dominant if the wife is older than her husband (as is the case in one of five marriages). One San husband told ethnographer Lorna Marshall that "if he wanted to go somewhere and his wife wanted to go somewhere else he might have to talk, talk, talk, talk, talk to persuade her" (Marshall 1959, 364). Divorce and remarriage are easy and carry no stigmas for women. Woman have considerable reproductive control and have a lower fertility rate than other tribes practicing natural fertility. Physical violence is rare, and rape is extremely rare. Woman participate in group decision-making discussions (although men do two-thirds of the talking, and tribe spokespeople are usually male) (Lee 1979, 447-54). Like the Pygmies, the San value cooperation, adaptation, and generosity. Ethnographer Elizabeth Thomas reports that a certain San band, driven to rather barren regions by more aggressive tribes, was once about to feast on the bounty of a successful hunt when they noticed another San band watching enviously. After a group discussion about the matter, the first band, intent on reducing envy and maintaining good relations, decided to give nearly all of the meat to their neighbors (1959; recounted in Lomax 1968, 203).

Another society in which the status of women is high is the Lovedu of South Africa. This society is not discussed by Lomax, but its ritual, music, and dance seem to correspond closely to that of Lomax's hunter-gatherers. The Lovedu practice simple agriculture in which the women hoe and the men plough and hunt, and while the women generally spend more time in the fields than the men, the contributions to subsistence of the respective sexes is complementary (Krige and Krige 1947, 40-41, 30-33).[6] The productive resources in this culture are inherited patrilineally. But the Lovedu have a queen who is the religious head and the nucleus of a network of political alliances. She is considered an embodiment of divine order, transformer of the clouds, changer of the seasons. She is allied with a group of district heads, most of whom are relatives and the most important of whom is also female (1947, 271, 172). The queen is not a political ruler, and it would be incorrect to say that Lovedu women have more political power than men. But ethnographers E. J. and J. D. Krige were taken with the "unusually exalted position" of women in Lovedu society. Both men and women are witch doctors, craftspeople, or storytellers, and women can own cattle and have wives (1947, 285). While the culture is polygynous, equal treatment of wives is expected and enforced (1947, 71). Lovedu girls are given a portion of their grandmother's garden to tend when they are ten or eleven, and the achievements of girls and women are given special recognition (1947, x). Premarital sex is tolerated, but discretion is expected. If an unmarried girl becomes pregnant, she is treated very well, while the man involved is treated severely (1947, 157). A bride's mother supervises the early marriage and determines when intercourse is appropriate (1947, 123). Both parties in a marriage may have discreet affairs, and old women sometimes have affairs with young men (1947, 157). Although there are menstrual taboos in Lovedu culture (possibly due to a fear of female power), women's sex organs are referred to as *vadimoni* (place of the gods), and those of old women as *khitugulo* (a charm made sacred by association with the gods) (1947, 290). Lovedu values are quite similar to those of Pygmies and the San. Reciprocity is the basis of relationships among district heads and in general, and reconciliation the method of settling differences. Modesty, dignity, and mature wisdom are valued, and fighting, boasting, arrogance, and assertion strongly discouraged (1947, 285-86).[7]

The analogies that can be drawn between the "aesthetics" of these societies and Göttner-Abendroth's matriarchal aesthetic are significant. None of the contemporary societies has a single goddess at the base of its mythology or culture, but both male and female ancestors are worshipped by the Lovedu, and there are powerful female figures in the stories and legends of the San (Krige and Krige 1947, 231; Lee and DeVore 1976, 310-16). Pygmies worship the forest or forest spirit, which is sometimes referred to as *eba* (father) but usually as *ema* (mother) (Turnbull 1961, 92-93; 1983b, 206). The matriarchal aesthetic emphasizes the relationship of magic, or deep emotion, to science and medicine in the healing of physical and social ills; this magic is cultivated in the dance. The Lovedu culture merges magic, religion, and medicine; dancing is used to heal the sick and the possessed and to promote the Lovedu pattern of reciprocity and cooperation (Krige and Krige 1947, 211, 242-43). The San *!kia*, or trance dance, is used for ritual healing and protection and for peacemaking after arguments or fights. Richard Katz states that *!kia* healing "is harmonious or synergistic with maintenance and growth on both the individual and cultural levels," and that the *!kia* increases social cohesion and solidarity. He also remarks that the emotions are aroused to an extraordinary level in *!kia*, and that the San most proficient at *!kia* are those with a highly emotional nature (Katz 1976, 284-89). In Pygmy society, dance forms the basis for religious expression, and dance, song, and play are used to promote unity and resolve conflict (Lomax 1968, 202).

The cycle of initiation, marriage, death, and return, which is fundamental to the structure of matriarchal myth, is also reflected in these cultures. The San consider a process of death and rebirth as critical to entering *!kia* (Katz 1976, 300). All three cultures have elaborate initiation ceremonies for males and females. The pygmy *elima*, or dance of life, is in celebration of the advent of menarche (Turnbull 1961, 185). The singing and dancing of the Lovedu *viali* is connected not only with initiation but with rain and fertility; its structure is based in part on the natural seasons (Krige and Krige 1947, 139). As described in the matriarchal aesthetic, everyone participates in the dance in these cultures. Men and women may dance separately, but they also dance and sing together, and virtually no one is systematically excluded. Göttner-Abendroth states that in matriarchal art, physical, mental, and emotional faculties combine to effect an ecstatic state. It seems appropriate to say that these faculties combine in the dances of foragers as well. The San *!kia* results in an ecstatic trance in which dancers walk on fires, effect cures, and claim X-ray vision (Katz 1976, 287). Pygmies consider the *elima* an event of great beauty and one of the most joyful occasions in their lives (Turnbull 1961, 187). As in the matriarchal aesthetic, the erotic element is prominent in the dance, song, and daily life of all three societies, and fertility is a social value. Art is not objectified, stored, or interpreted, and although dance, song, instruments, costume, and drama are used in the rituals, there are not separate artistic genres. As in the matriarchal aesthetic, there is no distinction in these cultures between art and nonart; the dance is simply a central part of everyday life.

Can all of these band characteristics be linked to the power or equality of women? The lack of distinction between art and life is thought to be typical of preindustrial societies in general. In complementary societies, however, this characteristic is linked with everyone having a "voice," both aesthetically and socially. In male-dominated societies, where aesthetic activity is chiefly the province of men, the activity tends to be integrated only with male life or experience. Lomax considers most of the other aesthetic characteristics listed above (participation by everyone in the dance, tendencies toward unity and integration, emphasis on fertility and the erotic) to be specific to complementary societies. And much of what Lomax reports about complementary societies is reminiscent of Göttner-Abendroth's aesthetic. "Varied synchrony," in which there is unity of dance and counterpoint but in which everyone sings and dances independently, with no one taking a dominant role, is remarkably similar to Göttner-Abendroth's description of matriarchal art and culture as "diversity in unity, where the unity is not dogmatic, the diversity not subjective." Lomax's description of varied or gross synchrony as representative of the complementary society's "dependence on a continual feed of empathy-producing, conflict reducing, unifying parallel behavior in interpersonal interaction" mirrors Göttner-Abendroth's vision. Varied synchrony is negatively correlated with all of the factors the matriarchal aesthetic seeks to overcome: masculine dominance and aggressiveness, rigid stratification, diffuse organization, repression of female sexuality. Lomax and Göttner-Abendroth used different methodologies to examine different egalitarian societies in time periods thousands of years apart, yet reached strikingly similar conclusions about the societies' social structures and "aesthetics."

Both of these aesthetics, and all of the cultures described, stress integration and inclusion rather than fragmentation, a unity of equal voices rather than hierarchism and stratification. Emotion, magic, and the dance serve to unite the individual, society, and nature; there is an integration of religion, art, healing, and life; emotion, intellect, and action combine to achieve an ecstatic state; process and continuous creation is stressed over objectification; there is a synthesis of the arts, and no divisions in the aesthetic sphere; the continuous cycle of life takes precedence over a focus on individual death; sexuality is (responsibly) free rather than exclusive; and everyone is included in aesthetic and other social activities. Significantly, however, this emphasis on synthesis, integration, and unity is not so total as to eliminate the self: the group consciousness and harmony with nature do not limit or repress individual consciousness but seem, rather, to nurture and support it. (This is not paradoxical but analogous to the harmony of individual themes in a piece of music.) Relationships between individuals and with the natural world are subject to subject rather than subject to object.

This tendency toward integration is one of the reasons I am inclined to consider the proposed aesthetic not only egalitarian but gynecentric. There are many examples in recent literature of the association of the integrative or synthetic with the experiences and activities of women. In "Toward a Feminist Aesthetic," Julia Penelope Stanley and Susan J. Wolfe (Robbins) suggest that the literary style of women is reflective of their thinking, a "discursive and conjunctive style rather than the complex and subordinating linear style of classification and distinction" (1978, 59, 67). Carol Gilligan has suggested that women's moral reasoning is oriented toward context and community rather than abstract, individual rights (Gilligan 1982). Nancy Chodorow has shown how girls tend to remain more interpersonally connected with their mothers, while boys tend to develop more discrete ego-boundaries (Chodorow 1978). Witken's "Embedded Figures Test" and "Rod and Frame Test" show that women tend to perceive a phenomenon as a whole, while men are more likely to isolate and focus on aspects of the phenomenon (Hyde and Linn 1986, ch. 4; Lloyd and Archer 1976, 169-71). I do not wish to contend that tendencies toward integration among women are biologically determined, for they are not peculiar to women, not all women exhibit them, and cultural factors may be responsible for them and can diminish them. Yet it is significant that these tendencies are strong in the societies described above. For because the women in these societies are relatively autonomous of men, their actions and expressions are likely to be authentic, to be based on female experience rather than to be imitations of men or actings out of male conceptions of the feminine.

The social structures of ancient or preliterate cultures would not be applicable to societies as large and complex as our own. Yet Eisler believes it is not only possible but essential, if our culture is to survive, to move from a "dominator" cultural model to a "partnership" one, a move she believes will come through empowering women (1987, ch. 13). If Lomax is correct about the relationships of aesthetic forms and social structures, such a social transformation would transform art and aesthetics as well. What form could a gynecentric aesthetic take in our complex society? Based on the material presented above, we may assume that the powerful emotion of dance and song would be used along with medicine and talk therapy to heal physical, social, and psychological ills. (Music, art, and dance therapists would be more plentiful, highly valued, and better paid.) Artistic activity would more often adapt to nature, rather than seek to express refinement or domination of nature. The division between intellect and emotion in aesthetic activity would lessen, and both would combine with action to achieve a synthesis of body and spirit. The erotic would be expressed as a vital, positive force and would be divorced from repression and the domination, submission, and violence of pornography. Artistic activity would be understood by and accessible to all; the authoritarian, hierarchical, and exclusionary nature of traditional artistic circles and performance groups would fall into decline. The emphasis would be off aesthetic objects to be coveted, hoarded, and contemplated, and on dynamic process, fully engaging and socially significant.

If Lomax's theories are valid, in such a culture the styles, structures, or processes of art itself would be transformed as well. Traditional ballet has revolved around overdisciplined (and often underfed) young women with bound feet and restricted movements controlled by authoritarian male choreographers. In the more gynecentric modern dance, which was conceived principally by Loie Fuller, Isadore Duncan, and Ruth St. Denis, choreographers work with dancers to achieve free, natural movement and a more personal, more erotic expression (Kendall 1979). Following Lomax's concept of "varied synchrony," gynecentric dance would not focus on principal dancers backed up by a group of subordinates but would involve a unified interaction or alternation of individual expressions.

Varied synchrony is particularly instructive for a feminist theory of musical form, an area that has yet to be developed. The concept suggests that gynecentric music would be composed of a unified, contrapuntal interaction of equal lines or voices, and not of principal and subordinate themes, or melody and accompaniment (a texture mirrored in musical performance as soloist and chorus, backup musicians or singers). Are there examples of varied synchrony in Western music history? Generally, Western polyphony or counterpoint is likely to have one or more parts prominent and others subordinate. When all voices are equally independent, they tend to treat what is basically the same material, and are thus unlikely to metaphorically exemplify a complex of personal or individual expressions.[8] A contrapuntal "egalitarianism," for example, might be thought to be characteristic of the avant-garde music of serialism, in which no one row is more prominent or important than any other row within a given piece. While all rows are equal, however, they are all essentially the same row; further, they are completely controlled or determined, totally subordinate to the overriding structure of the piece and the system. If, as Adorno has suggested, a row within a serial composition is taken as a model for an individual within a social structure, the individual in such a situation is clearly not free, has no individual voice; its identity is swelled up by the structure (Adorno 1985). The control and efficiency of serialism, and especially total serialism, reflects the Western association of progress with speed, control, and efficiency, a progress which seems to thrive on voiceless, alienated workers. In gynecentric polyphony, in contrast, individual, authentic voices would interact freely, contributing to the unification of the structure and being transformed through interaction with other voices and with the structure as a whole, but with no loss of identity in the process.

Western music in general is also distinct from the music of African foragers in that it is discipline-specific, separate from the other arts. It is also likely to be objectified, written out, and performed exactly as written. The performance of this music can be highly creative, of course, but the process-oriented, continuous creation of Pygmy or San music may be more conducive to personal expression and more reflective of the realities of the present. Post-avant-garde aleatoric or "change" music comes closer than serialism to the foraging and matriarchal aesthetics described above in its emphasis on mass or multi-media, on process of continuous creation in performance, and in its intent to adapt to rather than to control the natural world. John Cage urges us to let sounds be themselves, without trying to impose order on them; to "open our ears immediately, hear sounds suddenly, before one's thinking has a chance to turn them into something logical, abstract or symbolical" (Nyman 1974, 1). Unlike varied synchrony, however, there is no unity of equal voices in aleatoric music. Any sound, whether natural or human-made, can become a part of a musical composition or experience, and the very notions of unity, variety, and theme or subject are irrelevant. (The subject is allowed by the structure in serial music, but in aleatoric music there is no subject, period.) The foraging and "matriarchal" aesthetics are also distinct from aleatoric music in that they emphasize not only process but the stability of varied repetition and ritual, and in that aesthetic activity is inextricably linked to the stages and content of human life.

Formally speaking, a music that comes relatively close to the varied synchrony Lomax describes is jazz, specifically when it involves equal participation of all players and singers. The improvisational process in jazz is one of continuous creation, with each participant offering an individual expression while simulta- neously contributing to the unity of the whole. Jazz is also more open than traditional Western music to active participation of the audience, is likely to deal with the content of everyday life, and is often expressive of the erotic. It is significant, in our male-dominated society, that African American women have always been active participants in jazz, not only as singers of gospel and blues but as instrumentalists as well (Placksin 1982). Susan Cavin has shown that jazz grew out of the music of the Voodoo queens of nineteenth-century New Orleans (1975, 15). In view of the African roots of jazz, it is also significant that recent expositions of the African and feminine world views have been shown to be quite similar, especially in their respective emphases on the unity of the mind and body, the self and the natural world (positions summarized and critiqued in Harding 1986, 163-96). African societies in which women have powerful voices, however, are considered by Lomax to be most representative of his aesthetic.

In the Foreword to Catherine Clement's *Opera, or the Undoing of Women* (1988), Susan McClary describes some recent aesthetic contributions of women in music:

In the last few years, women of all kinds have emerged to participate in every sphere of musical production, to construct various models of femininity. Aretha Franklin's popular and gospel albums reveal her as a descendant of the great blues queens—a woman who sings with extraordinary power and physicality of longing, of satisfaction, of faith, of survival. Composer/performance artist Diamanda Galas draws upon the traditionally taboo figures of the madwoman, the temptress, the amazon to enact the ancient Mediterranean ritual of keening—for the politically oppressed and for victims of AIDS. Janika Vandervelde's piano trio *Genesis II* both deconstructs the phallic violence that underlies much of classical music and articulates an alternative erotic impulse that she identifies as feminine. And in the popular sphere, Madonna throws into confusion the virgin/whore dichotomy that has divided and contained women in Western society for centuries and takes on the features of the seductress Lulu, the exotic Carmen, the martyred Monroe, and leads them all to a moment of self-posses- sion and open celebration. No longer simply victim, toy, or dangerous essence, no longer forced to play dead within a male-controlled frame, this figure skips, dances, sings, and invites the audience—made up largely of young girls—to join in the festivities. (McClary 1988, xviii)

Some of these aesthetic expressions are soloistic and discipline specific, and most are understandably reactive to or reflective of male culture. Yet as in modern dance, there are features described in this passage that are reminiscent of the gynecentric aesthetic described above. Among these are female power in the face of domination, resistance to political oppression, an emphasis on both self-determination and community, and the connection of the aesthetic with spirituality, healing, and the erotic. These features reflect concerns that humanity in general can care about and share, and seem central to the aesthetic expression of strong, autonomous women.

The number of possible directions for a woman's art to proceed is unlimited, and the ones that emerge will result from the inspirations of particular artists, not from any conscious attempts to make art conform to aesthetic theory. But because the aesthetic offered here has emerged in various forms in cultures in which women have powerful voices, any contemporary manifestations of its aspects should be watched for, identified, and protected. Certain aspects of this aesthetic, such as the lack of structural complexity in artistic creation, the lack of specialization, and the de-emphasis of the visual arts, could be difficult for our contemporary culture to accept. Unlike ancient or foraging societies, however, a gynecentric aesthetic of the future would be influenced by the patriarchal art of our past, and perhaps retain some of its more desirable aspects. The fact that a high degree of structural complexity may not appear in the song of foraging cultures, for example, would not necessarily preclude its use in a gynecentric aesthetic of the present and future. The process of varied synchrony certainly allows for complex structures, which could be developed slowly to allow for assimilation by the community, and would be continuously transformed in "performance." A gynecentric culture would also inevitably include some individuals who are more inclined toward aesthetic activity than others, more aesthetically gifted and practiced than others. These individuals would be appreciated as they would be in any other culture, but would not be assigned any higher status in the community, nor serve to inhibit or stifle the expressions of others. The lack of emphasis on visual art is more disconcerting. The focus in the gynecentric aesthetic is on the process of continuous creation rather than on the production of art objects. The point is not that beautiful objects would not be made, however, but that they need not be made only for the sake of being beautiful. Perhaps the reason we place such high value on specialized art objects in contemporary culture is that aesthetic activity has been largely removed from everyday existence. Because workers cannot be concerned with making and doing things aesthetically when their jobs involve performing their duties as quickly and efficiently as possible, art and artistic activity in our culture has been relegated to the specialist, to the museum and the concert hall, and we are encouraged to satisfy our aesthetic needs by consuming beautiful objects. In the gynecentric culture envisioned here, everything made would be made with beauty, everything done would be done with beauty. Art would not be separate from the rest of life, and the entire society would be aestheticized.

Notes

1. Lomax was ahead of his time in making this claim in 1972. Based on a factor analysis of seventy-one measures of social and communicative structure, he noted a high degree of similarity between African and Australian gatherers despite extensive geographical and temporal separation. This lack of differentiation between widely separated groups is interpreted by Lomax as indicating the primacy of a gathering-based subsistence mode in early human prehistory. While this argument may not be persuasive to some, Lomax's conclusions are supported by Binford (1983) and the Dahlberg anthology (1983). Binford points out, for example, that foraging was the primary mode of subsistence for Australopithecines in Africa (c. 2.5 million years ago), who had neither the anatomy nor the culture (tools, etc.) to be bloodthirsty killers. What gave rise to male supremacy in complex societies? Agriculture is often assigned much of the blame. Ernestine Friedl shares Lomax's view that the status of women in a society is linked to their role in economic production. Female production levels diminished considerably when intensive agriculture, which requires considerable strength, became the principal mode of subsistence (Friedl 1987, 150-55). William Divale and Marvin Harris have suggested that the droughts and surpluses of agriculture gave rise to a need for raids and wars, and that war and violence is positively correlated with male supremacy (Divale and Harris 1976, 521-38). Eleanor Burke Leacock points out that male assertiveness "does not automatically flow from some psychologically conceived archetypical force, but it is related to a developing competition over economic prerogatives among men and between men and women in advanced cultural societies . . ." (1981, 246). She believes that women's oppression has resulted largely from the "transformation of their socially necessary labor into private service through the separation of the family from the clan" (Engels 1972, 41). Riane Eisler cites evidence to suggest that metallurgy, which led to more sophisticated weapons, played a significant role in the transition to male-dominated society (1987, 45-47). These theories imply that the increase in female production, the male sharing of responsibilities in the home, and moves to decrease institutionalized violence in contemporary society are facilitating the current rise in female power.

2. Some foragers are more egalitarian than others; Australian Aboriginal women, for example, do not fare as well as most African foraging women (Dahlberg 1983, 1-33).

3. As might be expected, Lomax has his supporters and detractors. Reviews of *Folk Song Style and Culture* in *American Anthropologist* (Nettl 1970), *Ethnomusicology* (Downey 1970), *Journal of American Folklore* (Merriam 1969), and *Science* (Naroll 1969) were strongly positive, while reviews by dance researchers in *CORD News* (Kealiinohomoku 1974) and *American Review of Anthropology* (Kaeppler 1978) were equally negative. Some of the dance researchers criticized Lomax's predilection for evaluation, synthesis and "grand schemes," maintaining that description and analysis is more appropriate for the discipline at this time. They took issue with his reliance on already-existing films instead of actual behavior, his assignment of one dance style for what was considered in some cases to be too broad a geographical area, and what they viewed as a relative lack of attention to intercultural influences and relationships. The positive reviews referred to Lomax's study as a "monument of our time" (*Science*), and "a major achievement in ethnomusicology and cross cultural method, regardless of the amount of criticism that may be levelled at the details" (*Ethnomusicology*). Alan Merriam (*Journal of American Folklore*) remarked that "Ethnomusicologists will ignore this book at their own peril." For more on Lomax, see McLeod (1979, 99-116).

4. The only societies Begler discusses that she considers truly egalitarian are the San and the BaMbuti Pygmies. She considers Australian Aborigines, which are egalitarian within the sexes but not between them, to be "semi-egalitarian." Other anthropologists continue to deny the existence of any truly egalitarian society. Michelle Rosaldo believes, for instance, that women are in some way subordinate to men in every known human culture, and will remain so as long as they are relegated to the domestic sphere (1974, 19).

But even if this is the case, it would remain that the Mbuti, San, and Lovedu societies discussed below would come very close to being egalitarian. And such a condition is sufficient for the critical point of this study: that the art of these cultures is reflective of their complementary tendencies.

5. The !Kung San will be referred to in this paper as the "San," the name they use to refer to themselves. The term "Bushman" has negative implications for the San.

6. Although over forty years old, this ethnography is still widely cited in anthropological research.

7. Other societies in which so-called "feminine" values are dominant and the status of women is high include the Montagnais-Naskapi of Canada, the Agta of the Philippines, the Washo of California, and the Navajo of Arizona and New Mexico (Leacock 1981, Part I; Dahlberg 1983, 121-52; Friedl 1987, 153; and Rosaldo and Lamphere 1974, 101-104. No information on dance or ritual is given in these studies.)

8. It should be pointed out that the music of the Pygmies and the San can have several individuals singing the same part, and that the music is often repetitive.

References

Adler, Margot. 1982. Meanings of matriarchy. In *The politics of women's spirituality*. See Spretnak (1982).

Adorno, T. W. 1985. *Philosophy of modern music*. Anne G. Mitchell and Wesley V. Blomster, trans. New York: Continuum.

Bachofen, J.J. [1854] 1973. *Das Mutterecht*. Bollingen Series 84. Princeton: Princeton University Press.

Bamberger, Joan. 1974. The myth of matriarchy: Why men rule in primitive society. In *Woman, culture and society*. See Rosaldo and Lamphere (1974).

Barstow, Anne L. 1988. The prehistoric goddess. In *The book of the goddess, past and present*. See Olson (1988).

Begler, Elsie P. 1978. Sex, status and authority in egalitarian societies. *American Anthropologist* 80 (3): 571-88.

Binford, Lewis. 1983. Man the mighty hunter? In *In pursuit of the past*. L. Binford, ed. New York: Thames and Hudson.

Binford, Sally R. 1982. Myths and matriarchies. In *The politics of women's spirituality*. See Spretnak (1982).

Brandel, Rose. 1973. *The music of Central Africa*. The Hague: Martinus Nijhoff.

Cavin, Susan. 1975. Missing women: On the voodoo trail to jazz. *Journal of Jazz Studies* 3 (1): 4-27.

Chodorow, Nancy. 1978. *The reproduction of mothering: Psychoanalysis and the sociology of gender*. Berkeley: University of California Press.

Clément, Catherine. 1988. *Opera, or the undoing of women*. Betsy Wing, trans. Minneapolis: University of Minnesota Press.

Dahlberg, Francis, ed. 1983. *Woman the gatherer*. New Haven: Yale University Press.

Davis, Elizabeth Gould. 1971. *The first sex*. New York: G. P. Putnam's Sons.

Divale, William T., and Marvin Harris. 1976. Population, warfare, and the male supremacist complex. *American Anthropologist* 78 (3): 521-38.

Donovan, Josephine. 1986. *Feminist theory*. New York: Ungar Publishing Company.

Downey, James. 1970. Review of *Folk song style and culture*. *Ethnomusicology* 14 (1): 63-67.

Eisler, Riane. 1987. *The chalice and the blade*. San Francisco: Harper & Row.

Engels, Friedrich. 1972. *The origin of the family, private property and the state*. Eleanor Burke Leacock, ed. New York: International Publishers.

Friedl, Ernestine. 1987. Society and sex roles. In *Anthropology 87/88*. E. Angeloni, ed. Guilford, CT: Dushkin Publishing Group.

Gilligan, Carol. 1982. *In a different voice: Psychological theory and women's development*. Cambridge, MA: Harvard University Press.

Gimbutas, Marija. 1982. *The goddesses and gods of old Europe, 6500-3500 B.C.* Berkeley: University of California Press.

Gimbutas, Marija. 1989. *The language of the goddess*. New York: Harper and Row.

Göttner-Abendroth, Heide. 1980. *Die Göttin und ihr Heros*. Munchen: Verlag Frauenoffensive.

Göttner-Abendroth, Heide. 1982. *Die tanzende Göttin*. Munchen: Verlage Frauenoffensive.

Göttner-Abendroth, Heide. 1986. Nine principals of a matriarchal aesthetic. In *Feminist aesthetics*. G. Ecker, ed. Harriet Anderson, trans. Boston: Beacon Press.

Graves, Robert. 1948. *The white goddess*. New York: Noonday Press.

Harding, Sandra. 1986. *The science question in feminism*. Ithaca, NY: Cornell University Press.

Harrison, Jane Ellen. 1922. *Prolegomena to the study of Greek religion*. Cambridge: Cambridge University Press.

Hyde, Janet Shibley, and Marcia C. Linn. 1986. *The psychology of gender*. Baltimore: Johns Hopkins University Press.

Jablow, Alta, and Dorothy Hammond. 1976. *Woman in the cultures of the world*. Menlo Park, CA: Cummings Publishing Co.

Kaeppler, Adrienne L. 1978. Dance in anthropological perspective. *American Review of Anthropology* 7: 31-49.

Katz, Richard. 1976. Education for transcendence. In *Kalahari hunter-gatherers*. See Lee and DeVore (1976).

Kealiinohomoku, J. W. 1974. Caveat on causes and correlations. *Council on Research in Dance News* 6 (2): 20-24.

Kendall, Elizabeth. 1979. *Where she danced*. New York: Alfred A. Knopf, Inc.

Krige, E. J. and J. D. Krige. 1947. *The realm of a rain queen*. London: Oxford University Press.

Leacock, Eleanor Burke. 1972. Introduction. In *Origin of the family, private property, and the state*. See Engels (1972).

Leacock, Eleanor Burke. 1981. *Myths of male dominance*. New York: International Publishers.

Lee, Richard B. 1979. *The !Kung San*. Cambridge: Cambridge University Press.

Lee, Richard B., and Irven DeVore, eds. 1976. *Kalahari hunter-gatherers: Studies of the !Kung San and their neighbors*. Cambridge, MA: Harvard University Press.

Lloyd, Barbara, and John Archer. 1976. *Exploring sex differences*. London: Academic Press.

Lomax, Alan. 1976. *Cantometrics: An approach to the anthropology of music*. Berkeley: California University Extension Media Center.

Lomax, Alan, with contributions by the cantometrics staff and with the editorial assistance of Edwin E. Ericson. 1968. *Folk song style and culture*. American Association for the Advancement of Science Pub. No. 88. Washington, D.C.

Lomax, Alan, and Norman Berkowitz. 1972. The evolutionary taxonomy of culture. *Science* 177: 230-38.

McClary, Susan. 1988. Foreword: Toward a feminist criticism of music. In *Opera, or the undoing of women*. See Clément (1988).

McLeod, Norma. 1979. Ethnomusicological research and anthropology. *Annual Review of Anthropology* 3: 99-116.

Marshall, Lorna. 1959. Marriage among !Kung bushmen. *Africa* 29 (4): 335-65.

Mellaart, James. 1967. *Çatal Hüyük*. London: Thames and Hudson.

Merriam, Alan. 1969. Review of *Folk song style and culture*. In *Journal of American Folklore* 82(326): 385-87.

Murdock, George P. 1967. *Ethnographic atlas*. Pittsburgh: University of Pittsburgh Press.

Naroll, Raoul. 1969. Review of *Folk song style and culture*. *Science* 166 (3903): 366-67.

Nettl, Bruno. 1970. Review of *Folk song style and culture*. *American Anthropologist* 72 (2): 438-41.

Neumann, Erich. 1963. *The great mother*. Ralph Manheim, trans. Bollingen Series XLVII. Princeton: Princeton University Press.

Nyman, Michael. 1974. *Experimental music*. New York: Schirmer.

Olson, Carl, ed. 1988. *The book of the Goddess, past and present*. New York: Crossroad.

Parsons, Jacquelynne E. 1980. *The psychobiology of sex differences and sex roles*. Washington: Hemisphere Publishing Corporation.

Placksin, Sally. 1982. *American women in jazz*. New York: Wideview Books.

Rosaldo, Michelle Zimbalist. 1974. Woman, culture and society: A theoretical framework. In *Woman, culture and society*. See Rosaldo and Lamphere (1974).

Rosaldo, Michelle Zimbalist, and Louise Lamphere. 1974. *Woman, culture and society*. Stanford: Stanford University Press.

Rubin, Gayle. 1975. The traffic in women: Notes on the "political economy" of sex. In *Toward an anthropology of women*. R. Reiter, ed. New York: Monthly Review Press.

Ruether, Rosemary Radford. 1985. *Womanguides*. Boston: Beacon Press.

Sherman, Julia. 1978. *Sex-related cognitive differences*. Springfield, Illinois: Charles C. Thomas.

Sjöö, Monica, and Barbara Mor. 1987. *The great cosmic mother: rediscovering the religion of the earth*. San Francisco: Harper and Row.

Spretnak, Charlene. 1978. *Lost goddesses of early Greece*. Boston: Beacon Press.

Spretnak, Charlene, ed. 1982. *The politics of women's spirituality*. New York: Anchor Press.

Stanley, Julia Penelope, and Susan J. Wolfe (Robbins). 1978. Toward a feminist aesthetic. *Chrysalis* 6: 57-76.

Starhawk [Miriam Simos]. 1979. *The spiral dance: A rebirth of the ancient religion of the great goddess*. San Francisco: Harper and Row.

Stone, Merlin. 1978. *When god was a woman*. New York: Harcourt Brace Jovanovich.

Stone, Merlin. 1980. *Ancient mirrors of womanhood: Our goddess and heroine heritage*. 2 vols. New York: New Syballine Press.

Stone, Ruth M. 1986. The shape of time in African music. In *Time, science and society in China and the West*. J. T. Fraser, ed. Amherst: University of Massachusetts Press.

Thomas, Elizabeth. 1959. *The harmless people*. New York: Knopf.

Turnbull, Colin. 1961. *The forest people*. New York: Simon and Schuster.

Turnbull, Colin. 1965. *Wayward servants: The two worlds of the African pygmies*. Garden City: Natural History Press.

Turnbull, Colin. 1983a. *The Mbuti pygmies*. New York: Holt, Rinehart and Winston.

Turnbull, Colin. 1983b. Mbuti womanhood. In *Woman the gatherer*. See Dahlberg (1983).

FOUR

Everyday Use
and Moments of Being
Toward a Nondominative Aesthetic

JOSEPHINE DONOVAN

Western aesthetic theory, especially since Kant, views art as material that has been extracted from the "real" world, as apolitical, and as governed by ideal aesthetic laws that are impressed upon it by the artist. In this dominative concept the imposition of form is seen as redemptive. Alternative aesthetic theory may be developed from feminist and Marxist theory, particularly that of Virginia Woolf and Theodor Adorno; its model is women's traditional domestic aesthetic praxis, art produced for everyday use. Such craft remains embedded in the everyday world but by virtue of its aesthetic character provides a political critique of the reified world of commodity exchange.

Western aesthetic theory, especially since Kant, has focused on the art object as a self-referential telos (*Zweckmässigkeit ohne Zweck*), divorced from the "real" world, apolitical, governed by ideal aesthetic laws. The artist takes a piece of reality and reworks it according to these rules, thus imprinting upon it his or her own design and setting it above the everyday. It is an imperialist dominative project. Usually the object—whether it be a painting or a work of literature—is eventually sold as an exchange-value commodity.

The basis for alternative aesthetic theory, one that provides for a relatively nondominative praxis, may be derived from feminist-Marxist theory—in particular from the epistemology (and implied aesthetic) developed by Virginia Woolf in *A Room of One's Own* modified and elaborated by Marxist theory, especially that of Theodor Adorno. From these sources one may propose an aesthetic of everyday use modeled on the nondominative process art of women's domestic aesthetic praxis, their use-value production.

Such art remains embedded in the everyday. It is not extracted and commodified as a "masterpiece," distinct from the everyday world. Because of this, the everyday world remains illumined by its beauty. Beauty and its ontological intensity—its sacrality—are not withdrawn, leaving the mundane workaday world all the more profane and providing aesthetic illumination only for an elite. Rather it remains a part of the worker's world, providing sacred, utopian space within that world and thereby commenting dialectically upon—offering a negative critique of—the profane reified world of commodity capitalism from the domestic standpoint.

Like much neoclassical theory, Kant's aesthetic is rooted in the mathematizing epistemology of the Cartesian-Newtonian worldview. Art, like the physical universe, operates according to ideal universal laws that are universally knowable and are disconnected from adventitious personal emotional interests. It is indeed through the forms of art that the everyday world is redeemed, just as contingent matter is made significant by the coherence given it by mathematical laws in the Cartesian-Newtonian view.

The aesthetic theory that governs Renaissance painting exemplifies this mathematical paradigm, as Erwin Panofsky points out in an important article, "Die Perspektive als Symbolische Form" ("Perspective as Symbolic Form"). Panofsky notes that objects in Renaissance painting take on significance according to their alignment on a perspective pyramid. "Their being," he says, is "functional but not substantial" (1927, 260, author's translation) and space is a mathematical construction (261). Thus, the sleeve on the virgin's dress is of significance because of its geometrical positioning and not because of its sacred being or ontic intensity. Panofsky calls this the triumph of a "distancing and objectifying sense of reality" (287).

Recently, Yaakov Jerome Garb has argued that the landscape perspective which emerged in the Renaissance governs our current Western attitude toward nature, which is one of alienation and domination. "[W]hen we step back to get a better view we create not only a physical distance but a corresponding psychic aloofness. The landscape perspective gives rise to (or is symptomatic of) a sense of detachment and spectatorship, for we become disengaged observers of rather than participants in the reality depicted" (1990, 266).[1]

This objectifying perspective sees matter or nature as dead;it is not perceived to have interests or indeed to have an existence apart from the subject whose mathematizing gaze is seen as redemptive. This allows the subject—whether it be artist or scientist—to manipulate matter or nature without retaining an empathy with or ethical respect for its independent existence. And it allows the subject to extract "significant" matter—that which corresponds to the subject's ideal conception—and elevate it, set it above the "trivial" matter of everyday life.

VIRGINIA WOOLF'S AESTHETIC THEORY

Virginia Woolf's A Room of One's Own is, among other things, a critique of the epistemology of Western science and its methodology of abstracting disembodied forms through mathematizing manipulation. Throughout she ridicules the possibility of extracting "a nugget of pure truth," of bringing closure to a topic, of saying, finally, this is that (Woolf 1957, 3). Rather, she sees truth (as well as beauty) as something embedded in the everyday, as something in process, as something revealed in glancing "moments of being."

In her quest for answers in the British Museum, which she sees as a repository of Western patriarchal knowledge and a locus of patriarchal methodology, she realizes one is expected there to "strain off what was personal and accidental in all these impressions and so reach the pure fluid, the essential oil of truth" (25). The properly trained male student from Oxbridge knows how to discipline his quest, where women, untrained in patriarchal methodologies, tend to exert less control over their material, allowing it to exist, untrammeled, on its own.

> The student who has been trained in research at Oxbridge has no doubt some method of shepherding his question past all distractions till it runs into its answer as a sheep runs into its pen. The student by my side, for instance, who was copying assiduously from a scientific manual was, I felt sure, extracting pure nuggets of the essential ore every ten minutes or so. . . . But if, unfortunately, one has had no training in a university, the question far from being shepherded to its pen flies like a frightened flock hither and thither, helter-skelter, pursued by a whole pack of hounds. (28)

While Woolf's tone is self-deprecatory here, it is clear her main satiric target is the Oxbridge methodology of forcing truth into preconceived patterns. Rather, Woolf proposes in its stead, here and elsewhere in *A Room*, a radical induction, an approach that allows reality to fly hither and thither, that does not cram it into a pen.

The analogy to humans controlling animals and nature cannot be ignored, for Woolf is clearly endorsing here a relatively laissez-faire attitude toward reality or nature, a let-it-be ecological approach. Unlike the student or Professor von X. (see below), Woolf does not elide the incidentals of her environment in order to get at a higher truth. Rather, she adopts an apparently random process, one that focuses on the incidentals of the everyday, not seeking to shepherd them into some redemptive category, allowing them an independent existence. In this example, for instance, she focuses on the student who *happens* to be sitting next to her. A manx cat who *happens* to wander by the window where she is dining at Oxbridge provokes other reflections (11). A newspaper that *happens* to have been left by an earlier tenant becomes the focus of her lunchtime deliberations while at the British Museum (33). "I take," she says, "only what chance has floated to my feet" (78). Throughout *A Room* Woolf arrives at partial, embedded illuminations by focusing on random, accidental events and situations.

Woolf's resistance to churning up reality and reworking it into man-made aesthetic categories may be further seen in her ruminations on the swamp that she imagines having been supplanted by the construction of Oxbridge. "Once, presumably, this quadrangle with its smooth lawns, its massive buildings, and the chapel itself was marsh too" (9). In reflecting on the construction of the university Woolf imagines an "unending stream of gold and silver" (9), thus connecting the patriarchal institution with capitalism. "Hence the libraries and laboratories; the observatories; the splendid equipment of costly and delicate instruments which now stands on glass shelves, where centuries ago the grasses waved and the swine rootled" (10). There is clearly the suggestion here that we might be better off with just the wild grasses, the prepatriarchal swamp. In a later use of this image Woolf unmistakably connects the rise of civilization with women's subordination and the concomitant rise of fascism and militarism, a theme she develops more fully in *Three Guineas* (1938).

Without women's historical subordination to men, without their having poured their energies into men, "without that power probably the earth would still be swamp and jungle. The glories of all our wars would be unknown. . . . The Czar and the Kaiser would never have worn their crowns or lost them" (36).

As Woolf proceeds with her inquiries in the British Museum, she finds herself "glancing with envy at the reader next door who was making the neatest abstracts, headed often with an A or a B or a C, while my own notebook rioted with the wildest scribble of contradictory jottings. It was distressing, it was bewildering, it was humiliating. Truth had run through my fingers. Every drop had escaped" (31).

In this state Woolf begins to fantasize a Professor von X., who is "engaged in writing his monumental work entitled *The Mental, Moral, and Physical Inferiority of the Female Sex*" (31). Woolf imagines "his expression" suggesting "that he was laboring under some emotion that made him jab his pen on the paper as if he were killing some noxious insect as he wrote, but even when he had killed it that did not satisfy him; he must go on killing it . . ." (31). Once again Woolf connects Oxbridge epistemology with the repression-destruction of the natural world, as she did in the swamp image. Woolf recognizes that such objectification and control serve to fortify the professor's ego and secure his identity. It is a matter of dominator/dominated. Later she speaks of the professor reaching "for his measuring-rods to prove himself 'superior' " (92) when confronted with new, anomalous evidence: he must tame it, control it, shepherd it into pens, objectify it, kill it.

Woolf resists the dualistic compartmentalization that the Oxbridge epistemology entails. Rather, her vision is holistic: one cannot separate mind and body. Indeed, it is women's impoverished material circumstances that have crippled them intellectually and spiritually—the central thesis of the book. "The human frame being what it is, heart, body, and brain all mixed together, and not contained in separate compartments . . . a good dinner is of great importance to good talk. One cannot think well, love well, sleep well, if one has not dined well" (18).

And art itself is not disconnected from material reality: "fiction is like a spider's web . . . attached to life at all four corners. Often the attachment is scarcely perceptible. . . . But when the web is pulled askew . . . one remembers that these webs are not spun in midair by incorporeal creatures, but are the work of suffering human beings, and are attached to grossly material things, like health and money and the houses we live in" (43-44).

But art does not simply reflect everyday reality—Woolf is not offering a mimetic theory; rather, it expresses the ontic illuminations that inhere in everyday life. For embedded within the material world is the spiritual, the transcendent, revealed in "moments of being." This is the reality that the writer seeks to discover and convey.

What is meant by "reality"? It would seem to be something very erratic, very undependable—now to be found in a dusty road, now in a scrap of newspaper in the street, now in a daffodil in the sun. It lights up a group in a room and stamps some casual saying. It overwhelms one walking home beneath the stars and makes the silent world more real than the world of speech—and there it is again in an omnibus in the uproar of Piccadilly. . . . Now the writer . . . has the chance to live more than other people in the presence of this reality. It is [her] business to find it and collect it and communicate it to the rest of us. (113-14)

In a later, only recently published article, "A Sketch of the Past," Woolf elaborates on this idea:

behind the cotton wool is hidden a pattern; that we—I mean all human beings—are connected with this; that the whole world is a work of art; that we are parts of the work of art. *Hamlet* or a Beethoven quartet is the truth about this vast mass that we call the world. But there is no Shakespeare; there is no Beethoven; certainly and emphatically there is no God; we are the words; we are the music; we are the thing itself. (1985, 72)

Thus, unlike the dominative view of the artist who stamps his or her form upon reality, redeeming it, civilizing it, Woolf sees the writer as one who is immersed in that reality, a part of it, who allows or enables Being to be expressed.

The "anonymity" that Woolf claims "runs in [women's] blood" (1957, 52) may thus be seen as a virtue, contrasting with the male imperialistic desire to put his name on everything. Unlike men, women "will pass a tombstone or a signpost without an irresistible desire to cut their names on it as Alf, Bert or Chas. must do" (52).[2]

Woolf's resistance to forcing reality into a preconceived order, shepherding it into a pen, is further illustrated in a comment she made about narrative structure in "Modern Fiction": "Let us record," she urged, "the atoms as they fall upon the mind in the order in which they fall, let us trace the pattern, however disconnected and incoherent in appearance, which each sight or incident scores upon the consciousness" (1966, 107).[3] Thus, rather than seeing form as redemptive of a threateningly chaotic reality—the assumption behind Kantian aesthetics—Woolf asks that the artist be faithful to that reality, not eliding its anomalies in a rush to preconceived pattern.

"On Re-reading Novels," in which she reviews Percy Lubbock's *Craft of Fiction*, further indicates Woolf's resistance to a traditional formalism, in particular Lubbock's insistence that "form" be considered the constitutive element of great literature. Woolf argues that the concept "form" comes between the reader and the emotions of a text as a kind of "alien substance" "imposing itself upon emotions which we feel naturally, and name simply" (1966, 126). Rather, she suggests, our sense of the meaning of a work as a whole comes to us in "moments of [emotional] understanding" that enable us to see what the overall point of a work is. Her emphasis is upon emotional meaning; it is that which gives significance to a text, not "form" per se.

Therefore the "book itself" is not form which you see, but emotion which you feel, and the more intense the writer's feeling the more exact . . . its expression in words. And whenever Mr. Lubbock talks of form it is as if something were interposed between us and the book as we know it. (126)

Woolf concludes that the form that matters in fiction is not a visual form such as one might find in Renaissance painting, but an emotional order: form in fiction means "that certain emotions have been placed in the right relations to each other" (129).

It is apparent that Woolf developed her own aesthetic theories in the context of Bloomsbury discussions of the subject. Two of her Bloomsbury friends, Clive Bell and Roger Fry, both developed formalist aesthetic theory in the tradition of autonomous art established by Kant and his English disciple Coleridge.

In *Art* (1913) Clive Bell coined the term "significant form" to explain his Kantian view of the art object as an end in itself:

> [H]aving seen [art] as pure form, having freed it from all causal and adventitious interests, from all that it may have acquired from its commerce with human beings, from all its significance as means, [one] has felt its significance as an end in itself. (53)

Bell sees art as having a religious or spiritual significance, an idea that has become synonymous with Bloomsbury aesthetics. "What is the significance of anything as an end in itself? That which is left when we have stripped a thing of all its associations, of all its significance as a means? . . . What but . . . 'the thing in itself' . . . [or] 'ultimate reality'?" (53-54). Thus, while Kant felt that the "thing itself" was unknowable, Bell believes it accessible through art, because of art's "significant form."

Bell's view that art "as pure form" be "freed" from all "adventitious interests . . . that it may have acquired from its commerce with human beings" is diametrically opposed by Woolf in *A Room of One's Own* where she rejects the idea that it is possible to "strain off" the "personal and accidental and so reach the pure fluid, the essential oil of truth." There and elsewhere she insists that truth and beauty (moments of being) are embedded, contextual, and in process, not something that can be extracted and expunged from the "suffering human beings" (1957, 44) who create and experience them. "We are the thing itself" (1985, 72).

While Woolf did not overtly criticize Bell's *Art*, it is clear that she found his formalism too extreme. In a 1914 letter to Bell she says "of course there are a great many things I don't agree with" (Nicolson and Trautman 1976, 46). And in a diary entry of May 28, 1918, she notes, Clive "seems to have little natural insight into literature" (Ann Olivier Bell 1977, 151). Conversely, Clive Bell did not like *A Room of One's Own* (Quentin Bell 1972, 150).

Roger Fry's *Vision and Design* (1920) proposed a Kantian aesthetic theory not far removed from Bell's. "We must," he urged, "give up the attempt to judge the work of art by its reaction on life, and consider it as an expression of emotions regarded as ends in themselves" (29). "The aesthetic emotion" he maintains, is "as remote from actual life and its practical utilities as the most useless mathematical theory" (302).

In elaborating on the notion of "significant form" Fry brings out the imperialistic impulse inherent in it. Significant form, he notes, "implies the effort [of the] artist to bend to our emotional understanding by means of his passionate conviction some intractable material which is alien to our spirit" (302). Here again we sense an image of the artist as one who wrenches reality, who forces reality to behave in accordance with a redemptive, mathematical order.

While Woolf did not overtly criticize *Vision and Design*, she did subtly indicate her disagreement in her biography of Fry, where she especially criticizes his attempt to apply the idea of significant form to literature (not unlike Percy Lubbock). "As a critic of literature," she notes, "he was not what is called a safe guide" (Woolf 1969, 240). And in a diary notation of December 19, 1920, she called his work "rudimentary" (Anne Olivier Bell 1978, 81). Nevertheless, in the conclusion to her biography Woolf approves of Fry's attempt to arrive at a "balance between the emotions and the intellect, between Vision and Design" (1969, 245).

This comment parallels somewhat her remarks in "On Re-Reading Novels" about an emotional hermeneutic.[4] In the above statement she appears to equate vision with emotion (and presumably with moments of being) and design with intellect and form. There are clearly connotations of feminine and masculine here, as historically in Western thought. Woolf appears to be concerned that the reality of the emotions, the feminine, not be distorted and imprisoned or colonized by masculine form.

THE NONDOMINATIVE AESTHETICS OF
CATHER AND JEWETT

The evolution of Willa Cather's artistic theory provides us with a model of a writer who early in her career embraced a dominative conception of aesthetics but moved in her later years toward a nondominative notion. In another article I suggested that the latter theory derives from a kind of women's art, meaning by that an art rooted in women's domestic craft labor and entailing such creations as quilts, bread, pottery, etc. (Donovan 1991a). As Cather's biographer Sharon O'Brien has noted, early in her career Cather made numerous statements where she equated writing with a kind of sadistic dominance. For the early writer "the links between [the] sword, the dissector's knife, the surgeon's scalpel, and the writer's pen are literal as well as metaphoric" (O'Brien 1987, 148; see also 149-54). "In the 1890s Cather considered technology's victory over nature analogous to the 'virile' writer's praiseworthy triumph over recalcitrant subject matter in the creative process" (O'Brien 1987, 389).

The identification of the writer with the scientist was a relatively common idea in the late nineteenth century—especially among the naturalists. Emile Zola, for example, develops the idea in *Le Roman expérimental* (1880).

Cather, however, moved away from this theory in her later work—perhaps, as O'Brien suggests, because of the influence of Sarah Orne Jewett, whose aesthetic theory provides for a nondominative artistic mode. One of Jewett's central contentions was that the writer should only minimally arrange the subject matter, transmitting it to the reader with the least intervention possible. On numerous occasions when giving advice to other writers she would state, "My dear father used to say to me very often, 'Tell things *just as they are!*' . . . The great messages and discoveries of literature come to us, they *write us,* and we do not control them in a certain sense" (Cary 1967, 52).[5] This idea of literature as discovery is similar to Woolf's notion that the writer perceives "moments of being" in the everyday.

Jewett believed the reader also engages in discovery and she resisted writers who, she thought, overly worked their material, leaving little for the reader to do except passively absorb. In her 1871 diary Jewett cited approvingly her father's idea that "a story should be managed so that it should *suggest* interesting things to the *reader* instead of the author's doing all the thinking for him, and setting it for him in black and white. The best compliment is for the reader to say 'Why didn't he put in "this" or "that" ' " (Jewett 1871-1879, n.p.). Jewett early saw Jane Austen as one who worked her material too much; Jewett complained, "all the reasoning is done for you and all the thinking. . . . It seems to me like hearing somebody talk on and on and on, while you have no part in the conversation, and merely listen" (Cary 1967, 21). Later, in complimenting a friend's reading of her story "Martha's Lady" (1897), Jewett noted, "You bring something to the reading of [the story] that [it] would go very lame without. . . . [I]t is those unwritable things that the story holds in its heart . . . and these must be understood, and yet how many a story goes lame for lack of that understanding" (Fields 1911, 112).

Jewett thus perceives the artist as one who is a relatively passive transmitter of "things as they are," who ideally imposes as little artifice as possible upon the material, so as to allow existential moments of discovery to happen for the reader. It is a collective process of recognition of the sacred embedded in the profane—similar to Woolf's ideas outlined above.

By the time Cather came to write her preface for a 1925 reprint of Jewett's *Country of the Pointed Firs* (1896), she had rejected the idea of the sadist-artist who manipulates the subject matter "by using his 'imagination' upon it and twisting it to suit his purpose" (O'Brien 1987, 388). Cather's new aesthetic is animated by "the 'gift of sympathy,' [the] ability to abandon the ego rather than to impose it upon her subject" (O'Brien 1987, 388). In that preface Cather praised Jewett's stories for their closeness to everyday reality. "They melt into the land and the life of the land until they are not stories at all, but life itself." Rather than dominating the material, the writer must surrender to it, Cather observes, as Jewett does: "If [the writer] achieves anything noble, anything enduring, it must be by giving [her]self absolutely to [her] material. And this gift of sympathy is [her] great gift; is the fine thing in [her] that alone can make [her] work fine" (Cather 1956, n.p.). Thus, like Woolf, Cather stresses fidelity to the random incidentals of the quotidian in her theory of aesthetic praxis.

In 1921 Cather commented, "The German housewife who sets before her family on Thanksgiving Day a perfectly roasted goose, is an artist" (Bennett 1951, 168).[6] By this time, thus, Cather has developed the idea that art is to be found in the everyday practices of the domestic woman—an idea amplified in Alice Walker's "In Search of Our Mothers' Gardens" (1974) (see below).

Elsewhere I have detailed the evolution of Cather's aesthetic ideas in her novels *The Song of the Lark* (1915), *One of Ours* (1922), and the *Professor's House* (1925) (Donovan 1991a). The essence of her theory is expressed by a character in the former novel who is meditating upon Indian women's pottery. "What was any art," she thought, "but an effort to make a sheath, a mould in which to imprison for a moment the shining elusive element which is life itself. . . . The Indian women had held it in their jars" (Cather 1978, 296). The Indian women's pottery, a use-value product, remains integrated with its environment and yet captures what Woolf called life's "moments of being."

THE DIALECTICAL AESTHETIC
OF THEODOR ADORNO

The central Marxist aesthetic tradition relies on the traditional Western idea of the artist as one who redeems contingent reality by giving it form. Indeed, Marx and Engels made transformative labor or praxis definitional to human identity. On the other hand, Marxist theory also offers the idea of art as "negative critique," which moves beyond formalism, recognizing that art is inherently political. This idea, I think, is one that can be used by those of us who are attempting to formulate a nondominative aesthetic.

First, let us recapitulate central aspects of Marx's aesthetic theory. In the *Economic and Philosophical Manuscripts* of 1844 Marx sees domination of nature as an essential characteristic of humans' "species-being": "The practical construction of an *objective world*, the *manipulation* of inorganic nature, is the confirmation of man as a conscious species-being." Unlike animals who also change and manipulate matter, humans do it "also in accordance with the laws of beauty" (Fromm 1969, 102). As Stefan Morawski remarks, Marx retains a Kantian theory of art where "the physical world is reworked to the harmonious standard, use, or measure (*Mass*) of humanity" (1974a, 13). In the *Grundrisse* Marx uses Kantian terms to explain his theory: medieval handicraft, he notes, "is still half artistic, it has still the aim in itself (*Selbstzweck*)" (Morawski 1974a, 16). In other words, its aesthetic character lies in self-referential autotelic form.

Art is a particular form of human labor that reshapes external reality in accordance with a preconceived aesthetic ideal. In *Capital* Marx notes that what distinguishes "the poorest architect . . . from the best of bees [is that] before [the architect] builds a cell in wax, he has built it in his head. The result achieved at the end of a labor process was already present at its commencement, in the *imagination of the worker, in its ideal form*. More than merely working an *alteration* in the form of nature, he also *knowingly works his own purposes into* nature" (Morawski 1974a, 54).

As Isaac D. Balbus has pointed out, traditional Marxism is really a philosophy of domination. In the *Grundrisse*, for example, Marx clearly shares the Enlightenment notion of progress as one of increasing human scientific "mastery over nature." He indeed applauds the advent of the capitalist stage in economic evolution because in its worldview "Nature becomes for the first time simply an object for making, purely a matter of utility." And he enthuses over the spread of "theoretical knowledge [that is] . . . designed to subdue [nature] to human requirements." "Communism," he maintains, "will entail 'the advent of real mastery over nature'" (Balbus 1982, 259, 273).

While traditional Marxist aesthetic theory remains within the confines of Western dominative aesthetics, there is a vein in contemporary Marxist thought that shifts the conception of art in a political direction, one that is compatible, I believe, with the nondominative aesthetic of everyday use that I am attempting to develop. This vein stems from the dialectical aspect of Marxist theory; it may be seen in such contemporary Marxist theorists as Ernst Bloch and Fredric Jameson who argue that art be seen as offering "anticipatory illuminations," or utopian glimpses; these are not far removed from Woolf's "moments of being." In *The Political Unconscious* Jameson asserts that, in addition to its "negative hermeneutic," Marxist criticism must offer a "positive hermeneutic, or a decipherment of the Utopian impulses of . . . cultural texts" (1981, 296).

Bloch developed the idea that literature and art provide "anticipatory illuminations" of an other and better world (1988, xxxiii-vi). Bloch was heavily influenced by Heidegger, whose theory of art as an "unconcealedness" of Being (*aletheia*) subtends Bloch's notion of *Vor-Schein* (see his "Origin of the Work of Art") (Heidegger 1984, 258-87). But since Bloch and Heidegger's intentions are problematic because of their associations with Stalinism and nazism respectively, I feel that their theories are compromised, and therefore prefer not to rely on them here.[7]

Rather, I turn to the dialectical theory of the "negative critique" developed by Theodor Adorno of the Frankfurt School of Marxism. In a 1964 conversation with Bloch, Adorno points out that "utopia is essentially in the determined negation of that which merely is, and by concretizing itself as something false, it always points at the same time to what should be" (Bloch 1988, 12). In an earlier article, "Reconciliation under Duress" (1958), Adorno explains that art provides a vantage point from which to criticize the world of commodity reification, because art "aims at a dialectical reconciliation of subject and object. In the form of an image the object is absorbed into the subject instead of following the bidding of the alienated world and persisting obdurately in a state of reification. The contradiction between the object reconciled in the subject . . . and the actual unreconciled object in the outside world, confers on the work of art a vantage-point from which it can criticize actuality. Art is the negative knowledge of the actual world" (1980, 160).

In his *Aesthetic Theory* (1970) Adorno amplifies that "art becomes a qualitatively different entity by virtue of its opposition, at the level of artistic form, to the existing world and also by virtue of its readiness to aid and shape that world. . . . [A]rt criticizes society just by being there. . . . This social deviance of art is the determinate negation of a determinate society" (1984, 2, 321).[8]

In his *Sociology of the Novel* Marxist critic Lucien Goldmann developed a somewhat similar idea, seeing the novel as a "critical and oppositional" form, harboring the personalist ethos of use-value production as a vantage point from which to criticize the increasingly "anesthetic" rationalism of the world of commodity production with its exchange-value ethic (1964, 52, 55, author's translation). Elsewhere I have argued that one of the reasons women gravitated to the novel form and used it as a critical vehicle was their traditional base in use-value production (Donovan 1991b).

Bettina Aptheker offers a similar theory in her recent book, *Tapestries of Life*. Focusing on the connections between women's "daily experience" and their "artifacts of daily life," Aptheker notes a theme of resistance emerging from women's literature and art (1989, 12).[9] Aptheker argues that the "women of each particular culture or group have a consciousness that is distinct from the way the men of the culture or group see things." This idea "that women have a distinct consciousness rests upon two assumptions. . . . [one, that] there is a sexual division of labor . . . [and, two, that] women are subordinated to men" (12).

Aptheker believes that women's work expresses a theme of resistance that is "shaped by the dailiness of women's lives" and "comes out of women's subordinated status" (173). In other words, women's economic base in use-value production and their political oppression provide a marginalized standpoint from which they resist the imposition of oppressive designs.

Aptheker sees Meridel Le Sueur's story "Harvest" (1929) as prototypical; it concerns the resistance of a farm woman to the use of a new mechanical harvester machine. "She was opposed to progress defined as 'power' and 'control' and 'conquest' over the land" (182). She felt "if you separate one thing from the whole . . . you upset the balance upon which all life depends . . ." (183).

My thesis in this article is somewhat different than Aptheker's, however; rather than arguing that women have a unique standpoint because of their historical social and economic situation—an entirely defensible idea, I believe—I am arguing in the vein of Adorno that art is inherently political in that it by definition offers a negative critique of commodity exchange reification.

This, of course, would be true of autotelic art as well as of the artisanal craft of women's domestic practice. However, the former retains a dominative character—and therefore is complicit in the very oppressions it may seek to criticize—while the latter does not. Women's craft or domestic art involves a nondominative praxis that nevertheless provides what Adorno calls a "negative critique." That critique derives from the "moments of being" that inhere in everyday art, which by their sacrality point up the profanity of our reified media environment.

Marxist critic Stefan Morawski, taking off, it appears, from Adorno, suggests that artisanal or use-value art may be seen to offer such a negative critique.

> Although they are in material substance or in use-value . . . a part of our world, they are at the same time opposed to this world. They provide territories in which . . . these given systems of qualities . . . subsist in themselves. A fine example is provided here by functional objects, which are changed into works of art if outfitted with special outward attributes such as color and proportion beyond the requirements of their use. . . . [There is] . . . a relative autonomy . . . where objects of everyday use or *objets trouvés* come to be looked upon as art. . . . It amounts simply to putting a given work or product in a context where, as a structure rendered conspicuous, it acquires an autotelic function. (Morawski 1974b, 106)

ALICE WALKER AND THE
AESTHETIC OF EVERYDAY USE

Alice Walker's story "Everyday Use" (1973) concerns many of the issues raised in this article. The conflict in the story is between a rural, black woman and her daughter, Dee, who has gone to the city and been educated into the ways of capitalism. She returns home an outside observer; she frames her old house and her mother aesthetically in terms of commodity values. On arrival, for example, she takes photos of the house and of her mother knowing they will be seen by others of her urban class as "quaint" commodities. The mother resists this objectification which she implicitly feels Dee imposing upon her and her world.

The pivotal clash in the story is over an old quilt. Dee looks at it—along with other craft items in the house, such as a butter churn—with new eyes. She sees it as an autotelic art object that has prize commodity value; it is something to be hung on the wall.

Her mother, on the other hand, sees it as an object of everyday use, one that is infused with personal and family value—therein lies its significance. She therefore decides to give the quilt to her other daughter who appreciates its family history and plans to use it on her bed. Thus, Walker implicitly rejects in this story the idea of art as a discrete masterpiece to be isolated from the real world—and therefore rejects a body of aesthetic theory that since Kant has dominated Western thinking. Rather, she proposes an art that is embedded in the everyday, that is infused with personal and local history, and whose interest lies in these so-called adventitious matters.

In her article "In Search of Our Mothers' Gardens" Walker amplifies this idea, looking at her mother's garden as a work of art: "Whatever rocky soil she landed on, she turned into a garden. A garden so brilliant with colors, so original in its design, so magnificent with life and creativity, that to this day people drive by our house . . . and ask to stand and walk among my mother's art." For her mother, Walker realizes, "being an artist has still been a daily part of her life" (1974, 105).

Thus, Alice Walker continues in the vein of such women theorists and artists of the past as Virginia Woolf, Willa Cather, and Sarah Orne Jewett, who similarly proposed an aesthetic theory where art remained embedded in and arose out of conversation with the contingent, everyday world. The artistic praxis each envisages is not of an artist stamping his or her mark upon material or of reshaping recalcitrant feminine matter into redemptive masculine form. Rather, it is of a practice that gives in to the environmental "material," that works with it in a dialogical fashion, that recognizes that moments of being inhere in the everyday world, seeing art as a means of momentarily capturing or highlighting or simply attending to those moments. Art is not transcendent, then, but rather part of the mortal process. The mother's quilt in "Everyday Use" will be worn out; it will not achieve immortal status but, like all women's domestic craft, will erode in the process of time.

Yet, the moments of beauty captured in this work remain as a "negative critique" of the reified world of commodity exchange, as a utopian glimpse of an other, sacred world. Dee's mother's decision not to accede to her daughter's desire to commodify the quilt is a gesture of resistance similar to that of the farm woman in Le Sueur's story "Harvest." Thus, women's domestic art remains political and yet does not engage in the dominative praxis seen in autotelic art forms. It therefore provides the basis for a nondominative aesthetic, an art of everyday use.

Notes

1. In *The Pornography of Representation* (Minneapolis: University of Minnesota Press, 1986), Susanne Kappeler also questions the idea of the disinterested artist/spectator who has no "responsibilities towards his subject matter, the woman 'material' " (56).

2. I owe this interpretation of the "anonymity" passage to Laura Lane.

3. On the question of women writers favoring an "inductive," paratactic narrative style see Josephine Donovan, "Sarah Orne Jewett's Critical Theory," in *Critical Essays on Sarah Orne Jewett*, Gwen Nagel, ed. (Boston: G. K. Hall, 1984), 213-14, 223, n. 7, and "Style and Power," in *Feminism, Bakhtin, and the Dialogic*, Dale Bauer and Susan Jaret McKinistry, eds. (Albany: SUNY Press, 1991).

4. Johnstone in *Bloomsbury Group* suggests that Woolf was influenced by Charles Mauron, *The Nature of Beauty in Art and Literature*, which applies Fry's ideas to literature and was translated by Fry in 1926 and published the next year by Hogarth Press. See also Mark Goldman's very useful discussion of Woolf's aesthetic theory in "Virginia Woolf and the Critic as Reader" (1965) in *Virginia Woolf: A Collection of Critical Essays*, Claire Sprague, ed. (Englewood Cliffs, NJ: Prentice-Hall, 1971), 155-68.

5. For a further elaboration of Jewett's theory see Josephine Donovan, "Sarah Orne Jewett's Critical Theory," 212-25, and "A Woman's Vision of Transcendence: A New Interpretation of the Works of Sarah Orne Jewett," *Massachusetts Review* 21, no. 2 (Summer 1980): 365-80. In a series of articles British novelist Iris Murdoch has articulated an analogous critique of the epistemological habit of forcing contingent reality into forms, a habit she sees as morally defective. Great artists, on the contrary, she maintains, are not "afraid of the contingent." ("The Sublime and the Beautiful Revisited," *Yale Review* 69 [December 1959]: 257.) For a further discussion of Murdoch's theories, see Josephine Donovan, "Beyond the Net: Feminist Criticism as a Moral Criticism," *Denver Quarterly* 17, no. 4 (Winter 1983): 54-57.

6. The comment is apparently from an interview with Cather by Eleanor Hinman, November 6, 1921, in the *Lincoln* [Nebraska] *Star*.

7. See Jack Zipes, "Ernst Bloch and the Obscenity of Hope," *New German Critique* 45 (Fall 1988): 3-8. On Heidegger see Victor Farias, *Heidegger and Nazism* (Philadelphia: Temple University Press, 1989).

8. See also Richard Wolin, "The De-Aestheticization of Art: On Adorno's *Aesthetische Theorie*," *Telos* 41 (1979): 105-27. The other major Frankfurt School theorist of "negative criticism" is Herbert Marcuse, but his aesthetic theories are infused with a kind of romantic Freudianism.

9. See also Josephine Donovan, "Toward a Women's Poetics," *Tulsa Studies in Women's Literature* 3, nos. 1/2 (Spring/Fall 1984). In "Still Practice: A/Wrested Alphabet: Toward a Feminist Aesthetic," Jane Marcus briefly introduces a similar aesthetic, which she calls "Penelope's Aesthetic"; "it does not separate art from work and daily life. . . . Penelope's art is work" (*Tulsa Studies in Women's Literature* 3, nos. 1/2 [Spring/Fall 1984]: 84).

References

Adorno, Theodor. 1980. Reconciliation under duress. In *Aesthetics and politics*, by Ernst Bloch et al. London: Verso.

Adorno, Theodor. 1984. *Aesthetic theory*. Gretel Adorno and Rolf Tiedemann, eds. London: Routledge and Kegan Paul.

Aptheker, Bettina. 1989. *Tapestries of life: Women's consciousness and the meaning of daily experience*. Amherst: University of Massachusetts Press.

Balbus, Isaac D. 1982. *Marxism and domination: A neo-Heglelian, feminist, psychoanalytic theory of sexual, political, and technological liberation*. Princeton, NJ: Princeton University Press.

Bell, Anne Olivier, ed. 1977. *The diary of Virginia Woolf*. Vol. 1, 1915-1919. New York: Harcourt.

Bell, Anne Olivier, ed. 1978. *The diary of Virginia Woolf*. Vol. 2, 1920-1924. New York: Harcourt.

Bell, Clive. 1913. *Art*. New York: Frederick A. Stokes.

Bell, Quentin. 1972. *Virginia Woolf: A biography*. Vol. 2, *Mrs. Woolf*. London: Hogarth.

Bennett, Mildred R. 1951. *The world of Willa Cather*. New York: Dodd, Mead.

Bloch, Ernst. 1988. *The utopian function of art and literature*. Cambridge, MA: MIT Press.

Cary, Richard, ed. 1967. *Sarah Orne Jewett letters*. Waterville, ME: Colby College Press.

Cather, Willa. [1925]. 1956. Preface to *The country of the pointed firs*. Garden City, NY: Doubleday.

Cather, Willa. [1915]. 1978. *The song of the lark*. Lincoln: University of Nebraska Press.

Donovan, Josephine. 1991a. The pattern of birds and beasts: Willa Cather and women's art. In *Writing the woman writer*. Suzanne Jones, ed. Philadelphia: University of Pennsylvania Press.

Donovan, Josephine. 1991b. Women and the rise of the novel: A feminist-Marxist theory. *Signs* 16 (3): 441-62.

Fields, Annie, ed. 1911. *Letters of Sarah Orne Jewett*. Boston: Houghton Mifflin.

Fromm, Erich, ed. 1969. *Marx's concept of man*. New York: Ungar.

Fry, Roger. 1920. *Vision and design*. London: Chatto and Windus.

Garb, Yaakov Jerome. 1990. Perspective or escape? Ecofeminist musings of contemporary earth imagery. In *Reweaving the world: The emergence of ecofeminism*. Irene Diamond and Gloria Feman Orenstein, eds. San Francisco: Sierra Club.

Goldman, Lucien. 1964. *Pour une sociologie du roman*. Paris: Gallimard.

Heidegger, Martin. 1984. The origin of the work of art. In *Art and its significance: An anthology*. Stephen David Ross, ed. Albany, NY: SUNY Press.

Jameson, Fredric. 1981. *The political unconscious: Narrative as a socially symbolic act*. Ithaca, NY: Cornell University Press.

Jewett, Sarah Orne. 1871-79. Manuscript Diary. The Houghton Library, Harvard University. Cited by permission of the Houghton Library.

Johnstone, J. K. 1954. *The Bloomsbury group: A study of E. M. Forster, Lytton Strachey, Virginia Woolf and their circle*. New York: Noonday.

Le Sueur, Meridel. 1977. *Harvest: Collected Stories*. Cambridge, MA: West End Press.

Morawski, Stefan, ed. 1974a. *Karl Marx and Frederick Engels on literature and art*. New York: International.

Morawski, Stefan. 1974b. *Inquiries into the fundamentals of aesthetics*. Cambridge, MA: MIT Press.

Nicolson, Nigel, and Joanne Trautman, eds. 1976. *Letters of Virginia Woolf*. Vol. 1, 1912-1922. New York: Harcourt.

O'Brien, Sharon. 1987. *Willa Cather: The emerging voice*. New York: Oxford University Press.

Panofsky, Erwin. 1927. Die Perspektive als Symbolische Form. In *Vorträge der Bibliotek Warburg Institut 1924-25*. Berlin: B. G. Tuebner.

Walker, Alice. 1975. Everyday use. In *Women and fiction*. Susan Cahill, ed. New York: Mentor.

Walker, Alice. 1974. In search of our mothers' gardens. *Ms.* 2 (11).

Woolf, Virginia. [1925]. 1966. Modern fiction. In *Collected essays*. Vol. 2. London: Hogarth.

Woolf, Virginia. [1922]. 1966. On re-reading novels. In *Collected essays*. Vol. 2. London: Hogarth.

Woolf, Virginia. [1929]. 1957. *A room of one's own*. New York: Harcourt, Brace.

Woolf, Virginia. [1940]. 1969. *Roger Fry: A biography*. London: Hogarth.

Woolf, Virginia. 1985. A sketch of the past. In *Moments of being*. 2d. ed. Jeanne Schulkind, ed. San Diego: Harcourt.
Woolf, Virginia. 1938. *Three Guineas*. London: Hogarth Press.

FIVE

Is There a Feminist Aesthetic?

MARILYN FRENCH

Literary art that is identifiably feminist approaches reality from a feminist perspective and endorses female experience. A feminist perspective demystifies patriarchal assumptions about the nature of human beings, their relation to nature, and the relation of physical and moral qualities to each other. To endorse female experience, the artist must defy or stretch traditional literary conventions, which often means offending or alienating readers. Traditional literary conventions are rooted in philosophical assumptions several thousand years old and still widely current. A third principle of feminist art—which not all feminists subscribe to—is accessibility. When feminist art is difficult, the reason usually lies not in purposeful obfuscation, but in the poverty of our language of feeling, and the difficulty of rendering feeling.

It is questionable whether the terms and issues of traditional aesthetics are applicable to feminist art. Some critics claim traditional aesthetic principles are universal, and that art is "above" sex, or at least, that sex is irrelevant to it. There is an art which is specifically feminist: that much is clear. Some, by virtue of its feminism, would deny it the title *art*, arguing that its political interest violates aesthetic standards. An aesthetics like Susanne Langer's, which defines what art creates and is indeed universal, fits feminist art as well as any other (Langer 1953). But most aesthetics are more prescriptive, and therefore more political: feminism has taught us that all critical approaches imply political standards, however tacitly. Before we can evaluate feminist art by any aesthetic principles, we need a definition of the art. In what follows, I will discuss the characteristics of feminist art as I understand them. For the sake of brevity, I will limit myself to the art I know best, literature; but the principles have parallels in the other arts.

The clearest proof of the existence of a feminist aesthetics is the distaste or rage feminists feel on encountering works that violate it. Sometimes a negative response seems to refer to subject matter—for example, I loathe lingering loving descriptions of mutilations of female bodies; yet when a writer like Andrea Dworkin treats such a theme, I feel it to be not offensive, but only unpleasant—it falls within the

Hypatia vol. 5, no. 2 (Summer 1990) © by Marilyn French

boundaries of "taste." So it is less subject-matter (content) than treatment (style) that is at issue (I will not here address the identity of style and content). Perhaps all a prescriptive aesthetic can be is a set of principles describing a particular style, a taste.

There are two fundamental, related principles that mark a work of art as feminist: first, it approaches reality from a feminist perspective; second, it endorses female experience. Each principle has several ramifications, so is more complicated than it sounds.

In a work with a feminist perspective, the narrational point of view, the point of view lying behind the characters and events, penetrates, demystifies, or challenges patriarchal ideologies. So much has been written about patriarchy in the last two decades that one tends to assume readers understand the term; yet I have met highly educated people who do not understand the feminist use of the term, so I'll explain it briefly. Patriarchy is a way of thinking, a set of assumptions that has been translated into various structures or ideologies. The assumptions are, first: males are superior to females. Their superiority may be granted by a deity or by nature, but it is absolute in conferring on men authority over women. Second: males have individual destinies; they are promised domination, a surrogate godhead, transcendence over the natural world through power in heroism, sainthood, or some form of transcendent paternity—founding a dynasty, an institution, a religion, or a state, or creating an enduring work of art or technology. Third: the form taken by patriarchy is hierarchy, a structure designed to maintain and transmit power from spiritual father to spiritual son. This form absolutely excludes females unless they "make themselves male" (the requirement Jesus places on women entering "the Life" in the gnostic Gospel of Thomas) (1977). Women control biological transmission, the ability to bring forth young passed from mother to daughter. Having this power, they must be excluded from institutional power—which was modeled on the biological sort—if they are not to overwhelm men. Females have only a "natural" destiny; interchangeable parts of nature's cycles, they are maids (in both senses), who become mothers, and finally widows (or hags), in which avatar they are expendable.

Finally, domination is divine, so to pursue it is noble, heroic, glorious. The material to be dominated is, essentially, nature—all women; the body and emotions; "bestial" men; and natural processes, the flux and transitoriness of time, material decay, life itself. Patriarchal works focus on individual males who pursue glory; lonely, self-made and self-defeating, men are isolated from community and exiled forever from the "female" fate of happiness.

Since almost all modern worlds are patriarchal, feminist literature necessarily depicts patriarchy. But it does not underwrite its standards. Feminist literature may show patriarchal attitudes destroying a character or a world, but the narrative does not approve the destruction. When, in *The Faerie Queene*, Guyon destroys the luscious female world called The Bower of Bliss, Spenser, who has used his highest imaginative skills to create the Bower, judiciously approves its ruin. This is true also of Vergil in *The Aeneid*. The poet sighs about the tears of things (*lacrimae rerum*), regretting that beauty and feeling (Dido and sexual love for instance) are destroyed in the pursuit of glory, yet approves Aeneas's desertion of Dido, and his slaughter of those who oppose his domination. Aeneas's destiny is to found Rome; it overrides humanitarian or emotional concerns. Clearly, despite their feelings, both poets uphold patriarchy.

It is less clear where Tolstoy stands in *Anna Karenina,* or Austen in *Pride and Prejudice.* Both authors accept the patriarchal societies in which they live. Yet the pity Tolstoy lavishes on Anna, and the acute irony with which Austen pricks upper-class pretention and the unctuous ambition of the middle-classes, subvert patriarchal standards. This sympathy is not in the eye of the reader; it is built-in. Tolstoy's novel induces readers to feel the world lessened by Anna's death, rather than to feel that it was necessary, like Dido's, to a greater purpose. Austen's heroines maintain self-respect and integrity (wholeness) even as they triumph within a patriarchal structure. Many works of the past three centuries stretch patriarchal standards in this way; they are not feminist, but do not wholly support patriarchy either.

The feminist perspective is partly a reversal of patriarchal views. Feminism sees women as at least equal to men, humanly if not politically or economically; it considers transcendence illusory or factitious and pursuit of power a fatally doomed enterprise, since it cannot ever be satisfied, and usually or always involves the destruction of vital qualities and even life itself. Domination is not divine but lethal to dominator and dominated. It harms the dominator by cutting him off from trust and mutuality, the foundations of friendship and love, the two primary values; it harms the dominated by forcing them into dependency, which precludes truth in relationships. Domination creates false forms of friendship (society) and love (conventional marriage) which mask power relations. And feminist art focuses on people as wholes; the human is made up of body and emotion as well as mind and spirit; she is also part of a community, connected to others; and—on the broadest level—to nature in both positive and negative aspects.

The second principle is equally complicated. To endorse women's experience, feminist art must present it honestly, wholly. This is difficult because literature, like all art, is made up of conventions which are particularly marked in the area of gender. Just as it would be startling to observe a painting of a male nude reclining seductively à la Maja, or Olympe, or of a clothed female Picasso contemplating a naked male with emphatic genitals, literary shifts in presentation of gender startle, distracting attention from *what* is being shown to *the fact* that it is shown. A work's political impact obliterates its other features. This means that either considerable time—decades or even centuries—must elapse before readers can concentrate on what is being shown, or the work will be forgotten without this ever happening. And conventions governing female characters in literature are extraordinarily powerful and tenacious.

One convention holds women's work trivial, insignificant, uninteresting. Indeed, even men's work was considered an inappropriate subject for literature until recently. Yet work fills our lives; domestic work *is* most women's entire life and takes up considerable time even for women who also work outside the home. What such work means to one's sense of self, of the larger world; how it affects a woman's relation to her children, mates, lovers, friends; its pleasures, pains, the personal and political consequences of endless work for which one is not paid: these experiences remain relatively unexplored because of convention.

Conventionally, women's stories had happy endings, usually marriage to a prince and living happily ever after—unless the heroine is guilty of a sexual transgression, in which case she is required to die. This convention has stretched to allow sexual women to survive, but readers still complain when a "good" woman does not live happily ever after. The assumption behind this convention seems to be that the world is ruled by a male bar of justice. All female characters come up before this bar, and males, being just, grant the good ones happiness—a female, not a male condition (male heroes almost never live happily ever after). If the author does not grant a virtuous female character eternal felicity, either she doesn't deserve it or the male bar is not just. Since in a patriarchal world the latter is unthinkable, her virtue must be deceptive. So male critics pore over Shakespeare's Cordelia searching for the hidden flaw that explains her fate and alter Edith Wharton's perception of her heroines (who *are* flawed), making them responsible for their own unhappiness.

If the definition of a "good" woman no longer involves chastity, heroines are still required to be sweet, vulnerable, *likeable*. Readers do not expect sweetness or honesty of male protagonists: they don't even have to be likeable: consider the heroes of *Under the Volcano, Notes from Underground, Look Back in Anger*. Authoritative, angry, rebellious heroines make most readers impatient; they tend to blame the character for not finding a way to be happy. I think about Andrea Dworkin's *Ice and Fire*, which could not at first find an American publisher, or my own *The Bleeding Heart*, which female and male reviewers (if not readers) uniformly condemned. Actual women, we ourselves, may walk around in a constant state of rage and yet reject heroines like us. The most lethal combination is authority and sexuality; it is almost impossible to depict a woman with both except as a villain.

I am very conscious of this because I am planning a novel with an authoritative, sexual woman character, who lives in rage and despair, and who may not be likeable—but who has real grounds for her feelings, and lives in pain, and is in some ways admirable. Someone like, say, Ivan Karamazov. I already know how she will be received, and I dread it. There should be room for every kind of female experience, even the inability to live happily ever after. There should be room for depictions of women who are monstrous. Again, difficulties occur in distinguishing portrayals of monstrous women from portraits drawn by woman-haters. Woman-hating nestles deep at the root of patriarchy; all of us, women and men, are probably infected by it to some degree. Women's own woman-hatred needs exploration in feminist art.

In portraying female experience, feminist art also portrays men, showing them as they impinge upon women or as they appear to women to be. There are no heroes who save women: not because men would not like to do this, but because it can't be done. This is not to say there is no heroism, male and female, in life; only that there are no princes. What men are in themselves or for other men may contradict what they are for women; women's dreams and hopes about men may be mere wishfulness; women may be complicit in male monstrousness. Feminist portraits of males must examine these realities, but there are serious dangers in doing so.

Although women (and even men) offer blanket condemnation of male treatment of females in conversation, such condemnation on a printed page is tantamount to mutiny (so wives' disobedience of husbands, in Shakespeare's era, was called "revolution") and leads to the work being dismissed.

These principles may sound limiting, as if feminist work could deal only and always with the middle ground, the mundane, the probable, eschewing flights of fancy, excessive characters, extremes of good and evil. This is not at all the case, although precisely that middle ground needs examination. Consider that for the 2,500-plus years of its existence, Western philosophy has looked at life strictly from a male perspective, and strictly as if men were constituted only of intellect, ambition, and political concern; as if they never had to deal with upset stomachs, irritation at their children, emotional dependency, hunger, or distress at growing bald. As Nietzsche pointed out, philosophy has ignored and dismissed the life of the body and the emotions, and—I would add—social involvement with women and children. It has been able to show men transcending only by pretending that the mundane does not exist and that other people do not matter.

In addition, for millennia, at least since fifth century BCE Athens, male thinking has divided human experience into two unequal categories. These may be mind/body, reason/sense, spirit/flesh (sexual desire), or intellect/emotion, but the two are always opposed like enemies, and one is always ascribed moral superiority— in the righteous man, mind (or reason, spirit, intellect) will triumph. By dividing experience this way, men have been able to build a world they claim is based on mind, reason, spirit, intellect, a culture which controls and belittles body, senses, desire, emotion; and have felt legitimate in using ruthless means to suppress people associated with what is disparaged. Valuing only certain talents and ignoring or denigrating others, certain men have created a science-based industrial-technological environment without giving a single moment of thought to its effect on living, feeling, and desire; and have disparaged, debased, and killed women of all sorts and men of discredited colors, religions, cultures, or backgrounds.

It is essential for the healing of a sick world that this division be mended. To begin with, it is false. Humans are of a piece, made up of thousands of intricate interconnections, mind body spirit sex sense intellect being only points in an indescribable continuum. Bodymind swirls around in us, without us; we contain it, it contains us. We can try to understand the processes by which we function, but we cannot control them. Every step at control is counteracted by the power of what is hidden; too many steps and we fall ill, off-balance.

Not only is each of us a complex network whose workings we barely understand, but each of us is connected to other people and ideas and things in equally complex ways. There is no such thing as a self-made man—or woman. Scientists are discovering more fully each decade that *nothing dominates*. No planet dominates the cosmos, no part of a cell dominates it, no single person, not even the boss, dominates any situation. The drive to control that informs patriarchy is an unremitting, relentless drive to an invulnerability, impregnability (consider the root of this word), that does not exist on earth. People spend their lives trying to reach a pinnacle of power from which they can affect others without being affected in return—one definition of god. But even a Stalin, who arguably controlled more, in terms of people and territory, than any other human in our century, lived within prison walls, with a taster to try his food, without the possibility of trust, without which both friendship and love are impossible. And bosses are afraid in direct proportion to the degree of control they possess—of those beneath them as well as those above. And are affected by them, in all kinds of ways. Power is a moment, a temporary station on a telephone line; tomorrow, the powerful man may be forced out even if he is president, chairman, Shah.

We have not yet created a language to describe interconnection: our language is based on fabricated dichotomies, and trying to speak about mind/body/senses all at once makes one feel she has a mouthful of marbles. But in whatever ways the genius of the artist can devise, feminist art suggests that things are connected as well as divided, that a person is not always at war with herself or her world, that in fact people seek to live harmoniously with themselves and their world *even though they can't control either*. Feminist work often focuses on groups, community, people as part of a context, and helps to remind us of a reality alternative to the Western tradition of individualistic, alienated man, lonely in a hostile, aggressive world.

So, a third kind of endorsement of female experience is showing a pluralistic reality made up of connection, flow, interrelation, and therefore equality—for when nothing dominates, all parts are equally necessary, and require equal attention. In the workings of the human being or of cosmic space, the puffing up of one part with claims of superiority leads to catastrophe for all parts. Human superiority is not a possibility, no matter how many have claimed it. Shakespeare may endow his kings and lords with social and political superiority, but he also regularly shows their underlings—a simple clown, a powerless girl—to be superior to them in common sense, morality, and understanding.

Works of art that assume the existence of human superiority are invariably anti-woman. I have been paying attention now for many years: works that presume that some people are and ought to be "better" than others betray contempt for those others on grounds of their identity—in Western literature, usually blacks or Jews. And when you find the one, you find the other: where there is contempt for any identity, there is also contempt for femaleness or things associated with female-ness—body, sex, desire, need—even in works written by women. Although writers of the late twentieth-century United States are inhibited from expressing anti-Semitism or racism, many, especially television writers, allow themselves the complacency of moral superiority in their literary treatment of prostitutes, who are not shown as people but as attractive subhumans, unworthy of humane consideration.

A third feminist principle, to which I myself am committed, is accessibility, language and style that aim at comprehensibility. I mention this separately because unlike the two principles already discussed, it is not a necessary condition of feminist art. It is, however, a standard about which I feel strongly.

For thousands of years, women were locked out of high culture. For example, sometime between 200 BCE and 550 CE, Hindu women were forbidden to learn Sanskrit, the language in which all the great Hindu religious and literary documents were composed. The rationale for this was that women were not capable of *moksha*, salvation, and so did not need to read about religion. But the prohibition kept women from learning the religious, mythic, and poetic backgrounds of their culture.

In the fifth century, Japan imported Chinese culture, philosophy, and language; at this time, Japanese women were still powerful. In later centuries, they were degraded and diminished, and male authorities forbade them to learn Chinese, by then the prestige language of Japan, the language of philosophy, government, and "high" literature. Ironically, in the eleventh century, while learned men trotted out tedious pretentious Chinese imitations, literary women writing in the vernacular produced some of Japan's greatest literature, including its masterpiece, the *Tale of Genji*, by Murasaki Shikibu.

Some societies refused to teach females how to read and write. But even if some women were literate, once a particular language became exalted, became the language of scholarship, poetry, diplomacy, or law, theology, and medicine, women were forbidden to learn it. When humanism swept Europe after the fourteenth century, and it became essential to cultivated discourse to know Latin and Greek, women were excluded from schools that taught Latin and Greek. As more lower-class men learned classical languages, a new literary form emerged: allegory, intended to separate the low from the high mind. The medieval allegorist prided himself on concealing spiritual meaning under a sensuous surface. Of course, this also permitted him to write splendid sensuous poetry, filled with sexual and chivalric exploits, while claiming to offer a more severe and exalted "kernel" of hidden significance to the truly learned. Often, poets were also offering serious moral instruction, usually about power, in this coded language.

In our own time, in our own country, our own language, English, is the prestige tongue, the one in which advanced scientific, social, philosophical, and technological documents are written. But these documents are rarely written in an English all of us can comprehend. Rather, each discipline has created a special language, a jargon accessible only to those who have been trained in the field. Women now learn these languages, and use them with it seems to me special pleasure, as if they knew they were using tools formerly sacrosanct, kept in the part of the temple forbidden to females. Some degree of specialist language is necessary; feminists who must use special languages can develop a critique of those languages, and acknowledge and renounce, even as they use them, the patriarchal assumptions implanted in their codes.

What I find non-feminist is intentional obfuscation, the kind of writing that purposes to impress the reader with the writer's knowledge or intellect or high style or "inness," the kind that makes a point of excluding all but the chosen few. With reservations, I love the work of James Joyce, T. S. Eliot, and Ezra Pound, writers who make frequent use of allusion, quoting fragments of poetry, namedropping, and otherwise referring to great poets and thinkers of the past. By this they accomplish several things: they add depth to their work, texturing, enriching it with allusions to a literary tradition. They also parade their learning, placing themselves above the perhaps less-learned reader, presenting themselves as distant and superior. And they legitimate themselves. Western poetry traditionally *required* citation of authority. By bringing in Homer, Cavalcante, Dante, Shakespeare, these men suggest that they are writing in the same tradition as the great men of the past; that they are the equals of these forebears; and that they deserve the same reverence.

Few women use such devices. In the first place, there are few female authorities and women do not seem to feel that males can legitimate them. Second, the device is itself patriarchal: patriarchy is about the transmission of power, the mantle handed from father to nonbiological son, a tradition excluding women. But most important, women seem to feel legitimated not by power and authority, as men do, but by experience itself. And experience is made up of feeling. Women seek legitimacy by finding ways to express what it feels like to live their particular reality. When women's writing is opaque, or what some might call inaccessible, it is because there is no language of expression of a context of emotion: each woman has to create a language for herself. So, some might find inaccessible Monique Wittig's *Les Guérillères* or Susan Griffin's *The Roaring inside Her*, or Luce Irigaray's *And the One Doesn't Stir without the Other*, or Lois Gould's *A Sea-Change* and *Subject to Change*, or Christa Wolf's *Cassandra* or *No Place on Earth*: but whatever inaccessibility exists in these works emerges not from pretention but from the difficulty of rendering the life of the emotions.

My own style is based on my decision, made after almost twenty years of (unpublished) writing in a different mode, to address the reader like a friend talking across a kitchen table, over coffee: I see the reader as an equal, who will out of friendship try as hard to understand the narrator's reality as she to express it. I believe that a healthy literature, one that attempts to create a healthy culture, is inclusive—of everyone— implicitly or explicitly. It is directed at an entire society, and considers everyone in it a member of that society. Choosing to write in such a style necessarily involves some loss and therefore some anguish. But any style requires sacrificing others.

Finally, there may be a distinction between patriarchal and feminist forms. In *Feeling and Form*, Susanne Langer describes the form of tragedy as expressing the rhythms of individual life as the hero realizes his potential and exhausts it, comparing it with comedy, the form of which celebrates vital continuity. In *Shakespeare's Division of Experience*, I draw on Langer's definitions to describe Shakespeare's tragedy and comedy as masculine and feminine forms respectively: tragedy focuses on an individual male, is linear, and leads to a destiny which must be death but suggests transcendence; comedy focuses less intensely on a female, is circular, communal, and leads to harmony and integration of an entire society (although in Shakespeare, the most seriously disruptive element may be excluded from the happy conclusion) (French 1981). Twentieth-century literature, patriarchal or feminist, rarely fits the categories of either traditional tragedy or comedy; yet I think a study of form in any art would yield similar conclusions.

The art I describe in these principles is a different entity from the art described by traditional aesthetics. Itself transcendent, embodying universal aesthetic principles, singular and useless except to move the sensibility exquisite enough to apprehend it, art as traditionally seen is the delicate flower expressing the spirit of a culture. But for feminists, as Lily Tomlin's baglady Trudy tries to work it out (in Jane Wagner's words, with Andy Warhol's image of cans of Campbell's soup), art is soup (Wagner 1986, 29). Art nourishes a society, feeds it; sturdy, not delicate, it arises from the life of a people like food from the ground, teaching us what we do not know, reminding us of what we tend to forget, emphasizing what is important, grieving over pain, celebrating vitality. It is useful and beautiful and moral—not moralistic.

The standards I hold for a feminist art are thus, as you have probably guessed, my standards in life. And that is what I believe an art, any art, ought to be: an expression of a vision that is at once a belief and a faith—belief in humanity and faith in its future. I have always accepted the Horatian definition of the purpose of art—to teach and to delight—and I believe feminist art can make us better, just as I think a feminist world would make us better. But art is not just a moral act. There is a last principle which is not feminist but truly universal: vitality. Art must create the illusion of "felt life," as Henry James suggested. Without it, the best-intentioned piece of work is mere words, a dead shell. And that is a quality for which no one can write prescriptions.

References

French, Marilyn. 1981. *Shakespeare's division of experience*. New York: Summit Books.
The gospel of Thomas. 1977. In *The Nag Hammadi Library in English*. J. M. Robinson, ed. New York: Harper & Row.
Langer, Susanne. 1953. *Feeling and form*. New York: Scribner's.
Wagner, Jane. 1986. *The search for signs of intelligent life in the universe*. New York: Harper & Row.

S I X

Suffrage Art and Feminism

ALICE SHEPPARD

Suffrage graphics constitute one of the first collective, ideological, artistic expressions by American women. Premised on the popular view of woman's nature as virtuous, responsible, and nurturant, this art nonetheless challenged traditional practices and demanded political change. Interrelationships between feminism, art, and the historical context are explored in this analysis of women's imagery.

> If the cartoon has never appealed to women
> workers, isn't it because it has never covered
> a class of interests with direct bearing on
> them?
> Lou Rogers 1913, in "A Woman Destined"

American women emerged as political cartoonists early in the twentieth century, with suffrage as their focus. An explanation of this delayed entry into the realm of political art was offered by feminist cartoonist Lou Rogers (1879-1952), who cited economic, social, educational, and professional deprivation as limiting women's appreciation of the cartoon form. To rectify the situation, Rogers herself developed an ideologically based art directed toward the enfranchisement of American women.

If we accept the definition that "feminist humor" "both elucidates and challenges women's subordination and oppression" (Walker 1988, 152), it is clear that Rogers's analyses and objectives readily conform to a modern position. The inspiration for her humorous art is the subjugation of women; she attacks the sources of social oppression and draws cartoons for the edification of women.

> It is not art as art that I am interested in. . . . It's art as a chance to help women see
> their own problems, help bring out the things that are true in the traditions that have
> bound them; help show up the things that are false. ("Lou Rogers—Cartoonist" 1913,
> 243)

Hypatia vol. 5, no. 2 (Summer 1990) © by Alice Sheppard

Figure 1. Transferring the Mother Habit to Politics. Woman Voter: "Are your hands clean, son?" Cartoon by Lou Rogers. *Judge* 31 (January 1914).

Having by this time published her work in national magazines and aspired to a career in cartooning (Rogers 1927), Rogers was prepared to perceive the advantages of using the cartoon form to promote suffrage.

> Better than almost any other medium, the picture can make a woman see the truth about the conditions into which her daughter and her neighbor's daughter go, and into which, through changes of circumstances, she herself may be forced to go. ("A Woman Destined" 1913, 77)

Rogers was a largely self-taught artist who contributed work to suffrage and socialist papers, as well as to the popular humor magazine *Judge*. She was skilled in symbolic imagery and adapted nineteenth-century cartooning conventions to convey her message. "Transferring the Mother Habit to Politics" (Figure 1) relies on the traditional woman's role as housekeeper/mother to extract virtue from her reluctant son (the politician). The female figure embodies strength and competence and, appropriate to the parent-child dyad, she is considerably larger than the male. In this cartoon and others Rogers incorporated a housekeeping motif to show how women would end corruption and purify the government. Additional symbolic housecleaning activities included bathing, dusting, scrubbing filth and corruption, and vacuuming faulty beliefs. Lou Rogers traced the position of women through various concrete issues—labor, government, economy, taxation, peace. She appealed to universal principles of humanity and foresaw a new social era accompanying women's participation in politics.

By 1911 the suffrage cartoon was a feature in the American women's press, including the *Woman's Journal* (published by the National American Woman Suffrage Association) and New York City's *Woman Voter*. Cartoons were usually placed on the front page of each issue, with additional ones often included inside. Artistic and entertaining, these graphics served several functions for suffragists. First, they were used to refute claims that women had no interest in politics, did not want the vote, or would be "unsexed" by the act of voting. A second group of arguments emphasized that women needed the ballot to protect themselves, combat the sources of their oppression, reduce government corruption, and promote children's welfare. There was a further rationale that true democracy dictated participation by *all* its citizens, typically exemplified by the rallying cry, "No Taxation without Representation [the vote]." Finally, cartoons served to stir feelings of confidence and conviction, portraying energetic women with suffrage banners or depicting suffrage victory as inevitable, often linked to the force of progress.

The portrayal of suffrage issues by women artists offered a distinctive perspective from men's, a fact reflecting their motivation and professional backgrounds. Male cartoonists who addressed suffrage were mostly newspaper artists, men who selected suffrage as one issue to tackle in their daily space. In contrast, female cartoonists were professional artists and amateurs for whom the suffrage campaign was an overriding passion. Only one, Edwina Dumm, was an editorial cartoonist for a newspaper (Caswell 1988).

Figure 2. Double the Power of the Home—Two Good Votes Are Better than One. Cartoon by Blanche Ames. *Woman's Journal* 23 (October 1915).

Figure 3. "Come to Mother." Cartoon by Nina Allender. *The Suffragist* 31 (March 1917). Courtesy of the National Woman's Party.

For centuries men had accepted the imagery of battle and conquest to describe their social achievements. Their cartoon images were male-dominated to the extent that women, if present, usually formed the supporting cast. The female form, however, provided suitable embodiment of abstract principles, such as Justice or Democracy. The nation itself was personified as a woman, Columbia, a commanding figure attired in loose, flowing robes, a crown upon her head. Elevated to goddess or relegated to background activities, woman was not an equal human partner in the traditional cartoon.

Characters and activities in women's cartoons remained close to their social experience. Woman figures were central and included crusader, amazon, mother, suffragist, young girl, and slum child. A few examples from this typology will be given.

Women as inspired crusaders were influenced by Pre-Raphaelite artistic conventions, particularly reliance on allegorical, medieval, and religious iconography. Pre-Raphaelite painters demonstrated a "preoccupation with the female form" (Marsh 1987, 10), though its interpretation was broadened in paintings by women associates. An example of suffrage art replete with classical allegorical symbols is "Lucy Stone's Vision" by Fredrikke Palmer. The drawing portrays Stone looking out her window at a desolate landscape in which a weary pilgrim has stopped to rest. Over the horizon a standard-bearer is approaching, carrying her banner marked "Woman's Suffrage." Another drawing depicted a medieval crusader sounding her trumpet to awaken New York City to the call of woman suffrage. This actually proved to be an American adaptation of a British suffrage poster published several years earlier (see Tickner 1988). Other inspiring images and slogans included, "Up for This Is the Day" and "The Dawn of Reason." Typically idealistic, if somewhat naive, depictions of the victorious day of women draw imagery from mythology and religion, viewing suffrage as the final crusade.

Amazon figures from a distant, if reinterpreted, past appeared in suffrage art. In a drawing by Nina Allender a female warrior carries a spear and clutches a shield marked, "The Vote." Other figures exemplify what we would now term androgyny, women whose strength enables them to hold up their half of the earth or to endure endless drudgery.

Women often portrayed a nurturing, nourishing, protector/guardian as their central motif. "Double the Power of the Home" by Blanche Ames (1878-1969) depicts woman's devotion to her children and home (Figure 2). The theme is traditional, providing an idealized view of motherhood as just the reason why women should have the ballot. The Rogers illustration reveals a similar psychology of gender differences, but her mother figure assumes a more active role in politics.

A further example of the "mothering" theme is a cartoon in which Jeannette Rankin, first woman elected to Congress, is portrayed as parent to the little girl "Susan B. Anthony Amendment" (Figure 3). The caption reads, "Come to Mother" and is supplemented by the parenthetical remark, "That child needs a woman to look after her." We find this woman politician, drawn by Nina Allender (1872?-1957), a far cry from the masculinized "Bloomer girl" image, against which men cartoonists solemnly warned should women enter the political arena. Rankin is portrayed as vibrant, young, and feminine.

The image of the suffragist underwent a parallel transformation at the hand of women artists, particularly Allender. Prior to 1912 the suffragist was typically a bespectacled, unattractive old maid, identified with a ubiquitous "Votes for Women" banner. In contrast, Allender portrayed an attractive, energetic, slender young suffragist, who displayed intelligence and dedication to her cause. In the words of one of her contemporaries:

> She [Nina Allender] gave to the American public in cartoons that have been widely copied and commented on, a new type of suffragist—the young and zealous women of a new generation determined to wait no longer for a just right. It was Mrs. Allender's cartoons more than any other one thing that in the newspapers of this country began to change the cartoonist's idea of a suffragist. (" 'The Suffragist' as a Publicity Medium" 1918, 9)

In the previous cartoon we also note the use of young girl as central symbol. An unpublished analysis of 338 suffrage cartoons in the *Woman Voter* revealed that male cartoonists depicted cartoon men and women in about the same proportion as did female, but that this balance did not hold for children. Specifically, female artists in the sample included girls in 8.3 percent of their cartoons, compared to 3.2 percent for males, a better than 2:1 ratio (Sheppard 1985). Women artists were thus more aware of the continuum of the female life cycle, extending from toddlerhood to old age.

Another example of a girl as central figure is "He ain't got no stockin's, he's poorer nor me" (Figure 4). Alice Beach Winter (1877-1970), a portrait painter, drew sentimental magazine covers and commercial advertisements before her ideological beliefs led her to join with the radical press. This illustration, drawn for the socialist magazine *The Masses*, depicts the girl as a victim of social class. She is sympathetically drawn, revealing depth of character, reflective powers, and a social conscience which allows her, mistakenly, to pity the little rich baby.

Ironically, as women artists joined the ranks of reformers, their sentimental drawings of children, for which they had initially been praised and encouraged, needed only superficial change in attire and context to become symbols of the plight of the working-class child. Rose O'Neill transformed images of sentimentality into a political statement when she contributed a parade of her famous Kewpies urging "Votes for our Mothers."

Early century sentimentality may not be as incompatible with feminism as it might initially appear. From analyses of literary genres, Zita Dresner concluded that nineteenth-century women writers created both sentimental fiction and humor capable of revealing an incipient feminist consciousness:

> Thus, many woman writers explored the problems of women as wives, mothers, and daughters—problems to which men were indifferent or which were discussed in ways that challenged male authority and dominance. (1985, 18)

They described issues of importance to women, diverging in content and even form from male writers, yet earning little recognition from critics.

Figure 4. "He ain't got no stockin's, he's poorer nor me." Cartoon by Alice Beach Winter. *The Masses*, January 1913. Courtesy of the Tamiment Institute Library, New York University.

It should not be surprising that creative productions by women of this period tended to follow gender-specific patterns, since the themes, attitudes, and perceptions that they expressed were linked to their life experience and role standards. Turn-of-the-century women were reared in a society that not only assigned sexual spheres but rationalized this practice by belief in an immutable psychological gender dimorphism. Strategically, activist women were less prone to challenge views of woman's nature than society's right to discriminate on the basis of sex. Full citizenship, equality, and representative government, after all, were touted by the founding patriots as inalienable rights. However, by the mid-nineteenth century, women's rights advocates proclaimed American woman a social slave.

Although suffrage artists in the United States relied extensively on imagery of the Constitution, Uncle Sam, political parties, state issues, etc., a major influence on their work arose from contact with women of other nations. England was, after all, the source of various strategies and nuisance tactics that were imported by Alice Paul and her radical vanguard (Irwin 1921). Art had already been used to promote suffrage in England through the Artists' Suffrage League and Suffrage Atelier (Tickner 1988). Though art committees and contests to promote suffrage art appeared on this side of the Atlantic, there was no American equivalent to the formal artists' suffrage societies.

The rise of socialism also influenced suffrage art. In terms of women's involvement in socialism and suffrage, Buhle considers them "twin heirs to the world view of the late nineteenth-century women's movement":

> Thus what Socialists termed "capitalism" and suffragists preferred to label "industrialism" became homologous concepts in a common theoretical framework that treated all questions of morality, rights, and duties not as static notions but as changing by-products of social evolution. (Buhle 1981, 219)

Socialism challenged the foundations of society, leading feminists to the optimistic conclusion that women could enjoy the higher consciousness resulting from major social change. It was their social duty to join the struggle.

Walter Crane, a British artist, promoted the concept of ideological graphics when he published *Cartoons for the Cause* ([1896] 1978), a collection of his own pro-socialist work. Using imagery that was heir to Pre-Raphaelite symbolism, it provided an innovative model of art allied to social movements. Crane's earth goddesses joined the socialist crusade against the vampire of capitalism, an iconography adaptable to any struggle between good and evil.

Feminism and socialism, uneasy partners at the organizational level, provided residents of Greenwich Village with a dual foundation for their radical lifestyles. Residents were united in an "intellectual community" that sought "to make abstract principles the basis for their actions" (Sochen 1972, 135). In the context of Village life, Sochen noted that suffrage was subsumed under feminism:

> Village feminists, however, saw the vote only as a modest stepping-stone to a larger goal: a cultural reorientation that would give all human beings an equal opportunity.

Figure 5. "We Accuse Society!" Cartoon by Cornelia Barns. *Birth Control Review* 17 (December 1917). Courtesy of the Sophia Smith Collection, Smith College.

Acting counter to the beliefs of most of their contemporaries, they saw feminism as the value system that would accompany the new socialist order. (1972, 5)

The Heterodoxy Club was the supreme feminist organization of the Village. Founded by Marie Jenney Howe, a Unitarian minister, its members included women of contrasting ages and life-styles, all devoted to feminism and suffrage (Schwarz 1986; Showalter 1989). Feminist philosophers, labor agitators, journalists, and artists were among those participating in bimonthly luncheons and lectures sponsored by the group. Heterodoxy also claimed two suffrage cartoonists: painter Ida Sedgwick Proper, art editor of the *Woman Voter*, and cartoonist Lou Rogers.

It is interesting to speculate how much of the quantity and forms of creative propaganda was influenced by mutual associations with Heterodoxy. For example, the slogan "Breaking into the Human Race" appeared as the caption to a Lou Rogers cartoon in 1911 and several years later as the title for a Feminist Mass Meeting sponsored by Heterodoxy (Schwarz 1986, 28).

Another radical movement centered in the Village was the crusade for family planning. Lou Rogers and Cornelia Barns had joined Margaret Sanger's organization and served as art editors for the *Birth Control Review* in 1917. It was there they published some of their strongest feminist statements, such as Rogers's message to Uncle Sam: "You are the only Nation on Earth that Makes Birth Control a Crime." Cornelia Barns (1888-1941) presented a powerful portrait of a distraught family approaching a judicial bench (Figure 5). Middle class, as indicated by tidy, fashionable attire, the figure of the mature mother, again pregnant, though her brood already numbers five, is captioned "We Accuse Society!" Her husband, standing slightly to the rear, appears supportive yet ineffectual. In the face of existing laws forbidding contraceptive information, both are victims of society, although in Barns's rendition, the woman initiates the confrontation.

The flourishing of the nineteenth-century art-school movement (Korzenik 1985) provided the fundamental prerequisite for women's political art. Women were increasingly celebrated as painters and illustrators; some even became newspaper cartoonists (see Robbins and Yronwode 1985; Sheppard 1984). Improved skills kindled ambition and a determination to overcome social prejudice and professional barriers faced by nineteenth-century women.

The art world of Greenwich Village contributed an intellectual alliance with feminism through *The Masses*. The radical magazine with its avant-garde graphics was brought to the Village in 1912 by Max Eastman and continued publication until suspended under the Espionage Act of 1917 for allegedly undermining the nation's war efforts. Its political art was significant from an aesthetic standpoint, and its contributors read like a contemporaneous who's who of art: John Sloan, Robert Henri, Boardman Robinson, Robert Minor, Art Young, Stuart Davis, etc. Renowned contributors, experimentation with new artistic styles, and quality reproductions characterized its art (Fitzgerald 1973; Zurier 1988). *The Masses's* radical, socialist premise held a ready appeal for feminist contributors.

Several artists published socialist art in *The Masses* before contributing to the suffrage press. Here and elsewhere socialism provided a training ground for feminist art. Alice Beach Winter and Cornelia Barns, two of the *The Masses* art editors, were members of the Socialist party (Zurier 1988). Barns, a talented and well-trained artist, defined her artistic role as pointing out contradictions and absurdities in a world governed by men. She employed visual humor, heightened by such captions as "Voters" and "Lords of Creation," to undermine self-assured male supremacy and to advance the suffrage cause. There was a class-consciousness in much of her work, images which depicted the labor conditions of women and children or the status of immigrants.

In examining the role of its women artists, particularly Cornelia Barns and Alice Beach Winter, Rebecca Zurier discovered few direct political assertions in their art. She concluded:

> The closest thing to a feminist statement by a woman *Masses* editor appears in the cartoons of Cornelia Barns, who refrained from any serious social analysis. (1988, 101)

Barns's style appeared outrageous and flippant, but her recurrent themes for *The Masses*, as well as her later artistic contributions to the National Woman's party and the Birth Control League, prove her a committed feminist. Writers and artists of *The Masses*, according to Leslie Fishbein, ranked among "the vanguard of the modern feminist movement." Prone to seek ideological justifications for their beliefs, these intellectuals believed

> that real feminine liberation could not be restricted to economic and political reform, that a transformation of consciousness must occur if women were to achieve true equality with men. (Fishbein 1988, 9)

The work of feminist cartoonists demonstrated an outlook which focused on women's perspectives, placed women in a particular social context, and called women to collective action. Some of the themes echoed a rhetoric carefully formulated by the leading thinkers of the movement. Others were emotional appeals for the means by which early century suffragists expected to transform the nation. In the span of a few years this art by women moved from a few sporadic efforts to rapid proliferation using sophisticated cartoon techniques and styles.

The art of the suffrage campaign contrasts with modern feminist art on several points. First, its ideology was distinct, though the rationale gradually shifted from principled to expedient grounds (Kraditor 1981). The majority of suffragists reaffirmed their nineteenth-century upbringing and its belief in psychological gender dimorphism. Women were morally superior, had mothering instincts, were concerned with the public welfare—all of which could only enhance the world of politics. Socialists, in particular, failed to observe the contradiction between a Marxist view that human characteristics and consciousness are embedded in social and economic relations and belief in a higher ethical sense, presumably innate, attributed to women.

Second, the target of their feminism was specific: attainment of the ballot (or other legislative changes such as legalization of birth control). Admittedly, the more reflective and radical among them saw the ballot as only the first step, but there was consensus regarding the initial goal. Finally, the organization for suffrage brought about a collective effort by women in their own interest. Suffrage societies were formed on the local, state, and national levels; the suffrage press encouraged participation and mutual contact and established complex communication networks.

Suffrage art, however, fails to speak directly to modern feminists, who are confused by its oblique references or frankly embarrassed by its sentimentality, class/race perspectives, and outdated psychology. Its reliance on humor, though an effective propaganda technique, adds a further degree of uncertainty if one seeks to probe its symbolic, double-edged code of meanings.

Can a feminist perspective in art transcend the place/time context in which it is embedded? Both perceptions and language change with time; the term "feminist" did not come into common use until around 1912 (Cott 1987). Just as the political perspective shifted from "woman's rights" to "suffragist," "feminist," and "women's libber," the standard of womanhood abandoned "true woman" for "new woman" and "modern woman." If turn-of-the-century women's political art is to take its place as the heritage of contemporary women artists, an interpretive framework must be established to encompass both commonalities and historic differences.

A further question is why feminist art reached a peak in the 1910s, unmatched in quantity until the 1970s. Attainment of the initial goal, suffrage, significantly altered the course of feminism. Without that tangible goal, the support groups and women's press lacked direction and became ineffective. The wave of progressivism, on which suffrage had ridden, declined with the entry of the United States into the Great War and again as the Red Scare cast suspicion on radical movements. Greenwich Village, which provided the supportive context in which much of this art was nurtured, lost its attraction for many at the decade's end.

Early century feminist art is a depiction of ideas and ideals, of singleness of purpose, that proved subsequently outmoded. Incomplete as it is in providing feminist ideology, its embryonic stages are a precursor to subsequent women's art and may provide insight into its nature. It is time to reconsider early century women's political art, which has been all but forgotten. And, as a final postscript, we should ask ourselves just why we seem more willing to accept grandma's refined embroideries and needlepoints than her feisty feminist cartoons.

Notes

Appreciation is expressed to Zita Dresner, Alice Marshall, Judith Schwarz, and Rebecca Zurier for information and helpful suggestions. Portions of this research were completed under a fellowship from the National Endowment for the Humanities.

References

Buhle, Mari Jo. 1981. *Women and American socialism, 1870-1920*. Urbana, IL: University of Illinois Press.

Caswell, Lucy. 1988. Edwina Dumm: Political cartoonist 1915-1917. *Journalism History* 15(1): 1-7.

Cott, Nancy. 1987. *The grounding of modern feminism*. New Haven: Yale University Press.

Crane, Walter. [1896] 1978. *Cartoons for the cause, 1886-1896*. London: Journeyman Press.

Dresner, Zita. 1985. Sentiment and humor: A double-pronged attack on women's place in nineteenth-century America. *Studies in American Humor* 4(1&2): 18-29.

Fishbein, Leslie. 1988. Introduction to *Art for the masses* by Rebecca Zurier. Philadelphia: Temple University Press.

Fitzgerald, Richard. 1973. *Art and politics*. Westport, CT: Greenwood.

Irwin, Inez Haynes. 1921. *The story of the woman's party*. New York: Harcourt Brace.

Korzenik, Diana. 1985. *Drawn to art*. Hanover: University Press of New England.

Kraditor, Aileen S. [1965] 1981. *The ideas of the woman suffrage movement, 1890-1920*. New York: Norton.

Lou Rogers—Cartoonist. 1913. *Woman's Journal* 44(31): 243.

Marsh, Jan. 1987. *Pre-Raphaelite women: Images of femininity*. New York: Harmony Books.

Robbins, Trina, and Catherine Yronwode. 1985. *Women and the comics*. Guerneville, CA: Eclipse Books.

Rogers, Lou [pseud.]. 1927. Lightning speed through life. *Nation* 124(3223): 395-97. See Showalter (1989).

Schwarz, Judith. 1986. *Radical feminists of heterodoxy*. Norwich, VT: New Victoria Publishers.

Sheppard, Alice. 1984. There *were* ladies present! American women cartoonists and comic artists in the early twentieth century. *Journal of American Culture* 7(3): 38-48.

Sheppard, Alice. 1985. Tactics of persuasion: Pro-suffrage cartoons by American women. Paper presented at meeting of National Women's Studies Association, Seattle.

Showalter, Elaine, ed. 1989. *These modern women*. New York: The Feminist Press.

Sochen, June. 1972. *The new woman: Feminism in Greenwich Village, 1910-1920*. New York: Quadrangle.

"The Suffragist" as a publicity medium. 1918, February 23. *Suffragist* 6(107): 9.

Tickner, Lisa. 1988. *The spectacle of women: Imagery of the suffrage campaign, 1907-1914*. Chicago: University of Chicago Press.

Walker, Nancy. 1988. *A very serious thing: Women's humor and American culture*. Minneapolis: University of Minnesota Press.

A woman destined—to do big things. 1913. *Cartoons* 3(2): 76-77.

Zurier, Rebecca. 1988. *Art for the masses*. Philadelphia: Temple University Press.

PART THREE

Interpretation and
Point of View

Feminine Perspectives and Narrative Points of View

ISMAY BARWELL

The search for a unified and coherent feminine aesthetic theory could not be successful because it relies upon "universals" which do not exist and assumes simple parallels among psychological, social, and aesthetic structures. However, with an apparatus of narrative points of view, one can demonstrate that individual narrative texts are organized from a feminine point of view. To this extent, the intuition that there is a feminine aesthetic can be vindicated.

In this essay I want to take another look at the question of whether there is such a thing as a feminine aesthetic and to argue both that it is there to be found and that it is worth the search. It is worth the search, because to be able to identify a woman in any text where there is one would allay fears that the systems of representation which are available within Western culture are so irredeemably male that a woman can only be heard if she adopts a male perspective, if she speaks as a man. These fears have been rendered acute by the influence of Lacan on a generation of French feminists and through them on the English-speaking world. The two dominant systems of representation which I have in mind are those of language, both spoken and written, and of visual imagery. I shall open the discussion by looking at the question of the degree of generalization that can be expected for a feminine aesthetic. This leads into a presentation of what is needed to show that a narrative text has aesthetic features that are feminine. Narratives can be constructed using language or imagery or both. I claim that a fictional narrative has feminine aesthetic features if the sequence of sentences or images is a part of a pragmatic system in which it is related to points of view, and the dominant point of view, i.e., the one in terms of which the narrative selections are made, is feminine.

In her 1979 article "Feminist Film and the Avant-garde," Laura Mulvey described the goal of the quest for a feminine aesthetic in this way: "Behind the work of research that went into these festivals, there lay a desire or an inspiration that, once discovered, films made by women would reveal a coherent aesthetic"

(1979, 181). But it seemed that even careful and sympathetic attention to them revealed nothing of the sort.

> Certainly the films made by women were predominantly about women, whether through choice or another aspect of marginalisation. But the question of whether a unified tradition emerged became increasingly in doubt, except on the superficial level of women as content. (Mulvey 1979, 181)

Like Mulvey, I assume that a feminine aesthetic must be present in the structural features of works. The search cannot be satisfied by the discovery of a tradition in which the works are merely produced by women and have women as their subject matter. Unlike her, I do not think that a feminine aesthetic must constitute a "unified" and "coherent" tradition.

The hope that works by women would exhibit such a coherent and unified aesthetic was based upon a belief in certain social "universals" and, in particular, the belief that from the advent of civilization, the social order has been patriarchal (Kelly-Gadol 1987, 22). Another very general feature of historical societies was the division of labor between the sexes, with women increasingly confined to domestic work and child raising, thereby creating a "woman's world," that of the household. The world constituted by men was the public world of politics and the marketplace, which stood in authority over that of women. Society was governed by the man's world, and it was there that the significant events which shaped people's lives began.

It seemed important that the "universals" upon which the tradition was to be based were found in social conditions because the alternatives to this were unacceptable. They required a highly doubtful metaphysical assumption, namely, that there was some female nature or essence responsible for the tradition. This essence would transcend all contingencies of race, class, and culture. Either it would be something like the transcendental ego of the phenomenologists, except that it was female and would not construct its gender as it constructed its other characteristics, or it would be a biological essence. The denial of essentialism would mean that any biological features which are relevant are relevant only insofar as they are mediated by social structures.

The desire for such a unified aesthetic was misplaced because of the way in which it used universals to guide its search and to justify its hopes. From the existence of the social universals it moved to the postulation of experiential universals and from there to the claim that women's art would reflect this common experience.

If there is to be any hope of finding aesthetic features that are distinctively feminine, the appeal to social conditions must be much more sensitive to specific conditions of class, race, and culture. It was not only the more obviously essentialist positions which could be charged with a falsifying ahistoricality. In nineteenth-century France, to be a woman of the working class was very different from being a woman of the bourgeoisie. In contemporary New Zealand, what it means to be a Maori woman is very different from what it means to be a Pakeha woman. And the difference is different in each case. To see the quest as involving categories which are not relativized to historical, cultural, racial, and class variables would leave it locked in, at best, just another stereotype—another set of constraints upon what a woman's work should be. At worst—and this is the more likely outcome—no aesthetic features which can be assigned to women will be discovered.

Furthermore, women's experience is not homogeneous in the way required if the hope for a unified aesthetic is to be fulfilled. Once the need for specific social conditions has been accepted, then the temptation to postulate universal features of women's experience becomes less strong. One realizes that the difference among women's experiences can be as important as, if not more important than, their similarities, with the consequence that the interesting and important distinctions between the works of women are no longer in danger of being obliterated.

The final mistake was that both the relationship between social conditions and actual experience and that between actual experience and aesthetic structure were conceived in a parallel fashion and according to an overly simple model. Actual experience does not simply "reflect" economic and institutional conditions, nor does the aesthetic structure of a work of art simply "mirror" the psychological structure of the individual or individuals who produce it. When the relationship between these is described as a "mirroring" or a "reflecting" the assumption seems to be that all of them exhibit the same structure—that the form of the work is isomorphic with the form of the relevant psychological structures in the producers of these works and that these are isomorphic with the social conditions which cause them. These mistakes point to a need for an adequate theory of how sexual differentiation is produced under variable conditions and how this sexual difference is related to features of paintings, sculpture, films, and literature.

The most influential theories of sexual differentiation have Freud as their historical source. All have as a crucial component the Oedipal stage where the child must reject the mother/feminine in favor of the father/masculine, thus positing an asymmetrical system in which the feminine is devalued. Actual women are assigned a position within a system of relations which divides the social world into two sorts of people with all the positive and active attributes belonging to the masculine side. If one accepts the Lacanian twist to this story, then the conclusion is that it is only by wearing the clothing of the other, by posing as a man, that women have been able to do anything at all. To speak, to write, even to look rather than to be looked at, is to adopt the masculine position.

The Lacanian version of psychoanalytic theory does offer an explanation of why there seems to be no coherent and unified tradition for women. But it might be pertinent to ask whether there is a need for such an explanation, given that the hope for such a tradition lay in the mistaken use of social and experiential "universals."

At the risk of dismissing the psychoanalytic approach too summarily, I shall not give it further consideration here. More discussion than I have given would certainly be appropriate since it is subtle, powerful, influential, and the only current theory of gender differentiation which has been worked out in any detail. Instead, I shall briefly consider some requirements which must be met by any theory that would be adequate for the successful completion of the quest, and then go on to investigate just how much can be done by being aware of the mistakes already discussed and by using the requirements as a guide.

The first requirement is that the theory should provide a conceptual framework which will permit the identification of some aesthetic structures as feminine. Without the spectacles of such a theory, it is likely that many of the relevant aesthetic features will go unnoticed. I assume that the conceptual framework will be derived from a theory which identifies some psychological structures as feminine on the basis of an account of gender differentiation. If this account is empirical, then it will have to be relativized to the variables of class, race, and culture. I make this point because it is very difficult to determine just how far Freudian and Lacanian theories are to be read as theories about the actual psychological processes of actual individuals and, thus, how far they should be taken to be empirical theories.

I do not believe that we have an adequate account of gender differentiation, and until we do, the plausibility of the features which are picked out as feminine must remain at the intuitive level. In what follows, I claim no more status than that for my own selections. The second and third requirements follow from this first. The second is that it should allow for a range of aesthetic features to be identified as feminine. The third is that the theory should explain why the aesthetic features are identified as feminine rather than masculine or ungendered. This last requirement will entail that there is some level of generalization to women as a group.

I shall be appealing to a feminine perspective, or point of view, in order to ground a claim that a certain work exhibits a feminine aesthetic structure. In the light of my previous remarks, it is important to realize that these do not involve an appeal to the experience of any actual woman who might read or see or make a work of art. Whether a work has feminine aesthetic features is not logically dependent upon anything occurring in the mind (conscious or unconscious) of she who is occupying the narrator role and she who is occupying the audience role. Although I claim that a text has a feminine aesthetic structure if it has a feminine point of view, this point of view may or may not be recognized or adopted by an individual. Whether she does will depend upon whether she understands the structure of the text, is willing to adopt the perspective "implied by" that structure, or is paying enough attention to the text. A feminine perspective may be adopted by a man if he fulfills the same conditions. This "may" is the may of logical possibility.

A point of view refers to a set of desires, beliefs, preferences, and values. This set must be sufficiently rich to provide reasons for, and thus explanations of, a set of selections. In fact, this is the function of a point of view. The notion of perspectives or points of view has been used recently in two areas within feminist philosophy. Carol Gilligan (1987) makes explicit that what In A Different Voice (1982) revealed was the existence of two moral perspectives. For her, a moral perspective is a set of organizing concepts and terms which provide the framework by means of which moral decisions and judgments are reached. These operate on the underlying nonmoral "facts" in an analogous way to that in which two sets of organizing concepts guide the interpretation of the black-and-white shapes to yield the perception of a rabbit picture or a duck picture. These two points of view are exclusive in that while one is looking at the shapes from the duck-picture perspective, one cannot also be looking at them from the rabbit-picture perspective, and vice versa. Not all points of view in my sense will be exclusive in this way. Some of them may include others. However, it is very important to realize that a point of view is just a set of psychological states and that the presence of some might exclude the presence of others. For some narrative points of view, it would be appropriate to require that they conform to a minimal level of rationality. This will involve some, probably vague, account of how people come to have the beliefs which they have from the evidence with which they are presented.

A notion of this kind has also been used in epistemology by Nancy Hartsock and Sandra Harding (Harding 1986). In "The Feminist Standpoint" (1983) Hartsock makes it clear that the position is to be understood as analogous to that of the proletariat in the Marxian analysis and for the same reasons. The claim is that the oppressed have available to them a vision which is not distorted by interests which arise with and are inseparable from power.

Up until now I have been emphasizing differences among women. When attention is directed exclusively to these the result is often skepticism about the capacity of gender concepts to provide a basis for a class of distinctive points of view. However, nothing that I have said need force this result. What is clear is that if gender can perform this analytic function, then the concept of a "feminine point of view" must be related to its instances as determinate to determinable.

What makes something a feminine point of view should be explained in terms of oppression of a particularly fundamental kind. Being oppressed is a condition which women share with other social groups. Being oppressed involves economic and political powerlessness, marginalization, and a vulnerability to violence. All of these are common to women's position, but they do not capture what is distinctive about it. Women are oppressed because that which gives them their identity as women is an oppressive concept. This identity is constructed in the interests of a dominant group which excludes them, and it is internalized by them. The subjectivity of individual women is structured by a concept which is oppressive and which supports other forms of oppression. Some class and race concepts may also operate in this way.

For my purposes, a point of view is feminine because it is a point of view which women (or a woman) in a specific social setting could have—if the values, priorities, foci of attention, expectations concerning gender-based social roles, etc., which make it up are assigned to one gender or the other in a specific social context. A point of view can be feminine even though it does not also have a political awareness concerning the social position occupied by the possessors of that gender—a feminine point of view need not also be a feminist point of view. There is a sense in which the conscious adoption of at least one of the gendered perspectives which I am now going to describe will be both feminist and also epistemologically advantageous, since it will facilitate the recognition of the gendered nature of the other perspectives, but I am not interested in questions of its overall superiority as an aesthetic standpoint.

Any point of view might be adopted by an actual person. When someone adopts a point of view, that person has, or pretends to have, the beliefs, attitudes, and preferences which make up the point of view. The amount of pretense involved will depend upon how close the point of view is to the point of view of the actual individual. In a situation where the point of view exactly matches the point of view of an actual individual there will be no pretence involved. However, in the normal case an actual person will have to pretend to some beliefs and preferences which she does not have. It is, of course, possible that she will have some of them after her encounter with the work.

Every fictional narrative text is a part of two systems involving points of view—a fictional and a hypothetical system. Both of these systems involve narrator and audience points of view. Every narrative text has a hypothetical narrator, and every fictional narrative text has, in addition, a fictional narrator. This is true even of those fictional narratives which are narrated from a third-person, "objective," point of view. I have put "objective" in scare quotes because even where the fictional narrator is the impersonal, omniscient perspective, he will still make choices which are guided by judgments about what is interesting and significant. Even texts with an "impersonal" narrator will be structured by a set of attitudes, interests, and prejudices. In fact, it is the realization of this which has revealed the possibility of recognizing that many more texts have a gendered voice than might seem to be the case at first.

I am here disagreeing with the views expressed by Kendall Walton. He claims that "it would be strained to recognize a narrator in some works, especially when, were a narrator recognized, he would have to be regarded as supernatural—as omniscient, omnipresent, or clairvoyant" (1976, 50). The narrator that he means is the actual (fictional) narrator. My disagreement is on two counts. I do not want the actual author to be a part of this scheme at all, and I maintain that wherever there is a fictional text then there is a fictional narrator, even when this narrator is not much like an actual narrator. It would be a mistake to identify the fictional narrator with either the point of view of the author or the hypothetical narrator. A hypothetical narrator may choose a fictional point of view for its contrast with his own or because it is very like his own. Even in the "impersonal" case, the narrative is structured by a set of desires, attitudes, and interests which guide the choices made, and these reveal the text to be gendered.

I have said that every narrative text has a hypothetical narrator. The gender of the hypothetical narrator is the gender of the text. This means that a narrative is feminine whenever its hypothetical narrator is feminine. The hypothetical narrator rationalizes the text with the organizing principles that a point of view provides and that yields reasons for the selection of the sentences or images of the narrative. Beliefs about the semantic content of the sentences selected will be one very important type of reason. For example, some sentences are made true by the occurrence of events, and they will be present in the narrative because of the sorts of event which make them true. If the narrative is composed out of images in whole or in part, then these will be chosen because of that which they are pictures of, i.e., their semantic content. Sentences and images will be chosen not just because of their individual semantic content but also for the relations in which they stand to one another—considerations of coherence and of symbolic significance are two very important types of reason.

More than this can be said—the sentences and images are chosen because of relations holding between the events and states of affair which make them true.

Traditionally (since Aristotle's *Rhetoric*), sentences and images are selected because of the narrative events which make them true, and narrative events are selected along the axes of *mythos* (story or plot), *dianoia* (theme), and *ethos* (character). What goes into a narrative will be constrained by the choices of the hypothetical narrator, and narrators in their turn will have some of their choices constrained by narratives. Where a narrative finds its place in a genre which is very directive about the kinds of events that are allowed within the narratives, there will be less scope for the selections to reveal a point of view and less scope for establishing a gender identity. In genres of this kind—an example would be the folktale—the role of the hypothetical narrator is very much restricted once the genre is selected. However, there will always be some choices to be made. In the most extreme cases, any attempt to establish a point of view rich enough to reveal a gender identity will have to rely on the inclusion of incidental descriptive details.

As well as the beliefs already discussed, the hypothetical narrator contains beliefs about the status of the narrative—beliefs about whether it is a documentary, history, or fiction, and, if it is fiction, whether it is a parody, a satire, or a "straight" narrative. When the hypothetical narrator is the hypothetical narrator of a fictional narrative, then for all the sentences of the text, the beliefs of the hypothetical narrator about whether they are being asserted or fictionally asserted are what determine their fictional status. Beliefs about whether the sentences are being asserted or not is one of the crucial differences between the hypothetical and fictional narrators. In many third-person narratives, it will be the main difference. In the standard case, the fictional narrator makes assertions, not fictional assertions. Thus, a crucial difference between the hypothetical and the fictional narrators is that the hypothetical narrator fictionally asserts the propositions of the narrative and knows that she is fictionally asserting them; the fictional narrator asserts the propositions of the narrative.

To assert fictionally is to pretend to assert where the pretence arises because the assertor's beliefs about the truth of what is asserted are irrelevant to the production of the act, and she intends that her audience should recognize this. The hypothetical narrator of a fictional narrative is not pretending that the narrative events really happened—that the narrative is true. She is pretending to assert that the narrative events really happened.

Another important aspect of the hypothetical narrator is that in it are to be found reasons for the choice of the fictional narrator. The hypothetical narrator chooses the fictional narrator in the sense that the hypothetical narrator chooses the point of view from which the narrative will be told. Even where the point of view is "impersonal," the narrative events and states of affairs reveal selections made on the basis of preferences which in their turn reveal judgments about what is interesting. By choosing a fictional narrator, the hypothetical narrator uses what someone says or sees in the fictional world to tell the story. A fictional narrator is "within" the world represented by the narrative and, in the simplest case, tells the narrative as a truth about that world. Fictional narrators can be chosen because they are boastful or biased, and the sentences of the text will be chosen to reveal this boastfulness or bias. Fictional narrators make assertions and thus purport to be telling a true story about the world that is actual to them, but the truth of the story may in fact, be doubtful. Fictional narrators do not have to be reliable about the truth of what they say or show. Wherever there is not a straightforward relation between the fictional narrator and the truth of what he says, there will be devices in the text which suggest or display this relation.

Whenever there is an embedded narrative, i.e., a story within a story, the relation of the fictional narrator to it will be that of a hypothetical narrator. If the story is a fictional narrative, the fictional narrator will be pretending to assert it. Where the fictional narrator is not reliable, or is deceived, e.g., where he seems to be engaging in unwarranted boasting or is suffering from an unacknowledged hallucination, then the fictional narrator has to be thought of as a person who is lying with the intention to deceive or a person who is telling a false story without full awareness of its falsity. The fictional narrator need not be clear about the status of the narrative she is telling, unless that narrative is a fiction within a fiction, when it is her authority which makes the embedded narrative fictional.

The hypothetical narrator has for its partner the ideal hypothetical audience. This is the point of view of an audience which understands and appreciates just what the hypothetical narrator wants them to understand and appreciate. They will believe just what the hypothetical narrator believes that they believe. For example, in order to appreciate the dramatic structure of the story, an ideal audience may need to know that certain characters and events in the represented world are based upon people and events in the actual world. An audience could only appreciate the dramatic structure of the movie *To Dance with a Stranger* if it knew that the protagonist was based upon a real woman who was hanged for murdering her lover. This is the audience which grasps the relation of the represented world to the actual world of the hypothetical narrator.

The way in which the ideal hypothetical audience is relevant to the question of the gender of texts is that in the hypothetical narrator will be found beliefs about the specific attitudes, evaluations, interests, and preferences of this audience. A narrative text is always produced for an audience, although this audience need not be precisely conceived. Beliefs about the audience will guide the selections made by the hypothetical narrator. Choices are made in order to ease the reception of the text by its intended audience. Sometimes it will be clear that the intended audience is of a specific gender. This will be the case even when there is no accompanying belief that the attitudes and beliefs by which the intended audience is picked out are gender-specific. The hypothetical narrator may attribute gender-specific interests and beliefs to his audience without realizing that they are gender-specific. He may take them to be the norm—to be human interests. The hypothetical narrator need not know that his intended audience is picked out by gender-specific interests, but beliefs about interests which are in fact gender-specific will be seen to be guiding the choices. Similarly, the hypothetical audience may not know that it has gender-specific interests—it just has those interests.

When a narrator does have a belief about the specific gender of his intended audience, he may fail to correctly characterize the attitudes, beliefs, and interests which are supposed to determine the gender specificity of that audience. The narrator may intend that his audience be or include women. He has a view about what women respond to, based upon a view about women's attitudes, beliefs, and interests. The ideal hypothetical audience will have the attitudes attributed to it. The audience may even believe that this is what women (at that time and place) are like. However, we may want to provide a perspective which offers a correction. This is another hypothetical point of view—the critical.

One must be wary of any simple move from beliefs about the attitudes, beliefs, and interests of the audience, which may include a belief about which gender has these interests, etc., to the attribution of a feminine or masculine point of view to the text as a whole. A text may be intended for women and be about women, but it may still have a masculine point of view because the beliefs in the hypothetical narrator point of view about women are masculine.

Before I introduce and explain the critical hypothetical point of view, I will give some examples of hypothetical narrator points of view which are feminine. In none of these examples are the perspectives strongly personal. They are not idiosyncratic or expressive of a personality. My first example comes from Dorothy Smith:

> We might take as a model the world as it appears from the point of view of the afternoon soap opera. This is defined by (though not restricted to) domestic events, interests, and activities. Men appear in this world as necessary and vital presences. It is not a woman's world in the sense of excluding men. But it is a woman's world in the sense that it is the relevances of the women's place which govern. Men appear only in their domestic or private aspects or at points of intersection between public and private as doctors in hospitals, lawyers in their offices discussing wills and divorces. Their occupational and political world is barely present. They are posited here as complete persons, and they are but partial. . . . (1987, 85)

The worlds represented in the novels of Jane Austen and Emily Eden are structured by a point of view similar to this.

There is a range of ways in which a represented world can be structured so that the concerns of the men in that world are marginalized. In some, for example, Alice Walker's *The Color Purple* and Zora Neale Hurston's *Their Eyes Were Watching God*, the world which is marginalized is not just that of men but of white people generally. All of them have a woman or women among the central characters, but it is not that alone which makes them feminine. Not all of them are structured by the concerns and interests of a demarcated social sphere—the domestic, though this is perhaps the most obvious example. Many of them "explore the bonding between women at all levels from sexual passion to neighbourliness" (Stuart 1988, 64)—a diversity which Adrienne Rich calls "the lesbian continuum" (1983).

Some representations show women operating in the public world on equal terms with men. Among these are Barbara Bradford Taylor's *A Woman of Substance* and the television series "Cagney and Lacey." In these the world of men is fragmented and subordinated to the women's interests. Women are often depicted reacting against the male world and male interests which seek to entrap them. In none of these works do they sweep aside the existing order, though sometimes they leave it (*Housekeeping, Coup de Foudre*, Henrik Ibsen's *The Doll's House*). More often they merely assert their own point of view in the face of the male one, and in so doing the male order is broken up and subverted.

I have already mentioned the possibility of another audience viewpoint—the critical. This would be one which does not simply accept the beliefs, values, and assumptions of the hypothetical narrator. I think that Elaine Showalter's "hypothesis of the female reader" (1979) is a hypothesis about a viewpoint of this kind. The critical female reader will have a set of beliefs and values which may conflict with those in the narrator, and thus the ideal audience viewpoints, and thereby reveal their conventional masculine bias. Adopting a critical perspective may reveal class or racial bias as well. As an oppositional perspective on a narrative, the critical perspective enables someone to recognize features which would have gone unnoticed from the ideal hypothetical point of view. (This is also the viewpoint from which deconstructive techniques are used on a text.)

The hypothetical critical perspective is importantly different from the other viewpoints because it is the only one not determined by the text. Essentially it is adopted in opposition to selected beliefs or assumptions in the narrator and ideal audience positions.

The remaining points of view which I will discuss are the critical fictional audience and the ideal fictional audience, a distinction made in somewhat different terms by Peter Rabinowitz (1977). However, Rabinowitz is not concerned to apply these points of view in order to clarify issues about the gender of texts. There will be a fictional audience position for every fictional narrative. This is the ideal fictional audience. One arrives at a characterization of this point of view by the same method that one arrives at a characterization of the ideal hypothetical audience, i.e., by seeing which of the beliefs that the fictional narrator has about his audience are guiding his narrative selections. One should arrive not only at the beliefs but also at the values, inclinations, and preferences that would have to belong to anyone who judged that the fictional narrator was giving a true and just account of events which occurred in her world.

In some texts there is an additional fictional audience. This is the critical fictional audience. This audience understands the beliefs, values, interests, and assumptions of the fictional narrator, including those that the fictional narrator has about his ideal audience, but does not share them all. This viewpoint emerges as doubts are cast on the narrator's claim to be giving a true and just account of her world. Very often a fictional narrator is employed as a device that opens up the possibility of a critical perspective within the fictional world.

A modified example of Rabinowitz's illustrates the three audience positions "implied" by the text: Jonathan Swift's A Modest Proposal satirizes political broadsheets of his time and proposes that the Irish poor could solve the country's problems of famine and poverty by selling their children to be eaten. In this text the ideal fictional audience is one which believes that the proposal is serious and that the beliefs and assumptions which it displays are acceptable. The critical fictional audience is one which believes that the proposal is serious but the values and assumptions are definitely peculiar. The ideal hypothetical audience is one which understands that the text is satirical and, therefore, the proposal is not to be taken seriously, although it might be making a serious political point.

I have introduced this apparatus of narrator and audience perspectives because I believe that it can be used to analyze texts in order to show how they have a gendered perspective. I have claimed that a narrative text is gendered if it is organized to reveal a feminine hypothetical perspective. There is more than one way in which a hypothetical perspective can reveal its gendered nature. One way is to make use of a gendered perspective within the story.

Having a female fictional narrator is clearly not sufficient for a text to be feminine. Daniel Defoe's Moll Flanders will do as an example. Here a fictional female narrator simply speaks as men have thought that women do or should. A similar situation can arise with a male fictional narrator. Something different occurs in Colleen Reilly's novel *The Deputy Head* where the male fictional narrator presents himself as possessing a paradigmatically reasonable and concerned masculine point of view, yet the text has a feminine and even a feminist point of view. The only masculine audience is the ideal fictional audience. The critical fictional audience departs from the ideal in this case by suspecting that what he says about the women in his life reveals a definite bias. His stories about the reactions and behavior of his wife, daughter, and girlfriend are all to be treated with reserve. The appearance of a critical fictional audience is a device used by the hypothetical narrator to comment upon the bias of points of view which are similar to that of the fictional narrator. This example illustrates my other point which is that a text is often organized with a specific audience in mind, which means that beliefs about the audience will be responsible for the selections made.

I hope this discussion is sufficient to show that with the right theoretical equipment it is possible to find aesthetic features that are recognizably feminine. This would mean that the intuitions which motivated the search for a feminine aesthetic can be justified.

References

Gilligan, Carol. 1982. *In a different voice*. Cambridge, MA: Harvard University Press.

Gilligan, Carol. 1987. Moral orientation and moral development. In *Women and moral theory*. Eva Kittay and D. T. Meyer, eds. Totowa, NJ: Rowman and Littlefield.

Harding, Sandra. 1986. *The science question in feminism*. Ithaca: Cornell University Press.

Harding, Sandra, ed. 1987. *Feminism and methodology*. Bloomington: Indiana University Press; Milton Keynes: Open University Press.

Hartsock, Nancy C. M. 1983. The feminist standpoint: Developing the ground for a specifically feminist historical materialism. In *Discovering reality*. Sandra Harding and Merrill B. Hintikka, eds. Dordrecht, Holland: D. Reidel.

Jacobus, Mary, ed. 1979. *Women writing and writing about women*. London: Croom Helm; New York: Harper and Row.

Kelly-Gadol, Joan. 1987. The social relations of the sexes. In *Feminism and methodology*. See Harding (1987).

Mulvey, Laura. 1979. Feminist film and the avant-garde. In *Women writing and writing about women*. See Jacobus (1979).

Rabinowitz, Peter. 1977. Truth in fiction: A reexamination of audiences. *Critical Inquiry* 4: 121-42.

Rich, Adrienne. 1983. Compulsory heterosexuality and lesbian existence. In *The signs reader: Women, gender and scholarship.* Elizabeth Abel and Emily K. Abel, eds. Chicago: University of Chicago Press.

Showalter, Elaine. 1979. Towards a feminist poetics. In *Women writing and writing about women.* See Jacobus (1979).

Smith, Dorothy. 1987. Women's perspective as a radical critique of sociology. In *Feminism and methodology.* See Harding (1987).

Stuart, Andrea. 1988. The color purple: A defence of happy endings. In *The female gaze.* Lorraine Gamman and Margaret Marshment, eds. London: The Women's Press.

Walton, Kendall. 1976. Points of view in narrative and depictive representation. *Nous* 10: 49-61.

E I G H T

Women, Morality, and Fiction

JENEFER ROBINSON AND STEPHANIE ROSS

We apply Carol Gilligan's distinction between a "male" mode of moral reasoning, focused on justice, and a "female" mode, focused on caring, to the reading of literature. Martha Nussbaum suggests that certain novels are works of moral philosophy. We argue that what Nussbaum sees as the special ethical contribution of such novels is in fact training in the stereotypically female mode of moral concern. We show this kind of training is appropriate to all readers of these novels, not just to women. Finally, we explore what else is involved in distinctively feminist readings of traditional novels.

In recent years, a trio of groundbreaking books has posited important differences between men and women. Dorothy Dinnerstein (*The Mermaid and the Minotaur*, 1976) and Nancy Chodorow (*The Reproduction of Mothering*, 1978) challenged the traditional psychoanalytic account of male and female development, while Carol Gilligan (*In a Different Voice*, 1982) challenged the reigning views of moral theory and moral development. Together, their studies suggest that men and women in our society today have significantly different interests, values, and habits of thought.

These feminist arguments for difference have profound implications. If men and women do differ in significant ways, then whatever the status of these differences—whether they are universal or occasional, hard-wired or culture-bound—we can expect them to affect all aspects of our cultural life. Feminist scholars are working out the implications of these arguments in various areas. For example, feminist epistemologists defend alternative ways of knowing, feminist moral theorists defend alternative ways of identifying duty and obligation, and feminist aestheticians defend alternative ways of construing the canon of great works of art.

In this paper, we investigate some aesthetic implications of Carol Gilligan's work. Our concern is with men's and women's responses to literature. After setting out some central themes of Gilligan's research, we sketch a claim about literary interpretation which seems to follow when Gilligan's conclusions are extended beyond the moral realm. We develop this claim in more detail by discussing some

Hypatia vol. 5, no. 2 (Summer 1990) © by Jenefer Robinson and Stephanie Ross recent work by Martha Nussbaum. We argue that what Gilligan identifies as a stereotypically female perspective is very close to the perspective which, on Nussbaum's view, is required by all good readers of a literary work. We then enquire whether the Gilligan-Nussbaum view will help us to distinguish between feminist and non-feminist readings of a literary text, and we conclude that it does not. We end with some speculation about what does make the difference between feminist and non-feminist readings.

GILLIGAN

In her pioneering book *In a Different Voice* (1982), Carol Gilligan attacks traditional accounts of moral development. She argues that psychologists since Freud have conceptualized psychological development in male terms. For example, Lawrence Kohlberg's six-stage account of moral development deems most women morally immature. The theory assigns them to the third level of moral development, concerned predominantly with "goodness" and with helping others, while men more often achieve levels five and six, which introduce universal rules and principles. Kohlberg's theory is based on a longitudinal study which tracked eighty-four boys for more than twenty years. Noting that "in the research from which Kohlberg derives his theory, females simply do not exist" (18), Gilligan claims that all such theories are biased since they take male patterns of development as the norm.

As a corrective to the developmental research which overlooked women, Gilligan conducted a trio of studies to investigate women's views about self-identity, morality, crisis, and choice.[1] She concluded that women are not deficient moral reasoners, as they seem when judged by male standards, but merely different moral reasoners when properly judged by their own distinctive standards.

Studying women's responses to both hypothetical and real-life dilemmas, Gilligan realized that men and women construe these situations quite differently. Women emphasize relationships and their thinking is contextual. That is, women emphasize the particulars of a situation (Gilligan 1982, 101) and reject appeal to universal principles. Overall, women conceptualize life as a web (48) while men instead see a succession or hierarchy of relationships. Thus Gilligan contrasts "male" morality—an ethics of rights—with "female" morality—an ethics of responsibility. The first emphasizes separation and individual rights. The second emphasizes attachment and the urge to care. Ultimately, Gilligan suggests, these two perspectives converge. A fully mature moral view would acknowledge the truths of both (165-67).

Gilligan supports her claims about women's moral reasoning by reference to experimental results that seem to confirm that men and women do indeed conceptualize the world differently, that they have different beliefs about the world and different emotional responses to it. According to Gilligan, these differences can be traced back to the underlying disparity which is her repeated theme: men's and women's opposing attitudes toward attachment and separation, attitudes which arise out of distinct patterns of personality development. (See Dinnerstein 1976; Chodorow 1978.)

One study which Gilligan cites in support of her view is Matina Horner's exploration of men's and women's attitudes toward competitive achievement. Horner found that women would create distressing conclusions for a story beginning, "After first term finals, Anne finds herself at the top of her medical school class." Gilligan reports that one version had Anne beaten and maimed for life by jealous classmates (1982, 40). While women introduce violence into stories involving competitive success, studies by Gilligan and others confirm that men instead project violence into stories involving intimacy. Gilligan describes one picture which elicited such responses as "a tranquil scene, a couple sitting on a bench by a river next to a low bridge" (39-40). More telling still was a picture of two trapeze artists performing high in the air without a safety net. This was the only picture in the experiment to show two people touching. In general women perceived the scene as safe, while men responded with various violent denouements.

Gilligan concludes from such experiments that men and women

perceive danger in different social situations and construe danger in different ways—men seeing danger more often in close personal affiliation than in achievement and construing danger to arise from intimacy, women perceiving danger in impersonal achievement situations and construing danger to result from competitive success. (42)

Thus men's and women's initially divergent experiences of attachment and separation generate a pattern of further difference. If Gilligan is right, she has uncovered important emotional and epistemic differences between men and women.

CRITICISM OF GILLIGAN

In her paper "Beyond Caring: The De-Moralization of Gender" (1987),[2] Marilyn Friedman argues that Gilligan is really defending two logically independent claims: (1) the "different voice" hypothesis ("that the care perspective is distinct from the moral perspective which is centered on justice and rights," and (2) the "gender difference" hypothesis ("that the care perspective is typically, or characteristically, a *woman's* moral voice, while the justice perspective is typically, or characteristically a *man's* moral voice" [Friedman 1987, 90]).

Friedman points out that there are a number of published studies which seem to disconfirm claim (2) (1987, 90). Moreover, it must be admitted that Gilligan's studies are somewhat anecdotal and that there is no control for key variables such as the age, class, and educational background of the men and women studied. Yet despite its shaky empirical foundation, researchers have noted that women readers of Gilligan's book have found it "to 'resonate . . . thoroughly with their own experience' " (93). Friedman explains this by suggesting that what Gilligan has uncovered may be not "actual statistical differences in the moral reasoning of women and men [but rather differences] in the moral norms and values culturally associated with each gender" (89), what Friedman calls differences in the *cultural stereotypes* associated with each gender. "Gilligan has discerned the *symbolically* female moral voice and has disentangled it from the *symbolically* male moral voice" (96). Moreover, Friedman notes that research in psychology and sociology confirms that both men and women do tend to conceive of the genders as "moralized" (95), that is, both sexes attribute to men and women different moral concerns and different modes of moral reasoning. In particular, the "ethic of care" is still the stereotypic moral norm for women (106).

Friedman also proposes a modification of (1), the "different voice" hypothesis. She argues that the two moral perspectives identified by Gilligan are better thought of as differences in the "primary form of moral commitment which structures moral thought" (1987, 109). What Gilligan calls the care perspective involves a primary commitment to "other persons in their wholeness and their particularity" (105), whereas the justice perspective involves a primary commitment to "general and abstract rules, values, or principles" (105). According to Friedman, care-reasoning and justice-reasoning need not be construed as incompatible modes of reasoning, and need not be identified with actual women and men respectively. Rather, care-reasoning and justice-reasoning define distinct patterns of moral concern, which are characteristically associated with women and men.

Although some of the details of Friedman's view are problematic, we find her central suggestions helpful. In particular, it seems to us useful (1) to think of the "ethic of care" in terms of a focus of moral attention and commitment (on the individual in all her particularity) and (2) to explain its attribution to women in terms of associations and cultural stereotypes rather than statistical correlations. We will now consider some aesthetic consequences of the claim that there is a stereotypically female moral perspective or orientation which can be spelled out in terms of a certain focus of attention and commitment.

READING AS A WOMAN

Gilligan's account of the stereotypical female moral perspective extends to the aesthetic realm because the attitudes and experiences which differentiate the care perspective from the justice perspective also figure in our responses to art. In her essay "Dancing through the Minefield" (1986), Annette Kolodny connects women's experience to distinctive literary and interpretive traditions. Kolodny quotes Elaine Showalter's assertion that the work of women writers demonstrates a unity of "values, conventions, experiences, and behaviors impinging on each individual" (1986, 243). Later, speculating on men's inability to appreciate this female countertradition, Kolodny remarks that "male readers who find themselves outside of and unfamiliar with the symbolic systems that constitute female experience in women's writings, will necessarily dismiss those systems as undecipherable, meaningless, or trivial" (245). Men are at a disadvantage because they cannot understand the "sex-related contexts out of which women write":

> The (usually) male reader who, both by experience and by reading, has never made acquaintance with those contexts—historically, the lying-in room, the parlor, the nursery, the kitchen, the laundry, and so on—will necessarily lack the capacity to fully interpret the dialogue or action embedded therein. (249)

Note the similarity to Gilligan's claims. Just as men seem unable to interpret women's accounts of their moral dilemmas in a way which makes the women seem like cogent moral reasoners, so too, according to Kolodny, men seem unable to interpret women's fiction in a way which makes women seem like gifted writers.

The quotes from Kolodny suggest that men simply lack the experience of certain contexts which are essential to understanding women's fiction. When put this baldly, the argument can't be right. Many men do have experience of typically female tasks; many women lack this. Short of endorsing an unattractive sort of biological determinism, we lack any grounds to support the blanket claim that women can, while men cannot, understand fiction set in these "sex-related contexts." Yet here as before we can speak of stereotypes. Friedman writes of a sexual division of labor which creates two separate spheres— one public and male, one private and female (1987, 94). Even though these spheres are now integrated to some degree, we still *think* stereotypically. That is, we view the domestic world as essentially female, while we view the economic and political worlds as essentially male, and this has a decided effect on readers' interests, concerns, and expertise.

We suggest that important epistemological differences underlie the two stereotypes adduced so far. Different aspects of a given situation are salient depending on one's moral orientation. Recall Gilligan's notion of caring. On her view, the caring conception of morality is marked by a more contextual mode of judgment, one which involves concern and emotional involvement with others rather than an impartial, impersonal assessment. Note that this account of caring can encompass caring for oneself; it is not limited to loving care for one's close friends and relations. Rather, caring means focusing on the particularities of a situation, regardless of who is involved. As Friedman notes, "The key issue is the sensitivity and responsiveness to another person's emotional states, individuating differences, specific uniqueness, and whole particularity. The 'care' orientation focuses on whole persons and de-emphasizes adherence to moral rules" (1987, 106). In fact, Gilligan observes that the person who has a caring conception of morality often has difficulty in making moral judgments at all: there is a propensity to see cases as insistently individual, and hence as unsusceptible to generalization.

Focusing on particularities rather than generalities, on context rather than principle, amounts to a distinct pattern of attention. Details that concern a care-reasoner would not interest a justice-reasoner, while commonalities compiled by a justice-reasoner would be passed over by a care-reasoner. For example, one subject in Gilligan's abortion study described her pregnancy as follows:

> It is a stress situation that brings out all the things in my relationship with [the father] that I had just been grinding along with all this time and just could have ground along with indefinitely. And now, wow, there it is, panorama, you cannot hide from it anymore. And so you might say that it becomes a very auspicious time. I am sorry. (1982, 117)

While this passage might be deemed incoherent on ordinary standards of moral reasoning, it clearly fits the pattern Gilligan ascribes to care-reasoners. The subject arrives at an abortion decision because myriad details of her relationship with the father of her child suddenly become clear. They force themselves on her, forming a picture ("a panorama") she cannot block out. Note that no mention is made of general principles whose relevance to her situation suddenly becomes clear. Rather, the details themselves, their accumulated weight, point to a decision.

In general, then, we find Gilligan (and Friedman) characterizing the "feminine" way of thinking and feeling as emphasizing the detailed rather than the general, connection rather than isolation, the contextual judgment rather than the universal principle. We contend that this "feminine" care perspective turns out to be just what is required for any good reading of a literary work. In this sense, to read well is always to read as a woman. Gilligan's insights can help us to understand what is required for *all* good readings, whether feminine, feminist, both, or neither. We approach our theme by focusing on some claims by Martha Nussbaum.

NUSSBAUM

In two recent papers (1983, 1987), Martha Nussbaum argues that certain works of literature are in fact works of moral philosophy. She claims that these works express important moral truths which it may be impossible to express in more traditional modes of philosophical writing, and that reading such works provides important practice in moral reasoning. Using Henry James's novel *The Golden Bowl* as her example, Nussbaum attempts to elucidate both the moral content of the text and the moral abilities required for reading and interpreting it (1983, 41).

On Nussbaum's Aristotelian view, moral deliberation is "first and foremost a matter of intuitive perception and improvisatory response," not a consultation of a "watertight system of rules or a watertight procedure of calculation" (1983, 43). Nussbaum stresses the particularity of moral response. She assimilates moral knowledge to perception rather than to the intellectual grasp of propositions or facts (Nussbaum 1987, 174), and she characterizes moral achievement as "learning the right sort of vision of the concrete" (185). Accused by Hilary Putnam of denying the importance to ethics of rules, obligations, and standing commitments, Nussbaum argues that concrete perception is prior to the application of rules. Someone armed only with general principles and rules would be unable to determine *where* they applied, unable to act on them *when* applied, and unable to cope with new or surprising situations (179-80). She concludes that "to confine ourselves to the universal is a recipe for obtuseness" (180), and that "a fixed antecedent ordering or ranking among values is to be taken as a sign of immaturity rather than of excellence" (1983, 43).

Nussbaum maintains that *The Golden Bowl* both illustrates and defends this view of moral deliberation and moral achievement. Describing James's moral ideal as "a respect for the irreducibly particular character of a concrete moral context and the agents who are its components; a determination to scrutinize all aspects of this particular with intensely focused perception; a determination to care for it as a whole" (1987, 186), Nussbaum argues that this ideal is expressed both within the fictional world and in our relation to it. Throughout the novel, James shows his characters struggling to "share the same pictures" (175), to achieve full and loving vision of one another. For example, Adam Verver acknowledges his daughter's sexuality, autonomy, and maturity when he pictures her as a sea creature "floating and shining in a warm summer sea . . . cradled upon depths, buoyant among dangers . . ." (172). At crucial junctures, characters connect by building a shared image. After Adam and Maggie achieve moral communication, James speaks of "the act of their crossing the bar" and of "having had to beat against the wind." Nussbaum notes that "we cannot say whose image for their situation this is. We can only say that it belongs to both of them . . ." (175). Later, discussing a crucial scene in which a conversation between Bob and Fanny Assingham merges their complementary moral outlooks, Nussbaum points out that the passage ends with an image of them sinking together, hand in hand, in a mystic lake (184).

Not only do James's characters often exemplify Gilligan's care perspective in their relations with one another, but we, as *readers* of the novel, relate to them in just the same way. That is, we too "engage [the characters] in a loving scrutiny of appearances . . . actively care for their particularity, and . . . strain to be people on whom none of their subtleties are lost, in intellect and feeling" (Nussbaum 1987, 186). For this reason, the attention we pay to works of art can sometimes be an instance of moral attention. Nussbaum claims that our attention to James's characters in *The Golden Bowl* "will itself, if we read well, be a high case of moral attention" (186). In other words, reading James's novels with appropriate attention gives us important schooling in moral deliberation.[3]

We seem to have identified an interesting coincidence of outlook between Gilligan and Nussbaum. Gilligan contrasts a universalist, justice approach to a moral situation with a particularist, caring approach, and she identifies one as male, the other as female. Nussbaum draws a similar distinction and then argues for the primacy of the "female" approach (though she doesn't label it as such) when responding to the moral situation of a Henry James novel. Nussbaum concludes that reading James gives us important practice in moral philosophy. We might amend this claim slightly: reading James gives us important practice in the stereotypically female moral response. Presumably this conclusion also extends to many other novels, for example, those of George Eliot and Joseph Conrad.[4]

This intriguing conclusion suggests that stereotypically female reading is a *good* kind of reading and that men who want to be good readers must to this extent learn to read as women. Of course it is undeniable that many fine male critics and writers (including Henry James) have been able to pay attention to the particular and the contextual in the way associated with women, but this does not affect the point that this way of reading *is* associated with women.

Now, if the modes of perception which James's heroine Maggie exhibits are those which women stereotypically employ, and if these are also modes of perception which any sensitive reader of James must cultivate, then must we all be feminine readers? It would seem that all of us—men and women alike—need to adopt a "caring, contextualist" approach if we are to understand a literary work. What then makes the difference between actual male and female readers of a text? And, more significantly, what makes the difference between *feminist* and non-feminist readings? The parallels linking Gilligan's care perspective and Nussbaum's reading of James—parallels concerning the characters' relations to one another and our relations to the characters—fall short of establishing anything about distinctively *feminist* interpretations of literature.[5] We would like to suggest that the contextualist moral orientation that Gilligan discovered among women is stereotypically female without being feminist. This contextualist approach, when applied to literature, is compatible with any number of political orientations. The sort of response which Gilligan describes, one which we have labeled that of a care-reasoner, does not guarantee a feminist interpretation either in life or in literature.

FEMINIST INTERPRETATION

We suggest that a feminist interpretation of either a literary work or a real-life situation is one which acknowledges differentials of power between men and women. Such an interpretation starts from the assumption that our society is patriarchally structured and that women in such a society are oppressed. Though analyses might differ on both the sources and the remedies for this pervasive oppression, all feminist analysis starts from this value-laden claim. A feminist and a non-feminist reader will therefore bring different assumptions to bear on a particular text and consequently they are likely to produce different—often incompatible—interpretations of the same text.

The recent rise of feminist criticism is connected to a simultaneous upsurge of interest in the *reader* in literary theory. Different theories have identified the reader in different guises, as an actual reader (Norman Holland), as an ideal reader (E. D. Hirsch), as an implied reader (Wayne Booth), as a narratee (Gerald Prince), and more (see Suleiman 1980; Culler 1982). What these very different theories all have in common, however, is the view that meaning is a function of the reader's experience and that differences in experience produce different—perhaps inconsistent—readings.[6] One major source of different readings is the different experiences of men and women in a culture. When people with different background experiences examine a situation, whether in real life or in a novel, they tend to see it differently: they see different moral implications, different ways in which the situation is ambiguous, etc., and consequently they offer quite different interpretations of it. Moreover, (female) feminists bring to a reading not only their experience as women but also a set of political assumptions about that experience. They bring too their interest in and commitment to the interests of women. Consequently, feminist readings are bound to reflect these feminist assumptions and perspectives. Furthermore, while the feminist stance is not restricted to women, it is nevertheless true that feminism in both men and women grows out of reflecting upon the experiences of *women*.

Since feminism arises from the distinctive experiences of women in a culture, one way to make vivid the literary and political assumptions on which a "traditional" reading has been based is to postulate a woman as "the reader" of a text. Judith Fetterley is a feminist critic who has used this strategy to uncover limitations in the critical interpretations offered by respected (male) critics of a number of works in the canon of American literature. At the same time, she has provided feminist readings which shed new insight on these classic texts. Consider Fetterley's interpretation of Ernest Hemingway's A *Farewell to Arms*. The (stereotypically) male reader of this novel can read it as a fairly straightforward tragic love story in which at the end "we" weep for the hero, Frederic Henry, whose beloved, Catherine, has just died in childbirth. According to Fetterley, however, there is a striking disparity between "the novel's overt fabric of idealized romance and its underlying vision of the radical limitations of love, between its surface idyll and its sub-surface critique. . . . If we explore the attitude toward women in *A Farewell to Arms*, we will discover that while the novel's surface investment is in idealization, behind that idealization is a hostility whose full measure can be taken from the fact that Catherine dies and dies because she is a woman" (1978, 49).

A Farewell to Arms resembles other novels Fetterley discusses in her book *The Resisting Reader* in that a woman who tries to read it sympathetically, in the way seemingly intended by the author, has to identify *against herself*—in this case to identify with Frederic in his hostility against women and against Catherine, the female protagonist. It is very difficult for readers who are both female and feminist to identify with Catherine, because she exists only to serve Frederic: [7] "her character is determined by forces outside her; it is a reflection of male psychology and male fantasy life and is understandable only when seen as a series of responses to the needs of the male world that surrounds her" (Fetterley 1978, 66). Nor can such readers identify with Frederic, as the book requires, since he is so exploitative of Catherine and contemptuous of women in general.

For generations, male critics have treated Frederic as a tragic hero rather than the self-pitying and hostile figure who emerges on Fetterley's reading. The male critics Fetterley attacks, however, are not lacking in perceptiveness or moral sensitivity. Rather, as she points out, their different background assumptions about men and women blind them to certain ways of construing the novel. When we read a novel, we focus on those things that are salient for us; our moral perceptions, too, are dependent on our background assumptions, expectations, and so on. Whereas the respected male critics whom Fetterley cites have assumed that their readings have universal validity, by postulating a woman as reader, she lays bare the particular (stereotypically male) assumptions that in fact govern these readings.

In emphasizing a characteristically female perspective, Fetterley claims to "give voice to a different reality and different vision" (1978, ix). The similarity in language here between Fetterley and Gilligan is striking, but whereas Gilligan's "different voice" is the characteristic voice of women, or the voice of the female stereotype, Fetterley's "different voice" is the voice of women who are more self-conscious about their gender and who have a feminist's concern for the interests of women. In both cases, however, the "different voice" arises out of differences in male and female experience, which in turn result in differences in the kinds of interest, commitment, and focus of attention that are characteristically associated with the two genders. Furthermore, it is by reflecting upon these differences that feminists arrive at claims about the differentials of power in a society.

In closing, we would like to draw one further aesthetic implication of these differences. This concerns the understanding of figurative language and literary symbolism.

FIGURATION

In her discussion of women's fiction and of the difficulties it presents to male readers, Annette Kolodny comments that, "The problem is further exacerbated when the language of the literary text is largely dependent upon figuration" (1986, 249). This is so because, as Ted Cohen notes, figurative language "can be inaccessible to all but those who share information about one another's knowledge, beliefs, intentions, and attitudes" (1978, 9). On Cohen's view, the use of metaphor establishes a certain intimacy between speaker and hearer, one requiring a "cooperative act of comprehension" (9). Cohen characterizes the use of figurative language as a transaction in which each participant employs a number of assumptions about the other's knowledge, beliefs, intentions, and attitudes. It follows from this analysis that figurative language can fail. That is, a metaphor can be inaccessible when conversants don't share the requisite information about one another or about a common core of cultural constants.

Cohen illustrates his point by comparing metaphors and jokes. Just as jokes can range from those which are widely understood within a culture to those which are radically esoteric, so too metaphors can vary in their accessibility. And, the more esoteric the assumptions on which a metaphor is based, the more select the community within which the metaphor establishes intimacy.

Note that Cohen's claims accord with Max Black's famous analysis of metaphor. Black maintains that understanding a metaphor depends on understanding the "system of associated commonplaces" which that metaphor evokes (1962, 230). For example, calling a man a wolf evokes the wolf-system of associated commonplaces,[8] and only those who share the wolf-system commonplaces will understand the remark. Nelson Goodman's analysis of metaphor is not dissimilar: "In metaphor . . . a term with an extension established by habit is applied elsewhere under the influence of that habit" (1968, 71). Again, understanding the metaphor depends upon sharing the habits of usage on which it is based.

Because men and women experience the world differently, they are likely to adopt different beliefs and attitudes, to embrace different systems of commonplaces, and to develop different habits of usage. Thus men and women are likely to employ different metaphors, and the same metaphors may signify differently for members of each sex. We do not claim that men and women are likely to form systematically different beliefs about straightforward empirical matters—when water boils, the color of a shirt, whether the cat is on the mat. It is only with issues that are value-laden, politicized, or connected with men's and women's reproductive or social roles that a marked divergence might be expected. An example which demonstrates this sort of disparity and which shows how our point about figurative language can be extended to apply to other cases of literary symbolism concerns Charlotte Perkins Gilmore's story *The Yellow Wallpaper*.

In her analysis of *The Yellow Wallpaper*, Annette Kolodny notes that the protagonist's mental breakdown takes place in an upstairs room with barred windows, which had once served as a nursery. Kolodny claims that this setting symbolizes the "progressive infantilization of the adult protagonist" (1986, 250). As she says, however, a reader unacquainted with the ways in which women have traditionally inhabited a household might not take the initial description of the setting as semantically relevant, and the progressive infantilization of the adult protagonist would thereby lose some of its symbolic implications. (250)

As a matter of fact, the symbolic significance of the nursery was missed by generations of critics who saw in *The Yellow Wallpaper* only a horror story in the genre of Poe. Here is a case where the associated commonplaces necessary to grasp a literary symbol seem to be available only—or chiefly—to women.

Jean Kennard has taken this argument one step further by introducing the notion of literary conventions and showing that these too are dependent on a community's practices, beliefs, and values. Kennard points out that a reading of any text is dependent on two things: (1) "the literary conventions known to the reader at any time" including "both reading strategies and associative clusters of meaning" and (2) "the choices the reader makes to apply or not any one of these conventions—these choices are dependent on what the reader is at the time" (1981, 72-73).

Acknowledging that conventions change over time, Kennard insists that this is due to *non*literary as well as to literary influences. "Rereadings" such as Kolodny's account of *The Yellow Wallpaper* have become possible only because there are "conventions available to readers of the 1970's which were not available to those of 1892" (Kennard 1981, 74), the year of the story's publication. For example, Kolodny's interpretation of the narrator's confinement in a room as "symbolic of the situation of women in patriarchal society" depends upon a knowledge of conventions—of "associative clusters of meaning"—which have been newly formed from contemporary experience. Kennard examines the conventions associated with four such concepts or meaning clusters—patriarchy, madness, space, and quest—and shows how they affect our reading of Gilmore's story.

Feminist readings are grounded in such concepts, for Kennard, because "when a convention is an agreement on the meaning of a symbolic gesture in a literary context rather than agreement to use a specific interpretive strategy . . . the question of value is made more obvious" (1981, 72). And, men and women, and feminists and non-feminists, are likely to disagree about fundamental questions of value. Thus Kolodny sees the protagonist's madness in *The Yellow Wallpaper* as a response to oppression; in her analysis of the same story Fetterley argues that in a sense the madness is an assertion of self-identity (1986). By contrast, a traditional male-centered analysis might interpret the madness as representing tragedy for the male hero. Similarly, whereas Hemingway in *A Farewell to Arms* employs the convention that a woman's dying represents tragedy for the male hero, Fetterley points out that a woman's dying for a man can also represent women's subservience to and oppression by men.

In general, then, the interpretation of metaphors and symbols, even the identification of what counts as figurative or symbolic, is highly variable and dependent on current conventions of reading, which are in turn dependent on the assumptions and perspectives of groups of readers. Men and women are likely, because of their diverse experiences, to have different assumptions and perspectives, and so too are feminists and non-feminists. Indeed, an important part of Kennard's point is that readings such as Kolodny's feminist reading of *The Yellow Wallpaper* only become possible through developments in contemporary thought, in particular, the growth of feminism. In short, it is not enough to have experience of the nursery in order to recognize the symbolic significance of the nursery in Gilman's story. After all, for years neither female nor male critics interpreted the nursery as representing the protagonist's infantilization. Rather, it is a modern *feminist* perspective which has produced these rereadings in feminist terms. What is salient to most women of the 1890s and what is salient to contemporary feminist women is very different. Certainly there is a community of understanding and intimacy which permits women of the same period and culture to read metaphors and symbols with mutual comprehension, but there is also a more select group from within this larger female population which, although sharing similar experiences with other women, has a different political perspective upon those experiences. The community of intimacy and understanding which underlies Kolodny's reading of Gilman's text is a community of modern feminists.

CONCLUSION

In this essay we have explored the notion that the "different voice" identified by Carol Gilligan as the characteristic voice of women has implications for the study of literature. We note the important similarities between Gilligan's idea of a caring, contextualist attention to the particular and Martha Nussbaum's account of the proper way to attend to a literary work such as *The Golden Bowl*, and we conclude that the correct perspective to take toward certain traditional literary works is indeed a stereotypically female perspective. We then pursue the question of what distinguishes good readings by actual women from good readings by actual men, or, more significantly, good readings that are feminist from good readings that are not. Drawing upon work by Judith Fetterley, Annette Kolodny, and Jean Kennard, we examine how the different experiences of men and women affect what is salient for them and how the political assumptions of feminists further affect their perspectives. Gilligan herself does not, we think, help us to understand what is distinctively feminist about a feminist reading, but by drawing our attention to the different habits of mind and different foci of commitment which are characteristic of women, she reinforces the general point that different experiences result in different interpretations, in literature as well as in life.

Notes

We would like to thank Ellen Peel and the editors of this collection for helpful comments on this essay.

1. One study investigated women only, since it followed the decisions of twenty-nine pregnant women who were contemplating abortion. The other two studies compared responses of men and women.

2. This paper was brought to our attention by Marcia Lind.

3. Nussbaum's account of moral progress and moral teaching is strikingly similar to Arnold Isenberg's account of the critic's task. Compare the following passages from "Finely Aware and Richly Responsible" and from Isenberg's famous essay "Critical Communication": "Progress comes not from the teaching of an abstract law but by leading the friend, or child, or loved one—by a word, by a story, by an image—to see some new aspect of the concrete case at hand, to see it as this or that" (Nussbaum 1987, 184). " . . . the critic's *meaning* is 'filled in,' 'rounded out,' or 'completed' by the act of perception, which is performed not to judge the truth of his description but, in a certain sense, to *understand* it. And if *communication* is a process by which a mental content is transmitted by symbols from one person to another, then we can say that it is a function of criticism to bring about communication at the level of the senses, that is, to induce a sameness of vision, of experienced content" (Isenberg 1979, 663).

4. Cf. F. R. Leavis 1962, which lists Austen, Eliot, James, Conrad, and Lawrence as forming the "great tradition" of English novels.

5. Indeed, this is not surprising, since in general the subjects Gilligan studied were not feminists.

6. Strictly speaking, ideal readers or implied readers, for example, do not have experiences because they are merely theoretical constructs, but although constructs, they are person-like constructs and hence "they" have constructed "experiences."

7. For example, when she first becomes Frederic's lover, Catherine says, "I'm afraid I'm not very good at it yet. . . . I'm good. Aren't I good? . . . You see? I'm good. I do what you want" (Fetterley 1978, 68).

8. "A suitable hearer will be led by the wolf-system of implications to construct a corresponding system of implications about [the man]. But these implications will *not* be those comprised in the commonplaces *normally* implied by literal uses of 'man.' The new implications must be determined by the patterns of implications associated with literal uses of the word 'wolf.' The wolf-metaphor suppresses some details, emphasizes others—in short, *organizes* our view of man" (Black 1962, 230).

References

Black, Max. 1962. Metaphor. In *Philosophy looks at the arts*. Joseph Margolis, ed. New York: Scribners.

Chodorow, Nancy. 1978. *The reproduction of mothering: Psychoanalysis and the sociology of gender*. Berkeley: University of California Press.

Cohen, Ted. 1978. Metaphor and the cultivation of intimacy. *Critical Inquiry* 5(1): 3-12.

Culler, Jonathan. 1982. *On deconstruction*. Ithaca: Cornell University Press.

Dinnerstein, Dorothy. 1976. *The mermaid and the minotaur: Sexual arrangements and human malaise*. New York: Harper and Row.

Fetterley, Judith. 1978. *The resisting reader*. Bloomington: Indiana University Press.

Fetterley, Judith. 1986. Reading about reading: *A jury of her peers, The murders in the rue morgue*, and *The yellow wallpaper*. In *Gender and reading*. Patrocino Schweickert and Elizabeth Flynn, eds. Baltimore: Johns Hopkins University Press.

Friedman, Marilyn. 1987. Beyond caring: The de-moralization of gender. In *Science, morality and feminist theory*. Marsha Hanen and Kai Nielsen, eds. Calgary: University of Calgary Press.

Gilligan, Carol. 1982. *In a different voice*. Cambridge, MA: Harvard University Press.

Goodman, Nelson. 1968. *Languages of art*. Indianapolis: Bobbs-Merrill.

Isenberg, Arnold. 1979. Critical communication. In *Art and philosophy*. W. E. Kennick, ed. New York: St. Martin's Press.

Kennard, Jean. 1981. Convention coverage or how to read your own life. *New Literary History* 13(1): 69-88.

Kolodny, Annette. 1980. A map for rereading: Or, gender and the interpretation of literary texts. *New Literary History* 11(3): 451-67.

Kolodny, Annette. 1986. Dancing through the minefield: Some observations on the theory, practice, and politics of a feminist literary criticism. In *Women and values: Readings in recent feminist philosophy*. Marilyn Pearsall, ed. Belmont, CA: Wadsworth.

Leavis, F. R. 1962. *The great tradition*. Harmondsworth: Penguin Books.

Nussbaum, Martha. 1983. Flawed crystals: James's *The Golden Bowl* and literature as moral philosophy. *New Literary History* 40(1): 25-50.

Nussbaum, Martha. 1987. Finely aware and richly responsible: Literature and the moral imagination. In *Literature and the question of philosophy*. Anthony J. Cascardi, ed. Baltimore: Johns Hopkins University Press.

Suleiman, Susan, and Inge Crosman. 1980. *The reader in the text*. Princeton: Princeton University Press.

NINE

Speaking in Tongues
Dialogics, Dialectics, and the Black Woman Writer's Literary Tradition

MAE GWENDOLYN HENDERSON

The multiple voices of black female characters in literature can be explicated through Bakhtin's dialogics of difference and Gadamer's dialectics of identity, as well as by reference to the scriptural notion of glossolalia or speaking in tongues. Characters from novels by Zora Neale Hurston, Sherley Anne Williams, and Toni Morrison demonstrate how both the differences and identities of female subjectivity structure the discourse of black women. Because of doubled otherness—not white, not male—black women are positioned to speak in a plurality of voices, transforming the glossolalia—of spiritual witness of a few—to "heteroglossia"—multiple tongues of public discourse accessible to many.

I am who I am, doing what I came to do, acting
upon you like a drug or a chisel *to remind you of your me-ness, as
I discover you in myself.*

—Audre Lorde, *Sister Outsider* (emphasis mine)

There's a noisy feelin' near the cracks
crowdin' me . . . slips into those long, loopin' "B's"
There's a noisy feelin' near the cracks
crowdin' me . . . slips into those long, loopin' "B's"
of Miss Garrison's handwritin' class;
they become the wire hoops I must jump through.
It spooks my alley, it spooks my play,
more nosey now than noisy,
    lookin' for a tongue
    lookin' for a tongue
    to get holy in.
Who can tell this feelin' where to set up church?
Who can tell this noise where to go?

A root woman workin' . . . a mo-jo,
just to the left of my ear.

—Cherry Muhanji, *Tight Spaces*

Some years ago, three black feminist critics and scholars edited an anthology entitled *All the Women Are White, All the Blacks Are Men, But Some of Us Are Brave,* suggesting in the title the unique and peculiar dilemma of black women (Hull, Scott, Smith 1982). Since then it has perhaps become almost commonplace for literary critics, male and female, black and white, to note that black women have been discounted or unaccounted for in the "traditions" of black, women's, and American literature as well as in the contemporary literary-critical dialogue. More recently, black women writers have begun to receive token recognition as they are subsumed under the category of woman in the feminist critique and the category of black in the racial critique. Certainly these "gendered" and "racial" decodings of black women authors present strong and revisionary methods of reading, focusing as they do on literary discourses regarded as marginal to the dominant literary-critical tradition. Yet the "critical insights" of one reading might well become the "blind spots" of another reading. That is, by privileging one category of analysis at the expense of the other, each of these methods risks setting up what Fredric Jameson describes as "strategies of containment," which restrict or repress different or alternative readings. (1981, 53). More specifically, blindness to what Nancy Fraser describes as the "gender subtext" can be just as occluding as blindness to *the race subtext* in the works of black women writers.[1]

Such approaches can result in exclusion, at worst, and, at best, a reading of part of the text as the whole—a strategy that threatens to replicate (if not valorize) the reification against which black women struggle in life and literature. What I propose is a theory of interpretation based on what I refer to as the "simultaneity of discourse," a term inspired by Barbara Smith's seminal work on black feminist criticism (1983, xxxii). This concept is meant to signify a mode of reading which examines the ways in which the perspectives of race and gender, and their interrelationships, structure the discourse of black women writers. Such an approach is intended to acknowledge and overcome the limitations imposed by assumptions of internal identity (homogeneity) and the repression of internal differences (heterogeneity) in racial and gendered readings of works by black women writers. In other words, I propose a model that seeks to account for racial difference within gender identity and gender difference within racial identity. This approach represents my effort to avoid what one critic describes as the presumed "absolute and self-sufficient" *otherness* of the critical stance in order to allow the complex representations of black women writers to steer us away from "a single and reductive paradigm of 'otherness' " (Rowe 1986, 67-68).

DISCURSIVE DIVERSITY: SPEAKING IN TONGUES

What is at once characteristic and suggestive about black women's writing is its interlocutory, or dialogic, character, reflecting not only a relationship with the "other(s)" but an internal dialogue with the plural aspects of self that constitute the matrix of black female subjectivity. The interlocutory character of black women's writings is, thus, not only a consequence of a dialogic relationship with an imaginary or "generalized Other" but a dialogue with the aspects of "otherness" within the self. The complex situatedness of the black woman as not only the "Other" of the Same but also as the "other" of the other(s) implies, as we shall see, a relationship of difference and identification with the "other(s)."

It is Mikhail Bakhtin's notion of dialogism and consciousness that provides the primary model for this approach. According to Bakhtin, each social group speaks in its own "social dialect"—possesses its own unique language—expressing shared values, perspectives, ideology, and norms. These social dialects become the "languages" of heteroglossia "intersect[ing] with each other in many different ways. . . . As such they all may be juxtaposed to one another, mutually supplement one another, contradict one another and be interrelated dialogically" (Bakhtin 1981, 292).[2] Yet if language, for Bakhtin, is an expression of social identity, then subjectivity (subjecthood) is constituted as a social entity through the "role of [the] word as medium of consciousness." Consciousness, then, like language, is shaped by the social environment. ("Consciousness becomes consciousness only . . . in the process of social interaction.") Moreover, "the semiotic material of the psyche is preeminently the word—*inner speech*." Bakhtin in fact defines the relationship between consciousness and inner speech even more precisely: "Analysis would show that the units of which inner speech is constituted are certain *whole entities . . . [resembling] the alternative lines of a dialogue.* There was good reason why thinkers in ancient times should have conceived of inner speech as *inner dialogue.*"[3] Thus, consciousness becomes a kind of "inner speech" reflecting "the outer word" in a process that links the psyche, language, and social interaction.

It is the process by which these heteroglossic voices of the other(s) "encounter one another and coexist in the consciousness of real people—first and foremost in the creative consciousness of people who write novels" (Bakhtin 1981, 292) that speaks to the situation of black women writers in particular, "privileged" by a social positionality that enables them to speak in dialogically racial and gendered voices to the other(s) both within and without. If the psyche functions as an internalization of heterogeneous social voices, black women's speech/writing becomes at once a dialogue between self and society and between self and psyche. Writing as inner speech, then, becomes what Bakhtin would describe as "a unique form of collaboration with oneself" in the works of these writers.[4]

Revising and expanding Teresa de Lauretis's formulation of the "social subject and the relations of subjectivity to sociality," I propose a model that is intended to address not only "a subject en-gendered in the experiencing of race" but also what I submit is *a subject "racialized" in the experiencing of gender* (Lauretis 1987, 2). Speaking both to and from the position of other(s), black women writers must, in the words of Audre Lorde, deal not only with "the external manifestations of racism and sexism" but also "with the results of those distortions internalized within our consciousness of ourselves and one another" (1984, 147).

What distinguishes black women's writing, then, is the privileging (rather than repressing) of "the other in ourselves." Writing of Lorde's notion of self and otherness, black feminist critic Barbara Christian observes of Lorde what I argue is true to a greater or lesser degree in the discourse of black women writers: "As a black, lesbian, feminist, poet, mother, Lorde has, in her own life, had to search long and hard for *her* people. In responding to each of these audiences, in which part of her identity lies, she refuses to give up her differences. In fact she uses them, as woman to man, black to white, lesbian to heterosexual, as a means of conducting creative dialogue" (1985, 209).

If black women speak from a multiple and complex social, historical, and cultural positionality which, in effect, constitutes black female subjectivity, then Christian's term "creative dialogue" refers to the expression of a multiple *dialogic of differences* based on this complex subjectivity. At the same time, however, black women enter into a *dialectic of identity* with those aspects of self shared with others. It is Hans-Georg Gadamer's "dialectical model of conversation," rather than Bakhtin's dialogics of discourse, that provides an appropriate model for articulating a relation of mutuality and reciprocity with the "Thou"—or intimate other(s). Whatever the critic thinks of Gadamer's views concerning history, tradition, and the like, one can still find Gadamer's emphases—especially as they complement Bakhtin's—to be useful and productive. If the Bakhtinian model is primarily adversarial, assuming that verbal communication (and social interaction) is characterized by contestation with the other(s), then the Gadamerian model presupposes as its goal a language of consensus, communality, and even identification, in which "one claims to express the other's claim and even to understand the other better than the other understands [him- or herself]." In the "I-Thou" relationship proposed by Gadamer, "the important thing is . . . to experience the 'Thou' truly as a 'Thou,' that is, not to overlook [the other's] claim and to listen to what [s/he] has to say to us." Gadamer's dialectic, based on a typology of the "hermeneutical experience," privileges tradition as "a genuine partner in communication, with which we have fellowship as does the 'I' with a 'Thou.' " For black and women writers, such an avowal of tradition in the subdominant order, of course, constitutes an operative challenge to the dominant order. It is this rereading of the notion of tradition within a field of gender and ethnicity that supports and enables the notion of community among those who share a common history, language, and culture. If Bakhtin's dialogic engagement with the Other signifies conflict, Gadamer's monologic acknowledgement of Thou signifies the potential of agreement. If the Bakhtinian dialogic model speaks to the other within, then Gadamer's speaks to *the same within*. Thus, "the [dialectic] understanding of the [Thou]" (like the dialogic understanding of the other[s]) becomes "a form of self-relatedness."[5]

It is this notion of discursive difference and identity underlying the simultaneity of discourse which typically characterizes black women's writing. Through the multiple voices that enunciate her complex subjectivity, the black woman writer not only speaks familiarly in the discourse of the other(s), but as Other she is in contestorial dialogue with the hegemonic dominant and subdominant or "ambiguously (non)hegemonic" discourses.[6] These writers enter simultaneously into familial, or *testimonial* and public, or *competitive* discourses—discourses that both affirm and challenge the values and expectations of the reader. As such, black women writers enter into testimonial discourse with black men as blacks, with white women as women, and with black women as black women.[7] At the same time, they enter into competitive discourse with black men as women, with white women as blacks, and with white men as black women. If black women speak a discourse of racial and gendered difference in the dominant or hegemonic discursive order, they speak a discourse of racial and gender identity and difference in the subdominant discursive order. This dialogic of difference and dialectic of identity characterize both black women's subjectivity and black women's discourse. It is the complexity of these simultaneously homogeneous and heterogeneous social and discursive domains out of which black women write and construct themselves (as blacks and women and, often, as poor, black women) that enables these women writers authoritatively to speak to and engage both hegemonic and ambiguously (non)hegemonic discourse.

Janie, the protagonist in Zora Neale Hurston's *Their Eyes Were Watching God* (1937), demonstrates how the dialectics/dialogics of black and female subjectivity structure black women's discourse. Combining personal and public forms of discourse in the court scene where she is on trial and fighting not only for her life but against "lying thoughts" and "misunderstanding," Janie addresses the judge, a jury composed of "twelve more white men," and spectators ("eight or ten white women" and "all the Negroes [men] for miles around") (274). The challenge of Hurston's character is that of the black woman writer—namely, to speak at once to a diverse audience about her experience in a racist and sexist society where to be black and female is to be, so to speak, "on trial." Janie speaks not only in a discourse of gender and racial difference to the white male judge and jurors but also in a discourse of gender difference (and racial identity) to the black male spectators and a discourse of racial difference (and gender identity) to the white women spectators. Significantly, it is the white men who constitute both judge and jury and, by virtue of their control of power and discourse, possess the authority of life and death over the black woman. In contrast, the black men (who are convinced that "the nigger [woman] kin kill . . . jus' as many niggers as she please") and white women (who "didn't seem too mad") read and witness/oppose a situation over which they exercise neither power nor discourse (225, 280).

Janie's courtroom discourse also emblematizes the way in which the categories of public and private break down in black women's discourse. In the context of Janie's courtroom scene, testimonial discourse takes on an expanded meaning, referring to both juridical, public, and dominant discourse as well as familial, private, and nondominant discourse. Testimonial, in this sense, derives its meaning from both "testimony" as an official discursive mode and "testifying," defined by Geneva Smitherman as "a ritualized form of . . . communication in which the speaker gives verbal witness to the efficacy, truth, and power of some experience in which [the group has] shared." The latter connotation suggests an additional meaning in the context of theological discourse where testifying refers to a "spontaneous expression to the church community [by whoever] feels the spirit" (Smitherman 1986, 58).

Like Janie, black women must speak in a plurality of voices as well as in a multiplicity of discourses. This discursive diversity, or simultaneity of discourse, I call "speaking in tongues." Significantly, glossolalia, or speaking in tongues, is a practice associated with black women in the Pentecostal Holiness church, the church of my childhood and the church of my mother. In the Holiness church (or as we called it, the Sanctified church), speaking unknown tongues (tongues known only to God) is in fact a sign of election, or holiness. As a trope it is also intended to remind us of Alice Walker's characterization of black women as artists, as "Creators," intensely rich in that spirituality which Walker sees as "the basis of Art" (1984, 232).

Glossolalia is perhaps the meaning most frequently associated with speaking in tongues. It is this connotation which emphasizes the particular, private, closed, and privileged communication between the congregant and the divinity. Inaccessible to the general congregation, this mode of communication is outside the realm of public discourse and foreign to the known tongues of humankind.

But there is a second connotation to the notion of speaking in tongues—one that suggests not glossolalia but heteroglossia, the ability to speak in diverse known languages. While glossolalia refers to the ability to "utter the mysteries of the spirit," heteroglossia describes the ability to speak in the multiple languages of public discourse. If glossolalia suggests private, nonmediated, nondifferentiated univocal-ity, heteroglossia connotes public, differentiated, social, mediated, dialogic dis-course. Returning from the trope to the act of reading, perhaps we can say that speaking in tongues connotes both the semiotic, presymbolic babble (baby talk), as between mother and child—which Julia Kristeva postulates as the "mother tongue"—and the diversity of voices, discourse, and languages described by Mikhail Bakhtin.

Speaking in tongues, my trope for both glossolalia and heteroglossia, has a precise genealogical evolution in the Scriptures. In Genesis 11, God confounded the world's language when the city of Babel built a tower in an attempt to reach the heavens. Speaking in many different tongues, the dwellers of Babel, unable to understand each other, fell into confusion, discord, and strife and had to abandon the project. Etymologically, the name of the city Babel sounds much like the Hebrew word for "babble"—meaning confused, as in a baby talk. Babel, then, suggests the two related, but distinctly different, meanings of speaking in tongues, meanings borne out in other parts of the Scriptures. The most common is that implied in 1 Corinthians 14—the ability to speak in unknown tongues. According to this interpretation, speaking in tongues suggests the ability to speak in and through the spirit. Associated with glossolalia—speech in unknown tongues—it is ecstatic, rapturous, inspired speech, based on a relation of intimacy and identifica-tion between the individual and God.

If Genesis tells of the disempowerment of a people by the introduction of different tongues, then Acts 2 suggests the empowerment of the disciples who, assembled on the day of Pentecost in the upper room of the temple in Jerusalem, "were filled with the Holy Spirit and began to speak in other tongues." Although the people thought the disciples had "imbibed a strange and unknown wine," it was the Holy Spirit which had driven them, filled with ecstasy, from the upper room to speak among the five thousand Jews surrounding the temple. The Scriptures tell us that the tribes of Israel all understood them, each in his own tongue. The Old Testament, then, suggests the dialogics of difference in its diversity of discourse, while the New Testament, in its unifying language of the spirit, suggests the dialectics of identity. If the Bakhtinian model suggests the multiplicity of speech as suggested in the dialogics of difference, then Gadamer's model moves toward a unity of understanding in its dialectics of identity.

It is the first as well as the second meaning which we privilege in speaking of black women writers: the first connoting polyphony, multivocality, and plurality of voices, and the second signifying intimate, private, inspired utterances. Through their intimacy with the discourse of the other(s), black women writers weave into their work competing and complementary discourses—discourses that seek both to adjudicate competing claims and witness common concerns.[8]

Also interesting is the link between the gift of tongues, the gift of prophecy, and the gift of interpretation. While distinguishing between these three gifts, the Scriptures frequently conflate or conjoin them. If to speak in tongues is to utter mysteries in and through the Spirit, to prophesy is to speak to others in a (diversity of) language(s) which the congregation can understand. The Scriptures would suggest that the disciples were able to perform both. I propose, at this juncture, an enabling critical fiction—that is, black women writers who are the modern-day apostles, empowered by experience to speak as poets and prophets in many tongues. With this critical gesture, I also intend to signify a deliberate intervention by black women writers into the canonic tradition of sacred/literary texts.[9]

A DISCURSIVE DILEMMA

In their works, black women writers have encoded oppression as a discursive dilemma; that is, their works have consistently raised the problem of the black woman's relationship to power and discourse. Silence is an important element of this code. The classic black woman's text, *Their Eyes Were Watching God,* charts the female protagonist's development from voicelessness to voice, from silence to tongues. Yet this movement does not exist without intervention by the other(s)— who speak for and about black women. In other words, it is not that black women, in the past, have had nothing to say, but rather that they have had no say. The absence of black female voices has allowed others to inscribe, write, and ascribe to, or read, them. The notion of speaking in tongues, however, leads us away from an examination of how the Other has written/read black women and toward an examination of how black women have written the other's(s') writing/reading black women.

Using the notion of "speaking in tongues" as our model, let us offer a kind of paradigmatic reading of two works which encode and resist the material and discursive dilemma of the black woman writer. Sherley Anne Williams's *Dessa Rose* (1986) and Toni Morrison's *Sula* (1975) are novels that emphasize respectively the *inter*cultural/racial and *intra*cultural/racial sites from which black women speak, as well as the signs under which they speak in both these milieus. Artificial though this separation may be—since, as we have seen, black women are located simultaneously within both these discursive domains—such a distinction makes possible an examination of black women's literary relations to both dominant and subdominant discourse. These works also allow us to compare the suppression of the black female voice in the dominant discourse with its repression in the subdominant discourse.[10] Finally, they provide models for the disruption of the dominant and subdominant discourse by black and female expression, as well as for the appropriation and transformation of these discourses.

The heroine of Sherley Anne Williams's first novel, *Dessa Rose*, is a fugitive slave woman introduced to the reader as "the Darky" by Adam Nehemiah, a white male writer interviewing her in preparation for a forthcoming book, *The Roots of Rebellion in the Slave Population and Some Means of Eradicating Them* (or, more simply, *The Work*). The opening section of the novel is structured primarily by notations from Nehemiah's journal, based on his interactions with the slave woman during her confinement in a root cellar while awaiting her fate at the gallows. The latter section, describing her adventures as a fugitive involved in a scam against unsuspecting slaveholders and traders, is narrated primarily in the voice of Dessa (as the slave woman calls herself) after she has managed, with the assistance of fellow slaves, to escape the root cellar. At the end of the novel, the writer-interviewer, Adam Nehemiah, still carrying around his notes for *The Work*, espies the fugitive Dessa.

Brandishing a poster advertising a reward for her recapture, and a physical description of her identifying markings (an R branded on the thigh and whip-scarred hips), Adam Nehemiah coerces the local sheriff into detaining Dessa for identification. Significantly, Adam Nehemiah, named after his precursor—the archetypal white male namer, creator, and interpreter—attempts not only to remand Dessa into slavery but to inscribe her experiences as a slave woman through a discourse that suppresses her voice. Like the Adam of Genesis, Nehemiah asserts the right of ownership through the privilege of naming. Not only is his claim of discursive and material power held together symbolically in his name, but his acts and his words conflate: Nehemiah not only wishes to capture Odessa (as he calls her) in words that are instructive to the preservation of slavery, but he wishes to confine her in material slavery. Just as the biblical Nehemiah constructed the wall to protect the Israelites against attack by their enemies, so Williams's Nehemiah sets out to write a manual designed to protect the American South against insurrection by the slaves. Ironically, the character of Nehemiah, a patriot and leader of the Jews after the years of Babylonian captivity, is reread in the context of the Old South as a racist and expert on the "sound management" of the slaves.[11]

Dessa fears that exposure of her scars/branding will confirm her slave status. As she awaits the arrival of Ruth, the white woman who abets in the perpetration of the scam, Dessa thinks to herself, "I could feel everyone of them scars, the one roped partway to my navel that the waist of draws itched, the corduroyed welts across my hips, and R on my thighs" (223). What interests me here is the literal inscription of Dessa's body, signified by the whip marks and, more specifically, the branded R, as well as the white male writer-cum-reader's attempt to exercise discursive domination over Dessa. Seeking to inscribe black female subjectivity, the white male, in effect, relegates the black woman to the status of discursive object, or spoken subject. The location of the inscriptions—in the area of the genitalia—signals an attempt to inscribe the sign *slave* in an area that marks her as *woman* ("Scar tissue plowed through her pubic hair region so no hair would ever grow there again"

[154]). The effect is to attempt to deprive the slave woman of her femininity and render the surface of her skin a parchment upon which meaning is etched by the whip (pen) of white patriarchal authority and sealed by the firebrand. Together, these inscriptions produce the meaning of black female subjectivity in the discursive domain of slavery.[12] Importantly, the literal inscription of the flesh emphasizes what Monique Wittig, insisting on "the *material* oppression of individuals by discourses," describes as the "unrelenting tyranny that [male discourses] exert upon our *physical* and *mental* selves" (emphasis mine) (1980, 105-106). Dessa is ordered by the sheriff to lift her skirt so that these inscriptions can be "read" by her potential captors. (Perhaps we should read the R on Dessa's thigh as part of an acrostic for *Read*.) The signifying function of her scars is reinforced when Dessa recognizes that "[Nehemiah] wouldn't have to say nothing. Sheriff would see [i.e., read] that for himself" (223). Her remarks also suggest that mortal consequence of such a reading, or misreading: [13] "This [the scars] was what would betray me . . . these white mens would kill me" (223).

If Williams's *Dessa Rose* contains a representation of the inscription of *black female* in the dominative white and male discourse, then Morrison's *Sula* contains a representation of *female* ascription in black subdominative discourse. If in the context of the white community's discourse Dessa is suppressed as woman *and* black, in the discourse of the black community she is repressed as woman.

Like Dessa, Sula is marked. Unlike Dessa, Sula is marked from birth. Hers is a mark of nativity—a biological rather than cultural inscription, appropriate in this instance because it functions to mark her as a "naturally" inferior female within the black community.[14] The birthmark, "spread[ing] from the middle of the lid toward the eyebrow" (Morrison 1975, 45), is associated with a series of images. For her mother, Hannah, Sula's birthmark "looked more and more like a stem and a rose" (64). Although in European and Eurocentric culture the rose is the gift of love as well as the traditional romantic symbol of female beauty and innocence (lily-white skin and rose blush), it is a symbol that has been appropriated by black women writers from Frances Harper, who uses it as a symbol of romantic love, to Alice Walker, who associates it with sexual love.[15]

Jude, the husband of Nel, Sula's best friend, refers to the birthmark as a "copperhead" and, later, as "the rattlesnake over her eye." If the image of the rose suggests female romantic love and sexuality, then the snake evokes the archetypal Garden and the story of Eve's seduction by the serpent.[16] The association is significant in light of the subsequent seduction scene between Jude and Sula, for it is Jude's perception of the snake imagery which structures his relationship with Sula, suggesting not only that the meaning he ascribes to the birthmark reflects the potential of his relationship with her but that, on a broader level, it is the "male gaze" which constitutes female subjectivity. At the same time, Morrison redeploys the role of Other in a way that suggests how the black woman as Other is used to constitute (black) male subjectivity.

The community, "clearing up," as it thought, "the meaning of the birthmark over her eye," tells the reader that "it was not a stemmed rose, or a snake, it was Hannah's ashes marking Sula from the very beginning" (99). (That Sula had watched her mother burn to death was her grandmother's contention and the community gossip.) If Jude represents the subject constituted in relation to the black woman as Other, the community represents a culture constituted in relation to the black woman as Other:

> Their conviction of Sula's evil changed them in accountable yet mysterious ways. Once the source of their personal misfortune was identified, they had leave to protect and love one another. They began to cherish their husbands and wives, protect their children, repair their homes and in general band together against the devil in their midst. (102)

Sula signifies, for the community, the chaos and evil against which it must define and protect itself. Convinced that she bears the mark of the devil because of her association with Shadrack, the town reprobate, the community closes ranks against one who transgresses the boundaries prescribed for women.

For Shadrack, the shell-shocked World War I veteran who has become the community pariah, Sula's birthmark represents "the mark of the fish he loved"—the tadpole (134). A symbol of the primordial beginnings of life in the sea, the tadpole represents potential, transformation, and rebirth. Such an image contrasts with the apocalyptic ending of life by fire suggested by the community's perception of Hannah's ashes.[17] As an amphibious creature, the tadpole has the capacity to live both terrestrially and aquatically. Etymologically, Sula's name is derived from the designation of a genus of seabird, again an image associated with a dual environment—aquatic and aerial. These contrasts suggestively position Sula at the crossroads or intersection of life and death, land and sea, earth and air. Thus both the mark and the designation are particularly appropriate for the black woman as one situated within two social domains (black and female) and, as such, implicated in both a racial and gendered discourse.

But it is the black community—the Bottom—which provides the setting for the action in Morrison's novel, and it is the men who have the final say in the community: "It was the men," observes the narrator, "who gave [Sula] the final label, who *fingerprinted* her for all time" (emphasis mine; 197). The men in the community speak a racial discourse that reduces Sula finally to her sexuality: "The word was passed around" that "Sula slept with *white* men" (emphasis mine; 97). It is thus her sexuality, read through the race relation, which structures her subjectivity within the male-dominated discourse of the black community.

The power of male discourse and naming is also suggested in the epithet directed to the twelve-year-old Sula as she, along with her friend Nel, saunters by Edna Finch's ice cream parlor one afternoon, passing the old and young men of the Bottom:

> Pigmeat. The words were in all their minds. And one of them, one of the young ones, said it aloud. His name was Ajax, a twenty-one-year-old pool haunt of sinister beauty. Graceful and economical in every movement, he held a place of envy with men of all ages for his magnificently foul mouth. In fact he seldom cursed, and the epithets he chose were dull, even harmless. His reputation was derived from the way he handled words. When he said "hell" he hit the *h* with his lungs and the impact was greater

than the achievement of the most imaginative foul mouth in town. He could say "shit" with a nastiness impossible to imitate. (43)

Not only does the language itself take on a special potency when exercised by males, but the epithet "pigmeat" which Ajax confers on Sula still has a powerful hold on her seventeen years later, when at twenty-nine, having traveled across the country and returned to the Bottom, she is greeted by the now thirty-eight-year-old Ajax at her screen door: "Sula . . . was curious. She knew nothing about him except the word he had called out to her years ago and the feeling he had excited in her then" (110).

The images associated with Sula's birthmark connote, as we have seen, a plurality of meanings. These images not only become symbols of opposition and ambiguity associated with the stemmed rose, snake, fire, and tadpole, but they evoke the qualities of permanence and mutability (nature and culture) inherent in the sign of the birthmark, the meaning and valence of which changes with the reading and the reader. At one point, Nel, Sula's complement in the novel, describes her as one who "helped others define themselves," that is, one who takes on the complementary aspect of the Other in the process of constituting subjectivity. As if to underscore Sula's signifying function as absence or mutability, Sula is described as having "no center" and "no ego," "no speck around which to grow" (103). The plurality and flux of meaning ascribed to the birthmark share some of the characteristics of the Sign or, perhaps more precisely, the Signifier. Sula's association with the birthmark gradually evolves, through synecdoche, into an identification between the subject/object and the Sign. Thus her entry into the subdominative discursive order confers on her the status of "a free-floating signifier," open to diverse interpretations.

The inscription (writing) of Dessa and the ascription (reading) of Sula together encode the discursive dilemma of black women in hegemonic and ambiguously (non)hegemonic discursive contexts. However, these works also embody a code of resistance to the discursive and material dominance of black women. To different degrees and in different ways, Williams and Morrison fashion a counterdiscourse within their texts.

DISRUPTION AND REVISION

In negotiating the discursive dilemma of their characters, these writers accomplish two objectives: the self-inscription of black womanhood and the establishment of a dialogue of discourses with the other(s). The self-inscription of black women requires disruption, rereading, and rewriting the conventional and canonical stories, as well as revising the conventional generic forms that convey these stories. Through this interventionist, intertextual, and revisionary activity, black women writers enter into dialogue with the discourses of the other(s). Disruption—the initial response to hegemonic and ambiguously (non)hegemonic discourse—and revision (rewriting or rereading) together suggest a model for reading black and female literary expression.

Dessa's continued rejection of Adam Nehemiah's inscription suggests that we must read with some measure of credence her claims of being mis-recognized. ("I don't know this master, Mistress," she says. "They mistook me for another Dessa, Mistress" [226-27].) Ultimately, Dessa's insistence on *meconnaissance* is vindicated in the failure of Nehemiah's attempts either to *con*fine her in the social system or *de*fine her in the dominant discourse.

Dessa not only succeeds in rupturing the narrator's discourse at the outset of the novel through a series of interventionist acts—singing, evasion, silence, non-acquiescence, and dissemblance—but she employs these strategies to effect her escape and seize discursive control of the story.[18] Moreover, Dessa's repeated use of the word *track* (a term connoting both pursuit and inscription) in reference to Nehemiah takes on added significance in the context of both her inscription and revision. Tracking becomes the object of her reflections: "Why the white man *track* me down like he owned me, like a bloodhound on my *trail*," and later, "crazy white man, *tracking* me all cross the country like he owned me" (emphasis mine; 225). In other words, Nehemiah *tracks* Dessa in an attempt to establish ownership—that is, the colonization—of her body. Yet tracking also suggests that Dessa's flight becomes a text that she writes and Nehemiah reads. His tracking (i.e., reading of Dessa's text) thus becomes the means by which he attempts to capture her (i.e., suppress her voice in the production of his own text).

If the pursuit/flight emblematizes a strategic engagement for discursive control, Dessa's tracks also mark her emergence as narrator of her own story. It is her escape—loosely speaking, her "making tracks"—that precludes the closure/completion of Nehemiah's book. The story of Dessa's successful revolt and escape, in effect, prefigures the rewriting of *the Work*—Nehemiah's projected treatise on the control of slaves and the prevention of slave revolts. The latter part of the novel, recounted from Dessa's perspective and in her own voice, establishes her as the successful author of her own narrative. Tracking thus becomes a metaphor for writing/reading from the white male narrator's perspective and a metaphor for revision (rewriting/rereading) from Dessa's. Creating her own track therefore corresponds to Dessa's assumption of discursive control of the novel, that is, the telling of her own story. In flight, then, Dessa challenges the material and discursive elements of her oppression and, at the same time, provides a model for writing as struggle.

Nehemiah's inability to capture Dessa in print is paralleled, finally, in his failure to secure her recapture. As Dessa walks out of the sheriff's office, Nehemiah cries: "I know it's her. . . . I got her down here in my book." Leaving, Dessa tells the reader, "And he reach and took out that little black-bound pad he wrote in the whole time I knowed him" (231). But the futility of his efforts is represented in the reactions of the onlookers to the unbound pages of Nehemiah's notebook as they tumble and scatter to the floor:

[Sheriff] Nemi, ain't nothing but some scribbling on here. . . . Can't no one read this.
[Ruth] And these [pages] is blank, sheriff. (232)

Finally, in two dramatic acts of self-entitlement, Dessa reaffirms her ability to name herself and her own experience. In the first instance, she challenges Nehemiah's efforts to capture her—in person and in print: "Why, he didn't even know how to call my name—talking about Odessa" (emphasis mine; 225). And in the second, after her release, she informs Ruth, her white accomplice and alleged mistress, "My name Dessa, Dessa Rose. Ain't no O to it" (232). She is, of course, distinguishing between Odessa, an ascription by the white male slavemaster and used by both Nehemiah and Ruth, and Dessa, her entitlement proper. Her rejection of the O signifies her rejection of the inscription of her body by the other(s). In other words, Dessa's repudiation of the O (Otherness?) signifies her always already presence— what Ralph Ellison describes as the unquestioned humanity of the slave. She deletes nothing—except the white male other's inscription/ascription.[19]

At the conclusion of the novel, Dessa once again affirms the importance of writing oneself and one's own history. It is a responsibility that devolves upon the next generation, privileged with a literacy Dessa herself has been denied: "My mind wanders. This is why I have it down, why I has the child say it back. I never will forget Nemi trying to read [and write] me, knowing I had put myself in his hands. Well, *this* the childrens have heard from our own lips" (236). Yet, as Walker might say, the story bears the mother's signature.[20]

While Dessa, through interventions and rewriting, rejects white male attempts to write and read black female subjectivity, Sula, through disruption and rereading, repudiates black male readings of black female subjectivity. (Significantly, black males, like white females, lack the power to *write* but not the power to *read* black women.) If it is her sexuality which structures Sula within the confines of black (male) discourse, it is also her sexuality which creates a rupture in that discourse. It is through the act of sexual intercourse that Sula discovers "the center of . . . silence" and a "loneliness so profound *the word itself had no meaning*" (emphasis mine; 106). The "desperate terrain" which she reaches, the "high silence of orgasm" (112), is a modal point that locates Sula in the interstices of the closed system of (black) male signification. She has, in effect, "[leapt] from the edge" of discourse "into soundlessness" and "[gone] down howling" (106). Howling, a unary movement of nondifferentiated sound, contrasts with the phonic differentiation on which the closed system of language is based. Like the birthmark, which is the symbolic sign of life, the howl is the first sound of life—not yet broken down and differentiated to emerge as intersubjective communication, or discourse. The howl, signifying a prediscursive mode, thus becomes an act of self-reconstitution as well as an act of subversion or resistance to the "network of signification" represented by the symbolic order. The "high silence of orgasm" and the howl allow temporary retreats from or breaks in the dominant discourse. Like Dessa's evasions of interventions, Sula's silences and howls serve to disrupt or subvert the "symbolic function of the language." It is precisely these violations or transgressions of the symbolic order that allow for the expression of the suppressed or repressed aspects of black female subjectivity. The reconstitutive function of Sula's sexuality is suggested in the image of the "post-coital privateness in which she met herself, welcomed herself, and joined herself in matchless harmony" (107). The image is that of symbiosis and fusion—a stage or condition represented in psychoanalysis as pre-Oedipal and anterior to the acquisition of language or entry into the symbolic order.[21]

It is through the howl of orgasm that Sula discovers a prediscursive center of experience that positions her at a vantage point outside the dominant discursive order. The howl is a form of speaking in tongues and a linguistic disruption that serves as the precondition for Sula's entry into language. Unless she breaks the conventional structures and associations of the dominant discourse, Sula cannot enter through the interstices.[22] (This reading of *Sula,* in effect, reverses the biblical movement from contestorial, public discourse to intimate, familial discourse.)

In contrast to the howl, of course, is the stunning language of poetic metaphor with which Sula represents her lover and the act of love:

> If I take a chamois and rub real hard on the bone, right on the ledge of your cheek bone, some of the black will disappear. It will flake away into the chamois and underneath there will be gold leaf. . . . And if I take a nail file or even Eva's old paring knife . . . and scrape away at the gold, it will fall away and there will be alabaster. . . . Then I can take a chisel and small tap hammer and tap away at the alabaster. It will crack then like ice under the pick, and through the breaks I will see the [fertile] loam. (112)

It is an eloquent passage—not of self-representation, however, but of representation of the male other. If Sula cannot find the language, the trope, the form, to embody her own "experimental" life, she "engage[s] her tremendous curiosity and her gift for metaphor" in the delineation of her lover. The poetic penetration of her lover through the layers of black, gold leaf, alabaster, and loam signals that her assumption of a "masculine" role parallels the appropriation of the male voice, prerequisite for her entry into the symbolic order. (Such an appropriation is, of course, earlier signaled by the association of the birthmark with the stemmed rose, the snake, the tadpole—a series of phallic images.)

I propose, however, in the spirit of metaphor, to take it one step further and suggest that the imagery and mode of the prose poem form a kind of model for the deconstructive function of black feminist literary criticism—and to the extent that literature itself is always an act of interpretation, a model for the deconstructive function of black women's writing—that is, to interpret or interpenetrate the signifying structures of the dominant and subdominant discourse in order to formulate a critique and, ultimately, a transformation of the hegemonic white and male symbolic order.

If Williams's primary emphasis is on the act of rewriting, then Morrison's is on the act of rereading. Perhaps the best example of Sula's deconstructive rereading of the black male text is exemplified in her reformulation of Jude's "whiny tale" describing his victimization as a black man in a world that the "white man running":

> I don't know what the fuss is about. I mean, everything in the world loves you. White men love you. They spend so much time worrying about your penis they forget their own. The only thing they want to do is cut off a nigger's privates. And if that ain't love and respect I don't know what is. And white women? They chase you all to every

corner of the earth, feel for you under every bed. . . . Now ain't that love? They think rape soon's they see you, and if they don't get the rape they looking for, they scream it anyway just so the search won't be in vain. Colored women worry themselves into bad health just trying to hang on to your cuffs. Even little children—white and black, boys and girls—spend all their childhood eating their hearts out 'cause they think you don't love them. And if that ain't enough, you love yourselves. Nothing in this world loves a black man more than another black man. (89)

Adrienne Munich points out that "Jude's real difficulties allow him to maintain his male identity, to exploit women, and not to examine himself." Sula, she argues, turns "Jude's story of powerlessness into a tale of power." Through a deconstructive reading of his story, Sula's interpretation demonstrates how Jude uses "racial politics [to mask] sexual politics" (1985, 245-54).

If Sula's silences and howls represent breaks in the symbolic order, then her magnificent prose poem looks to the possibilities of appropriating the male voice as a prerequisite for entry into that order. Dessa similarly moves from intervention to appropriation and revision of the dominant discourse. As the author of her own story, Dessa writes herself into the dominant discourse and, in the process, transforms it. What these two works suggest in variable, but interchangeable, strategies is that, in both dominant and subdominant discourses, the initial expression of a marginal presence takes the form of disruption—a departure or a break with conventional semantics and/or phonetics. This rupture is followed by a rewriting or rereading of the dominant story, resulting in a "delegitimation" of the prior story of a "displacement" which shifts attention "to the other side of the story."[23] Disruption—the initial response to hegemonic and ambiguously (non)hegemonic discourse—and the subsequent response, revision (rewriting or rereading), together represent a progressive model for black and female utterance. I propose, in an appropriation of a current critical paradigm, that Sula's primal scream constitutes a "womblike matrix" in which soundlessness can be transformed into utterance, unity into diversity, formlessness into form, chaos into art, silence into tongues, and glossolalia into heteroglossia.

It is this quality of speaking in tongues, that is, multivocality, I further propose, that accounts in part for the current popularity and critical success of black women's writing. The engagement of multiple others broadens the audience for black women's writing, for like the disciples of Pentecost who spoke in diverse tongues, black women, speaking out of the specificity of their racial and gender experiences, are able to communicate in a diversity of discourses. If the ability to communicate accounts for the popularity of black women writers, it also explains much of the controversy surrounding some of this writing. Black women's writing speaks with what Mikhail Bakhtin would describe as heterological or "centrifugal force" but (in a sense somewhat different from that which Bakhtin intended) also unifying or "centripetal force" (Bakhtin, 271-72). This literature speaks as much to the notion of commonality and universalism as it does to the sense of difference and diversity.

Yet the objective of these writers is not, as some critics suggest, to move from margin to center, but to remain on the borders of discourse, speaking from the vantage point of the insider/outsider. As Bakhtin further suggests, fusion with the (dominant) Other can only duplicate the tragedy or misfortune of the Other's dilemma. On the other hand, as Gadamer makes clear, "there is a kind of experience of the 'Thou' that seeks to discover things that are typical in the behaviour of [the other] and is able to make predictions concerning another person on the basis of [a community] of experience" (1975, 321). To maintain this insider/outsider position, or perhaps what Myra Jehlen (1983) calls the "extra-terrestrial fulcrum" that Archimedes never acquired, is to see the other, but also to see what the other cannot see, and to use this insight to enrich both our own and the other's understanding.

As gendered and racial subjects, black women speak/write in multiple voices—not all simultaneously or with equal weight, but with various and changing degrees of intensity, privileging one *parole* and then another. One discovers in these writers a kind of internal dialogue reflecting an *intrasubjective* engagement with the *intersubjective* aspects of self, a dialectic neither repressing difference nor, for that matter, privileging identity, but rather expressing engagement with the social aspects of self ("the other[s] in ourselves"). It is this subjective plurality (rather than the notion of the cohesive or fractured subject) that, finally, allows the black woman to become an expressive site for a dialectics/dialogics of identity and difference.

Unlike Bloom's "anxiety of influence" model configuring a white male poetic tradition shaped by an adversarial dialogue between literary fathers and sons (as well as the appropriation of this model by Joseph Skerrett and others to discuss black male writers), and unlike Gilbert and Gubar's "anxiety of authorship" model informed by the white woman writer's sense of "dis-ease" within a white patriarchal tradition, the present model configures a tradition of black women writers generated less by neurotic anxiety or dis-ease than by an emancipatory impulse which freely engages both hegemonic and ambiguously (non)hegemonic discourse (Bloom 1973; Gilbert and Gubar 1979; Skerrett 1980). Summarizing Morrison's perspectives, Andrea Stuart perhaps best expresses this notion:

> I think you [Morrison] summed up the appeal of black women writes when you said that white men, quite naturally, wrote about themselves and their world; white women tended to write about white men because they were so close to them as husbands, lovers and sons; and black men wrote about white men as the oppressor or the yardstick against which they measured themselves. Only black women writers were not interested in writing about white men and therefore they freed literature to take on other concerns (1988, 12-15).

In conclusion, I return to the gifts of the Holy Spirit: 1 Corinthians 12 tells us that "the [one] who speaks in tongues should pray that [s/he] may interpret what [s/he] says." Yet the Scriptures also speak to interpretation as a separate gift—the ninth and final gift of the spirit. Might I suggest that if black women writers speak in tongues, then it is we black feminist critics who are charged with the hermeneutical task of interpreting tongues?

Notes

This essay first appeared in *Changing Our Own Words: Essays on Criticism, Theory, and Writing by Black Women*, edited by Cheryl A. Wall. Copyright © 1989 by Rutgers, The State University. It is reprinted by permission of the author, and of Rutgers University Press.

1. The phrase "gender subtext" is used by Nancy Fraser (and attributed to Dorothy Smith) in Fraser's critique of Habermas in Nancy Fraser, "What's Critical about Critical Theory?" (1987, 42).

2. Bakhtin's social groups are designated according to class, religion, generation, region, and profession. The interpretative model I propose extends and rereads Bakhtin's theory from the standpoint of race and gender, categories absent in Bakhtin's original system of social and linguistic stratification.

3. V. N. Volosinov (Mikhail Bakhtin) 1973, 11, 29, 38. Originally published in Russian as *Marksizm I Filosofija Jazyka* (Leningrad, 1930). Notably, this concept of the "subjective psyche" constituted primarily as a "social entity" distinguishes the Bakhtinian notion of self from the Freudian notion of identity.

4. According to Bakhtin, "The processes that basically define the content of the psyche occur not inside but outside the individual organism. . . . Moreover, the psyche "enjoys extraterritorial status . . . [as] a social entity that penetrates inside the organism of the individual personal" (1973, 25, 39). Explicating Caryl Emerson's position on Bakhtin, Gary Saul Morson argues that selfhood "derives from an internalization of the voices a person has heard, and each of these voices is saturated with social and ideological values." "Thought itself," he writes, "is but 'inner speech,' and inner speech is outer speech that we have learned to 'speak' in our heads while retaining the full register of conflicting social values" (1986, 85).

5. While acknowledging the importance of historicism, I can only agree with Frank Lentricchia's conclusion that in some respects Gadamer's "historicist argument begs more questions than it answers. If we can applaud the generous intention, virtually unknown in structuralist quarters, of recapturing history for textual interpretation, then we can only be stunned by the implication of what he has uncritically to say about authority, the power of tradition, knowledge, our institution, and our attitudes" (1980, 153). Certainly, Gadamer's model privileges the individual's relation to history and tradition in a way that might seem problematic in formulating a discursive model for the "noncanonical" or marginalized writer. However, just as the above model of dialogics is meant to extend Bakhtin's notion of class difference to encompass gender and race, so the present model revises and limits Gadamer's notion of tradition (Gadamer 1975, 321-25). My introduction to the significance of Gadamer's work for my own reading of black women writers was first suggested by Don Bialostosky's excellent paper entitled "Dialectic and Anti-Dialectic: A Bakhtinian Critique of Gadamer's Dialectical Model of Conversation," delivered at the International Association of Philosophy and Literature in May 1989 at Emory University in Atlanta, Georgia.

6. I extend Rachel Blau DuPlessis's term designating white women as a group privileged by race and oppressed by gender to black men as a group privileged by gender and oppressed by race. In this instance, I use "ambiguously (non)hegemonic" to signify the discursive status of both these groups.

7. Black women enter into dialogue with other black women in a discourse that I would characterize as primarily testimonial, resulting from a similar discursive and social positionality. It is this commonality of history, culture, and language which, finally, constitutes the basis of a tradition of black women's expressive culture. In terms of actual literary dialogue among black women, I would suggest a relatively modern provenance of such a tradition, but again, one based primarily on a dialogue of affirmation rather than contestation. As I see it, this dialogue begins with Alice Walker's response to Zora Neale Hurston. Although the present article is devoted primarily to the contestorial function of black

women's writing, my forthcoming work (of which the present essay constitutes only a part) deals extensively with the relationship among black women writers.

8. Not only does such an approach problematize conventional categories and boundaries of discourse, but, most importantly, it signals the collapse of the unifying consensus posited by the discourse of universalism and reconstructs the concept of unity in diversity implicit in the discourse of difference.

9. The arrogant and misogynistic Paul tells us, "I thank God that I speak in tongues more than all of you. But in church I would rather speak five intelligible words to instruct others [i.e. to prophesy] than ten thousand words in a tongue." Even though we are perhaps most familiar with Paul's injunction to women in the church to keep silent, the prophet Joel, in the Old Testament, speaks to a diversity of voices that includes women: "In the last days, God says, I will pour out my Spirit on all people. Yours sons and *daughters* will prophesy. . . . Even on my servants, both men and *women*, I will pour out my Spirit in those days, and they will prophesy" (emphasis mine). I am grateful to the Rev. Joseph Stephens whose vast scriptural knowledge helped guide me through these and other revelations.

10. I draw on the distinction between the political connotation of *suppression* and the psychological connotation of *repression*. Suppression results from external pressures and censorship imposed by the dominant culture, while repression refers to the internal self-censorship and silencing emanating from the subdominative community.

11. Nehemiah, a minor prophet in the Old Testament, is best remembered for rebuilding the walls around Jerusalem in order to fortify the city against invasion by hostile neighbors of Israel. Under his governorship, Ezra and the Levites instructed the people in the law of Moses "which the Lord had commanded for Israel." He is represented as a reformer who restored the ancient ordinances regarding proper observance of the Sabbath and the collection of the tithes; he also enforced bans against intermarriage with the Gentiles. He is perhaps most noted for the reply he sent, while rebuilding the walls, to a request from his enemies, Sanballat and Gesham, to meet with him: "I am doing a great *work* and cannot go down" (emphasis mine). Williams's Nehemiah, like his prototype, is devoted to the completion of a project he calls *The Work*—in this instance a book entitled *The Roots of Rebellion in the Slave Population and Some Means of Eradicating Them*. Significantly, the name of Williams's character, Adam Nehemiah, reverses the name of Nehemiah Adams, author of *A South-side View of Slavery* (1854), and a Boston minister who wrote an account of his experiences in the South from a point of view apostate to the Northern antislavery cause.

12. The mark of the whip inscribes Dessa as a slave while she remains within the discursive domain of slavery—a domain architecturally figured by the prison from which she escapes, but also a domain legally and more discursively defined by the Fugitive Slave Act, the runaway ads, and the courts and depositions of the nation. Note, however, that within the northern lecture halls and the slave narratives—the spatial and discursive domains of abolitionism—the marks do not identify an individual but signify upon the character and nature of the institution of slavery.

13. Although the status of slave is not a "misreading" within the discursive domain of slavery, it is clearly a misreading according to Dessa's self-identification.

14. One might describe Sula's birthmark as an iconicized representation rather than, strictly speaking, an inscription. For our purposes, however, it has the force of a sign marking her birth or entry into black discourse.

15. Morrison's epigram to the novel highlights the cultural significance of the birthmark by quoting from Tennessee Williams's *The Rose Tattoo*: "Nobody knew my rose of the world but me. . . . I had too much glory. They don't want glory like that in nobody's heart." In "The Mission of the Flowers," Harper describes the rose as "a thing of joy and beauty" whose mission is to "lay her fairest buds and flowers upon the altars of love." Walker's protagonist Celie compares her own sex to the "inside of a wet rose." See Frances E. W. Harper, *Idylls of the Bible* (1901) (quoted in Stetson 1981, 34-36); and Alice Walker, *The Color Purple* (1982, 69). In naming her own character Dessa Rose, Williams not only plays on the above connotations but links them, at the same time, to the transcendence implicit in "arising" and the insurgence suggested in "uprising."

16. Signifying perhaps on Hawthorne's short story "The Birthmark," Sula's mark can be reread as a sign of human imperfection and mortality, a consequence of Eve's seduction by the serpent in the Garden.

17. The fire and water image, associated with the tadpole and ashes, respectively complement and contrast with that of the snake—a symbol of death and renewal—and that of the stemmed rose—an image suggesting not only love and sexuality, but the beauty and brevity of life as a temporal experience.

18. I do not develop here the interviewer's misreadings of Dessa in the early part of the novel, nor the specific insurgent strategies with which Dessa continually outwits him. These details are treated extensively, however, in my article on Williams's "Meditations on History," the short story on which the novel is based. It appears in Kauffman 1989.

19. Williams also uses onomastics to signify upon a less rebellious female heroine, somewhat more complicitous with female ascription by the Other. See Kaja Silverman's excellent discussion of Pauline Reage's *The Story of O* (in Silverman 1984).

20. Williams, in her earlier version of this story, "Meditations on History," privileges orality (rather than writing)—as I attempt to demonstrate in my article "W/(R)iting *the Work* and Working the Rites" (in Kauffman 1989).

21. Positing a kind of "mother tongue," Julia Kristeva argues that "language as symbolic function constitutes itself at the cost of repressing instinctual drive and continuous relation to the mother." This order of expression, she contends, is presymbolic and linked with the mother tongue. According to Nelly Furman's interpretation, the existence of this order "does not refute the symbolic but is anterior to it, and associated with the maternal aspects of language. This order, which [Kristeva] calls 'semiotic,' is not a separate entity from the symbolic, on the contrary, it is the system which supports symbolic coherence." Continuing, Furman quotes Josette Feral in establishing a dialogical relationship between the semiotic and symbolic orders "which places the semiotic *inside* the symbolic as a condition of the symbolic, while positing the symbolic as a condition of the semiotic and founded on its repression. Now it happens that the Name-of-the-Father, in order to establish itself, needs the repression of the mother. It needs this otherness in order to reassure itself about its unity and identity, but is unwittingly affected by this otherness that is working within it" (Furman 1985, 72-73).

22. In contrast to Dessa, who disrupts the dominant discourse, Sula would seem to disrupt not only discourse but, indeed, language itself.

23. Rachel Blau DuPlessis uses these terms to describe the "tactics of revisionary mythopoesis" created by women poets whose purpose is to "attack cultural hegemony." "Narrative displacement is like breaking the sentence," writes DuPlessis, "because it offers the possibility of speech to the female in this case, giving voice to the muted. Narrative delegitimation 'breaks the sentence'; a realignment that puts the last first and the first last has always ruptured conventional morality, politics, and narrative" (1985, 108).

References

Bakhtin, Mikhail. 1981. Discourse in the novel. In *The dialogic imagination: Four essays by M. M. Bakhtin*. Michael Holquist, ed. Austin: University of Texas Press.

[Bakhtin, Mikhail] Volosinov, V. N. 1973. *Marxism and the philosophy of language*. New York: Seminar Press. Orig. pub. 1930.

Bloom, Harold. 1973. *The anxiety of influence: A theory of poetry*. New York: Oxford University Press.

Christian, Barbara. 1985. The dynamics of difference: Book review of Audre Lorde's *Sister outsider*. In *Black feminist criticism: Perspectives in black women writers*. New York: Pergamon Press.

DuPlessis, Rachel Blau. 1985. *Writing beyond the ending*. Bloomington: Indiana University Press.

Fraser, Nancy. 1987. What's critical about critical theory? In *Feminism as critique*. Seyla Benhabib and Drucilla Cornell, eds. Minneapolis: University of Minnesota Press.

Furman, Nelly. 1985. The politics of language: Beyond the gender principle? In *Making a difference: Feminist literary criticism*. Gayle Greene and Coppelia Kahn, eds. London: Methuen.

Gadamer, Hans-Georg. 1975. *Truth and method*. New York: Seabury Press.

Gilbert, Sandra M., and Susan Gubar. 1979. *The madwoman in the attic: The woman writer and the nineteenth-century literary imagination*. New Haven: Yale University Press.

Harper, Frances E. W. 1901. *Idylls of the bible*. Philadelphia: George S. Ferguson.

Henderson, Mae Gwendolyn. 1989. W(R)iting *the work* and working the rites. In *Feminism and institutions: Dialogues on feminist theory*. Linda Kauffmann, ed. London: Basil Blackwell.

Hull, Gloria, and Patricia Bell Scott, and Barbara Smith, eds. 1982. *All the women are white, all the blacks are men, but some of us are brave*. Old Westbury: Feminist Press.

Hurston, Zora Neale. 1937. *Their eyes were watching god*. Rept. Urbana: University of Illinois Press, 1978.

Jameson, Fredric. 1981. *The political unconscious: Narrative as a socially symbolic act*. Ithaca: Cornell University Press.

Jehlen, Myra. 1983. Archimedes and the paradox of feminist criticism. Reprinted in *The Signs reader: women, gender and scholarship*. Elizabeth Abel and Emily K. Abel, eds. Chicago: University of Chicago Press.

Lauretis, Teresa de. 1987. *Technologies of gender*. Bloomington: Indiana University Press.

Lentricchia, Frank. 1980. *After the new criticism*. Chicago: University of Chicago Press.

Lorde, Audre. 1984. Eye to eye. Included in *Sister outsider*. Trumansburg, NY: Crossing Press.

Morrison, Toni. 1975. *Sula*. New York: Alfred A. Knopf, 1973; rept. Bantam.

Morson, Gary Saul. 1986. Dialogue, monologue, and the social: A reply to Ken Hirshkop. In *Bakhtin: Essays and dialogues on his work*. Gary Saul Morson, ed. Chicago: University of Chicago Press.

Munich, Adrienne. 1985. Feminist criticism and literary tradition. In *Making a Difference*. See Furman (1985).

Rowe, John Carlos. 1986. To live outside the law, you must be honest: The authority of the margin in contemporary theory. *Cultural Critique: International Journal of Cultural Studies* I (2), Oxford University Press.

Silverman, Kaja. 1984. Histoire d'O: The construction of a female subject. In *Pleasure and danger: Exploring female sexuality*. Carole S. Vance, ed. Boston: Routledge and Kegan Paul.

Skerrett, Joseph T. 1980. The Wright interpretation: Ralph Ellison and the anxiety of influence. *Massachusetts Review* 21: 196-212.

Smith, Barbara, ed. 1983. *Home girls: A black feminist anthology*. New York: Kitchen Table: Women of Color Press.

Smitherman, Geneva. 1986. *Talkin and testifyin: The language of black america*. Detroit: Wayne State University Press.

Stetson, Erlene, ed. 1981. *Black sister*. Bloomington: Indiana University Press.

Stuart, Andrea. 1988. Interview with Toni Morrison: Telling our story. *Sparerib*. April.

Walker, Alice. 1982. *The color purple*. New York: Harcourt Brace Jovanovich.

Walker, Alice. 1984. In search of our mothers' gardens. In *In search of our mothers' gardens: Womanist prose*. New York: Harcourt Brace Jovanovich.

Williams, Sherely Anne. 1986. *Dessa Rose*. New York: William Morrow.

Wittig, Monique. 1980. The straight mind. *Feminist Issues* I.

Feminist Film Aesthetics
A Contextual Approach

LAURIE SHRAGE

This essay considers some problems with text-centered psychoanalytic and semiotic approaches to film that have dominated feminist film criticism and develops an alternative contextual approach. I claim that a contextual approach should explore the interaction of film texts with viewers' culturally formed sensibilities and should attempt to render visible the plurality of meaning in art. I argue that the latter approach will allow us to see the virtues of some classical Hollywood films that the former approach has overlooked, and I demonstrate this thesis with an analysis of the film Christopher Strong.

At the beginning of *Narration in Light*, George Wilson claims that "[t]here are moments in some films which suddenly force us to reconsider, for at least an instant, our complacent ways of watching at the cinema" (1986, 1). The following film segment had this effect on me. In the 1933 film *Christopher Strong*, Katherine Hepburn plays an aviator named Cynthia Darrington, who begins an illicit romance with a married man (Sir Christopher Strong). Near the end of the film, there is a sequence of shot/reverse shot close-ups in which Elaine Strong, Christopher's wife, takes Cynthia aside at an afternoon tea party and offers her a "mother's sincerest thanks" for her role in causing Christopher's "change of heart." This change, Elaine believes, prevented them from wrecking their only child's life. The close-ups focus our attention on each woman's facial gestures: Elaine appears genuine, warm, and buoyant; Cynthia appears tense, pained, and awkward.[1]

The "change of heart" to which Elaine has referred concerns her husband's decision to approve their daughter's marriage to her lover Harry Rawlinson—a man who courted her while he was married to another woman. Elaine had remained opposed to this match but, seeing her daughter (Monica) beaming and pregnant, she concedes to Cynthia that she and Christopher "managed things much better" than Elaine herself would have done and "for that reason alone [they] all owe [Cynthia] a great deal."

Hypatia vol. 5, no. 2 (Summer 1990) © by Laurie Shrage

Ironically, Cynthia has helped clear the way for Monica's marriage by committing adultery with Christopher (Monica's father and Elaine's husband), for it is this adulterous relationship which transforms his initial intolerance toward Monica's imprudent courtship to one of sympathy. Both the audience and Elaine know of Christopher's affair with Cynthia and of the emotional torment it has caused Elaine. Thus, Elaine appears, in this peculiar scene, to be acknowledging, with exceptional composure and generosity, a debt of gratitude to Cynthia for having a sexual relationship with her husband because of its beneficial side-effect. In other words, if we take Elaine's display of gratitude to be sincere (and I have indicated some evidence for this), then we have a story in which a loving, jealous, and insecure wife is nevertheless appreciative of her husband's mistress for her valuable assistance to her daughter, and thus—at least to some degree—gives her approval to her husband's adulterous affair.

In a society that generally sees adult women as sexual rivals—especially wives and mistresses—and in one that is inclined to see a mistress's function as disruptive rather than constructive, this scene appears rather odd. On numerous occasions when I have shown this film to students and have raised the issue of Elaine's implicit approval of her husband's adultery, my students repeatedly and nearly unanimously have rejected this interpretation. However, none has been able to offer another reading that makes sense of this film segment in the context of the entire movie. My students' rejection of this interpretation seems simply based on the fact that it contradicts their "cultural common sense": a set of principles and beliefs which is deeply ingrained in the thinking habits of members of our society, and which structures our perceptions and social interaction. A movie dealing with adultery that resonates closely with our culturally formed common sense is the recent *Fatal Attraction* (1987). This movie ends with the wife participating in the brutal murder of the contemptible mistress, which elicits from the audience an enthusiastic response for this marriage-saving act. By contrast, at the end of *Christopher Strong* when Cynthia heroically takes her own life, the audience experiences her death as tragic.

Feminist film critics have lumped *Christopher Strong* together with movies that possess the qualities of *Fatal Attraction*: movies which reinforce the dominant ideologies of our society, in this case ideologies regarding the worthiness of bourgeois patriarchal marriage (see Suter 1979). In doing so, they have failed to see some of the ways that *Christopher Strong* contributes to a liberatory cultural politics. I will argue that feminist critics have missed some of the aesthetic and political virtues of a range of classical Hollywood movies because they have predominantly adopted a textual rather than a contextual approach to film.

CONTEXTUAL CRITICISM

Using psychoanalytic and semiotic frameworks, feminist criticism of the '80s has generally focused on the structures of address and communication in film texts that control their meaning and account for their appeal. Feminist critics who employ this approach have attempted to demonstrate that Hollywood films of the '30s and '40s inscribe a masculinist perspective and create conditions that satisfy male psychological projects—the latter conceived in Freudian terms. Feminist criticism of the '70s was text-centered as well. Critics of this era tended to reduce the issue of sexism in film to the absence or appearance of positive or negative images of women in a text and, not surprisingly, they too found little pleasing in classical narrative cinema (see Haskell 1974). My contention is that, by abstracting cinematic texts from their social and cultural contexts, feminist critics have dismissed many Hollywood films prematurely.

Recently several feminist critics have stressed the need to consider contextual features when assessing the political significance of a film. According to Annette Kuhn:

> [Q]uestions of context can easily become evacuated in favour of the formalism that is readily privileged in semiotic and psychoanalytic approaches to cinema. Whether such approaches are inherently impervious to contextual analysis, or whether the focus on meaning foregrounded by the semiotic model can be brought to bear on an analysis of the historical and social conditions and contexts of individual films, is very much an open question. Approaches which in some way bring the two together are often regarded as desirable, even essential, ways forward for cultural analysis. . . . The point about this issue, however, is that it can only be resolved by actual historical/analytical work: we will not know whether a semiotic-based contextual analysis of the institution of cinema from a feminist standpoint is possible until it has been seriously attempted. This, I believe, is the point at which feminist film theory now stands. (1982, 83)

A contextual analysis of film should render visible the relativity and ambiguity of meaning in art: the plurality of perspectives from which a work can be viewed. It should not make meaning a simple function of a work's historical context of production. Because contextual analysis must encompass a certain amount of relativism and pluralism in regard to meaning, I, like Kuhn, question whether it is compatible with psychoanalytic criticism.

Psychoanalytic criticism tends to treat the structures of masculine and feminine subjectivity as human universals. Critics who employ this approach tend to ignore how subjectivity is raced, classed, and inflected by the categories of ethnicity, sexual orientation, age, and so on (Gledhill 1978, 482). According to Carmine Coustaut (1989), to conceptualize "woman" as the fetishized object of the male gaze may accurately reflect the experience of white women, but not of black. A contextual criticism must recognize that the interpretive principles of those who psychologize are often valid only for members of the dominant culture.

Many semiotic studies tend to overemphasize the role of signifying practices in the construction of gender difference and often ignore how the category "woman," for instance, is shaped by processes of social interaction other than textual production and reception. According to Christine Gledhill,

> The ultimate problem, it seems to me, lies in the attempt to make language and the signifying process so exclusively central to the production of the social formation. Under the insistence on the semiotic production of meaning, the effectivity of social, economic, and political practice threatens to disappear altogether. (1978, 491)

Mary Ann Doane raises a similar issue regarding the tendency of feminist critics, when theorizing about female subjectivity, to overlook the role of social or material factors in the maintenance of hierarchy, and to focus exclusively on the role of psychical or symbolic processes. According to Doane:

> Frequently, [the terms "female spectator"] do not even refer to the spectator as a social subject but, rather, as a psychical subject, as the effect of signifying structures. Historically, the emphasis on issues of spectatorship in film theory derives from a psychoanalytically informed linguistics, not from a sociological based analysis. It has been the task of feminist theory to point out that this spectator has been consistently posited and delineated as masculine. Feminist theory therefore necessarily introduces the question of the social subject, but unfortunately, it frequently and overhastily collapses the opposition between social and psychical subjects, closing the gap prematurely. There has never been, to my mind, an adequate articulation of the two subjects in theory (which is another way of saying that psychoanalysis and a Marxist analysis have never successfully collaborated in the theorization of subjectivity). (1987, 8)

In short, there is one subject "constructed in language" and another "produced by historical, social and economic forces" (Gledhill 1978, 483). Contextual criticism must be able to give an account of how symbolic and nonsymbolic processes contribute to a film's significance and value.

Contextual criticism should aim to describe features of the context of reception of a piece of art and to explicate how those features interact with some aspects of the artwork. In regard to film, some important feature of the context of reception might include an audience's cinematic habits. These habits generate expectations regarding, for instance, appropriate plot development, degree of narrative coherence and transparency (see Wilson 1986), the handling of space and time, and so on—expectations which are, in part, controlled by genre rules. We usually become aware of these expectations when they are thwarted: for example, Jim Jarmusch's *Stranger Than Paradise* (1984) is a strange film because, among other things, it violates our assumption that something interesting should happen in the first hour or so of a film. George Wilson coins the notion "epistemic distance" to refer to the extent our ordinary beliefs about the world and about film are helpful to us in understanding a particular film (1986, 4). Certain films challenge or force us to suspend our commonsense beliefs, and a contextual criticism should explore the ramifications of this epistemic distancing.

Contextual film criticism should explore the interaction of film texts with socially ingrained principles of cinematic viewing, principles which, unlike the psychological structures identified by psychoanalytic criticism, are historically and culturally specific. Moreover, these principles may not carry the same authority for persons differently positioned by gender, race, class, and so on, but nonetheless, like the rules of standard English, they inform and render meaningful our symbolic exchanges. Contextual criticism should explore how the authority of these principles varies in accordance with gender, race, sexual orientation, and so forth.

I began this essay with a description of how the movie *Christopher Strong* betrays our culturally formed expectations both about the treatment of mistresses in narrative and the nature of relations between mistresses and wives. I will end this study by considering how *Christopher Strong* challenges our ordinary beliefs about the institution of marriage. In particular, I want to consider the bizarre depiction of marriage that is offered in this film, and how it interacts with certain cultural myths regarding women and their desire for marriage. Before I attempt this, though, some general issues regarding desire and film need to be clarified.

FILM AND FEMALE DESIRE

Feminist psychoanalytic theorists have claimed that the primary function of women in classical Hollywood films is to bring into play and signify male desire (Mulvey 1975, 11). On this view, female desire is generally absent, passive, or evil. This situation is not accidental but reflects these films' inevitable conformity to patriarchal logic, a logic in which there is no space for active female thought, looking, or desiring. Naomi Scheman has tried to show that there are cracks in this logic which create a space for a genuine female perspective—a perspective which is not reducible to women adopting the male gaze, or to women adopting socially prescribed female forms of desire, but one that embodies an oppositional feminist gaze (1988, 64). According to Scheman, this gaze is not inscribed in classical Hollywood films themselves or in their terms of address, but is nevertheless available for looking at the classical Hollywood cinema (89).

The quest for a genuine female gaze is made imperative by the following kind of question: if all knowledge and seeing is structured by culture and language, and culture and language are male, and furthermore "women" are the products of culture and language, then how is feminist knowledge and seeing possible? Rather than accepting this paradox, I will argue that it contains a claim that needs to be rethought or qualified: the assumption that language and culture are male, or inextricably infused with a patriarchal logic. The problem with this idea is that it does not recognize cultural variability with respect to the power and forms of patriarchy. Yet patriarchy may be experienced differently in accordance with race, class, nationality, religion, and so forth. To recall Coustaut, black women do not find themselves in film the fetishized object of the male gaze, and a theory that makes patriarchy seamless, all-encompassing, and universal cannot account for this.

Nevertheless, feminist critics have identified an important quality of a range of Hollywood films in their consideration of female desire. With one important modification, I think much of the analysis produced is extremely helpful. The modification I propose is that we regard the absence, passivity, or treacherousness of the female gaze, not as the inevitable product of global patriarchy, but as a local variant inscribed in the viewing habits of Euro-American audiences and in certain films themselves. Since I do not assume patriarchy to be monolithic and universal, I am also prepared to find the inscription of a masculinist framework in classic Hollywood films incomplete.

Stanley Cavell offers us a perspective on female desire that recognizes a genuine female voice in the classical cinema. According to Cavell,

[F]ilm . . . is from first to last more interested in the study of individual women than of individual men. . . . Men are, one could say, of interest to it in crowds and in mutual conflict, but it is women that bequeath psychic depth to film's interests. (1987, 29)

Cavell's claim, in part, rests on his analysis of ten films that make up the genre he calls "the melodrama of the unknown woman." These films contain heroines with complex spiritual and romantic desires and are concerned with the lack of fulfillment of these desires. According to Naomi Scheman, however, these films reflect the male framing of female desire. Scheman shows that, in some of Cavell's films, a tension is set up between the mother/daughter bond and heterosexual desire, which inevitably forces one type of relationship to be sacrificed to the other. Moreover, women's heterosexual desire is essentially passive in these films: women learn to desire men who desire them. In the remainder of this essay I will try to show that female desire in *Christopher Strong* is not entirely framed by a masculinist perspective, for whether a film's perspective is masculinist or feminist is a function of how the projected pieces of celluloid resonate with viewers' culturally formed sensibilities.

MARRIAGE IN *CHRISTOPHER STRONG*

In *Christopher Strong*, Monica's love for Harry initially ruptures her relationship with her mother. Nevertheless, as Monica's and Elaine's relationship is splintered, Monica enters into a surrogate mother/daughter relationship with Cynthia, her father's mistress. Monica repeatedly seeks Cynthia's help in managing her illicit relationship with Harry, and Cynthia genuinely assists her. Yet, when Monica succeeds in waiting out Harry's divorce and marrying him, her interests as a wife and (later) mother-to-be become realigned with her mother's. Now she, like Elaine, is threatened both by marital infidelity, which Cynthia represents, and by the loss of their common male provider, Christopher. The dramatic action of this film is resolved when Monica switches her allegiance to her mother, which she shows both by being rude to Cynthia and by telling Harry and Elaine that her father will dine with them that particular evening, for she will "make him throw everything else over."[2] Indeed, by fulfilling Monica's desire and dining with his family, Christopher breaks a dinner engagement with Cynthia, who awaits his arrival to share with him the news that she, like Monica, is pregnant. This action signifies the breaking of his attachment to his mistress and their love child, and Cynthia interprets it as Christopher's inability to place love before duty. As a result, Cynthia plots her own destruction.

While the incompatibility of Monica's and Cynthia's desires needs to be analyzed, I want to focus on the compatibility of Monica's and Elaine's interests. In this regard, the film provides an instance of the ability of heterosexual love (i.e., Monica's love for Harry), sanctioned by marriage, to re-cement the mother/daughter relationship. Monica is shown instructing Harry to be "terribly nice" to her mother and reprimanding Cynthia for taking a man away from a woman who is an angel—a woman he had always loved. Moreover, Monica's heterosexual desire is active: she desires Harry not because he desires her but apparently because he is someone with whom she can have a good time. Similarly, Cynthia desires Christopher for the moral virtues he represents, and not because of his active desiring. Indeed, if any desire is passive in this film, it is male desire, for Cynthia's and Monica's desires predominantly drive the action forward.[3]

In discussing the body of work of the film's director, Dorothy Arzner, Claire Johnston states,

> [T]he woman in Arzner's films determines her own identity through transgression and desire in a search for an independent existence beyond and outside the discourse of the male. . . . In *Christopher Strong* we are presented with the epitome of this desire for transgression in the character of Cynthia Darrington. . . . (1975, 4)

While Johnston focuses on the transgressive nature of female desire in Arzner's films, my analysis of *Christopher Strong*, like Cavell's analysis of the melodrama of the unknown woman, focuses on the failure of fulfillment of female desire.[4] I will argue that the frustration of female desire can focus an audience's attention on the inequitable nature of particular social institutions, and thereby enable a feminist critique of these institutions.

In *Christopher Strong*, Cynthia's desire for a secure union with Christopher remains unrealized. Moreover, we cannot even be sure that Monica's desire to form a permanent union with Harry has been fulfilled, because the film continually emphasizes the fragility of marital bonds. For example, the dialogue ironizes Harry's tendency to be unfaithful when Harry jokes that his wedding with Monica was the nicest wedding he's ever had, and she snaps back "it's your last, I hope." Similarly, in a scene where Elaine is informed that Monica is pregnant and says to Harry "of course, you want a boy," he retorts "not at all, I've liked girls all my life." Moreover, the humiliation women must suffer in order to preserve the marital bond is suggested by Monica's aunt's statement: "If every wife would only keep her misgivings to herself and her fingers crossed, marriage might sometimes be a success." In an early segment, the insecure and degrading nature of marriage is stressed when, in a scene in the Strongs' home, Elaine announces she must apply some stuff to her face that claims it "positively keeps away wrinkles." What Elaine must do to deserve her husband's steady affection is connected to what the cream falsely promises to do for her. Indeed, Christopher does not remain loyal to Elaine in the film, suggesting that loyalty and affection in patriarchal monogamy, like wrinkle prevention, are illusions difficult to keep. Finally, the incompatibility of this bond with female freedom and accomplishment is emphasized when, in a scene representing the consummation of Cynthia and Christopher's affair, the screen is filled up with Cynthia's hand wearing a bracelet Christopher has given her and on the soundtrack we hear Cynthia say "I'm shackled."

In commenting on the treatment of desire, Pam Cook states,

> The films of Dorothy Arzner are important in that they foreground precisely this problem of the desire of women caught in a system of representation which allows them at most the opportunity of playing on the specific demands that the system makes on them. (1979, 225)

Johnston makes a similar point:

> Unlike most other Hollywood directors who pose "positive" and "independent"
> female protagonists . . . in Arzner's work the discourse of the woman, or rather her
> attempt to locate it and make it heard, is what gives the system of the text its structural
> coherence, while at the same time rendering the dominant discourse of the male
> fragmented and incoherent. (1975, 4)

While Cook and Johnston insist on the hegemony of a male discourse or "system
of representation" within Arzner's texts, both seem to allow for the counterhegemo-
nic force of her films. In *Christopher Strong*, Arzner's ability to create a space for an
oppositional female voice is evident in the film's handling of Monica. Though the
dominant discourse is often silent on woman's desire, Monica manages to manipulate its constraints to realize her own ends. Her manipulation consists in making
the satisfaction of her desires a necessary condition for the satisfaction of her father's
desires. For example, by threatening to engage in imprudent behavior which her
father would desire to prevent, Monica manages to convince her father to accompany her to the party where he meets Cynthia. Earlier we see Monica tell a
skeptical-looking Harry that she will get her father to come to the party, and we
are surprised when, after his strong protestations, he does indeed go. Monica's action
initiates a sequence of events that ends with her father having an affair, and thereby
coming to approve of her own affair. Her role in causing her father's infidelity is
emphasized by the film's dialogue. After Cynthia and Christopher are introduced,
Monica refuses to leave her aunt's party. Her impudence forces her father to accept
a ride home from Cynthia, to which Monica says, "yes, Father, go home with the
pretty lady." The indirect causal efficacy of Monica's desire is again illustrated when
Monica exploits her mother's and father's desire to end her temporary depression,
which begins when her mother forbids her to see Harry. She promises to get over
her unhappiness if her father will accompany her to Cynthia's air meeting in Paris.
Her coercion leads to Cynthia's joining the family on their vacation in Cannes and,
ultimately, to Cynthia and Christopher falling more deeply in love.

However, the cost of achieving some of her desires is that Monica is ultimately
rendered a moral hypocrite. At least this is one possible interpretation of Monica's
antagonism toward Cynthia, when she discovers her affair with her father. Yet
Monica's abrupt switch from rebellious child to dutiful daughter, which gives rise
to her seemingly hypocritical antagonism toward Cynthia, might force us to see her
contradictory interests as mistress and wife rather than attribute to her the holding
of a double standard. Similarly, Elaine's awkward speech of gratitude to Cynthia
might force us to see her contradictory interests as mother and wife rather than
attribute to her a great tolerance for adultery. (Here is an alternative explanation
of the scene described at the beginning of this paper.) Monica and Elaine are simply
playing on the specific demands the film's system of representation makes on them,
to echo Cook's words. This symbolic system forces Monica to embody contradictory
values: as a mistress she epitomizes the pursuit of selfish interest above family
commitment and marital faithfulness and later, as a wife, she represents unselfish
daughterly devotion and marital fidelity. The contradictory and awkward posture

Monica assumes is a function of a representational system not designed to accommodate a woman's desire.

The film's emphasis on the anomalous nature and frustration of female desire does not provide evidence of the anti-feminist framing of this desire. To dismiss films for this would involve an error similar to the one that feminist critics of a previous decade committed when they dismissed films for failing to contain realistic images of women. The latter critics assumed that the value of a film, from a feminist perspective, would come from its provision of authentic female characters with whom women viewers could identify. The problem with this is that the requirement of authenticity sees "women" in essentialist terms and fails to see the social and historical nature of the signified as well as the signifier, to use Saussurian concepts. Similarly, to dismiss films that fail to depict successful female desiring as masculinist is to see female desire in universalist terms and to assume that a film's value only comes from its ability to provide the conditions of vicarious enjoyment for any female viewer.

In speaking of another Arzner film (*Dance, Girl, Dance*), Cook comments,

[I]t would be a mistake to read the film in "positive" terms as representing the progress of its heroine to "maturity" or "self-awareness." The value of the film lies not in its creation of a culture-heroine with whom we can finally and fully identify, but in the ways in which it *displaces* identification with the characters and focuses our attention on the problematic position they occupy in the world. (Emphasis in original) (1979, 225)

When *Christopher Strong* legislates the satisfaction of Cynthia's desires as impossible and she becomes suicidal, a viewer may experience her transformation as displacement. Our disappointment at Cynthia's inability to resolve her situation in a constructive way displaces our identification with her and refocuses our attention on the problematic position she occupies. In this way, the film reinforces a broader political perspective on Cynthia's problems, implying with Cynthia's death that the avoidance of this tragedy is a matter for social, and not merely individual, action.

By disrupting our identification with Cynthia and her envisioned exceptional success, we see that the problematic position Cynthia occupies is a function of the disappointing nature of marriage for women in our society. Outside of patriarchal marriage a woman can have excitement (e.g., Cynthia's flying), but no secure love object (e.g., Cynthia eventually loses Christopher and their love child). Yet, inside marriage, the objects of a woman's affection are only slightly more secure (e.g., Christopher returns to Elaine), and she has no excitement (e.g., the cessation of Cynthia's flying in her illicit "marriage"). For a viewer who assumes both that women desire marriage and that, in marriage, this desire as well as many others are satisfied, this movie will be perplexing. In this way, *Christopher Strong* interrupts the ongoing naturalization of patriarchal monogamy, and does not valorize this institution, as Jacqueline Suter has claimed (1979, 137).

By focusing our attention both on women who fail to achieve certain conventional and unconventional ends and on problematic aspects of the social system that impedes them (e.g., patriarchal marriage), *Christopher Strong* challenges the alleged ubiquitousness of male discourse. While *Christopher Strong* is not an entirely satisfactory film from a feminist perspective, it should disturb patriarchal sensibilities enough to insure our enjoyment of it, and I suspect this applies to a number of other Hollywood films.

Notes

I would like to thank the Pacific Division of the Society for Women in Philosophy for the opportunity to present this paper at the spring 1989 meeting. I am grateful to Daniel Segal, Edward Rocklin, and the *Hypatia* reviewers for their comments on an earlier draft of this work, and to many classes of students in Philosophy 465 for their willingness to discuss *Christopher Strong* with me. Cal Poly Pomona's Affirmative Action Released Time Program provided me with the time necessary to complete this paper.

1. For a different analysis of this film segment, see Suter (1979, 138).

2. In a scene where Monica and Harry are celebrating their marriage, the dialogue ironically foreshadows this change of alliance when Monica exuberantly flatters Cynthia by saying, "Don't think I'll ever forget all you've done for me, darling," and Cynthia replies with modesty, "Oh, nonsense."

3. My students have often questioned the appropriateness of the title of this film, and I think it is because of Christopher's passivity.

4. Nevertheless, I do not want to include *Christopher Strong* in this genre of Cavell's because Cynthia is not fundamentally transformed or remade by her love for Christopher, as Cavell's genre rules require. See Cavell (1987, 17).

References

Cavell, Stanley. 1987. Psychoanalysis and cinema: The melodrama of the unknown woman. In *Images in our souls: Cavell, psychoanalysis, and cinema*. Vol. 10 of *Psychiatry and the Humanities*. Joseph H. Smith and William Kerrigan, eds. Baltimore: Johns Hopkins University Press.

Cook, Pam. 1979. Approaching the work of Dorothy Arzner. In *Sexual strategems: The world of women in film*. Patricia Erens, ed. New York: Horizon.

Coustaut, Carmen. 1989. Unveiling our image: Black women film makers. Paper given to the Embodied & Engendered Conference, April 1. Sponsored by the Intercollegiate Department of Black Studies of the Claremont Colleges, Claremont, California.

Doane, Mary Ann. 1987. *The desire to desire: The woman's film of the 1940s*. Bloomington: Indiana University Press.

Gledhill, Christine. 1978. Recent developments in feminist criticism. *Quarterly Review of Film Studies* 3(4): 457-93.

Haskell, Molly. 1974. *From reverence to rape: The treatment of women in the movies*. New York: Holt, Rinehart and Winston.

Johnston, Claire. 1975. Dorothy Arzner: Critical strategies. In *The work of Dorothy Arzner: Towards a feminist cinema*. Claire Johnston, ed. London: British Film Institute.

Kuhn, Annette. 1982. *Women's pictures: Feminism and cinema*. Boston: Routledge and Kegan Paul.

Mulvey, Laura. 1975. Visual pleasure and narrative cinema. *Screen* 16: 6-18.

Scheman, Naomi. 1988. Missing mothers/desiring daughters: Framing the sight of women. *Critical Inquiry* 15: 62-89.

Suter, Jacquelyn. 1979. Feminine discourse in *Christopher Strong*. *Camera Obscura* 3-4: 135-50.

Wilson, George. 1986. *Narration in light: Studies in cinematic point of view*. Baltimore: Johns Hopkins University Press.

ELEVEN

A Woman on Paper

SAN MACCOLL

The work of Georgia O'Keeffe has been regarded as distinctively female since she first exhibited, but I will show that there are different underlying assumptions about this in the interpretations of her work in the '20s and the '70s. I want to suggest that her work expresses a conception of the body, subjectivity, and sexuality which challenges traditional dichotomies of mind/body and subject/object and provides us with a model for a positive alternative.

The claim that Georgia O'Keeffe's work showed Woman expressed on paper is attributed to Alfred Stieglitz on his first viewing of the charcoal drawings, which he proceeded to show in a joint exhibition (without her permission). Whether or not he said, on January 1, 1916, "At last a woman on paper," as is sometimes claimed,[1] certainly *Camera Work*, which he published, reports: " '291' had never before seen woman express herself so frankly on paper" (Anon. 1916, 12). He did write, in a letter a year later, when his 291 gallery had closed: "The little room was never more glorious than during its last exhibition—the work of Miss O'Keeffe—a Woman on Paper" (quoted in Giboire, 1990, xxiii).

The title has already been used by Anita Pollitzer for her biography of O'Keeffe, which appeared in 1988 (*A Woman on Paper*), after O'Keeffe had discouraged her from publishing it earlier (Lisle 1986, x). Pollitzer had a special role in the O'Keeffe story. In 1915, O'Keeffe was teaching art in South Carolina and corresponding with Pollitzer, who was her student friend at Teachers College in New York. It was to her that she sent the roll of her charcoal drawings which arrived on January 1, 1916. Pollitzer, who frequented 291, took them there that afternoon and showed Stieglitz, even though O'Keeffe had told her not to show them around at Teachers College.

Stieglitz was visibly impressed, and Pollitzer wrote immediately to O'Keeffe that he said to tell her the drawings were the "purest, finest, sincerest things that have entered 291 in a long while" (quoted in Lisle 1986, 84) and that he wouldn't mind showing them sometime. It is surprising that, if Stieglitz did make the famous remark on that occasion, Pollitzer did not report it to O'Keeffe.

I have taken up the title because O'Keeffe's work has been considered distinctively female since she first exhibited, and also because the idea of O'Keeffe as a woman on paper has a particular resonance for current views of sexed subjectivity.

I propose to examine claims about O'Keeffe's work as distinctively female, focusing on two specific periods—one early in her career, from 1916 through the '20s, and one later, during the '70s—to uncover the assumptions made about the female in regard to subjectivity, the body, and sexuality.

The claims of the early period, which I refer to for convenience as the '20s, in fact range from the time of her first exhibition in 1916 to her first visit to New Mexico in May 1929. These claims relate to her abstractions, the landscapes of Manhattan, Lake George, and other places she visited, fruit, rocks, shells, and the large flowers of 1924 on. They exclude work of the New Mexico period from 1929 on, of bones, calico flowers, shells, hills, the patio, and also the roads, rivers, and clouds of the period after 1960 when she began flying. The claims of the '70s relate to almost her entire output, since she painted very little after 1971 when her eyesight all but failed.

What emerges are significant differences in the two sets of assumptions. In the '20s interest is in female sexuality from a mostly male point of view. This interest is dominated by the impact of psychoanalytic theory against a background of the achievements of the suffragist movement and the idea of the New Woman. O'Keeffe's work was regarded as the expression of female sexuality, hitherto taken to be unknown or inexpressible or both. In the '70s, when O'Keeffe's work was treated as distinctively female, it was explored for an autonomous female subjectivity in the context of feminist theory. Her imagery is taken to express the bodily centering of a woman. The emphasis is on what is distinctive of the female, based on sexuality, but not limited to it.

THE CLAIMS OF THE '20s

Certainly the idea of a woman on paper caught on, and critics were quick to repeat it. In the notice of that first exhibition in 1916, Henry Tyrrell said:

> Miss O'Keeffe looks within herself and draws with unconscious naivete what purports to be the innermost unfolding of a girl's being [O'Keeffe was twenty-eight years old at the time], like the germinating of a flower. (1916, 10)

This is the only specific remark about what was exhibited, which interestingly consisted of charcoal drawings which were mostly abstract and included no flowers.

The following year, reviewing her first solo exhibition, Tyrrell was even more fulsome about it:

> Miss O'Keefe [sic] . . . has found expression in delicately veiled symbolism for "what every woman knows" but what women heretofore have kept to themselves . . . dealing with what hitherto has been deemed the inexpressible in visual form at least. . . . Now, perhaps for the first time in art's history, the style is the woman. (1917, 10)

He is not forthcoming with details of this symbolism except for an explicit reference to line drawings which symbolize a man's and a woman's lives (see e.g., "Blue Lines

X" 1916 in Cowart and Hamilton 1987, P1.9), which does not seem to sustain his earlier claim.

His theme, however, set the tone for much later writing. It is picked up in a 1921 article by Paul Rosenfeld, which upset O'Keeffe (see Robinson 1989, 240-41). He contrasted O'Keeffe to her fellow artists in the Stieglitz stable, John Marin and Arthur Dove, who were said to instance in their work the unification of the male. He said that in O'Keeffe's work is found:

> the woman polarizing herself, accepting fully the nature long denied, spiritualizing her sex. Her art is gloriously female. Her great painful and ecstatic climaxes make us at last to know something the man has always wanted to know. For here, in this painting there is registered the manner of perception anchored in the constitution of the woman. The organs that differentiate the sex speak. Women, one would judge always feel, when they feel strongly, through the womb. (1921, 666)

Another 1921 article upset O'Keeffe greatly: "I almost wept. I thought I could never face the world again," she said (quoted in Glueck 1970, 24). Marsden Hartley had written:

> With Georgia O'Keeffe one . . . [can] see the world of a woman turned inside out. . . . The pictures of O'Keeffe . . . are probably as living and shameless private documents as exist, in painting certainly, and probably in any other art. By shamelessness I mean unqualified nakedness of statement. (1921, 116)

Despite all the hype, critics were coy in the extreme when it came to detail. Their idea of "feeling through the womb" is very abstracted. We can only assume that they are referring to such things as O'Keeffe's womb-like spaces which seem to burst into cascading droplets, or surround rising and swelling forms, and to the forms of her color abstractions which also conjure up sexual organs.

These quotes are a selection from very early influential reviews of 1916-1921, which were themselves later quoted, and echoed. Excerpts in a similar vein between 1922 and 1927 follow.

Rosenfeld, in 1922, spoke of the "essence of very womanhood" which permeated her pictures and of how every stroke of her brush was "arrestingly female in quality." He said that in her painting the universe and life cycles were conveyed "through the terms of a woman's body" and that the "principle of woman's being" was expressed, and nothing more profane than that (1922, 112).

In 1923 Alexander Brook said: "these things of hers seem to be painted with her very body" (1923, 132) and Herbert Seligmann referred to "hitherto unattempted truths of a woman's sensibility" (1923, 10).

Helen Read was one of the very few women art critics at this time, and she wrote in 1924: "It happens that O'Keeffe's femininity is not of the fan-carrying sort. It is intensely, primitively womanly." Blanche Matthias, also a woman, said in 1926:

> No woman artist in America is so daringly herself in all that she does, which fact in itself is enough to provoke widespread discussion and comment. . . . O'Keeffe's simplicity was profoundly feminine. (1926, 14)

In 1927, Lewis Mumford claimed that O'Keeffe had produced a new set of symbols and opened up "a whole area of human consciousness which has never, so far as I am aware, been so completely revealed in either literature or in graphic art" (1927, 42). He claimed, however, that these symbols could not be formulated in words, but that in her paintings she had found "a language for experiences that are too intimate to be shared." The nearest he got in explaining this was to say that these symbols revealed "the sense of what it is to be a woman" and "the intimacies of love's juncture."

Alongside this are O'Keeffe's own references to her work. Referring to one of her first drawings shown to Stieglitz, she said, in a letter to Pollitzer of January 4, 1916: "The thing seems to express in a way . . . essentially a woman's feeling" (Cowart and Hamilton 1987, 147). She spoke of herself as making her unknown known (see, e.g., Cowart and Hamilton 1987, 174). She said publicly in a debate in 1930, referring to the oppression of women:

> Before I put a brush to canvas, I question, "Is this mine? . . . Is it influenced by some idea which I have acquired from some man?". . . I am trying with all my skill to do a painting that is all of women, as well as all of me. (quoted in Lisle 1986, 238)

Another consideration, of course, is her reaction to certain accounts of her work. Two articles in 1921 which displeased her have already been mentioned. In general she was unhappy with the way most critics, who were male, discussed her work in the early '20s. In 1925 she asked her friend and critic Mabel Dodge Luhan to write about her work, because she said: "I feel there is something unexplored about women that only women can explore" (Cowart and Hamilton 1987, 180). She moved to painting flowers when talk about her abstractions upset her, but the flowers attracted similar notice. She wrote in her 1939 catalog statement: "You hung all your own associations with flowers on my flower" (quoted in Lisle 1986, 170). The story is recounted much later of her defense against what she regarded as misinterpretations. She took to saying: "When people read erotic symbols into my paintings they're really talking about their own affairs" (quoted in Glueck 1970, 24).

In 1926, Searchlight, a pseudonym for Waldo Frank, defended O'Keeffe against over-interpretations, asking "How could you expect New York to admit that what it likes in O'Keeffe is precisely the fact that she is clear as water? cool as water?" (1926, 32-33).

Her reaction to interpretations of her work seems to be partly against the prevalent Freudianism and partly related to her deep dislike of exhibiting and the invasion of her self entailed in reviews of her work. While she recognized the need for publicity, which was organized and controlled by Stieglitz while he was alive, she retreated from engaging with what was said.

Almost everything written about her work in this early period regarded it as distinctively female. This selection I have presented brings out some prominent themes. She is said to express what had not been expressible before, to make known what had been unknown, to capture the essence of woman, and to paint with the body.

EXPRESSING THE INEXPRESSIBLE, MAKING
THE UNKNOWN KNOWN

It isn't clear whether what O'Keeffe expressed had been inexpressible before, for social reasons—as a matter of propriety either because it was sexual or because it was female, or both; or even just for technical reasons. But the sexual nature of what O'Keeffe expressed and its frankness were not usually separated, though critics were remarkably inarticulate about just what it was, or even what the symbols were.

When O'Keeffe herself talks of making her unknown known and the satisfaction this gives her, it sounds like a matter of self-discovery linked to her being a woman. Other writers see it as a revelation for the benefit of men—" 'what every woman knows' but what women heretofore have kept to themselves" (Tyrrell 1917, 10). "Make us at last to know something the man has always wanted to know" (Rosenfeld 1921, 666).

Either way the idea of making the unknown known is easily linked to Freud's view of woman as "a 'dark continent' for psychology" ([1926] in Strachey 1961, vol. XX, 212). Sexuality attracted great interest at this time in New York intellectual circles, due largely to the influence of Freud and Lawrence, and certainly Stieglitz was intensely interested in the sexual sources of being and artistic inspiration. Further, it was good business to have O'Keeffe talked about. O'Keeffe reported later: "Eroticism. . . . It wouldn't occur to me. But Alfred talked that way and people took it from him" (quoted in Seiberling 1974, 54). The extent to which he influenced what was written about O'Keeffe's work at the very beginning should not be underestimated (see Lynes 1989, 17, 25).

Here is a sample of Stieglitz "talking that way," from a letter to S. Macdonald Wright dated October 9, 1919, with his notes on "Woman in Art," which he had been asked for:

As for the Advent of Woman in the Field of Art . . . Woman feels the World differently than Man feels it . . . elemental feeling—Woman's & Man's are differentiated through the difference in their sex make-up. . . . The Woman receives the World through her Womb. That is the seat of her deepest feeling. Mind comes second. . . . (Norman 1973, 136-37)

The popularity of psychoanalytic theory among the Stieglitz set in New York at the time she first arrived was no doubt partly responsible for the reception her work had. The general influence of psychoanalysis through the '20s is also apparent. In 1926, a reviewer in the *New Yorker* said: "Psychiatrists have been sending their patients up to see the O'Keeffe canvases" (quoted in Lisle 1986, 171). Women particularly were said to have a shock of recognition on seeing her works. Even at the time it was recognized to some extent not to be quite sexual in the usual sense of being erotic, or of being feminine (of the fan-carrying sort), and it was awkwardly described as "primitively womanly," "Woman" capitalized, or as the essence or principle of womanhood.

THE ESSENCE OF WOMANHOOD, THE BODY

Some part of her achievement was taken to be the capturing of an essence or principle in paint. The recognition of the abstract nature of what she was believed to be expressing is clear in the references to the "truths of a woman's sensibility," "the essence of womanhood," "the principle of woman's being." This began with the early charcoal drawings and abstractions. Some of what is said relates to O'Keeffe's technical achievement in form, color, and style. She is credited with expressing in paint what had not been expressed before in painting, or perhaps even in any medium. She is sometimes taken to parallel in painting D. H. Lawrence's achievements in the novel.[2]

What is striking and of special interest for my purposes is that this essence of woman is related to bodily experience. To repeat from earlier quotes, O'Keeffe is taken to show "the innermost unfolding of a girl's being, like the germinating of a flower," as Tyrrell put it; or as Rosenfeld put it, himself echoing Stieglitz:

> there is registered the manner of perception anchored in the constitution of the woman. The organs that differentiate the sex speak. Women, one would judge, always feel, when they feel strongly, through the womb. (1921, 666)

As others said, "the world of a woman turned inside out"; and "these things of hers seem to be painted with her very body."

There is, however, an aspect of writing on O'Keeffe which confuses the issue. It was frequently noted that her appearance and her personality were reflected in her painting. For example: "It is to a singularly conscious and singularly integrated personality that these canvases refer us" (Rosenfeld 1922, 112). Or, again, in a review: "so impregnated are they [her paintings] with her own personality, so moulded and transformed by her inner conception." Or, in another example: "Each picture is in a way a portrait of herself," with reference to her clearcut features, simplicity of manner, and spirituality (Read, March 1924, 2B). And finally: "O'Keeffe's heart, soul and body are in her work" (Read, April 1924, 4).

The observation of the relation of her paintings and her self is one way in which the theme of expressing the essence of woman comes out. In part it is the suggestion that her work involves self-discovery, expression of inner feelings, etc. In part it is the recognition of her individuality and freedom from other influences (especially the European painting tradition and male artists). But there is another conspicuous aspect in the early '20s (which recurs in a slightly different form in the '70s). In the early '20s the artist and her work were equally well known. Schwartz records:

> O'Keeffe's fame was special in that it was based equally on what people knew of her work and of her life. As the most famous couple in American art, she and Alfred Stieglitz each glamorized the other's career in his photographs of her—a legendary series of pictures, roughly five hundred in number, made during the years 1917 to 1937. (1978, 88)

O'Keeffe was known intimately through Stieglitz's 1921 exhibition of forty-five of his photos of her, which had made a great impact (see Robinson 1989, 239). This impact was increased when Stieglitz put a $5,000 price tag on one of his nude photographs of O'Keeffe. As Lynes says:

> whether he intended to do it or not, by implying that this fascinating woman and artist was his high-priced and exclusive property, he objectified O'Keeffe even more than his photographs may have on their own. (1989, 44)

It is notable that reviews of her shows often featured as illustration a Stieglitz photograph of the artist, rather than an example of her own work, or sometimes both (see Anon., July 1922, 50; Rosenfeld 1922, 56; Anon. 1924, 49; Searchlight 1926, 30).

This double exposure of O'Keeffe through her own work and Stieglitz's photographs and the sort of treatment it generated bring out the ambiguity of O'Keeffe's position at this time as a woman artist. A woman artist was breaking with the artworld tradition where women figured as the subject of representation. A woman artist was representer rather then represented, an active subject and not a passive object. Yet O'Keeffe was both—because she was an artist and by virtue of Stieglitz's photographic representations of her. It is surprising how few of Stieglitz's many photos acknowledge O'Keeffe the artist.

This ambiguity in her prominent position in the artworld as both represented and representer is significant. The tension between the two roles is clear. It meant that reactions did not always focus directly on her work. It meant that her self and her body were public property. This may partly account for the way she avoided publicity later in her life, turning her back to photographers literally in one notable instance, which is reproduced on the back cover of *Georgia O'Keeffe*, and rightly described as unpleasantly arch (by Schwartz 1978, 90).

OUTLINE OF HER PAINTING LIFE

Interpretations in the '20s place consistent emphasis on her work as distinctively female in terms of revealing female sexuality. To bridge the gap between the '20s and the '70s let me give a brief outline of O'Keeffe's painting life. O'Keeffe exhibited for the first time in 1916 jointly with Charles Duncan and Rene Lafferty in Stieglitz's 291 gallery, and her first solo exhibition followed in 1917. She worked prolifically and by the mid-1920s was firmly established. She married Stieglitz quietly in 1924. Her series of small calla lilies brought a record-making price in 1928. The strains of success told, however. She didn't paint at all for a few years and had a breakdown in 1932. But Stieglitz regularly exhibited past work, and by 1936 she was again producing solidly. Throughout the '30s and '40s she was well known, and between 1929 and 1949 she worked regularly in New Mexico, moving there permanently in 1949 after she settled Stieglitz's estate following his death in 1946.

There was something of a lull and a slow period then, and during the '50s she had only three exhibitions at the Downtown Gallery in New York. But in 1960 she had a major museum exhibition, her first in fourteen years, at the Worcester Art Museum, Massachusetts (curator Daniel Rich), and she began to receive frequent honors and awards. (In 1962 she was elected to the American Academy of Arts and Letters.) With the 1970 Whitney retrospective (curators Lloyd Goodrich and Doris Bry), which traveled to Chicago and San Francisco to huge audiences, she was in the mainstream of modern art. However, there were few new paintings after 1971, when her eyesight became increasingly worse.

THE CLAIMS OF THE '70s

O'Keeffe was a celebrity in the '70s. The 1970 Whitney retrospective was an immense success across the country. In 1976 her book *Georgia O'Keeffe* with 106 illustrations appeared and was an instant sellout and widely reviewed. Her ninetieth birthday in 1977 brought a lot of publicity, and a television documentary ("Georgia O'Keeffe," producer Perry Miller Adato) was made and shown for the occasion. In 1978 the Metropolitan Museum of Art in New York put on an exhibition of fifty-one Stieglitz photos of O'Keeffe. In 1980 her first biography appeared (Lisle 1986).

The '70s were a period of strong feminist activity, and in the arts there was lively discussion on the issue of a female aesthetic and feminine sensibility.[3] A feminist art program was first taught at Fresno State College by Judy Chicago in 1970. Chicago, a founding figure in the women's art movement, championed O'Keeffe as the best example of female imagery (Schapiro and Chicago 1973, 11; Chicago 1977). This increased O'Keeffe's already great popularity and significance among feminists.

Writings on O'Keeffe's work in the '70s range broadly from those concerning exhibitions, her book, and her ninetieth birthday to specifically feminist discussions. Whereas in the '20s her work is almost universally treated as distinctively female, this was not the case in the '70s. Claims for her work as distinctively female were prominent in feminist circles, but these need to be considered against a broader background. Overall the writings fall into three categories: those ignoring or downplaying the female in her work; those lauding her individuality; and those celebrating the female.

THE GREAT ARTIST: DOWNPLAYING THE FEMALE

Lloyd Goodrich in the introduction to the catalog for the Whitney show says:

> Georgia O'Keeffe is a unique figure in contemporary American art. Her art is an individual one, expressing personal emotions and perceptions in a style that combines strength and crystalline clarity. The sources of her imagery lie in the world of nature. . . . (1970, 7)

Later on, he says:

> In the flower paintings nature's organisms often bore sexual associations. The forms were flower forms, but they also suggested the forms of the body, its subtle lines, its curves, folds and hidden depths . . . this sexual magnetism. . . . (18)

Barbara Rose, who has consistently advanced O'Keeffe's position in modern American art, said: "O'Keeffe seems constantly to be in touch with life's deepest secrets" (1977, 144). In a long review of the Whitney exhibition she focused on the new sixties paintings and emphasized the mystical in O'Keeffe's works:

> There is no question of the authenticity or singularity of O'Keeffe's vision. To those qualities she adds in the paintings of the sixties an authority which results from the complete mastery of her own idiom, and the extension of her expressive range to include both the most universal and the most contemporary experiences. . . . Not much has been said of the intrinsically mystical content of O'Keeffe's work, yet to ignore it would, I believe, miss the essential center of her work. (1970, 42)

She connects the theme of infinity in the clouds, road, and patio works with a "profoundly mystical content" which she claims is also found in earlier works such as "Shelton with Sunspots" (1970, 44; 1926).

Several years later, in reviewing *Georgia O'Keeffe*, she develops an account of O'Keeffe's debt to the American transcendentalist writers Emerson and Thoreau and her affinities with Eastern art (1977, 29-33). Rose has commented on how little has been seriously written about O'Keeffe given her great popularity, yet the tendency seems to continue. There was almost no response to Rose's account until Weisman (1982/1983, 10-14).

These views represent the tendency in the '70s to shy away from the female in O'Keeffe's work and to assert her importance in terms of more general achievements. In Goodrich female sexuality is important as one element among others; in Rose her significance is in metaphysical terms. In many other substantive accounts or interviews female sexuality is not mentioned, or not given any emphasis (e.g., Glueck 1970, 24; Tomkins 1974, 40-66; Heller and Williams 1976, C1, C3; Schwartz 1978, 87-93), or is referred to in passing by quotes from the '20s (e.g., Munro 1979, 76).

In the art history context, this tendency seems to be evasive, and sometimes even defensive. Sarah Peters explicitly counters the claim for the female in O'Keeffe's work:

> Her work since 1915 has been labelled "feminine" by many critics because of its many associative connections with the female body. But the wide range of her artistic language would seem to gainsay this simple description. (1977, 302)

Rose, making reference to Freudian interpretations of O'Keeffe, says: "It is as if a rose is a rose if a man paints it, but it must be something else in a painting by a woman" (1977, 32). Contrast this to Lucy Lippard's statement: "But the time has come to call a semisphere a breast if we know damn well that's what it suggests, instead of repressing the association and negating an area of experience . . ." (1976, 148). These remarks reflect tensions within feminism at this time, which I will look at shortly.

The other two alternatives which need to be considered are the way in which the distinctively female in O'Keeffe's work was taken as an autonomous and positive feature, and used in establishing a notion of female imagery; and the way in which O'Keeffe was taken as a model for independence and self-assertion.

AUTHENTIC INDIVIDUALITY

This approach takes O'Keeffe and her work as a model of self-assertion by virtue of her independence. She was often singled out for her individuality and authenticity as an artist. Her self-assertion and independence made her a role model for women artists in the '70s. Alexandra Johnson, comparing O'Keeffe with Rembrandt and Cezanne, says:

> Each exercised the courage and imagination to believe that the sovereignty of his [sic] own voice was as persuasive as the external influences which he needed to reject in order to free his genius. . . . Few artists have succeeded in doing this better than Georgia O'Keeffe whose impact on modern American art is as impressive as the individuality of her style. (1977, 24)

She concludes with the description of O'Keeffe as "a person whose presence is remarkably centered, whose power and stature is totemic, whose vision is clear, clean and free."

Another example is Sanford Schwartz, who says:

> Her painting, with its images of romantic isolated purity, became an embodiment of an individual who was strong enough to live out her life exactly as she wanted to. . . . O'Keeffe was a living symbol of self-assertion. (1978, 88)

References to O'Keeffe in *Women Artists' Newsletter* show the esteem in which O'Keeffe and her work were held. They published a glowing account of a meeting with her (Edelheit 1977, 3, 8, 9). Their questionnaire asked readers "If you have role models, historical or contemporary, who are they?" and O'Keeffe was the most popular overall, and across all age groups.

O'Keeffe provides a clear role model for feminist artists, and women generally, by virtue of her independence and individuality. She asserted herself in her art and in her life. Her work shows remarkably little influence of anything but herself and her environment. She did not in her training, or her early years, follow the European tradition of visiting Europe (until she was sixty-five years old in 1953), which was unusual for that time among artists in New York. She tells of how in 1915 she put aside all her earlier work because it had been influenced by others in order to start again for herself:

> I locked myself up in my room and held a private exhibition of everything I had painted. I noticed which paintings had been influenced by this painter, and which by that one. Then I determined which of the finished pieces represented me alone. From that moment forward I knew exactly what kind of work I wanted to do. (Quoted in Seiberling 1968, 52)

In her life, similarly, she seemed to do as she pleased (although not without difficulty sometimes; for example, in leaving Stieglitz for summers in New Mexico). She lived a life she chose from 1949 in seclusion in New Mexico. Her livelihood was secure and she was not constrained by influences from the art market. In fact, she kept much of her work.

A caveat has to be entered here, however, on Stieglitz's influence in the period 1916-1929, when he was the more established artist. Stieglitz had control over the exhibition and sale of her works all his life. Her enormous dedication to the importance of his work and well-being is matched only by the strength of her commitment to her own work.

There are striking similarities here between O'Keeffe and Frida Kahlo in this regard which cannot pass unnoticed. They both showed great dedication to their lover's "genius": O'Keeffe from the beginning of her painting career until Stieglitz's death; Kahlo to Diego Rivera from an early age until her own death. This was despite the despair each felt over their lover's other loves: Stieglitz's affair with Dorothy Norman contributed to O'Keeffe's breakdown in 1932, Rivera's affair(s) contributed to the drastic step of divorce and a two-year separation before their remarriage to each other. At the same time O'Keeffe and Kahlo both displayed a fierce determination and a powerful sense of themselves and the self-sustaining force of their commitment to their own work. O'Keeffe has said that it was work which gave the whole center to life. Kahlo took up painting while hospitalized in her youth, and was still struggling up from her deathbed, amputated, into the wheelchair to paint for three hours until her energy failed her (see Herrera, 1983).

The view in the '70s of O'Keeffe's individuality as an artist might seem to be one just of independence and self-assertion, and perhaps it is sometimes meant as that. What is important is the realization that this depends on what is distinctively female in her work. In eschewing traditional influences on her painting, which would have been almost entirely male, and in wanting to find her own self, what she found and expressed so clearly was herself as a woman.

FEMALE IMAGERY: CELEBRATING THE FEMALE

The claims I particularly want to consider are those that treat O'Keeffe's work as distinctively female. The theoretical claim for a distinctive female imagery appeared in 1973. Miriam Schapiro and Judy Chicago said:

> O'Keeffe began. She painted a haunting, mysterious passage through the black portal of an iris, making the first recognized step into the darkness of female identity. . . . She painted out of an urgency to understand her own being and to communicate as yet unknown information about being a woman. . . . [T]here is now evidence that many women artists have defined a central orifice whose formal organization is often a metaphor for a woman's body. The center of the painting is the tunnel; the experience of female sexuality. (1973, 11)

This central core imagery, as it came to be known, was to be distinguished from "vaginal" or "womb" art in a simplistic sense (Schapiro and Chicago 1973, 14). It is sexual imagery[4] in a symbolic sense, suggestive of the experience of the female body but not involving images of the body as such. (Indeed, O'Keeffe is unusual for the almost complete lack of human figures in her painting.) It expresses the body as the basis of feeling, sexuality, and spirituality. The imagery is about the centering of a female in her experience, which provides an autonomous and positive sexual identity. It was explicitly intended to bring about a reversal in the cultural image of women by emphasizing *their* view of their identity and sexuality.

It is imagery used to describe a female perception of reality. In her autobiography, Chicago argues the need for this because all imagery to date (including abstract art and the art of many women) had been based on a male view of the world explicitly or implicitly. She recounts the dilemma she had experienced between expressing her identity as a woman in her art and failing to be understood, or suppressing her womanliness to get recognition as an artist. The difficulty of finding a way to express herself authentically as a woman is resolved "through the flower":

> I used the flower as the symbol of femininity, as O'Keeffe had done. But in my images the petals of the flower are parting to reveal an inviting but undefined space, the space beyond the confines of our own femininity. These works symbolized my longing for transcendence and personal growth. They were my first steps in being able to make clear, abstract images of my point of view as a woman. (1977, 141)

The relationship in O'Keeffe's work (and Chicago's) between the centered image and the body is not literal. What is distinctively female in this imagery is abstract and symbolic. It is not suggested that O'Keeffe's paintings are depictions of parts of the female body. Rather, in a variety of different ways, the flower, bone, hill, and patio paintings express the embodiment of her subjectivity, what is constitutive of her female sexual identity.

The common '20s view of the impact of her work as sexualized imagery which is erotic contrasts markedly with this. There the emphasis is primarily on what sexuality is for a female. Here the emphasis is rather on what a female identity is and how that is imbued with sexuality.

There is a clear tension between different approaches in feminist writing about O'Keeffe in the '70s. One approach is to ignore the female in her work and the other is to celebrate it. There was a tendency, in art history especially, to claim O'Keeffe as a great artist (not a great woman artist), and this involved downplaying any suggestion of the distinctively female in her work, or relegating it to a minor part of her oeuvre. This is a natural response to sexist art criticism from which O'Keeffe and all women artists have suffered at the hands of a male-dominated art establishment (see Mitchell 1978, 681-87). Interestingly, Read made a similar defense of O'Keeffe in the '20s (1928, 76-77). This response coincides with O'Keeffe's rejection of the second-class status of being the best woman painter. "The men like to put me down as the best woman painter," she said in 1943. "I think I'm one of the best painters" (quoted in Lisle 1986, 173).

Something similar is going on in taking her as a model of individuality without recognizing that her achievements depended on what was distinctively female in her work. The connection between O'Keeffe's authenticity and individuality and distinctively female expression is not coincidental. In expressing her own authenticity and individuality without the confines of male traditions, the self she expresses is clearly female.

In that way she perfectly exemplifies Chicago's argument about being a woman and an artist in a male-dominated world:

> Their self-images did not correspond to society's definition of women. Asserting their own self definitions was an implicit step toward challenging the culture and demanding that it adjust its definition of women to correspond to the reality of women's lives. (1977, 158)

Some of what is paradoxical in O'Keeffe's views about being an artist and a woman is explicable in the light of this consideration. She did not want to succeed as a woman artist because that was a second-rate category, and it was used as a put-down (see Lisle 1986, 173). "I have always been very annoyed at being referred to as a 'woman artist' rather than an 'artist,' " she said (quoted in Kotz 1977, 43), and she was well aware of discriminatory treatment against women:

> All the male artists I knew, of course, made it very plain that as a woman I couldn't hope to make it—I might as well stop painting. (Quoted in Glueck 1970, 24)

She has been a reluctant model for the feminist theory for which her work provided the basis, e.g., permission was refused for reproductions of her paintings to appear in Chicago's *Through the Flower* and she is said to have rejected feminist interpretations of her work (Drobojowska 1986, 120). She is reported as saying that a book on women artists was a silly topic and that the only people who had helped her were men (Zito 1977, C3). However, this should not be taken to imply that she did not support the cause of women or want to help other women, as has been suggested (by Moss, e.g., 1973, 8). In 1926 she addressed a dinner of 500 in Washington for the National Woman's Party to which she belonged for thirty years until she left New York (see Lisle 1986, 163, 323) and at different times she helped other individual women artists. Her attitude in the '70s is not entirely a matter of being negative about women as it has been assumed. But she was an uncooperative heroine and this partly relates to her general view of interviewers and her public image and her refusal to be co-opted.

She also showed an awareness of trying to express herself as a woman and was well aware of the difference that involved. This is clear where she said (quoted earlier) that her work expressed "essentially a woman's feeling" and that she tried to do a painting "that is all of women, as well as all of me." Most revealing is what she wrote in a letter to Jean Toomer on February 14, 1934, while she was convalescing in Bermuda after her breakdown. She said that she wanted to "be just a woman . . . it is this dull business of being a person that gets one all out of shape" (quoted in Lisle 1986, 267).

THE '20s AND THE '70s

I want to compare the claims of what is distinctively female in O'Keeffe's work in the two different periods. There is an interesting parallel in the influence of Stieglitz's promotion of O'Keeffe's work in the '20s and in the influence of Chicago in the '70s. In the '20s Stieglitz was a leading advocate of modern American art in a milieu greatly interested in sexuality against the intellectual background of the New Woman, Freudian theory, and the writing of D. H. Lawrence.[5] In the '70s, Chicago was at the forefront of developing the notion of female imagery in her own art and in feminist art theory. In Chicago's large-scale work "The Dinner Party" of 1979, O'Keeffe was the only living artist accorded a place at the table.

By considering the interpretations of O'Keeffe's work current in the '20s and the '70s, I hope to bring out how discussions of her work as distinctively female operate with different underlying assumptions about the body, subjectivity, and sexuality. This also illustrates how the theoretical background of a period functions in the construction of the prevailing paradigm of the female or the feminine. A contributing factor is the work done later than the '20s. However, what always attracted most attention were the large flower paintings first done in the '20s.

The '20s were a time when it was a matter of curiosity that a woman was a subject with a sex, and that there was another kind of sex. O'Keeffe's work was intriguing because it addressed directly what even critics, although often given to extravagant talk, were pretty coy about. But it is clear that she was taken as expressing female sexuality in a fairly literal sense. "Feeling through the womb" is taken to distinguish woman and to have priority over mind in interpretations by Stieglitz and Rosenfeld. The standard social conceptions of woman as other, mysterious, different, and interesting perhaps, but inferior, inform the view of what is taken to be distinctively female, and O'Keeffe's work is interpreted accordingly.

The emphasis tends toward female sexuality as a variant of what was familiar about male sexuality, or as a complement to it in the more high-flown rhetoric. This is not surprising given the majority of writers were male and the cultural milieu largely male-dominated. Female artists were very rare. But it should not be forgotten, though it didn't get much direct voice, that O'Keeffe's work was very popular with women in exhibitions and sales (see McBride 1923, 7; 1924, 13).

The '70s were a time when interest in what was distinctively female was feminist. The significance of sexual difference, rather than human equality, was an issue. Psychoanalysis was an important tool. The exploration of a distinctively female identity was centered on sexuality, not for the sake of sex itself, but because a conception of female subjectivity was impossible without it, unlike the detached, anonymous, rational, bodyless subject of traditional philosophical theorizing, who was implicitly male. In feminist theorizing subjectivity was imbued with sexuality, and sexuality was rooted in the body. This was the focus of the lived body of experience.

O'Keeffe's work was central to the concept of female sexual imagery in the '70s in providing a whole range of images symbolic of woman's experience through the body. The feminist emphasis was a positive one of what is distinctively female for its own sake. In the '20s O'Keeffe's work was seen as full of female sexuality and sexualized imagery. In the '70s it was taken to present a female subjectivity imbued with sexuality and implicitly to articulate a female view of the world.

The difference then between the claims about O'Keeffe's work is that in the '20s the distinctively female was a matter of a subject with a sex, whereas in the '70s it was a matter of sexed subjectivity.

TAKING THE BODY SERIOUSLY

I want finally to elaborate on the useful alternative suggested in O'Keeffe's life and work for contemporary feminist philosophy. O'Keeffe has embodied in her work an idea of sexed subjectivity which gives us a positive alternative to the traditional conception of the body and the subject. She gives us a clear, and distinctively female, example to challenge dichotomies of mind/body and subject/object.

The lived body is beautifully expressed in O'Keeffe's work, and a distinctively female subjectivity is illustrated in her life and work, and especially in the relation between them. There is no division between mind and body, or subject and object, no neutral body, no anonymous subject, no separation of mind and feeling, of self and other. She personifies in her work a subjectivity where sex is constitutive. This is also recognized by Roxana Robinson in her recent biography, when she says:

> The sexuality in O'Keeffe's painting is inextricably related to her integrated view of life. Sexuality was a central force, celebrated but not separated from the rest. (1989, 283)

The significance of the body comes out in two important ways in O'Keeffe's work. First, it is integrated into, and fundamental to the nature of, her subjectivity—"she paints with her body." There are many clear examples of this in her work which capture different aspects of female sexual and bodily experience. Her world is experienced through the body, and that bodily presence is acknowledged in various ways. Even in paintings which might seem to have little bodily presence there is a marked way in which she constructs distance that has to do with the projection of the body into the paintings. Rose has remarked on this (1970, 46) in the late paintings such as "Sky with Clouds" series (1963-1965) where her preoccupation is with infinity. She positions us bodily, in relation to the clouds, so as to produce the sensation of floating and moving.

Second, this body which pervades her subjectivity is sexually specific. O'Keeffe's expression of this sexual specificity, which was discussed in the '70s in terms of female imagery, ranges from the soft rounded shapes of her abstractions, to the undulating openings and depths of her flowers, to the folds and crevasses of her hills, to the cavities and centeredness of her bones, to the interiority of her patios.

In O'Keeffe's work we have an expression of how female subjectivity is sexed through our experience of the body. Over the wide range of her paintings many aspects of this are explored. Her female imagery is of the morphology of a body which relates to its anatomy but is not restricted to it (see Irigaray 1977, 64). O'Keeffe's work expresses a conception of the distinctively female that is not just sexual but encompasses contemporary feminist concerns in philosophy.

Notes

1. E.g., in Willard (1963, 92) and Seiberling (1968, 52); see also Pollitzer (1988, 164) and Lisle (1986, 83).
2. *Women in Love* was topical in the '20s and Stieglitz had a censored copy of *Lady Chatterley's Lover* around 1927.
3. See Orenstein 1975, esp. 519, 521.
4. This became overlooked. As Lippard points out: "Of course, 'female imagery' was first used, and should continue to be used, to mean female sexual imagery. That wasn't understood and it all got confused" (1976, 81).
5. This is detailed in Lyne's study (1989) of critics in the '20s, which also reproduces their writings.

References

Anon. 1916. *Camera Work* 47: 12-13.
Anon. 1922. The female of the species achieves a new deadliness. *Vanity Fair*, July, 18: 50.
Anon. 1922. "I can't sing, so I paint! . . ." *New York Sun*, Dec. 2: 22.
Anon. 1924. We nominate for the Hall of Fame. *Vanity Fair*, July, 49: 49.
Anon. 1979. Who is your role model? *Women Artists News* 5(2-3): 3.
Brook, Alexander. 1923. February exhibitions. *The Arts*, Feb. 3: 126-35.
Chicago, Judy. 1977. *Through the flower: My struggle as a woman artist*. New York: Doubleday Anchor.
Cowart, Jack, and Juan Hamilton, eds. 1987. *Georgia O'Keeffe: Art and letters*. Washington: National Gallery.
Dobrojowska, Hunter. 1986. Georgia O'Keeffe 1887-1986. *Art News* 85 (6): 119-21.
Edelheit, Martha. 1977. Georgia O'Keeffe: a reminiscence. *Women Artists' Newsletter* 3 (Dec.): 3, 8, 9.
Freud, Sigmund. [1926] 1961. *The question of lay analysis*, tr. and ed. James Strachey. The standard edition of the complete psychological works of Sigmund Freud. London: Hogarth Press.
Giboire, Clive, ed. 1990. *Lovingly, Georgia*. New York: Simon and Schuster.
Glueck, Grace. 1970. "It's just what's in my head. . . ." *New York Times*, Oct. 18: 24.
Goodrich, Lloyd, and Doris Bry. 1970. *Georgia O'Keeffe*. New York: Praeger.
Hartley, Marsden. 1921. *Adventures in the arts*. New York: Boni and Liveright. 112-19.
Heller, N., and J. Williams. 1976. Georgia O'Keeffe: The American Southwest. *American Artist* 40: 76-81, 101.
Herrera, Hayden. 1983. *Frida: A biography of Frida Kahlo*. New York: Harper and Row.
Irigaray, Luce. 1977. Women's exile. *Ideology and Consciousness* 1: 62-76.
Jonson, Alexandra. 1977. An influence on oneself. *Christian Science Monitor*, Nov. 15: 24.
Kotz, Mary Lynn. 1977. Georgia O'Keeffe at 90. *Art News* 76(10): 36-45.
Lippard, Lucy. 1976. *From the center*. New York: Dutton.
Lisle, Laurie. 1986. *Portrait of an artist: A biography of Georgia O'Keeffe*. New York: Washington Square Press.
Lynes, Barbara Buhler. 1989. *O'Keeffe, Stieglitz and the critics 1916-1929*. Ann Arbor: UMI Press.
Matthias, Blanche. 1926. Georgia O'Keeffe and the intimate gallery: Stieglitz showing seven Americans. *Chicago Evening Post*, Mar. 2: 1, 14.

McBride, Henry. 1923. Curious responses to work of Miss Georgia O'Keefe [sic] on others. *New York Herald*, Feb. 4: 7.

McBride, Henry. 1924. Stieglitz, teacher, artist: Pamela Bianco's new work. *New York Herald*, Mar. 9: 13.

Mitchell, Marilyn Hall. 1978. Sexist art criticism: Georgia O'Keeffe—A case study. *Signs* 3(3): 681-87.

Moss, Irene. 1973. Georgia O'Keeffe and "these people." *Feminist Art Journal* 2(2): 8.

Mumford, Lewis. 1927. O'Keefe [sic] and Matisse. *The New Republic* 50 (Mar. 2): 41-42.

Munro, Eleanor. 1979. *Originals: American women artists*. New York: Simon and Schuster.

Norman, Dorothy. 1973. *Alfred Stieglitz: An American seer*. New York: Aperture.

O'Keeffe, Georgia. 1976. *Georgia O'Keeffe*. New York: Viking.

Orenstein, Gloria Feman. 1975. Art history. *Signs* 1(2): 505-25.

Peters, Sarah. 1977. O'Keeffe. In *Women artists 1550-1950*. Ann Harris and Linda Nochlin, eds. New York: Knopf, 300-306.

Pollitzer, Anita. 1988. *A woman on paper*. New York: Simon and Schuster.

Read, Helen Appleton. 1924. Georgia O'Keefe [sic] again introduced by Stieglitz at the Anderson Galleries. *Brooklyn Daily Eagle*, Mar. 9: 2B.

Read, Helen Appleton. 1924. Georgia O'Keeffe—woman artist whose art is sincerely feminine. *Brooklyn Daily Eagle*, April 6: 4.

Read, Helen Appleton. 1928. The feminine viewpoint in contemporary art. *Vogue* 71 (June 15): 76-77.

Robinson, Roxana. 1989. *Georgia O'Keeffe*. New York: Harper.

Rose, Barbara. 1977. *American painting from the colonial period to the present*. New York: Rizzoli.

Rose, Barbara. 1970. Georgia O'Keeffe: The paintings of the sixties. *Artforum* 9(3): 42-46.

Rose, Barbara. 1977. O'Keeffe's trail. *New York Review of Books* 24 (Mar. 31): 29-33.

Rosenfeld, Paul. 1921. American painting. *The Dial* 71: 649-70.

Rosenfeld, Paul. 1922. The paintings of Georgia O'Keeffe. *Vanity Fair* 19: 56, 112, 114.

Schapiro, Miriam, and Judy Chicago. 1973. Female imagery. *Womanspace Journal* 3: 11-14.

Schwartz, Sanford. 1978. Georgia O'Keeffe writes a book. *New Yorker*, Aug. 28: 87-93.

Searchlight. 1926. *Time exposures*. New York: Boni and Liveright.

Seiberling, Dorothy. 1968. Horizons of a pioneer. *Life* 64-65. (Mar. 1): 39-53.

Seiberling, Dorothy. 1974. The female view of erotica. *New York*, Feb. 11: 54-58.

Seligmann, Herbert. 1923. Georgia O'Keeffe, American. *Manuscripts* 5 (Mar.): 10.

Tomkins, Calvin. 1974. The rose in the eye looked pretty fine. *New Yorker*, Mar. 4: 40-66.

Tyrrell, Henry. 1916. New York art exhibitions and gallery news. *Christian Science Monitor*, June 2: 10.

Tyrrell, Henry. 1917. New York art exhibition and gallery notes. *Christian Science Monitor*, May 4: 10.

Weisman, Celia. 1982/1983. O'Keeffe's art: Sacred symbols and spiritual quest. *Woman's Art Journal* 3(2): 10-14.

Willard, Charlotte. 1963. Georgia O'Keeffe. *Art in America* 51(5): 92-96.

Zito, Tom. 1977. Georgia O'Keeffe. *Washington Post*, Nov. 9: C1, C3.

PART FOUR

Philosophical and Critical Legacies

Beautiful Exiles

MARY BITTNER WISEMAN

This essay distinguishes between a woman's identifying herself in philosophers'
writings about women and men and identifying what a woman is from these writings.
It suggests a way of reading those texts that alienate women from humanity: it is
reading as a woman or as an innovating stranger. A woman can read as a man,
saying "we" with Kant when in the Observations on the Feeling of the Beautiful
and the Sublime *(1763) he identifies women with the beautiful and men with the*
sublime and declares women incapable of acting on principle, and saying further that
she is not a woman if that is what women are. One can read as a woman, however,
where this is to read in a way that discovers itself to whomever the text alienates, and
confront the fact that Kant is talking about her and that this is what he says. In doing
so the reader deliberately excludes herself from the languages into which she was born
and repeats Socrates' and Descartes's distancing themselves from and refusing to
inherit their traditions.

Two displacements pertinent to the place of women in philosophy and in language
were made during philosophy's golden ages in classical Greece and Enlightenment
Europe. One displacement, resulting from theories about the difference between
women and men, tends to be ignored; the other is not ignored at all but seems not
to have anything to do with women. This first is Aristotle's and Kant's not allowing
women to enter the moral arena, the second Socrates' and Descartes's distancing
themselves from the scene of the languages and beliefs of their traditions. Philosophers'
metalanguages at times have the effect of excluding women from the object
languages in which ordinary lives are spoken, and philosophers at times displace
themselves from the ordinary languages spoken by the members of their tribe.

Women learn to speak the languages into which they were born and later learn
to read their signs: they know that words and strings of words say more and different
things from those their speakers use them to say and that "man," for example, means
"male" as well as "human being" regardless of what the speaker has in mind. For
they hear the words, not the speaker's intentions, hearing "male" when they hear
"human" also. Women can estrange themselves from their culture's languages even
as they speak them, saying with Socrates "I am quite a stranger to the language of
the place; and therefore I would have you regard me as if I were really a stranger"

(Plato 401). They gain a curious power thereby, for exiles from language can know better than its speakers what are its powers, what it can do and what it can say. An alien interlocutor can find in natives' words divisions they never dreamed were there: ambiguities such that one reading makes the words say the opposite of what another makes them say. One can, for example, read Aristotle and Kant as a man or as a woman. To read as a woman is to read in a way that discovers itself to whomever the text alienates, as it alienates women from humanity by denying them entrance into the kingdom of ends. It is to trick the master language by estranging oneself from it, by saying with Socrates "I am a stranger to the language of the place."

BEYOND THE PALE

Kant

Consider now not women's making the philosopher's liberating gesture of excluding themselves but their reading works in which they are excluded. Consider also what happens to the concept of woman in one of these works, Kant's *Observations on the Feeling of the Beautiful and Sublime* (1763).[1] Several identity questions present themselves. One has to do with a woman's identifying *herself* in the works and turns on a plausible reconstruction of what occurs when a woman reads Kant's words about her, the other with anyone's identifying *what a woman is* from what Kant says in light of the way in which the intentional concept of the feminine moves further and further away from the causal concept of the female as he elaborates the distinction between the feminine and the masculine along the lines drawn between the beautiful and the sublime. What emerges is a structural opposition whose transformations include sense/reason, inclination/duty, particular/ general, and measurable/measureless, as well as feminine/masculine and beautiful/sublime. A reader asking what a woman is may see the boundaries of the concept of the feminine go so wild as the feminine becomes a member of a set of exchangeable ordered pairs of values that woman under this description is nothing identifiable. No reader can identify what a woman is from Kant's *Observations*, for woman there is figured as a function of sense, inclination, and the beautiful, where these are the other side of reason, duty, and the sublime, respectively. Woman figures both as the value whose variables are the marked members of certain oppositions, as the site through which the members pass, and as the field within which the oppositions are inscribed.

Kant's pre-critical *Observations on the Feeling of the Beautiful and Sublime* was written "more with the eye of an observer than of a philosopher" (Kant 45), an eye that cast itself over the objects and attributes that excite the feeling and over the distinction of the beautiful and sublime in the interrelations of the sexes and in the characteristics of people from different nations. He functions there as a grand taxonomer, assigning virtually all human attributes and types either to the beautiful, the sublime, or some combination of the two. The result of this classifying passion is that the beautiful and the sublime are introduced not by the definitions that are forthcoming in *The Critique of Judgment* (1790) but by the objects and attributes with which they are associated and by the oppositions between items on the list of things beautiful and their counterparts on the list of things sublime.

There are in play no conceptions of the beautiful or the sublime independent of their being feelings of enjoyment that tend to be aroused by items from the paradigm of the beautiful or the sublime. For example, the beautiful just is that by virtue of which wit and artfulness are like each other and different from understanding and courage, which in turn are sublime (51). That wit and understanding, artfulness and courage are associated with a feeling of enjoyment is what Kant observes, but he does more than merely observe when he names what wit and artfulness occasion, the *feeling of the beautiful*, and what understanding and courage occasion, the *feeling of the sublime*. He opposes wit to understanding and artfulness to courage as he opposes the sight of "flower-strewn meadows, valleys with winding brooks and covered with grazing flocks" to that of "a mountain whose snow-covered peak rises above the clouds" (47). Whatever understanding is, it is to be grasped in its difference from wit; whatever the appeal of the mountain whose peak is lost in the clouds, it is precisely not the appeal of the valley in which everything is in plain view. One casts about for matrices of which these opposing pairs are transformations, but none show themselves.

Again, "the sublime *moves*, the beautiful *charms*" (47). "Sublime attributes [are those that] stimulate esteem, beautiful ones, love" (51), where attributes are sublime because they are esteemed rather than esteemed because they are sublime and beautiful because loved rather than loved because beautiful. The pairs proliferate, each exchangeable with all and all with each, and there seems to be no reason to privilege one over another. Any one is as telling, as important, as any other. One can speak as well of the moving or the charming as of the estimable or the lovable as of the sublime or the beautiful. There is one pair, however, that I would like to single out for the reason that it bears a special relation to the readers of the *Observations*. It is masculine/feminine, given in Section Three, "Of the Distinction of the Beautiful and Sublime in the Interrelations of the Two Sexes." The relation it bears is special in that readers may or may not at times in their lives move or be moved, charm or be charmed, esteem or be esteemed, love or be loved, but they *are* gendered and can no more not be gendered than they cannot be human beings. According to Kant, their gender relates them to either the beautiful or the sublime. For beauty is the mark of a woman, sublimity the mark of a man: "certain specific traits lie especially in the personality of this [female] sex which distinguish it clearly from ours and chiefly result in making her known by the mark of the beautiful. . . . All the other merits of a woman should unite solely to enhance the character of the beautiful, which is the proper reference point; and on the other hand, among the masculine qualities the sublime clearly stands out as the criterion of his kind" (76-77).

The beautiful and the sublime are first of all feelings, however, introduced in the *Observations* by examples of what in nature provokes them and how they manifest themselves. "Temperaments that possess a feeling for the sublime are drawn gradually, by the quiet stillness of a summer evening as the shimmering light of the stars breaks through the brown shadows of night and the lonely moon rises into view, into high feelings of friendship, of disdain for the world, of eternity. The shining day stimulates busy fervor and a feeling of gaiety" (47). Beauty and sublimity are provoked by and manifest in the human as well as the natural order, however. Inclinations may be beautiful, principles sublime. The senses may charm, sublime reason move. The epistemological and the moral both know the distinction between the feminine and the beautiful, on the one hand, and the masculine and the sublime, on the other. Indeed, it is in the relation of the two sexes to knowledge that the distinction's full evaluative force manifests itself. For Kant holds that it is perverse and improper for women to presume to know what men know.

> The fair sex has just as much understanding as the male, but it is a beautiful understanding, whereas ours should be a deep understanding, an expression that signifies identity with the sublime. . . . Deep meditation and a long-sustained reflection are noble but difficult, and do not well befit a person in whom unconstrained charms should show nothing else than a beautiful nature. Laborious learning or painful pondering, even if a woman should greatly succeed in it, destroy the merits that are proper to her sex, and because of their rarity they can make of her an object of cold admiration; but at the same time they will weaken the charms with which she exercises her great power over the other sex. (78)

The power of women over men is the power of the senses over reason, of inclination over duty, and no more can the senses know or the inclinations have moral worth than can the power of women be ought but resisted, contained, and constrained. Anyone who would know and do the right, proper man and perverse woman alike, must resist feminine, sensuous, feeling beauty. So great, Kant says, is men's weakness before the natural charms of women that a "single sly glance sets them [men] more in confusion than the most difficult problem of science," and were a woman to do science, men in their generous indulgence to her would not let her see how perverted was her taste for speculation cold and abstract. "The content of woman's great science, rather, is humankind, and among humanity, men. Her philosophy is not to reason, but to sense" (79).

The transformations of beautiful/sublime in the moral register have the effect of identifying humankind with men. The inclinations of sympathy and complaisance are said by Kant to be beautiful but to become trifling when without the support of principles. They are not true virtues because they are based on feelings, whereas "true virtue can be grafted only upon principles such that *the more general they are, the more sublime and noble it becomes*. These principles . . . are the consciousness of a feeling that lives in every human breast and . . . is the *feeling of the beauty and the dignity of human nature*" (first emphasis added) (60). Virtue that rests upon principles is called genuine virtue, while the beautiful inclinations are called adoptive virtues, for "ennobled by the relationship with [genuine virtue], even they gain its name" (61). The genuine is privileged over the adoptive and lends its name to the less privileged, as man lends but does not give his name to woman when he includes her in mankind. The more directly related to principles, the more genuine a virtue is, and the more general a principle, the more sublime.

The beautiful, the mark of a woman, is here identified with feelings such as sympathy and complaisance, and the sublime, the mark of a man, is identified with principles. Feelings exist in their occurrence. They are particular and concrete; they show themselves as the flowers, winding brooks, and grazing cattle show themselves in the valley called beautiful for what it shows. Principles, on the other hand, are general and abstract, most sublime when most like peaks of mountains lost in the clouds. They can move men to act, but not women, who are moved instead by what pleases. "Women will avoid the wicked not because it is unright, but only because it is ugly; and virtuous actions mean to them such as are morally beautiful. Nothing of duty, nothing of compulsion, nothing of obligation! Woman is intolerant of all commands and all morose constraint. They do something only because it pleases them, and the art consists in making only that please them which is good. I hardly believe that the fair sex is capable of principles" (81).

Since Kant's morality is one of law, not virtue, and since the moral law is the imperative to act only on those maxims that one can will as universal laws of nature, not to be capable of acting on principles or universal laws is not to be capable of obeying the categorical imperative. Entertaining ends and directing one's actions toward them involves acting on principle rather than on inclination. Because they cannot act on principle, women can neither exercise true virtue nor belong to the kingdom of ends. Exiled from the kingdom, they are exiled from humanity.

A woman reading Kant cannot help but know that when he says "we" and means men, this word is not hers. But she knows too that the word is not men's either. For since the paired concepts masculine/feminine belong to the same paradigms as do the pairs sublime/beautiful, science/sense, duty/inclination, they have a common logic. Stern duty commands because seductive inclination challenges reason's sway over men's will: there is duty only because there are inclinations and duty is their overcoming. Similarly, science is the mastery of what the senses show and the sublime what overreaches all that beauty circumscribes. Beauty inhabits the surfaces of things and lives in its own appearing, whereas sublimity lives in the hidden—night is sublime; in the out of reach or out of sight—great heights and great depths are sublime, as are mountain tops lost in mist; in what cannot be sized—raging storms. Man is the measure, Protagoras said, but Kant's sublime is precisely what defies man's measure in any familiar sense of "man." Measurable/measureless becomes now a transform of particular/general, where the measureless is the utterly general in the sense of being what is out of this world with its men who measure, what has thrown away the ladder leading up from the particular case.

Man is familiar, included in Kant's "we," whereas woman is estranged from the language in which ordinary lives are spoken. Yet one matrix of which beautiful/sublime and feminine/masculine are transformations is here/beyond, where what is here is familiar, not strange. Although Kant excludes women from "we," they reenter his language from the place of their exile and mime it. Actors, strangers, they are in position to know better than he where they are and why they are there. Women are excluded from morality not because they are incapable of it but because they are characterized precisely in terms of the exclusions necessary for there being anything like morality. Kant's "we," naming what can be moral, what can do philosophy and science, carries within itself the exclusion of inclination, of sense, of the female, the feminine, the feeling, the beautiful, and so is no more men's word than it is women's because there is nothing that identifies men, masculine, male other than their difference from women, feminine, female, where the latter concepts are prior and the former constructions out of them. The concept of the masculine is an operation on that of the feminine, an overcoming, necessary because of the power of the feminine, where this is the power of nature, of all that man would subdue in order to assert himself and his power. Woman becomes the figure for all that is subject to the law of reason made practical: she is the immediately present before it is transcended, nature before it is reduced to rule, desire before it is right or wrong, feelings before they are constrained by principles. Woman marked by beauty becomes the condition for the possibility of male man's being able to be fully human, to be fully rational, to be dutiful.

Aristotle

Aristotle like Kant characterizes the difference between men and women in such a way as to make women incapable of morality and, therefore, incapable of rationality in practice and of humanity. Aristotle distinguishes male from female along the precise line that divides active from passive, saying that "a woman is as it were an infertile male; the female, in fact, is female on account of an inability of a sort, viz., it lacks the power to concoct semen out of the final state of the nourishment" (Mahowald 1978, 62).[2] Aristotle's *Politics* inscribes the biological within the political: "For that which has the capacity, in virtue of its intelligence, of looking forward, is by nature the ruling and master element, while that which has the capacity, in virtue of its body, of carrying out this will of the superior is the subject and slave by nature. And for this reason the interests of the master and the slave are identical. Now it is by *nature* that the woman and the slave have been marked out as separate . . ." (Mahowald 1978, 66).

Aristotle continues: "For the slave, generally speaking, has not the deliberative faculty, but the woman has it, though without the power to be effective; the child has it, but in an imperfect degree. . . . We must suppose that all ought to have some share in [the moral virtues], though not in the same way, but only so far as each requires for the fulfillment of his own function. . . . [T]he same kind of temperance does not belong to women and men, nor the same courage and justice (as Socrates thought), but the one is the courage of the ruler, the other the courage of the subject. And similarly with the other virtues" (Mahowald 1978, 68). Since practical wisdom entails all of the other virtues, it is the highest virtue and the mark of the moral. The practical wisdom of the ruler man is superior to that of the subject woman, who does not, then, bear the mark of the moral: for the moral is the highest. Nor does she bear the mark of the rational in the highest sense: she is rational only in being subject to man's ruling reason. Subject, not ruler, she does not perform the fully human function and is, then, not fully human.

Nothing active without something passive, and in light of Aristotle's identification of the male principle with activity and the female with passivity, this may be recast: no active male without passive female. The exclusion of the female from maleness is necessary, for there must be something passive on which the active principle can act. It is not so the other way around, however; passive is passive whether acted on or not. Aristotle's exclusion of the female from the full exercise of practical wisdom bears witness to the power of the female. It is precisely the female's displacement from the reigning center that gives the ruler something to rule, and passive female becomes in the words of Aristotle as well as Kant the figure for all that is subject to the law of reason made practical. Passive female becomes the condition for the possibility of male man's being able to be fully human, to be fully active, to be the ruling principle.

Reading as a Woman

Women and men read and discuss Aristotle and Kant, but it would not be wide of the mark to say that they read different books or read them in different ways. Men read books *about* themselves, women read books *about* men, about those capable of the highest moral virtues and the moral law, about those fitted by nature to mastery. And men read the books as themselves. How does a women read them? As a man. Gender informs and complicates both the reading and the writing of texts: in supposing the categorical imperative to be within her reach, for example, a woman reads herself as a man. And when she reads Kant's words about women, a woman is apt to think that he is not talking about her. *She* is not a woman if that is what women are. Familiar strategies of reading turn on the notion that reading is saying silently to oneself the authors' words, and when the author is a man and says "we," the woman reader leaves her gender aside and says "we" too.

There are different strategies of reading, however, and they tend to engender different stories. One can foreground what a certain blindness has put into the background. One can deny the claim that Kant was just being silly when he said what he said about women. One can take what an author says about the sexes to be as important for the whole of his thought as what he says about anything else. One can read as a woman, confronting the fact that Kant *is* talking about her and that *this* is what he says. His language shuts her out. Excluded from the moral, a woman is excluded from the mastery of both herself and the merely natural in her, for this is what morality is. Excluded from mastery, she is excluded from the master's language, from God's language, where language is patriarchal insofar as it regards authors as fathers, begetters of meanings, and tries to assure the legitimacy of meaning by prohibiting illegitimate interpretations. Neither the language nor the morality of patriarchy is hers, for she is not a father.

Excluded from morality, from mastery, from language, is she exempt from them and free to find her own new way to act, to speak, to write? Or should she take the second place, the place in the shadows cast by the natural light of reason in its practical use, assigned her by those who claim women incapable of ruling reason and deep understanding? But the voice that puts her in the second place is not hers. Should she claim the first place, claim the right to reason, claim to be a patriarch? But she is not a patriarch: she can at best imitate one. And here lies a way to cheat, trick, evade, avoid mastery by the master's language: the woman like an actor says words and makes moves that are not hers; speaking and acting the only languages there are, the ones she was born into, she nonetheless *remains elsewhere*. The trickery is necessary because if she speaks a tongue that is utterly new she cannot be heard and if she speaks the father tongue she complies with its exclusion of her.

To play with mimesis is . . . for a woman to resubmit herself . . . to ideas—notably about her—elaborated in and through a masculine logic, but to "bring out" by an effect of playful repetition what was to remain hidden: the recovery of *a possible operation of the feminine in language*. It is also to unveil the fact that if women mime so well they are not simply reabsorbed in this function. They also *remain elsewhere*. (Emphases added) (Irigaray 1985, 76)

What might be the operation of the feminine in language? Kant's feminine works where words charm and seduce, bewitch and fascinate other words and where, finally, language compels its users not by reason but "by a secret magic with which she makes our passion inclined to judgments favorable to her" (Kant 76). Aristotle's female is there in the materiality of language, in signifiers, material words in thrall not now to transcendental signifieds, to meanings of a different stuff from words that mean, but to other material words.

INNOVATING STRANGERS

Socrates

Plato's *Apology* suggests that estrangement from the languages of the tribe is a necessary condition for birthing the new. Socrates has spent the years since he heard the oracle's message introducing new gods to the Athenians—the forms and the soul that can know them—and is now on trial for trying to replace tradition's gods. He begins his defense by asking that he be regarded as a stranger: "For I am more than seventy years of age, and appearing now for the first time in a court of law, I am quite a stranger to the language of the place; and therefore I would have you regard me as if I were really a stranger, whom you would excuse if he spoke in his native tongue, and after the fashion of his country" (Plato 401). A stranger to the language, he will speak the tongue native to another place, not to Athens. Two languages, then, one a mirror of the other; and in the mirror world that is the *Apology* everything changes into its opposite and back again. Reversal rules. Socrates corrupts *and* benefits the young; the state helps *and* harms itself in killing Socrates; the state inflicts the greatest evil upon Socrates *and* harms him not at all; Socrates makes the young worse *although* no one can make another person worse; he both issues in the new *and* upholds the old.

Think now of women's exile from the canonical ethics of the moral realm and the subsequent need for a different ethics through which to work and worry Socrates' questions about rights and wrongs, about how to live and what to be. Exile is itself a moral relation, for it involves a stripping away or refusing of rights, where a right is an entitlement, a license to exercise a designated power. To be in exile is to be outside the jurisdiction of the power from which one is exiled: in exercising the right to exclude, the exiling agent forgoes all other rights over the exile, and in exercising the right to exclude oneself, one forgoes all claims against the place one has left. The question of the ground of any institution's right to exclude is not ready of answer because it is precisely by acts of exclusion that institutions are constituted, classifications are made, sounds signify, intelligibility is won. These inaugurating exclusions themselves cannot then be authorized within any of the instituted systems of intelligibility.

Only something beyond the pale of the constituted, classified, significant, intelligible can be invoked as the source of the right to put things in their proper places. Call what is beyond the pale "God," God the father, author of everything, and all fathers will henceforth be in the image of the divine patriarch, God, who rank orders all of creation, and all authorizing, originating, lawmaking power will be an image of the power of God. On this account all power is patriarchal and hierarchical, where the hierarchy is one of kinds: women are inferior to men on the grand scale, blacks to whites, slaves to masters, the slow to the swift, bronze to gold, and so on. To reject hierarchies, then, is not to hold that no comparative evaluations may legitimately be made but to hold that an individual does not count as inferior or superior simply by virtue of belonging to a certain so-called natural kind.

What would another ethics, an ethics in which women are counted and have a voice, look like? The way Socrates handles the charge about the gods breathes the hint of an answer to the question about how a woman, excluded from morality, from mastery, from language, might find a new way to act, to speak, to write. To do so it is at least necessary not to try to name the new. Socrates neither acknowledges that he replaces the storied gods of Athens with other divine things nor names the replacements. How could he name them in the same language? The sense of "divine" has shifted utterly. Socrates enters the discourse of the ordinary Athenian only to turn it on its head: he tricks, avoids, evades the accusers' questions; questions couched in the language of Athens are answered in the different language of the man who warned his audience that he was a stranger to its language. There is little communication between natives and strangers, and in effecting a profound dislocation between the languages, in playing with mimesis, Socrates enacts the dislocation that occurs when one *reads as a woman* the words that women are not moral, not rational, not human. Reading these words, one need not be co-opted by them: one can do as Socrates did and remain elsewhere.

Descartes

There is in Descartes, as in Socrates, a *refusal to inherit* the beliefs and values of the past, and there is in Descartes opposition between the mind that he is and the body he inhabits, between natural believer and formal doubter, as there is in Socrates between the language of Athens, which he must speak in order to be heard at all, and the language of the gods, the guides, the sages, the oracles that speak through him, which the Athenians do not understand. Descartes wants to inherit nothing, no beliefs, from the past, lest they turn out to be false, but finds it difficult in the extreme not insensibly to slip back into the old beliefs, to vacillate between habitual acceptance and the effort to suspend belief. During the empty time when he has managed to shake himself free from inherited beliefs and has not yet refined a mechanism for generating new ones, he is nowhere, at sea, lost in a dream: "I am like a slave who, enjoying an imaginary liberty during sleep, begins to suspect that this liberty is only a dream; he fears to wake up and conspires with his pleasant illusions to retain them longer. . . . I feel as though I were suddenly thrown into deep water, being so disconcerted that I can neither plant my feet on the bottom nor swim on the surface" (Descartes 22-23). He finds it difficult but not impossible to refuse to inherit the beliefs of his time, and the purity and strength of his desire for a set of beliefs not vulnerable to what the future will discover, in short, not vulnerable to time, works to allay the difficulty of refusing.

Because it is difficult to refuse to inherit the language into which they were born, to refuse its accents, its emphases, because it is difficult to negotiate the necessary awkwardness that threatens to disable the feminist critic at the start as she balances one foot on the conceptual map and the other in the margins, women may refuse to locate themselves on the map. But it is not impossible to negotiate the awkwardness. The purity and strength of their desire to be something in their own right, to have their own jurisdiction, enables them to play the deadly serious game of conceptual remapping, deadly because victory in the game spells defeat for the maps by which they steer and because once they begin to play they can neither trust the maps they have nor stop the play.[3]

Notes

One portion of this paper appeared in the American Philosophical Association, *Newsletter on Feminism and Philosophy: Feminism and Aesthetics* 89, no. 3 (Spring, 1990), under the title "Beautiful Women, Dutiful Men," and another appeared in *The Women's Anthology of St. John's College* (Annapolis: St. John's College, 1990) under the title "Reading as a Woman."

1. Kant, *Observations on the Feeling of the Beautiful and Sublime*, trans. John T. Goldthwait (Berkeley: University of California Press, 1960). Page references to this work are made in the body of the paper.

2. From Aristotle, *On the Generation of Animals*, trans. A. L. Peck (Cambridge, MA: Harvard University Press, 1942), quoted in Mary Briody Mahowald, *Philosophy of Woman* (Indianapolis: Hackett Publishing Company, 1978).

3. This paper was read at a Philosophy and Literature Colloquium at the Graduate Center of the City University of New York on January 7, 1988, in reply to a paper by Professor Jane Marcus, whom I wish to thank for raising the questions treated here.

References

Descartes, Rene. *Meditations on first philosophy*. Laurence J. Lafleur, trans. Indianapolis: Bobbs-Merrill, 1960.

Irigaray, Luce. 1985. *This sex which is not one*. Catherine Porter, trans. Ithaca: Cornell University Press.

Kant, Immanuel. *Observations on the feeling of the beautiful and sublime*. John T. Goldthwait, trans. Berkeley: University of California Press, 1960.

Mahowald, Mary Briody. 1978. *Philosophy of woman*. Indianapolis: Hackett Publishing Company.

Plato. "Apology." In *The dialogues of Plato*. vol. 1. B. Jowett, trans. New York: Random House, 401-27, 1937.

THIRTEEN

Discipline and Silence

Women and Imagination in Kant's Theory of Taste

JANE KNELLER

*In what follows I want to sketch out some similarities between Kant's charac-
terization of taste and his characterization of properly feminine women. I will argue
that these similarities suggest that Kant's theory of taste, like his account of femininity,
is steeped in what might be labeled a "masculinist" view of human experience, that
is, in a view that limits the importance to that experience of anything closely tied to
sensibility, including the imagination. I argue that Kant's account of taste may
therefore be of questionable value in attempting to find close links between his
aesthetic theory and his moral theory, where such attempts are seen as ways of
rescuing Kant's moral theory from charges of arid formalism and reintroducing the
role of feeling into morality.[1] I will conclude by suggesting that an aspect of his
aesthetic theory that is more promising in this regard is his account of the powerful
"reformative" imagination that may be found in the morally "interested" manifestations of artistic production and reception.*

Typically, Kant scholars have politely ignored Kant's derogatory remarks about
women, with the implicit understanding that they are inessential to the core of his
philosophy and are merely historical appendages to an otherwise humane philosophy.[2] Nor are students of Kant's aesthetic theory likely to turn immediately to his
scattered remarks about women in order to elucidate difficult questions raised by
Kant's attempt to deduce the validity of judgments of taste. Nevertheless, there are
interesting and, I believe, significant connections between Kant's views on women
and his theory of taste that need to be considered by anyone interested in Kant's
theory of the beautiful for its own sake or for the sake of the contemporary theories
that owe so much to it.[3] These connections suggest that Kant's theory of taste, like
his account of the nature of women, is not without personal and historical bias.
Moreover, the deep affinities between Kant's influential account of taste and of
"feminine qualities" suggest that his views on women may not, after all, be

completely extra-theoretical, and that they thus merit serious consideration and critique.[4]

In what follows I will discuss three similarities between taste and femininity in Kant's philosophy: (1) both are seen as means to further culture and hence civilization; (2) both are set up as socially organized and imposed practices ("disciplines") that involve a subtle form of self-perpetuating subordination; and (3) both are thereby effectively "silenced" as voices that could determine moral and social experience.

FEMININITY AND TASTE AS CIVILIZING INFLUENCES

The most striking similarity between Kant's account of femininity and that of taste is that both share the common aim of furthering human culture. As the production in a rational being of "an aptitude for purposes generally," Kant says that culture in human beings is characterized by "the more refined feelings" of *sociability* (a "fitness and propensity" for society), and by decorum.[5] In civil society,[6] Kant tells us, women are nature's instruments of culture:

> [Nature] made woman man's ruler through her modesty and her eloquence in speech and expression. It made her precociously shrewd in claiming gentle and courteous treatment by the male, so that he finds himself imperceptibly fettered by a child through his own generosity and led by it, if not to morality itself, at least to its clothing, the cultivated propriety that is the preparatory training for morality and its recommendation. (*Anthro.* 306)

Similarly, taste also leads to culture by cloaking human activity in the semblance of morality:

> Ideal taste has a tendency to promote morality in an external way. Making a man (*Mensch*) well-mannered as a social being falls short of forming a *morally good* man, but it still prepares him for it by the effort he makes, in society, to please others (to make them love or admire him). (*Anthro.* 244).[7]

Feminine ways ("Weiblichkeiten") and taste thus both exhibit the ability to promote culture and "prepare" men for morality without being *necessarily* connected to morality. In the case of women, Kant's claim that feminine ways are not necessarily moral ones may be understood as an expression of the prevailing eighteenth-century view that the female sex is naturally weaker in rational capacity. The feeble connection of *taste* with morality is, I believe, largely due to Kant's account of judgments of taste as being "free" of all interest. It is this "disinterested" attitude that distinguishes judgments of taste from what Kant calls judgments of sense, that is, from reports of the immediate and unreflective sensuous pleasure we may take in an object.[8] Kant introduces this concept of reflective taste in the first two introductions to the third *Critique* and at the end of the first moment, where he defines taste as "the faculty of judging of an object or a method of representing it by an entirely disinterested satisfaction. The object of such satisfaction is called beautiful."[9]

Since taste, for Kant, is not directly concerned with empirical or moral truth, but only with "outward appearance," i.e., with the formal properties of an object, it may at best provide the *garb* of morality in the form of manners, politeness, and propriety, but it is no guarantee of genuine moral virtue:

> To show taste in our conduct (or in judging other people's conduct) is very different from expressing our moral way of thinking. For this contains a command and gives rise to a need, whereas moral taste only plays with the objects of liking without committing itself to any of them. (CJ 210)

Kant goes on (CJ 211) to define taste as the ability to judge in this "playful" and morally uncommitted way, and his deduction of taste depends upon this condition.[10] The object of the judgment of taste (the beautiful) is thus carefully segregated from its counterpart (the morally good) in moral judgment. At best, the former is said to be capable of providing a "transition" to "habitual moral interest" (CJ 354), but how this passage from taste to morality takes place remains obscure in Kant's aesthetics. Kant attempts to explain the "transition" in terms of beauty's capacity to serve as a symbol of morality, inasmuch as the beautiful is in several respects *analogous* to the morally good (CJ 353-54). At the very end of the "Critique of Aesthetic Judgment" Kant vaguely asserts that taste is the ability to judge "by means of a certain analogy" ("*einer gewissen Analogie*") about the way moral ideas are made sensible, but for Kant, the actual task of making moral ideas sensible is a function of "Geist," i.e., of genius and the creative imagination, and not, as will be argued, of the sort of imagination to be found in taste.[11]

Whatever their value with respect to Kant's account of the validity of judgments of taste, his views on the relationship of taste to morality are worth comparing with his views on the relationship of femininity and morality. If taste is supposed somehow to prepare the way to morality, women lead men to morality, or its trappings, in a way that is left similarly vague, even mysterious: "Nature's foresight put more art into the make-up of the female than of the male"; she "does not betray her secrets," but nevertheless leads the man "imperceptibly fettered" to "cultivated propriety," the "clothing" of morality (*Anthro.* 303-306).[12] Despite Kant's assurances that they are necessary to the development of culture, taste and femininity are both systematically contrasted with and ultimately subordinated to individual morality and masculinity, respectively. The reason for this, it seems, is that for Kant neither taste nor femininity are principled enough to order and hence shape experience. Kant contrasts the mere play of taste with the legitimate authority of the moral law (CJ 210), just as he argues that women, who, like children, beguile and cajole in order to get men to do their bidding, have no authority to shape the decisions and actions that constitute the "objective" realm of public experience. In his discussion of timidity and fortitude in the *Anthropology* it is men, in contrast to women (and Native Americans), whose actions in the face of danger are courageous, i.e., ruled by principle (258).[13] Kant's women are creatures of inclination (*Anthro.* 309), concerned with outward appearance (*Anthro.* 308).

What femininity and taste can do, at their best, is to make human experience more polite and decorous. They do not, however, constitute part of the very structure of moral experience. That is to say, for Kant, a world without "feminine" and tasteful human beings would not necessarily be a world without morals.

The nonconstitutive status that Kant assigns to taste and femininity vis-à-vis morality can be explained in part by his ambivalence about the desirability of culture itself. In the same passage where he argues that the fine arts and the sciences "make man, not indeed morally [sittlich] better for society, but still civilized [gesittet] for it," he admits that highly refined taste brings with it "a preponderance of evils" by creating insatiable desires in human beings (CJ 433). He makes an interesting parallel remark in his discussion of the sexes:

> When refined luxury has reached a high level, a wife shows herself virtuous only under constraint and makes no secret of her wish that she were a man, so that she could give her inclinations wider scope and freer play. (Anthro. 307)

Thus, refinement is not unconditionally good, but requires in addition the *discipline* of the inclinations (CJ 433). Taste and femininity contribute to culture only when they exhibit discipline and restraint.

DISCIPLINING THE IMAGINATION AND DISCIPLINING WOMEN

Kant's unwillingness to give a constitutive role to taste or women in the determination of the moral realm no doubt has its deepest root in his profound distrust of sensibility.[14] The human being's "propensity to the senses" is a "tyranny" that unlawfully interferes with the sovereign rule of reason (CJ 433). Both taste and femininity for him are "aesthetic," that is, both involve the sensuous in the form of inclination (in the feminine) and feeling (in taste).

In the case of femininity, the connection to sensibility is biological. Due to their role in reproduction, women are more tied to the physical than are men. In order to best guarantee the preservation of the species, Kant argues, nature implanted in women "fear in the face of *physical* harm and timidity in the face of physical dangers" (Anthro. 306). Whereas men, as was seen, manifest their independence from the realm of the senses via the "rational" virtue of courage, women at their best display the feminine virtue of patience—they try to lessen pain by getting used to it (Anthro. 256-57). Thus, for Kant, women are thoroughly "aesthetic" in their submission to pain and fear of physical harm.

Taste *also* involves sensibility insofar as it requires imagination, which for Kant mediates between sensibility and the understanding and whose product is "always in itself sensible."[15] Taste requires a special relation between imagination and understanding, a relation of what Kant calls "free play," which gives rise to a *feeling* that is universally communicable.[16] No matter how "disinterested," taste is never abstract but is always *aesthetic*, that is, *felt*.

Of course, just because imagination and women are closely linked with sensibility in Kant's philosophy does not mean that for Kant they are unimportant or even peripheral to the economy of his system. Among its many functions in human experience, imagination is absolutely essential to cognition insofar as it must mediate between what is given in sensation and the understanding. And, apart from their "feminine" role in society, women are required for the preservation of the species. In this way, both imagination and the female sex are necessary components of human experience. But for Kant, we are *human* animals only insofar as inclination is controlled by the "higher cognitive faculties." Taste and femininity, for Kant, far from being "original," are the results of a certain kind of control of imagination and control of the female, respectively. That is, they are the result of the disciplining of the imagination and the female sex by "higher" rational powers. It is for this reason that Kant claims that both taste and femininity only arise in society,[17] where such discipline can be methodically instituted.

It is therefore no surprise that Kant's account of socially proper marital relations is extremely well suited to characterizing the relationship between imagination and understanding that gives rise to taste:

> Who, then, should have supreme command in the household? . . . I would say, in the language of gallantry (but not without truth): the women should *reign* (*herrschen*) and the man *govern* (*regieren*); for inclination reigns and understanding governs. The husband's behavior must show that his wife's welfare is the thing closest to his heart. But since the man must know best how his affairs stand and how far he can go, he will be like a minister to his monarch who thinks only of amusement . . . so that the monarch can do all that he wills, but on one condition: that his minister lets him know what his will is. (*Anthro.* 309-10)

It may be objected that such a comparison is unfair, since the relation of "free play" between understanding and the imagination in judgments of taste is a relation of equals, bearing little resemblance to the subtle oppression of the wife by her husband in Kant's ideal marriage. The validity of judgments of taste depends upon the relationship between the understanding and the imagination in which these two faculties work together in the harmonious way required "for cognition in general," where "we need imagination to combine the manifold of intuition, and understanding to provide the unity of the concept uniting the presentations" (*CJ* 217-18). But in the judgment of taste, cognition, i.e., the actual application of a concept to the manifold under reflection, is waived in favor of reflection simply upon the feeling that the play of the imagination and the understanding produce in the subject when they harmonize in this way. But closer scrutiny of the "free" play of the imagination with the understanding reveals that in judgments of taste the imagination is far from free. The relationship itself "belongs to cognition in general" ("*zum Erkenntnis gehört*"), Kant says (*CJ* 217), and cognition is under the sovereign rule of the understanding. Imagination is not *absolutely* free, but rather is "freely lawful,"[18] with the understanding setting its limits:

> And yet to say that the *imagination* is *free* and yet *lawful of itself*, i.e., that it carries autonomy with it, is a contradiction. The understanding alone gives the law. (*CJ* 241)

  It is fairly clear, then, where the real freedom, or at least the real control, lies in the relation between imagination and understanding in the judgment of taste. As in any harmonious marriage, Kant believes, "it is not enough for two people to associate as they please; one party must be *subject* to the other and, reciprocally, one must be the *superior* of the other in some way, in order to be able to rule (*beherrschen*) and govern (*regieren*) him" (*Anthro.* 303). In judgments of taste the imagination resembles nothing so much as the docile wife of Kant's proper marriage: it exhibits the appearance of freedom (it "reigns"), but it is the understanding that sets the boundaries, or "governs" the imagination's play.

  So just as women need to be disciplined by being "feminized," imagination for Kant must be disciplined if it is to serve nature's purpose and become "tasteful." At section 50 of the *Critique of Judgment* Kant identifies genius with the imagination and taste with judgment, and continues:

> Taste, like the power of judgment in general, consists in disciplining (or training) genius. It severely clips its wings, and makes it civilized, or polished; but at the same time it gives it guidance as to how far and over what it may spread while still remaining purposive. (188)

Discipline, as we saw, is essential to culture. Taste and femininity, as social practices that uphold and perpetuate culture, are in this sense "disciplines." But taste and femininity are complex social phenomena, embracing both sensuous and intellectual aspects of "human nature." In both, on Kant's account, a tension exists between sense (inclination or feeling) and understanding that is resolved by the submission of the former to the governance of the latter. And in both cases this subordination is veiled by the *apparent* autonomy of inclination or feeling. These similarities in the relationships that define taste and femininity in Kant's philosophy suggest that both serve as theoretical constructs for the resolution of a power struggle in which unfettered imagination and unfettered "womanhood" are domesticated by a "masculine" understanding.[19]

SILENCING THE IMAGINATION
AND SILENCING WOMEN

It may also be objected that this account of femininity and taste as in essence an oppressive means of socializing women and the human imagination neglects the high value Kant attaches to sociability in his philosophy. Given that, it may be argued, the roles of taste and femininity are for Kant much more positive and important than I have made them out to be. Sociability, he says, combines the qualities of "the universal feeling of sympathy, and the ability to engage universally in very intimate communication," and it "distinguishes [our humanity] from the limitation of animals" (*CJ* 355). In "Speculative Beginning of Human History," Kant argues that taste in the form of decency, "as the proper foundation of all true sociability—gave the first hint of man's formation into a moral creature," and he traces the development of this sort of taste to its origins in sexual instinct.[20] Thus it may be argued that sociability includes taste and femininity, and hence, since morality and sociability are genetically related for Kant, so too are morality and the "disciplines" of taste and femininity.

But even if this approach could be made to square with other, more important aspects of Kant's moral theory,[21] it is important to bear in mind the forms that sociability in fact takes on for Kant in the "civilized" society. In the case of women they are infamous. Given their association with inclination, women are not *as* rational as men. They are immature (*unmündig*) and hence dependent creatures who require male guardianship. As we saw, Kant allows women a modicum of "free play" within the domestic realm. But the price for this recreation is legal dependency. A woman, Kant says, should have no voice outside the domestic realm, either in defending her civil rights (men should do it for her) or in the shaping of public policy (*Anthro*. 209).

Kant's model woman, of course, is not a household *servant* (although there are many resemblances). She is allowed to take part in social gatherings with men, and, Kant admits, she is even quite glib (*Anthro*. 209). Her "eloquence in speech and expression," however, is primarily directed toward subtly influencing men to fulfill her inclinations, or perhaps, at the skillful manipulation of a dinner conversation (*Anthro*. 278n). Thus the sociability furthered by properly "feminine" women perpetuates these women's role as ornaments of social life and hinders their development into genuine creators of that life.

If we look at the role of the imagination in Kant's judgment of taste, we find a similar process of "domestication," here of the imagination by the understanding. Just as for Kant it was unthinkable that women could possibly enter the public sphere without wreaking havoc, it us unthinkable for him that imagination could create anything of value without the constraints of the understanding:

> it is necessary that the imagination in its freedom be commensurate with the lawfulness of the understanding. For if the imagination is left in lawless freedom, all its riches produce nothing but nonsense, and it is judgment [taste] that adapts the imagination to the understanding. (*CJ* 319)

Judgments of taste have the distinction of being universally communicable, and hence of being able to make claims to the agreement of others. And taste's object, the beautiful, may serve to symbolize, but not instantiate, the good. But this sort of validity and symbolic value in fact amounts to little more than a right to sit at table with cognition and morality. Taste is "universally communicable" only insofar as it is silent on these serious topics, and the beautiful is after all only a symbol, not a schema, of the morally good. Imagination in Kant's theory of taste is indeed given a voice, but only to speak of the formal aspects of cognitive and moral experience, not the substance of that experience.

Given Kant's account of the properly feminine woman and the properly disciplined, "tasteful" imagination, it is understandable that he bans both from entering the moral and political realm. Children and "wild things" are not in a position to responsibly shape moral and political reality, and I, no less than Kant, would hate to see *his* ideal women in positions of power and responsibility. But this is simply to say what one would hope is obvious, namely that the notion of femininity at work in his philosophy is severely misguided.

What may not be so obvious, and what I hope to have shown, is that the close and interesting connections between Kant's notion of femininity and his account of taste force similar serious questions about the value to moral theory of the highly domesticated imagination of Kant's theory of taste. Disengaged aesthetic observation is still very much a part of the standard experience of art, and, for that matter, of nature. The problem with "disinterested" taste, however, is precisely the problem of Kant's account of femininity. A potentially very important contributor to social experience, the imagination, is relegated to a limited sphere of influence and effectively silenced in the moral realm. That is to say, the imagination of taste may adorn, but not create, social reality.

REFORMATIVE IMAGINATION
AND THE IDEAL OF BEAUTY

Kant's account of taste precludes the possibility that the sort of imagination involved in judgments about beauty could itself be creative, that is, productive of visions of genuine alternatives to the status quo, whether in art or in society as a whole. Especially when seen in light of the parallels to his views on femininity, Kant's theory of taste appears to be far too restrictive to allow human experience of the beautiful to also determine the moral realm. Granted, as was already mentioned, in section 59 of the third *Critique*, entitled "On Beauty as the Symbol of Morality," Kant argues that there are important analogies between experience of the beautiful and of the moral such that the beautiful might well serve as a preliminary form of moral education (CJ 230). He also suggests that the activity of imagination in judgments of beauty may allow us to draw analogies to morality through symbols (CJ 227), where symbols are defined as intuitive presentations (of the imagination) that exhibit the object by analogy to another "entirely different object." They are carefully distinguished from schemata inasmuch as they proceed by "mere analogy," whereas schemata exhibit their concepts in *a priori* but nonetheless sensible form (CJ 227n). This is just to say, however, that imaginative symbols make no "real" connection with sensibility. Imagination may *help* us "make the transition from sensible charm to a habitual moral interest without making too violent a leap" (CJ 230), but morality does not *require* imagination as a bridge to sensibility.

However, Kant's aesthetic theory involves a great deal more than just a theory of taste. In section 17 of the *Critique of Judgment*, Kant argues for the possibility of exhibiting the rational idea of humanity "as an aesthetic idea fully *in concreto* in a model image" (CJ 81). He maintains that it is possible for the imagination to exhibit an idea of reason in a concrete image:

> Hence that archetype of taste, which does indeed rest on reason's indeterminate idea of a maximum, but which still can be presented not through concepts but only in an individual exhibition [*Darstellung*], may more appropriately be called the ideal of the beautiful. (CJ 80)

It is important to recognize that the ideal of beauty is not a symbol but rather the concrete "model" of "that which has the purpose of its existence within itself," or in other words, of a self-determining being—a human being (81). In the last paragraph of this section he argues unequivocally for the possibility of "the visible expression of moral ideas" through imagination, in a manner that, while "taken only from experience," nevertheless transforms that experience:

> these moral ideas must be connected, in the idea of the highest purposiveness, with everything that our reason links with the morally good: goodness of soul, or purity, fortitude, or serenity, *etc.*; and in order for this connection to be made visible; as it were, in bodily expression (as an effect of what is inward), pure ideas of reason must be united with a very strong imagination in someone who seeks so much as to judge, let alone exhibit, it. (CJ 84)

Such a presentation is not a symbol of morality, since it is not the re-application of a rule appropriate to one object to an entirely different object, as in Kant's example of the handmill that symbolizes the state (CJ 227). In the case of the ideal of beauty, a single "object," the human being that for Kant is essentially dual-natured, is artistically presented or "modeled" as the physical embodiment of its own moral (nonphysical) character. Thus in this section Kant suggests that although imagination may not be able to schematize morality, i.e., to realize it in the physical world, it can nevertheless do more than simply "play" in a disinterested way with objects of sense. Judgment according to an *ideal* of beauty is no longer a "mere judgment of taste" (236). Here there is no talk of the rule of the understanding or of the limitation of imaginative freedom to the conditions of cognition in general. Judgments involving this sort of visionary imagination are connected with a moral interest and are rather the presentation of the *possibility* of the realization of moral ideas in model form.

It seems to me that this somewhat obscure section of the third *Critique* is of genuine significance to Kant's moral theory. The ability to realize the possibility of a schematized morality that is of a moral world existing in nature is, according to Kant himself, a necessary condition of the moral law's validity. In the *Critique of Practical Reason* Kant claims that the moral law requires human beings to "further the highest good" (113-14), where the "highest good" (*summum bonum*) means "happiness in exact proportion to morality" (111). He concludes that

> the impossibility of the highest good must prove the falsity of the moral law also. If, therefore, the highest good is impossible according to practical rules, then the moral law which commands that it be furthered must be fantastic, directed to empty imaginary ends, and consequently inherently false. (114)

In the second *Critique* Kant goes on to argue that we can only think the possibility of a genuinely moral world's existence if we postulate the existence of God and immortality. Section 17 of the *Critique of Judgment*, however, suggests that "imaginary ends" are by no means always "empty." Inasmuch as the ideal of beauty is an actual model image of a moral idea, it may serve to provide mere mortals with the vision they need to believe in the possibility of a moral idea (e.g., the highest good) being realized in the sensible world.[22]

Moreover, the importance of the ideal as an instrument of self-improvement is established already in the first *Critique*, where Kant defines the ideal as "the idea, not merely *in concreto*, but *in individuo*, that is, as an individual thing, determinable or even determined by the idea alone" (A568/B596). Kant claims that such ideals "have *practical* power (as regulative principles) and form the basis of the possible perfection of certain *actions*" (A569/B597).

Kant contrasts the ideas of virtue and complete human wisdom "in its purity" with the ideal of the "wise man of the stoics" who, though existing "only in thought" nevertheless "conforms" to the idea of wisdom and serves as the

archetype for the complete determination of the copy; and we have no other standard for our actions than the conduct of this divine man within, with which we compare and judge ourselves, and so *reform* ourselves, although we can never attain to the perfection thereby prescribed. (A569/B597; emphasis added)

Kant goes on to argue that these ideals, although without objective reality, are nevertheless *indispensable* to reason as standards against which to judge objects. Then, in a move directly contradicting his later position in section 17 of the third *Critique*, Kant denounces as "impracticable" and even "absurd and far from edifying" all attempts to "realize the ideal in an example, that is in the field of appearance, as, for instance, to depict the [character of the perfectly] wise man in a romance. . . ." Such attempts, he says, "cast suspicion on the good itself . . . by giving it the air of being a mere fiction" (A570/B598).

Kant holds that the ideal of reason is not a product of the imagination primarily because he believes that an aesthetic, i.e., merely felt, ideal can only be an "incommunicable shadowy image" (A570/B598). But as the "Critique of Aesthetic Judgment" shows, Kant was to change his mind about the possibility of universally communicable feelings. Moreover, as was seen, he argues in section 17 that it is precisely the artist and receiver in possession of "great imagination" who are capable of communicating the aesthetic ideal of human perfection.

Finally, and perhaps most importantly, in the third *Critique* it is the imagination which becomes the faculty of "re-form":

For the imagination ([in its role] as a productive power) is very mighty when it creates, as it were, another nature out of the material that actual nature gives it. . . . We may even restructure [*umbilden*] experience; and though in doing so we continue to follow analogical laws, yet we also follow principles which reside higher up, namely, in reason. . . . In this process we feel our freedom from the law of association . . . for although it is under that law that nature lends us material, yet we can process that material into something quite different, namely, into something that surpasses nature. (CJ 182)

Here again the imagination is not "productive" in the sense of creating schemata to fit concepts to sensible things. It cannot, that is, by itself create a morally restructured world. But through its capacity to model the real possibility of such ideas imagination can be "reformative": it makes the attempt to improve ourselves and our world appear "sensible."[23]

Notes

1. A noteworthy attempt to do so recently can be found in Paul Guyer (1990).

2. Mary Gregor's introduction to her translation of Kant's *Anthropology from a Pragmatic Point of View* (*Anthro.*) is a good case in point. When touching on his account of the sexes, she focuses on Kant's characterization of women as instruments of culture and civilization. She makes no allusion to the less positive aspects of his account of women's nature, which includes a particularly contemptuous view of women's scholarly abilities. (See Gregor 1974, xxiv.) To some extent I am following suit by not analyzing Kant's pre-critical piece "Observations on the Feeling of the Beautiful and the Sublime" in this paper. Although this piece contains a wealth of material for feminist criticism, and although it is clear that Kant still maintained his views on women to the very end of his life, my point is that Kant's *critical* aesthetic theory still raises systematic problems from a feminist perspective. I have therefore focused on comparing his account of taste as put forth in the *Critique of Judgment* and in his account of femininity in the *Anthropology*. Although the *Anthropology* lectures span a time embracing both pre-critical and critical periods in Kant's philosophy, there is nothing in the student lecture notes to indicate that Kant ever changed his views on women and femininity during this time.

3. I refer here primarily to aesthetic attitude theories, such as that of Bullough, and to formalist accounts of art.

4. For a more optimistic view of Kant's account of women, see Ursula Pia Jauch (1988).

5. Relevant texts here include *Critique of Judgment* (CJ 431 and also 296-97) and *Anthropology from a Pragmatic Point of View* (306).

6. Woman's femininity, her "proper nature," Kant says, is to be distinguished from the way she is when existing in a pre-civilized state: "In the crude state of nature we can no more recognize her proper nature than we can that of the crab apple and the wild pear, which reveal their diversity only when they are grafted or inoculated; for while civilization does not produce these feminine qualities, it allows them to develop and, under its favoring conditions, become discernible" (*Anthro.* 303).

7. This passage continues: "In this way we could call taste morality in one's outward appearance—though this expression, taken literally, contains a contradiction—because good breeding includes the look or bearing of moral goodness, and even a degree of it: namely, the tendency to put a value on even the semblance of moral goodness" (*Anthro.* 244). Thus Kant here seems to be suggesting that good breeding, and hence taste, contain or include moral goodness insofar as the propensity to value *apparent* moral goodness is itself a form of moral goodness.

8. Even here there may be more similarity than is at first obvious. As will be seen, there is a real sense in which the wife in Kant's ideal marriage may be said to be quite "disinterested" in moral considerations, i.e., she is unconcerned with moral "goods" such as honor, and is concerned more with outward appearance. A good example of this may be found in Kant's lectures on anthropology, where he cites the anecdote of Milton's disagreement with his wife over whether he should accept a certain government post as an example of the triumph of masculine moral virtue (honor) over feminine domestic virtue (social appearances) (*Anthro.* 308).

9. References to "taste" in this paper are to that "taste of reflection" defined by Kant in both introductions and in the summary definition of the first moment. In the second introduction to the *Critique of Judgment* Kant first introduces the concept of taste as "the faculty of judging by means of such a [universally shareable] pleasure." In the first introduction to the *Critique of Judgment* Kant's first reference to the notion of taste comes in the form of an announcement that "aesthetic reflective judgments will be analyzed hereafter under the name of judgments of taste" (1965, 239). At *Critique of Judgment* section 7 he refers somewhat misleadingly to "the taste of the tongue, the throat and the palate" or more generally the "taste of sense" (sections 7 and 8), distinguishing it from the "taste of reflection." Having pointed out what are by now two clearly different usages in his account, Kant continues to refer to judgments about the beautiful as judgments of taste, and to judgments about "the pleasant" as "judgments of sense" (although given that the latter involve no reflective activity they might better be called "reports" of sense [section 8]). And given that they involve no *a priori* principle, there certainly can be no *theory* of these sense reports. For Kant the latter are only called taste in a loose and popular sense and cannot serve as the subject of critique.

10. Cf. *CJ* 292ff, and see also Werner Pluhar's translator's introduction to *CJ* lxvff.

11. On Kant's account of taste, imagination is an *element* necessary to the operations of the faculty of taste but is not to be identified with it, nor does it play the same role that imagination plays in other judgments. Paul Guyer has argued that "Aesthetic as well as teleological judgment assist in this enterprise [moral practice] by offering both sensible representation of morality as well as opportunities for the cultivation of the moral feeling" (1990, 139-40). But it is not clear that the "connections between aesthetic judgment and the cultivation of moral feelings" are as "direct" as Guyer suggests (140), at least not where taste is concerned. The ability to render moral ideas sensible is certainly a very important function, and I have argued elsewhere that it is indeed a necessary condition of what Guyer calls moral "practice and comprehension." But the capacity for "sensible representation" of the moral is not that of the imagination in judgments of taste, but of the productive imagination in "genius" or "Geist," which *latter*, for Kant, is the "ability to exhibit aesthetic ideas" (*CJ* 313-14). At *Critique of Judgment* section 48 (313) Kant explicitly states that "Taste is merely an ability to judge, not to produce." (Cf. also *CJ* sec. 60, 356: "taste is basically an ability to judge the [way in which] moral ideas are made sensible . . .") ("Da aber der Geschmack im Grunde ein Beurteilungsvermögen der Versinnlichung sittlicher Ideen . . . ist . . ."). And at section 50, Kant contrasts taste identified as judgment, on the one hand, and genius identified with imagination, on the other, arguing that taste must discipline genius (319).

12. As mentioned above (n. 7), Kant does suggest that "cultivation" is important because even the desire to appear to be moral is to a degree itself moral (*Anthro.* 244). Still, given his statement in the *Critique of Judgment* that "moral taste" in the form of manners, politeness, or propriety is not *committed* to the morally good, but only plays with it, it is hard to see how moral taste in general, and feminine social decorum in particular, can be a component of genuine morality.

13. This is not an unimportant point, given that for Kant courage and industry are conditions of thinking for oneself—of autonomous thought. Cf. Kant, "What Is Enlightenment?" In *Foundations of the Metaphysics of Morals*, trans. Lewis White Beck (Indianapolis: Bobbs-Merrill: 1959), 85-92: "Laziness and cowardice are the reasons why such a vast majority of people . . . happily remain immature all their lives" (My translation) ("Faulheit und Feigheit sind die Ursachen, warum ein so großer Theil der Menschen . . . gerne zeitlebens unmündig bleiben . . .").

14. Hartmut and Gernot Böhme (1985, 387-423) and Robin Schott (1988, ch. 7 and ch. 8) both suggest that this suspicion may best be seen as a socially and historically grounded, but nevertheless pathological, aversion to the body, and fear of sickness.

15. *Critique of Pure Reason*, trans. Norman Kemp Smith (New York: St. Martin's Press, 1965), A124.

16. *Critique of Judgment*, 62 (218).

17. *Anthropology from a Pragmatic Point of View*, 303-304; *Critique of Judgment*, 205n, 296-97, and note 6, above.

18. Kant speaks of the *"freie Gesetzmäßigkeit der Einbildungskraft"* ("free lawfulness of the imagination") (1987, 240).

19. There may be important differences between the relationships of imagination to the understanding, on the one hand, and to reason, on the other. Reason may provide the rational idea of the highest social good, as well as of individual virtue, for imagination to "model" in the form of an aesthetic idea. See Kneller (forthcoming), and also Kathleen M. Wheeler (1989, 42-56), on the occasional synonymy of reason and imagination.

20. Kant, *Perpetual Peace and Other Essays*, 113.

21. There are major problems with making Kant's accounts of the progressive moral development of the human species square with central aspects of his moral theory, especially with his view that morality is an individual affair. See Paul Stern (1986).

22. Rudolf Makkreel argues for the thesis that Kant's account of aesthetic ideas and the ideal of beauty serve "interpretive functions" which, as part of what he calls "reflective interpretation," "enrich and specify" our initial understanding (of a given whole) (1990, 5). He also argues that these "ideas of the imagination" involve "the coordination of contingency and necessity" (113), which lends support to the argument that the creative aesthetic imagination, if not the imagination of taste, could represent the possibility of a moral world where happiness and virtue coincide.

23. I would like to thank Hilde Hein and Carolyn Korsmeyer for their helpful suggestions on an earlier version of this paper, and also Karl Ameriks, Sally Sedgwick, and Thomas Wartenberg for helpful comments on the first section.

References

Böhme, Hartmut, and Gernot Böhme. 1985. *Das Andere der Vernunft: Zur Entwicklung von Rationalitätsstrukturen am Beispiel Kants*. Frankfurt am Main: Suhrkamp.

Guyer, Paul. 1990. Feeling and freedom: Kant on aesthetics and morality. *Journal of Aesthetics and Art Criticism* 48: 2 (Spring).

Jauch, Ursula Pia. 1988. *Immanuel Kant zur Geschlechterdifferenz*. Auflklärische Vorurteilskritik und bürgerliche Geschlechtervormundschaft. Vienna: Passagen Verlag.

Kant, Immanuel. 1974. *Anthropology from a pragmatic point of view*. Mary Gregor, trans. The Hague: Martinus Nijhof (Akademie edition, vol. VII).

Kant, Immanuel. 1987. *Critique of judgment*. Werner S. Pluhar, trans. Indianapolis: Hackett (Ak V).

Kant, Immanuel. 1956. *Critique of practical reason*. Lewis White Beck, trans. New York: Liberal Arts Press.

Kant, Immanuel. 1965. *Critique of pure reason*. Norman Kemp Smith, trans. New York: St. Martin's Press (Ak IV, V).

Kant, Immanuel. 1965. *First introduction to the critique of judgment*. James Haden, trans. Indianapolis: Bobbs-Merrill (Ak XX).

Kant, Immanuel. 1983. Speculative beginning of human history. In *Perpetual peace and other essays*. Ted Humphrey, trans. Indianapolis: Hackett (Ak VIII).

Kant, Immanuel. 1959. What is enlightenment? In *Foundations of the metaphysics of morals and what is enlightenment?* Lewis White Beck, trans. Indianapolis: Bobbs-Merrill (Ak VIII).

Kneller, Jane. Forthcoming. Imagination and the possibility of moral reform in the critique of aesthetic judgment. *Proceedings of the 7th International Kant Society*.

Makkreel, Rudolf. 1990. *Imagination and interpretation in Kant*. Chicago: University of
    Chicago Press.
Schott, Robin. 1988. *Cognition and eros*. Boston: Beacon Press.
Stern, Paul. 1986. The problem of history and temporality in Kantian ethics. *Review of
    Metaphysics* 39: 505-45.
Wheeler, Kathleen M. 1989. Kant and romanticism. *Philosophy and Literature* 13: 42-56.

FOURTEEN

Aestheticism, Feminism, and the Dynamics of Reversal

AMY NEWMAN

Postmodern aestheticism is defined as a way of thinking that privileges the art of continual reversal. The dynamics of reversal operate according to a theoretical model that, historically speaking, has been the vehicle for blatantly masculinist ideologies. This creates problems for feminist thinking that would appropriate the postmodern conception of the subjectivity of the artist or the aestheticist dissolution of the distinction between life and art.

Contemporary aestheticism advocates the dissolution of the distinction between art and life. It is "an attempt to expand the aesthetic to embrace the whole of reality . . . a tendency to see 'art' or 'language' or 'discourse' or 'text' as constituting the primary realm of human experience" (Megill 1985, 2). As with all metatheories, aestheticism has a hidden agenda, and it is this agenda that I want to explore. I shall do this by analyzing some apparent points of conjunction between postmodern aestheticism and some trends in recent feminist thinking, particularly trends that emphasize the lives of women as constituting a primary realm of human experience and focus upon the transformational potential of this experience. As a "transformational politics," contemporary feminism has as its focus the creation of "new ways of viewing the world" (Bunch 1987, 302-303). This transformation is to be accomplished not only through embracing the vast diversity of methods that women know for subverting and replacing the text that is phallocentric reality, but also through the creation of new kinds of texts.[1] Many feminists contend that this creative project should privilege the perspectives of marginalized women, especially non-Western women and women of color. This latter emphasis is based upon a recognition of the extent to which a woman's sense of her own body and the location of a woman's body in the world (literally, geographically) are determinative for her understanding of life. This recognition has led some feminists to associate feminist creativity with female corporeality as such.[2]

In what follows, I shall focus upon some tendencies within postmodern aestheticism that seem to me to be problematic from a feminist perspective. At the heart of my concern is the fact that, at least historically, aestheticist thinking has been a vehicle for blatantly masculinist ideologies privileging a certain kind of aesthetic experience, that arising within male corporeality. The theoretical model according to which this way of thinking is organized operates according to the requirements of a binary logic. Binary logics are formal systems structured in terms of oppositional polarities, within which one term is privileged over its opposite, or within which oppositional terms are alternately idealized and devalued.

I think that whenever it appears feminists are implementing theoretical models previously used to justify privileging the experience of males, some questions need to be raised.

> Every binary split creates a temptation to merely reverse its terms, to elevate what has been devalued and denigrate what has been overvalued. To avoid the tendency toward reversal is not easy—especially given the existing division in which the female is culturally defined as that which is not male. In order to challenge the sexual split which permeates our psychic, cultural, and social life, it is necessary to criticize not only the idealization of the masculine side, but also the reactive valorization of femininity. What is necessary is not to take sides but to remain focused on the dualistic structure itself. (Benjamin 1988, 9)

This is a sensitive issue, but a crucial one for the future of feminism.

A related concern that this essay will address is the way in which the subjectivity of the artist is portrayed within postmodern aestheticism. Of particular interest in this respect is a phenomenon that has become a focal point for postmodern discourse: the phenomenon of self-fragmentation. I shall suggest that this phenomenon comes most clearly into the foreground when the dualistic structure of domination is activated within theoretical models that operate according to the dynamics of reversal. The questions I want to raise in this regard have to do with the interrelationships between sadomasochistic power relations, contemporary manifestations of social psychopathology, and the phenomenon of fragmented subjectivity.

THE CONCEPT OF AESTHETICISM

Historically, the origins of postmodern aestheticism may be traced to a late nineteenth-century reversal of Romantic aestheticism. This movement is paradigmatic in that it illustrates the character of aestheticism in general as "a continual movement between two poles," that of immediacy (corporeality) and that of detachment (ideality) (Megill 1985, 203). Romantic aestheticism advocated "art for art's sake," which was to be created and evaluated in isolation from ethical, social, or political considerations—as a pure expression of human nature that bursts forth independently and individualistically. However, near the end of the nineteenth century, a new understanding of human nature began to emerge that involved a transference of the aestheticist idealization of an essentialist concept of human nature to "life as it is lived." "Life" thus conceived became a dominant theme in German philosophy between 1880 and 1930:

> The banner of life led the attack on all that was dead and congealed, on a civilization which had become intellectualistic and anti-life, against a culture which was shackled by convention and hostile to life, and for a new sense of life, "authentic experiences"— in general for what was "authentic," for dynamism, creativity, immediacy, youth. . . . The difference between what was dead and what was living came to be the criterion of cultural criticism, and everything traditional was summoned before "the tribunal of life" and examined to see whether it represented authentic life, whether it "served life," in Nietzsche's words, or inhibited and opposed it. (Schnädelbach 1984, 139)

Art historian Carla Gottlieb notes a similar trend in the aestheticism dominant in French thought during this same period. Again, the employment of the term "life" in this context was polemical in nature, highly determined by concrete historical circumstances.

> Aestheticism was born out of the disappointment suffered by the French intelligentsia and middle class when the revolution of 1848 turned out to be the stepping stone that led to the abolishment of the republic. The disillusioned fighters for the rights of the individual buried their hopes and, turning away from participation in the life of the community, dedicated themselves to providing a substitute for the unattainable dreams they had sought to make real through the revolution. (Gottlieb 1976, 402)

What fin-de-siècle aestheticism substituted for revolutionary dreams was intensity of experience; aesthetic experience was conceived as a kind of visceral, sensuous rush (*Rausch*). Postmodern aestheticism has revived this interpretation of aesthetic experience. An artist's success is measured by her or his ability to produce and recreate the aesthetic experience at will (and to evoke it in an observer). This interpretation of aesthetic experience is often coupled with a sort of "negative idealization" of the artist as a decadent, maligned, misunderstood misfit— marginalized and oppressed by the dominant culture, at the mercy of his or her oppressors *except* in her or his unique ability to engage in aesthetic ecstasy (or agony) at will.

> Here are the "men of profusion," the "masters" of today: marginals, experimental painters, pop, hippies, and yippies, parasites, madmen, binned loonies. One hour of their lives offers more intensity and less intention than three hundred thousand words of a professional philosopher. (Lyotard 1978, 53)

By assigning highest value to the immediate (psycho-physiological) experience of the artist, and interpreting this experience as the primary mode of artistic expression, postmodern aestheticism effects a dissolution of the distinction between artist, art object, environment, and spectator. Linguistic (literary/textual), visual (painting, sculpture), or auditory (musical) exercises—or some combination thereof (e.g., performance art, poetry)—which evoke an aesthetic experience are conceived as the most effective modes of social criticism and action. In effect, subjective intensity of experience substitutes for political action. Through the dissolution of the distinction between artist and political activist, the intellectual and the person on the street, the transformation of society becomes a textual, visual, or auditory reality. Aestheticism provides a pleasurable haven from the unbearable tension which builds up in response to an unrelentingly oppressive social and historical reality (and thus the mode of immediacy advocated is at the same time a dissociative mode of being). Even feelings of victimization are transformed into artistic triumph by a mythology that portrays them as a form of aesthetic experience, and thus as a personally gratifying and effective form of social criticism.

The problem inherent in postmodern aestheticism that begins to emerge at this point is a very deep one and revolves around the question of the extent to which the subversion of texts, for example, substantially changes the living conditions of those who neither read nor write, or changes the minds of their oppressors. When the distinction between art and life is dissolved, the oppressors, as much as the oppressed, become artists in their own right—and those with the upper hand in the game of dominance are, for the most part, profoundly uninterested in, and their victims unaffected by, the methodological cleverness of privileged, artistic intellectuals. The cultivation of an acute sensitivity to the *ekstasis* of the artistic moment (even when this is identified with political consciousness) can signify a disengagement from the kind of decisive action required for concrete social change. Not only this, but the aestheticist tendency to romanticize immediate experience translates easily into a trivialization or idealization of suffering (as, for example, when the painful immediacy of those with severe mental disorders is identified with aesthetic experience).

THE WILL TO POWER AS ART

Nietzsche's concept of the will to power as art and Heidegger's interpretation of his thinking in this respect are pivotal for any discussion of postmodern aestheticism. Heidegger's fascination with Nietzsche from 1936 to 1946 will serve as my point of departure. During this period, Heidegger taught four courses on Nietzsche at the University of Freiburg. "The Will to Power as Art" (Heidegger 1979) was the first lecture course in this series, taught during 1936-37.[3] This course was based upon the sections (794-853) of Nietzsche's *The Will to Power* with the same name.[4]

In defining his concept of the will to power as art, Nietzsche makes a radical distinction between a "woman's aesthetics" and a masculine aesthetics: "Our aesthetics hitherto has been a woman's aesthetics to the extent that only the receivers of art have formulated their experience of 'what is beautiful?' " (1967, 811). Nietzsche views this as unfortunate, inasmuch as women "have no conscience for art" (838). He asks a rhetorical question: "Would any link at all be missing in the chain of art . . . if the works of women were missing?" (817). Heidegger, in turn, defends Nietzsche on this point: "True, Nietzsche speaks against feminine aesthetics. But in so doing he speaks for masculine aesthetics, *hence for aesthetics*" (Emphasis mine) (Heidegger 1979, 77).

Nietzsche's virile, masculine artist "affirms the *large-scale economy* which justifies the *terrifying*, the *evil*, the *questionable*—and more than merely justifies them"

(Nietzsche 1967, 852). The "and more than merely justifies them" alludes to his conviction that the artist-philosopher must go beyond the Romantic tendency to cosmeticize reality, involving himself actively in the cycle of destruction and creation. The artist must cultivate "*the art of the terrifying,*" because "a *preference for questionable and terrifying things* is a symptom of *strength*" (852).

> Life itself recognizes no solidarity, no "equal rights," between the healthy and the degenerate parts of an organism: one must excise the latter—or the whole will perish.—Sympathy for decadents, equal rights for the ill-constituted—that would be the profoundest immorality, that would be antinature itself as morality! (734)

This sadomasochistic preoccupation is central to Nietzsche's concept of the will to power as art. The quality and intensity of the male artist's "victorious energy" is measured by his ability to experience both suffering and cruelty as pleasure. The creative instinct excites both "a desire to harm *ourselves,* self-violation," and a desire to harm others: "To those human beings who are of any concern to me I wish suffering, desolation, sickness, ill-treatment, indignities—I wish that they should not remain unfamiliar with profound self-contempt, the torture of self-mistrust, the wretchedness of the vanquished" (802, 910).

> The great creators abominate everything that interferes with the full expression of their will to power; they are not egalitarians, democrats, or refined and tolerant appreciators of the poems of their competitors. . . . [Nietzsche's] invocation of the blonde beast and continent-wide bloodletting is a terrifyingly lucid expression of his poeticist politics. The bestiality of the blonde beast may be understood . . . as a consequence of Nietzsche's fundamental identification of Being and history. This identification makes possible the exalted status given by Nietzsche to art or creativity. (Rosen 1969, 106-107)

Heidegger, for his part, puts to Nietzsche the ultimate question with which he believes all philosophizing is concerned: "What is Being itself?" Nietzsche's answer, in Heidegger's view, would be that the Being of beings is the will to power as art.

> Art, thought in the broadest sense as the creative, constitutes the basic character of beings. Accordingly, art in the narrower sense is that activity in which creation emerges for itself and becomes most perspicuous; it is not merely one configuration of the will to power among others but the *supreme* configuration. Will to power becomes genuinely visible in terms of art and as art. (Heidegger 1979, 72)

"Until now," Heidegger says elsewhere (in a contemporaneous text), "art presumably has had to do with the beautiful and beauty, and not with truth." But *now*: "Art is truth setting itself to work"—it is "*the becoming and happening of truth*" (1971, 36, 39, 71). And "truth," for Heidegger, is constituted by "agreement with what *is*" (36-37). Later (ca. 1946-47), Heidegger elaborates on this notion of truth: What *is,* is *Being,* and there comes from Being itself "the assignment of those directions that must become law and rule for man." One's "assignment" is "contained in the dispensation of Being" and only this assignment "is capable of dispatching man into Being" (Heidegger 1977, 238).

This sense of the inescapable necessity of accepting one's "assignment" in the face of "what *is*" (a rule Heidegger conscientiously observed during the period in question) lies at the heart of Heidegger's dissolution of the distinction between philosophy and literature, and between art and life. Language, like art, is "the setting-into-work of truth" (Heidegger 1971, 75). Language is not used in order to think; rather, Being thinks with and through language. And for Heidegger, the truth that unfolds in Being (and thus in both language and art) is that human existence is primarily being-to-death: "Being nihilates—as Being" (Heidegger 1977, 238).

Heidegger thus reverses Nietzsche's aggressive aestheticism, in which the artist-philosopher initiates destruction for the sake of creation. Heidegger's preference, in contrast, is for methodological passivity—he assumes a submissive posture in relation to what is given. This stance has much in common with the philosophy of Wittgenstein (and existential phenomenology in general), for whom the task of philosophy was purely descriptive: "Here we can only *describe* and say: this is what human life is like" (Wittgenstein 1979, 63). Forms of language, like Wittgenstein's "forms of life," impose themselves upon one. "Language 'speaks' and that is that. We should not try to dominate it; we should not try to improve it; we simply follow it" (Gier 1981, 215).

Heidegger's reversal of Nietzsche on this point also constitutes a reversal of Nietzsche's valuation of the role of corporeality in the production of aesthetic experience. A clue as to the meaning of this reversal may be found in Nietzsche's and Heidegger's divergent views of the body. Nietzsche, on the one hand, interprets aesthetic experience as a physiological phenomenon. He associates artistic creativity with human reproduction: "Making music," he says, "is another way of making children." He equates "the creative instinct of the artist and the distribution of semen in his blood," and calls the urge to create "an indirect demand for the ecstasies of sexuality communicated to the brain" (Nietzsche 1967, 800, 805). Heidegger, in contrast, rejects this concept of art-as-physiology and returns to a denial of the body (a denial which within the Western tradition serves as metaphor for a devaluation of women, women's bodies, and female sexuality). He calls Nietzsche's aesthetics "extreme," in that Nietzsche proceeds "to the farthest perimeter of the bodily state as such," and maintains that it is precisely at this point that "*a sudden reversal* [Umschlag] *occurs*": "While the bodily state as such continues to participate as a condition of the creative process, it is at the same time what in the created thing is to be restrained, overcome, and surpassed" (emphasis mine) (cf. Haar 1988) (Heidegger 1979, 129).

The dynamic relationship between Nietzsche's aestheticism and that of Heidegger is paradigmatic for the art of continual reversal that defines postmodern aestheticism. Whereas Nietzsche's reliance upon a binary logic is evidenced in his idealization of a fragmented, distorted conception of masculinity, coupled with a devaluation of an equally distorted concept of femininity, Heidegger's reliance on a similar logic is manifest in his attempt to ward off corporeality as such. Splitting off parts from the whole (as in Nietzsche's lopsided depiction of the masculine artist-philosopher) or dissociation from the physical structure (as in Heidegger's attempt to overcome physicality altogether) results in a lack of cohesiveness in one's sense of self—as corporeality itself provides this sense of cohesiveness. In either case, what begins to come into the foreground in this struggle between immediacy and detachment is the phenomenon of self-fragmentation.

REVERSAL AND FRAGMENTATION

Nietzsche sounds very contemporary when he refers to "the antagonism of the passions," and, alluding to Goethe's *Faust*, maintains that there are "two, three, a multiplicity of 'souls in one breast' " (1967, 778). He goes on to say that this situation is unhealthy except where "one passion at last becomes master." This one passion, of course, is the will to power, and "the most interesting men, the chameleons, belong here." This phenomenon of simultaneous multiple self-reference has become thematic for postmodernism, which privileges the ability "to refer to *ourselves*, in a singular way, while attributing to ourselves incompatible desires, aims, expectations, and, most importantly, perspectives or points of view" (Prado 1985, 30). Similarly, postmodernism embraces "the irreducible plurality of incommensurable language games and forms of life, the irremediably 'local' character of all truth, argument, and validity" (Baynes 1987, 3-4). The chaotic plurality of human experiences and values is interpreted as evidence of the fragmentary nature of human reality in general.

Deconstruction is the methodological expression of this "triumph of a disintegrating 'I.' "[5] That is, deconstructive methodology undermines the interpretive field by transforming the phenomenon of self-diffusion into a methodological approach. The rationalizing ego is replaced by the fragmented self, who then controls the epistemological field by continually undermining meaning and value. This is a logical maneuver that attempts to displace conflict by introducing multiple alternative positions within the system of bias itself. Deconstruction challenges philosophical orthodoxy, for example, by subverting the rules of discourse in the construction of the text. Each text becomes a demonstration of the meaninglessness of traditional discourse.

Derrida has remarked that "Reason keeps watch over a deep slumber in which it has an interest" (1978, 252).[6] *But over what deep slumber does deconstructive methodology keep watch?* We are given a clue as to the nature of this slumber when Derrida advocates a mode of consciousness that "makes us dream of an inconceivable process of dismantling and dispossession"; this dreaming consciousness produces the sense of a spatial and temporal "dislocation of our identity" (82). It is this sense of dislocation that evokes, in turn, the experience of self-diffusion. Identification with any particular historical locale, for example, is replaced by a nomadic departure "from the Greek site and perhaps every site in general" (82), and temporal consciousness dissolves into "a series of perpetual presents" (Sarup 1989, 134). It is this quality of awareness—often identified in the literature of postmodernism with madness or "schizophrenia" (cf. Deleuze and Guattari 1983)—that deconstructive methodology objectifies, idealizes, and aestheticizes.

As a starting point, this methodological approach serves as a useful way of revealing the potentially devastating effects of binary logic. But conceived as an "end" in itself, it becomes yet another version of this logic. The reason for this is that the concept of self-diffusion serves as metaphor for a reversal of the privileging of affectless, rationalizing awareness.[7] Deconstructive methodology, that is, constitutes an objectification of a reversal of the Cartesian disembodied cogito, and as such exists as *a valorization of the passive and damaged victim-stance within the structure of domination*. This reversal is justified by a metapsychology that portrays the fragmented self as technically (methodologically) indispensable.[8] This aura of indispensability, in turn, is enhanced by a passive-aggressive, masochistic mythology in which the fragmented self decides the fate (the end) of philosophy itself.

While this mythology reverses (at least theoretically) the relationship between oppressor and oppressed, it does so without coming to terms with the fact that such a role reversal merely reproduces the structure of domination, since reversible unequal complementarity is the basic pattern for every form of domination (Benjamin 1988, 220).[9] "One moves from passive object of others' hostility and power to the director, ruler; one's tormenters in turn will be one's victims" (Stoller 1975, 106). Aesthetic rationalizations of compulsive, methodical reversal (of one's own position, and of any values) serve the process of denial, obscuring the symbiotic relationship which exists between this ("schizophrenic") activity and the structure of domination.

FEMINISM AND AESTHETICISM

Jessica Benjamin contends that even feminists "frequently shy away from the analysis of submission, for fear that in admitting women's participation in the relationship of domination, the onus of responsibility will shift from men to women, and the moral victory from women to men" (1988, 9). Clear vision at this point is compromised by the logic of domination, which not only pervades our culture but also has become embedded in our deepest selves. "The anchoring of this structure so deep in the psyche is what gives domination its appearance of inevitability, makes it seem that a relationship in which both participants are subject—both empowered and mutually respectful—is impossible" (8).

It is with the need for a deeper analysis of submission in mind that I would like to return to the issue with which I began: the question of the relationship between feminism and postmodern aestheticism. Though feminism is often identified as "an instance of postmodern thought" (Owens 1983, 62), I would like to suggest that at least three characteristic features of postmodern aestheticism reveal a fundamental incompatibility between feminism and postmodernism.

First, postmodern aestheticism's conception of the subjectivity of the artist, which assigns highest value to intensity and immediacy, allows even (or especially) the social psychopathology associated with victimization and brutalization to be interpreted as a variety of aesthetic experience. While an emphasis on immediacy and corporeality can serve as a needed corrective to the dissociative tendencies of the Western male intellectual tradition, difficulties arise when this includes privileging female corporeality for its own sake. A woman is likely to find (much like the schizophrenic) that "fearfulness will color her organs" (Benjamin 1988, 124). For this reason, merely substituting "a female representation of desire derived from the image of a woman's organs" for the image of the phallus may actually serve to reinforce the structure of domination. Feminists must come to grips with the fact that the perspective of the body cannot always be privileged, because some bodies are desensitized to pain, or eroticize suffering, or reproduce disintegrating anxiety. Not only this, but "woman's body is endlessly objectified in all the visual media. The element of agency will not be restored to woman by aestheticizing her body—that has already been done in spades" (Benjamin 1988, 124).

Second, postmodern aestheticism's romanticization of victimization devalues the subjectivity of others. Although postmodernism has been at the forefront of a revival of interest in recovering the perspective of the "other," the concept of subjectivity lying at the heart of postmodernism negates this "otherness" even as it coaxes it out into the open. In portraying fragmentation as a universal human condition, postmodernism creates a world in which "one whole person never relates to another whole person because there is no such thing as the 'whole person' "—in other words, there can be no authentic human relationships characterized by mutual recognition. (Cf. Sarup 1989, 103.) But contradictorily, postmodernists also want to claim this schizophrenic condition as a clever and deliberate methodological innovation. Thus we find such claims as that "the schizophrenic deliberately seeks out the very limit of capitalism" (Deleuze and Guattari 1983, 35). This methodological appropriation of the concept of "schizophrenia" manages simultaneously to ignore several decades of brain research, to trivialize the suffering of the schizophrenic, and to deny the possibility or desirability of psychic health. (From this perspective, for example, there can be no such thing as—nor would it be desirable for there to be—an "other" who feels good about herself and her body and communicates this in a coherent manner.) Such polemical distortions of the experience of the schizophrenic expose the sadomasochistic dimension of the postmodern aesthetic: in the case of schizophrenia, it objectifies and aestheticizes this concept, effectively and systematically distorting, manipulating, and annihilating the subjectivity of real, flesh-and-blood schizophrenics (and others) in the process.

Running parallel to this tendency to trivialize and devalue the subjectivity of others is the attempt within postmodernism to dissolve the distinction between "art" and "life." This approach can represent a gross denial of the existence of fundamentally unbearable living conditions that should not be romanticized or aestheticized. There are circumstances where to call life "art" is to exhibit a crass insensitivity and misunderstanding: "I'm not afraid anymore," says an 18-year-old woman who was sprinkled with gasoline and set afire by the Chilean military police. "When one has come so close to death, it is impossible to feel fear again" (Torres and Martin 1988, 7). Here Nietzsche's (and the Anglo-European male intellectual tradition's) valorization of the evil and the ugly, portrayed as biologically normative, loses its appeal, and any Heideggerian acquiescence to life as it stands becomes an affront.

Finally, the metaphysical standpoint of postmodern aestheticism is problematic. In reaction to the tendency of romantic aestheticism to promote forms of art that created the illusion of wholeness against the backdrop of a chaotic social and political reality, postmodern aestheticism assigns highest value to forms of art which promote the metaphysical viewpoint that reality is fundamentally and irreversibly chaotic and meaningless. The experience of reality in general is portrayed as one of spatial and temporal fragmentation: "a departure from every site," . . . "a series of perpetual presents." Persons are portrayed as being at the mercy of powerful (internal and external) forces and desires beyond their control and thus they can really do nothing about their living conditions, since change requires the ability to commit oneself to temporal and spatial continuity. That is, the post-modern standpoint represents a profound cynicism in regard to the possibility of unified, coordinated social action among persons who can come to some rational agreement concerning a preference for some ways of thinking and being over others.

Feminism, in contrast to postmodernism, promotes the restoration of the independent subjectivity of both self and others, accompanied by a sense of agency. This implies, among other things, the conscious and deliberate cultivation of a firm sense of spatial and temporal existence. Spatial agency is constituted by the ability to experience one's own corporeal subjectivity—one's own desire(s)—without "impingement, intrusion, or violation" (Benjamin 1988, 128). Temporal agency is the establishment and maintenance of the sense of a continuity of existence— which implies an awareness of an accumulation of effective actions in the past, alongside positive strategies for the future. A basic feminist assumption is that it is both possible and desirable for women and other oppressed groups to pursue substantive changes in their living conditions and thus also in the quality of their subjective experience.

Moving beyond the structure of domination cannot be accomplished by simply recreating the binary logic on a new axis: valorizing immediacy as opposed to detachment, diversity as opposed to identity, multiplicity rather than singularity, marginality instead of centrality. Whenever it appears that feminists are employing the dynamics of reversal in order to argue their case, this may indicate an incomplete analysis of the logic of domination—specifically, an incomplete analysis of submission.

Notes

1. For example, Jeffner Allen (1988) has outlined a "poetic politics" which seeks to nullify the mandatory separation of the poetic and the political through "textual action."

2. There are many examples: Sara Ruddick (1989) associates feminist creativity with "maternal thinking," i.e., with female reproduction and mothering; Monique Wittig (1976), on the other hand, privileges the lesbian body.

3. I am aware of the textual difficulties presented by the posthumous editing process to which Der Wille Zur Macht was subjected; however, it is Heidegger's use and interpretation of the text, thus edited, that is of interest to me here.

4. References to The Will to Power will indicate section numbers; all other references are to page numbers.

5. A phrase from an aphorism by E. M. Cioran (1987), brought to my attention by Rafael C. Castillo.

6. The context is an essay on Bataille, with oblique reference to a remark that Bataille makes in regard to "*the sleep of reason—which produces monsters.*" (Cf. Bataille 1989, 113.)

7. In her editorial comments on my paper, Hilde Hein suggests that "this is the ironic triumph of the Jewish intellectual (Derrida) over the authoritarian Nazi (Heidegger)."

8. I am thinking here of what Bat-Ami Bar On (1982) calls "the masochist control rule." This rule "provides the masochist with the power to limit the behavior and authority of the sadist, and calls upon the sadist to comply with the limitations set by the masochist" (78-79). This negative power stems from the dependence of the oppressors on the oppressed and protects an oppressed class against total destruction. In the psychiatric literature on the "masochistic contract," see especially Smirnoff (1970).

9. Nor does this mythology come to terms with clinical evidence indicating that identity diffusion is distinguished by an overhwelming etiological association with severe trauma, which triggers defensive operations (such as denial, splitting, dissociation, fragmentation of affects, grandiosity, and devaluation) resulting in the formation of multiple contradictory representations of self and others (Kernberg 1984). For example, recent research conducted by the National Institute for Mental Health indicates that 97 percent of patients diagnosed with multiple personality disorder—the most extreme form of the experience of self-fragmentation—experienced severe trauma (especially sexual abuse and violence) as children, and these patients are disproportionately female (some clinicians report a female to male ratio of 9: 1) (Putnam 1989).

References

Allen, Jeffner. 1988. Poetic politics: How the Amazons took the Acropolis. *Hypatia* 3(2): 107-22.

Bar On, Bat-Ami. 1982. Feminism and sadomasochism: Self-critical notes. In *Against sadomasochism: A radical feminist analysis.* Robin R. Linden, et al., eds. San Francisco: Frog in the Well.

Bataille, Georges. 1989. *Theory of religion.* Robert Hurley, trans. New York: Zone Books.

Baynes, Kenneth, James Bohman, and Thomas McCarthy, eds. 1987. *After philosophy: End or transformation?* Cambridge, MA: MIT Press.

Benjamin, Jessica. 1988. *The bonds of love: Psychoanalysis, feminism, and the problem of domination.* New York: Pantheon.

Bunch, Charlotte. 1987. *Passionate politics: Feminist theory in action.* New York: St. Martin's Press.

Cioran, E. M. 1987. Exasperations. *Frank: An International Journal of Contemporary Writing and Art* 6/7: 22-24.

Deleuze, Gilles, and Felix Guattari. 1983. *Anti-oedipus: Capitalism and schizophrenia.* Robert Hurley, Mark Seem, and Helen R. Lane, trans. Minneapolis: University of Minnesota Press.

Derrida, Jacques. 1978. *Writing and difference.* Alan Bass, trans. Chicago: University of Chicago Press.

Gier, Nicholas. 1981. *Wittgenstein and phenomenology: A comparative study of the later Wittgenstein, Husserl, Heidegger, and Merleau-Ponty.* Albany: State University of New York Press.

Gottlieb, Carla. 1976. *Beyond modern art.* New York: Dutton.

Haar, Michel. 1988. Heidegger and the Nietzschean "physiology of art." In *Exceedingly Nietzsche: Aspects of contemporary Nietzsche interpretation.* David Farrell Krell and David Wood, eds. New York: Routledge.

Heidegger, Martin. 1971. The origin of the work of art. In *Poetry, language, thought*. Albert Hofstadter, trans. New York: Harper and Row.

Heidegger, Martin. 1977. Letter on humanism. In *Basic writings*. David Farrell Krell, ed. New York: Harper and Row.

Heidegger, Martin. 1979. *Nietzsche: The will to power as art*. David Farrell Krell, trans. New York: Harper and Row.

Kernberg, Otto F. 1984. *Severe personality disorders*. New Haven, CT: Yale University Press.

Lyotard, Jean François. 1978. Notes on return and kapital. *Semiotext(e)* 3(1): 44-53.

Megill, Allan. 1985. *Prophets of extremity: Nietzsche, Heidegger, Foucault, Derrida*. Berkeley: University of California Press.

Nietzsche, Friedrich. 1967. *The will to power*. Walter Kaufmann, ed. Walter Kaufmann and R. J. Hollingdale, trans. New York: Random House.

Owens, Craig. 1983. The discourse of others: Feminists and postmodernism. In *The anti-aesthetic: Essays on postmodern culture*. Hal Foster, ed. Port Townsend, WA: Bay Press.

Prado, C. G. 1985. Reference and the composite self. *International Studies in Philosophy* 17(1): 25-33.

Putnam, Frank W. 1989. *Diagnosis and treatment of multiple personality disorder*. New York: Guilford Press.

Rosen, Stanley. 1969. *Nihilism: A philosophical essay*. New Haven, CT: Yale University Press.

Ruddick, Sara. 1989. *Maternal thinking: Toward a politics of peace*. Boston: Beacon Press.

Sarup, Madan. 1989. *An introductory guide to post-structuralism and postmodernism*. Athens: University of Georgia Press.

Schnädelbach, Herbert. 1984. *Philosophy in Germany 1831-1933*. Eric Matthews, trans. New York: Cambridge University Press.

Smirnoff, V. N. 1970. The masochistic contract. *International Journal of Psycho-analysis* 50: 665-71.

Stoller, Robert J. 1975. *Perversion: The erotic form of hatred*. Washington, D.C.: American Psychiatric Press.

Torres, Carmen, and Christine Martin. 1988. What can they do to me now? *Connexions* 27: 6-7.

Wittgenstein, Ludwig. 1979. Remarks on Frazer's *Golden Bough*. In *Wittgenstein: Sources and perspectives*. C. G. Luckhardt, ed. Ithaca, NY: Cornell University Press.

Wittig, Monique. 1976. *The lesbian body*. David LeVay, trans. New York: Avon.

Modernism, Postmodernism, and the Problem of the Visual in Afro-American Culture

MICHELE WALLACE

While Afro-American music is widely recognized for its influential place in traditions of American music, Afro-American visual art remains isolated. This is sharply illustrated in the case of modernist painting, which borrowed heavily from African art while insisting upon its difference and distance from it. This putative distance obscures the fact that Afro-American visual art also has a modernist period and is symptomatic of what Ralph Ellison has called the general "invisibility" of Afro-American visual culture. In the complex dynamic of invisibility in both modernism and postmodernism, the subjectivity of black women virtually disappears. The continued failure to incorporate Afro-American artists in the visual traditions of postmodernism suggests that a critical area for analysis remains the most occluded subject of visual arts: the intersection of race and gender.

In 1954 in the case of *Brown vs. the Board of Education*, the Supreme Court ruled that segregated schools were inherently unequal, discriminatory, and illegal. The case made by the NAACP included the findings of Kenneth and Mamie Clark, black Ph.D.s in social psychology who had been using a doll test and a coloring test to measure how racism and segregation damaged the self-esteem of black children ranging in age from three to seven. They found, among other things, that black children—I don't know how many of them were girls or if anyone thought about the fact that only girls generally play with dolls—preferred white dolls to black dolls, and the black children had a tendency to use a white or yellow crayon to color both a same-sex figure said to be themselves and an opposite sex figure said to be a friend (Kluger 1979, 398-403).

There has been much debate within the fields of psychology and sociology about the meaning of the Clarks' research, most of it focused upon the scientific validity of the testing methods (Kluger 1979, 446-48). However, it is not at all unusual for the media to refer back to this research as evidence that racism is an unambiguously deprivational experience, while completely ignoring what the visual implications of such findings might be. In fact, in the summer of 1989 there was a TV special called *Blacks in White America,* entirely produced by black journalists at ABC (Minerbrook 1989, 33). The documentary opened with a present-day reenactment of the Clarks' research showing small black children choosing a white doll over a black one, and interpreting a stereotypical line drawing of a blond little white girl as prettier or cleaner or nicer. It closed with the narrator's voice—a black female journalist—telling us that she had been one of the little girls who had participated in the Clarks' original research in the early fifties. She confessed that she, too, had preferred the white doll over the black one.

The documentary interpreted this information as corroboration of the fact that blacks are still comparatively poor and disenfranchised in comparison to whites. Profiles of a black regiment of fighter pilots in World War II and of the newly appointed black Chairman of the Joint Chiefs of Staff, Colin L. Powell, were offered as correctives. Amazingly, neither art nor beauty nor aesthetics nor high culture nor pop culture nor media were raised as significant precipitating factors in this process.

Of course, poverty and powerlessness feed a child's perception of what it means to have black skin, but this process is much more complex than a direct correlation could encompass. Rather, it is society's always already operative evaluation of images, further inscribed by skin color (dark or light, white or black or yellow or red) that would most affect a child's opinion of race. Not only the presence of "negative" black stereotypes in schoolbook illustrations, posters, religious imagery, and advertising images, as well as movie and television images, but the absence of black images in mass media in general is the crucial dynamic never accounted for.

The power of the image—as well as the word—seems to be the very thing addressed so well by Toni Morrison's use of the Dick and Jane text in order to characterize white hegemony in *The Bluest Eye.*[1] After all, this was an elementary school reader whose illustrations were at least as unforgettably repetitive and stifling to the imagination as its text. The absence of black images in the reflection of the social mirror, which such programmatic texts (from "Dick and Jane," to Disney movies, to "The Weekly Reader") invariably construct, could and did produce the void and the dread of racial questions that the Clarks found in the fifties, particularly in Northern black children who were already attending integrated schools. Their studies related how these children sometimes cried when asked to identify the doll that was "Negro" or that was the same race as them. On the other hand, Southern children who attended segregated schools displayed less ambivalence, which the Clarks interpreted as a cynicism inappropriate to childhood: " 'Oh, yeah, that's me there—that's a nigger,' they'd say. 'I'm a nigger' " (Kluger 1979, 448).

We all know in our hearts, as any mere child in our midst today must know, that "nigger," "black," and "schwartze" are often used interchangeably in our language to mean an abject "other," and yet we persist in denying it, just as Kenneth and Mamie Clark, the NAACP, and the Supreme Court denied it in 1954. In 1979, when Donald Neuman designated his exhibition of charcoal drawings at Artist Space as "Nigger Drawings," and in 1989 when Jackie Mason called mayoral candidate David Dinkins a "schwartze," sizable downtown New York controversies followed precisely in order to continue this charade, which has become one of the principal tenets of bourgeois humanism, that color is an innately trivial matter, which does not signify.

How one is seen (as black), and, therefore, what one sees (in a white world), is always already crucial to one's existence as an Afro-American. The very markers that reveal you to the rest of the world, your dark skin and your kinky/curly hair, are visual. However, *not* being seen by those who don't want to see you because they are racist, what Ralph Ellison called "invisibility," often leads racists to the interpretation that *you are unable* to see.

This has meant, among other things, that Afro-Americans have not produced (because they've been prevented from doing so by intra-racial pain and outside intervention) a tradition in the visual arts as vital and compelling to other Americans as Afro-American tradition in music (West 1989, 274). Moreover, the necessity, which seems to persist of its own volition in Afro-American Studies, for drawing parallels or alignments between Afro-American music and everything else cultural among Afro-Americans stifles and represses most of the potential for understanding the visual in Afro-American culture. For if the positive scene of instruction between Africans and Europeans in the U.S. (Levine 1977; Baraka 1963) is located in what is now triumphantly called the "tradition" of Afro-American music, the negative scene of instruction is in its visual tradition.[2] This "negative scene of instruction" (so much more common in Afro-American experience) was one in which white teachers refused to teach black students who were in turn just as reluctant to learn from them. As even the smallest child seems to instinctively understand, institutionalized education has always been, first and foremost, a means of transmitting social values, not knowledge or power.

It appears that the only reason black artists aren't as widely accepted as black writers (and this is far from widely enough) is because shifts in art historical judgment result in extraordinary economic contingencies. Consequently, the closed economic nepotism of the art world perpetuates a situation in which, as Howardena Pindell has pointed out, "artists of color face an industry-wide 'restraint of trade,' limiting their ability to show and sell their work" (1988, 160).

If black writers had had to rely on the kinds of people and developments that determine the value of art, if writing had to be accepted into rich white people's homes and into their investment portfolios in the manner of the prized art object, I suspect that none of us would have ever heard of Langston Hughes, Richard Wright, Zora Neale Hurston, Ralph Ellison, Amiri Baraka, Sonia Sanchez, John Edgar Wideman, Ishmael Reed, Alice Walker, Adrienne Kennedy, Toni Morrison, Ntozake Shange, August Wilson, George Woolfe, and Trey Ellis. Indeed, we are lucky to have heard of Jacob Lawrence, Betye Saar, Romare Bearden, Richard Hunt, Sam Gilliam, Daniel Johnson, Mel Edwards, and Faith Ringgold.

I was two years old in 1954. And, perhaps because my mother was pursuing a master's in art education until I was nine, I grew up being aware of the Clarks' research. I also grew up watching a television on which I rarely saw a black face, reading Archie and Veronica comics, Oz and Nancy Drew stories, and *Seventeen* magazine, in which "race" was unmentionable. At the same time, I always had black dolls and I was always given a brown crayon to take to school as an encouragement to color my people brown as I did at home.

In the spring of 1961 my mother, who wanted to be an artist, graduated from City College of New York with her master's in art education. That summer my mother planned and carried out an elaborate tour of the art treasures of Italy and France with my grandmother, my sister, and myself in tow. I remember the virtually endless streams of white faces not only in paintings and sculpture but also in the operas, film, theater, and television we saw that summer. I can also remember a French saleswoman being asked by my mother to find a black doll at the Galleries Lafayette in Paris, and being relieved when she succeeded in producing one. I can still recall that doll, which was blacker than most American black dolls.

"Race" was frequently discussed in my family's home, although "racism" was not. As far as I know, no such word had entered common parlance. Moreover, and more personally, any discussion of "race" in the presence of people who were not black embarrassed me. I can remember giving a report on the "races of the world" in my seventh grade class and being so embarrassed by my subject matter that I could hardly speak. I said "colored" to refer to my own people. A black boy in my class corrected me by saying "Negro." I was mortified, for "Negro" was then considered to be the more militant word. My grandmother never used "Negro" at all, although my mother and her friends did. Of course, "black," as a description of race, was still the ultimate and virtually unspeakable insult.

So you can see I came by my fascination with the visual quite automatically. Visual production has always been an obsession in my life, because I was a child of the 1954 Supreme Court decision, a child of Kenneth Clark's research—Dr. Kenneth Clark, who taught at CCNY where my mother was a graduate student and, together with his wife, ran the Northside Psychological Testing Service, which shared a building with the private school I attended from the seventh grade on.

I saw Kenneth and Mamie Clark often. If I didn't actually know them, I felt as though I did and was enormously proud of them, as was everyone in my family. For they were part of this whole business of being a Negro, I well knew, this whole self-conscious business of something that would later be called "The Black Aesthetic" but that, for right now, confined itself to this problem of not liking dolls of the same color as yourself unless carefully educated to do so. This I understood even then, for I was also a child of television, comic books, and magazines, although I was carefully instructed by my parents and teachers to know that the pleasure these gave was counterfeit, not to be taken seriously.

Moreover, my mother and my grandmother were artists. My paternal grand- mother, Momma T from Jamaica, West Indies, was a Sunday landscape painter. My maternal grandmother, Momma Jones, was a fashion designer. I modeled in all her fashion shows while growing up and was constantly being photographed by the two or three black photographers she always had on hand to document even the most trivial events. Later she would collaborate on quilts and other kinds of fabric art with my mother, the "fine" artist.

In the work of the women in my family, it is actually in the career of my mother, Faith Ringgold, that fashion and fine art were finally conjoined. But for quite a long time before she became interested in the questions of a black aesthetic and a feminist aesthetic, she was a painter who tried to take seriously her relationship to the tradition of Western painting, particularly its culmination in cubism. Our home revolved around the tension this challenge created in her and in her work. I remember in particular when I was very young, a very bad (postmodern?), often wet Picasso-esque "study" that contained a *mise-en-abîme* effect of endless doors within doors, which occupied in our home the space which should have been occupied by a dining room table and chairs.

According to Raymond Williams in *Marxism and Literature*, a hegemony is a process that relies upon the mechanisms of traditions and canons of Old Masters in order to waylay the utopian desires that are potentially embodied in cultural production (1977, 115-17). The underlying structure of the very concept of "tradition" lies in wait behind contemporary variations on "tradition"—whether they are named feminist, Afro-American, or Eskimo—in that they are inevitably radically selective in favor of maintaining the dominance of a brutal status quo despite their best intentions to subvert it.

I cannot recall a time during which I didn't perceive Western art and Western culture as a problem in ways that seem to me now akin to the manner in which modernism, postmodernism, and feminism raise such problems. On the other hand, thanks to my mother's unrelenting ambition to be a successful artist and her political interpretation of the continuing frustration of that ambition, I can't remember a time during which I didn't know that artmaking and visual production were also deeply problematic in Afro-American culture. For these reasons and more, James Baldwin's statement in *Notes of a Native Son* that he "despised" black people "possibly because they failed to produce Rembrandt" (1955, 7) had profound resonance as I was growing up.

More specifically it was Picasso (not Rembrandt) and modernism, in general, that epitomized the art historical moment of greatest fascination. The debate was precisely situated in the paradox that Picasso, cubism, and subsequent modernists had borrowed heavily from African art. In other words, as it was widely interpreted among a black middle-class intelligentsia in the '50s and '60s, "they," or white Euro-American high modernism, had borrowed from "us," the African peoples of the world, even if "they" were incapable of admitting it.

My interest in modernism only accelerated once I had become knowledgeable enough about the visual and literary production of both Afro-Americans and white Europeans and Americans in this country (no small task) to know that modernism actually took place in the Afro-American as well as in the white American-European milieu. Afro-American modernism is both the same and different, as imitative as it is original, which is consistent with Henry Louis Gates's notion of "critical signification," an attempt to describe the mechanical relationship between Afro-American culture and Euro-American culture. According to Gates—and he has employed "critical signification" almost exclusively in the context of literature and the question of Afro-American literacy—Afro-American culture imitates and reverses the terms of Euro-American culture. This relationship can also usefully be described as dialogical, or as one of intertextuality.[3]

But the problem remains the unilateral unwillingness of Euro-American culture to admit and acknowledge its debt, or even its relationship, to African and Afro-American culture. In fact, this problem—which lies at the heart of the problem of the visual in Afro-American culture—has such a long and convoluted history that its enunciation has become one of the telling features of Afro-American modernism. One of the early practitioners of Afro-American literary modernism, Ralph Ellison, even gave it a name: invisibility.

In *The Invisible Man* (1952), Ellison catalogs the dilemma. According to the myth of blackness, it is the opposite of whiteness, or it is so much "the same" that it is "invisible." Both dynamics are, in fact, aspects of this "invisibility's" inevitable and structural binary opposition. On the one hand, there is no black difference. On the other, the difference is so vast as to be unspeakable and indescribable. Invisibility, a visual metaphor, is then employed as a way of presenting a variety of responses to racism and cultural apartheid; there is the problem of translating a musical/oral Afro-American tradition into a written history and literature; there is the problem of Eurocentrism; and there is the problem of not being seen, in all its various connotations.

There is also the problem of being viewed as an object whose subjectivity is considered as superfluous as that of the dancing, grinning Sambo doll that the formerly political Clifton sells on the street corner in downtown New York. And finally, there is the problem of being the patriarch of a black family whose role must be defined in opposition to that of the patriarch of the white family. Therefore, myth constructs the black family on a model contrasting with the Freudian/Oedipal/modernist drama of individuation, so that, early in the novel, the illiterate storyteller/farmer, Trueblood, impregnates both his wife and his daughter, and thereby gains cachet in the white community which pays him, again and again, to tell them the story of how it happened (Ellison 1952). However, perhaps the most psychologically damaging residual of this story is that in the process of its unfolding, the subjectivity of the black woman becomes entirely unimaginable.

In *Invisible Man*, "women" are generally "white," and while the text is not especially sympathetic or kind to white women, it seems entirely engaged by the assumption that from a white male progressive point of view, or from the perspective of Euro-American modernism (I am not suggesting that these are necessarily synonymous), the problem of the female (white) "other" and the problem of the black (male) "other" are easily interchangeable. In Euro-American modernism, and in Afro-American modernism as well, for that matter, the position of the "other" is as unitary and as incapable of being occupied by categories more diverse than "women and blacks" as was the formerly unified, omniscient subject from which it split.

It seems to me not entirely irrelevant to mention here that Ellison's prediction wasn't at all accurate, in that it is a handful of black women writers who follow in the tradition of Trueblood, in being well paid by a white (post-feminist?) audience to tell the stories of the Oedipal transgressions of black men. I don't mean to suggest that either black men or black women are doing anything wrong, for the Oedipal transgressions of the black male are as inevitable as the black woman's need to break her silence about them (and I am not referring only to incest). But the motives of the whites who are ostensibly being entertained by this storytelling are not neces-sarily much different from those whites who paid Trueblood to tell his tale, or who stood on the corner watching Clifton's grinning, dancing Sambo dolls. The differ-ence in the motivation is only a function of the extent to which the performance and consumption of these texts are interrogated by a critical discourse emanating from white and black (and brown) feminist and Afro-Americanist discourses. The relative scarcity of such interrogation in the media and in academia is as telling as the relative scarcity of a multicultural "other" presence in the various fields of visual production, from museum administration to films. It is telling us, in fact, that the fabric of invisibility has not altered, that it makes little difference in our hegemonic arrangements if Trueblood is now a woman.

But if we move now from the Afro-American modernist novel par excellence to the Afro-American postmodernist novel par excellence, Ishmael Reed's *Mumbo Jumbo*, there is an interesting black female character who comes into view.[4] It is the dancer and vaudevillian and Folies Bergere star Josephine Baker, who shares with African art, and with Picasso and the cubists, a mutual location in the Paris of the '20s. Reed's novel brings all of these variables into dramatic dialogues or juxtaposition with each other during the Harlem Renaissance.[5] Yet the "idea" of Josephine Baker in *Mumbo Jumbo*, and in most of what has been written about her, remains the old-fashioned one wherein she becomes the muse of the white man, whether that is resented, as it is by Reed, or celebrated, as it is by many others who have written about her (Rose 1989; Hammond and O'Connor 1988).

When one arrives at the postmodern scene, marked as it is by reproduction and simulation, the rampant exploitation of international capitalism, not to mention much speculation regarding the death of the subject, the death of history, and the total blurring of lines between pop culture and high culture, spinoffs of the Josephine Baker model proliferate. Tina Turner, Grace Jones, Jody Watley, Whitney Houston, Diana Ross, and Donna Summer (as well as Michael Jackson?) all follow in her tracks. Baker's much photographed performances are not the only starting point, however, of this fascination with black women's bodies—the site upon which blackness was conceptualized as an aspect of the white personality and white Euro-American achievement. There was also the popularity in Europe of an ethnographic photography issuing from the process of the colonial/anthropological exploitation of a Third World Asia and Africa that proceeded and overlapped with a burgeoning interest in Europe in African and Oceanic art which was really about an interest in other ways of seeing and looking that had not before occurred to the West.

Sander L. Gilman points out that in the early decades of the 1800s, even before photography's ascendancy, there was a general fascination in Europe with the "Hottentot Venus," as represented by series of black women who were imported from South Africa and exhibited in the major cities of Europe because of their large and fatty buttocks. In this way, representations of black women with large and fatty buttocks came to signify not only black women but all other categories of women, such as prostitutes, who were thought to be as sexually wanton as black women.

According to Gilman, Manet paints the white courtesan *Nana* with protruding buttocks for this reason, and in *Olympia*, the presence of the clothed buxom black female servant allows for the transgressive sexuality of Olympia. In 1901, Picasso painted a parody of *Olympia* in which she is a fat black woman with the huge thighs of the Hottentot Venus. Gilman describes this painting as a prolegomena to the intersection of issues of race and sexuality in *Les Demoiselles d'Avignon* of five years later (1986, 251-53). *Les Demoiselles* might be seen as illustrating the occasional advantage of art over institutionalized history or science in that it seems to represent the desire to both reveal and repress the scene of appropriation as a conjunction of black/female bodies and white culture—a scene of negative instruction between black and white art or black and white culture.

Unlike the positive scene of instruction of Afro-American and Euro-American music, in which mutual influence and intertextuality is acknowledged (although not without struggles that further enrich the transmutation), in the negative scene of instruction of Afro-American art and Euro-American art the exchange is disavowed and disallowed—no one admits to having learned anything from anyone else. Subsequently, Euro-American postmodernism emerges as the lily white, pure-blooded offspring of an inbred and dishonest (in the sense of not acknowledging its mixed blood) modernism and post-structuralism. And, more or less simultaneous with this subtle but effective metamorphosis, the black aesthetic emerges as the unambivalent, uncompromised linkup between Africa and the "New World" in which Euro-American influences are superfluous and negligible.

Griselda Pollock (1990), following Julia Kristeva's lead in "Woman's Time," has proposed that there is a third position in feminist discourse beyond the simplistic mechanics of the struggle for equality for (white) women and the celebration of (white) female difference. This third position is the most difficult to describe because it encompasses many positions and strategies still *in potentia*. Its goal, however, is to deconstruct the discursive formations which define the hegemonic process and which define, as well, the subversive limitations of previous feminist approaches. Herein lies my opportunity to usher forth "new knowledge," as Pollock names it, in conceptualizations of the visual in Afro-American culture that would consider the interdependency in issues of ethnicity and sex. This "new knowledge" would be constituted in the excavation of the black artistic versus the white artistic experience under the historical headings of modernism and postmodernism—on the theory that this is, in fact, the genuinely counter-hegemonic thing to explore at this particular art historical moment. The purpose of this would be to subvert the most persistent arrangement of present-day cultural hegemony, with its cultural apartheid and "separate development" as Trinh Minh-ha has described it (1989, 80). Instead of being concerned with commonalities in the developments of Afro- and European American communities in the '20s (or in subsequent periods), each camp of canonizers, whether white or black, male or female, is only interested in claiming autonomous achievement. What gives "modernist primitivism" any critical import in this cultural revisioning of the visual is the fact that it appears to be an ongoing category in modernist, postmodernist, and feminist discourses, a fundamental way of discounting the "blackness" of the occasional black artist who is accepted within its ranks (as in the case of Jean-Michel Basquiat and Martin

Puryear), while rejecting the category of black artist in general (Schjeldahl 1989, 214-16; Brenson 1989, 37).

This said, there also exist in this postmodern moment the problems encountered, for example, by black British filmmaker Isaac Julien, who has experienced the opposition of the Langston Hughes estate for his counter-historical and counter-hegemonic vision of the Harlem Renaissance in his most recent film, *Looking for Langston*. Ostensibly the estate objects to the implication that Hughes was gay, but the film is really about the erasure of the gay black subject and, in the process, the erasure of the body and of sexuality in the dominant discourse. This film made me aware, as I had not been before, of how disembodied cultural figures of the Harlem Renaissance generally are made to appear within black critical discourses, compared with those black artists, such as Louis Armstrong, Bessie Smith, and Josephine Baker, who have been cast in "primitivist" or neo-primitivist terms and who, as such, have always been of more interest to white criticism.

This disembodiment, with its attendant desexualization of black literature and high culture, occurs in response to the over-sexualization of black images in white mass culture. It is an effort, in part, to block the primitivization of the black subject by white critics (this is particularly relevant in Afro-American literary criticism), resulting in the not surprising though still devastating outcome of, once again, marginalizing or erasing as irrelevant or unworthy the female subject. If this process of desexualization and deprimitivization had not been assimilated in the consolidation of black high culture within Afro-American studies, many more black female artists, writers, and blues singers—whose gender seems of paramount importance here—would figure in the discussion of black culture. To focus on the intersections of gender and sexuality would be to bring into relief the terms not only of the sexual victimization of black women (rape, etc.) but of black men (lynchings, etc.) in the South in the '20s, and evidence how the dread of such scenarios fed into the literary and visual production and the modernist aspirations of the artists, writers, and intellectuals of the Harlem Renaissance.

On the other hand, the absence of black voices in the debate over the primitivism show at the Museum of Modern Art in 1984 was no accident. William Rubin, the curator of the show, would have us think that modernism is the culmination of universal aesthetic values and standards. Therefore, it should come as no surprise that, in a few isolated instances, so-called primitive art would be as good as Western art, for the people who make these objects are people too (Rubin 1984). Thomas McEvilley (1984), his respondent in *Artforum*, would have us shed Western aesthetics for Western anthropology, although, as James Clifford points out in his contribution to the debate, both discourses assume a primitive world in need of preservation or, in other words, no longer vital and, needless to say, incapable of describing itself.

Clifford is right when he says, "The fact that rather abruptly, in the space of a few decades, a large class of non-Western artifacts came to be redefined as art is a taxonomic shift that requires critical historical discussion, not celebration" (1988, 196). Yet I am not convinced that "minority" artists of color in the West, who are, in some sense, along with African and Third World artists, the rightful heirs to the debate around "primitivism," will ever surface in the discussion.

Black criticism was blocked from the discussions of modernism, which are defined as exclusively white by an intricate and insidious cooperation of art galleries, museums, and academic art history, and also blocked from any discussion of "primitivism," which has been colonized beyond recognition in the space of the international and now global museum. At this juncture one is compelled to ask, "Is multiculturalism, as it is being institutionally defined, occupying the same space as 'primitivism' in relationship to postmodernism?" For me, a response to such a question would need to include a careful scrutiny of the history of black popular culture and race relations, and account for the sexualization of both, thus defining the perimeters of a new knowledge which I can only name, at this point, as the problem of the visual in Afro-American culture.

For this reason, more suggestive to me is Hal Foster's reading of the stakes of the debate on primitivism in his book of essays *Recodings*, in which he describes *Les Demoiselles* as the landmark of a crisis in phallocratic culture. Primitivism becomes the "magical commodity" whereby white European art will appropriate the ritual function of tribal art and resist the process, which the museum space makes inevitable, of being reduced to a lifeless commodity. "On the one hand, then," Foster writes,

> the primitive is a modern problem, a crisis in cultural identity, which the west moves to resolve: hence the modernist construction "primitivism," the fetishistic recognition-and-disavowal of the primitive difference. This ideological resolution renders it a "nonproblem" for us. On the other hand, this resolution is only a repression: delayed into our political unconscious, the primitive returns uncannily at the moment of its potential eclipse. The rupture of the primitive, managed by the moderns, becomes our postmodern event. (1985, 204)

And yet finally there is only an implied entry way here for the artist or the critic of color who is not a member of a postcolonial intellectual elite, because we who are subject to internal colonization, we who are called "minorities," suffer the problems of the modern and of cultural identity, perhaps more than anyone, and the unified, unmarked subject of this, and so far most other analyses of the postmodern, never mind the modern, continue to render us "invisible" and silent.

Gayatri Spivak ventures the point in "Who Claims Alterity?" that postcolonial intellectuals have the advantage over minorities subject to "internal colonization" because of the tendency for those who control theory to conflate the two spheres (1989, 274). To me the potential difference for white intellectuals is between one's somewhat dark past and one's absolutely dark future. While a white art world may debate the nature of the relationship between "primitive" art and modern art, black artists and intellectuals widely assume that a white world is simply unable to admit that art from Africa and elsewhere in the Third World had a direct and profound influence on Western art because of an absolutely uncontrollable racism, xenophobia, and ethnocentrism.

The so-called discovery of tribal objects by Modernism is analogous to an equally dubious discovery of the "New World" by European colonization. What was there was not, in fact, "discovered" but rather appropriated and/or stolen. But more to the point, the dynamic that emerged was born not only from the probability that European civilization would first repudiate and deny and then revise and reform that which they would eventually label "tribal" or "primitive," but from the even greater probability of a new kind of civilization or art, no longer strictly European, which would be revitalized by its proximity to and contact with an internal alternative. In other words, both European and non-European cultures were transformed by their "new" and closer relationship to one another in the "New World." For the most part, the relationship was one of exploitation, appropriation, oppression, and repression. But it is also true that something came into and is coming into being: something neither "primitive/tribal" nor European modern.

While the most concrete sign of that something new is generally referred to as postmodernism, unfortunately this move usually carries along with it the reinscription of modernism's apartheid. Although the negation of their former powers to explain the world is potentially useful to counter-hegemonic strategies, invariably European-influenced theorists are so preoccupied with the demise of the Hegelian dialectic that they never really get to anything or anyone other than white men who share similar feelings. Moreover, there is another sign just as indicative of novelty which is best represented by the cultural contributions of Afro-Americans to popular culture.

The temptation is great to subsume and reify this contribution under the heading of "primitivism," or neo-primitivism, following the pattern of modernist criticism. But it is the kind of development that will only occur because white males continue to absolutely dominate and control all aspects of postmodern criticism. In other words, it is not the kind of choice that black critics or black feminist cultural critics are likely to endorse.

Notes

This essay first appeared in *Out There: Marginalization and Contemporary Culture*, ed. Russell Ferguson, Cornel West, Trinh Minh-ha, Martha Givers (The New Museum and MIT, 1990). It is reprinted here with permission of the author and the MIT Press.

1. "Here is the house. It is green and white. It has a red door. It is very pretty. Here is the family. Mother, Father, Dick, and Jane live in the green-and-white house. They are very happy. See Jane. She wants to play. Who will play with Jane? . . ." (Morrison 1970, 7).

2. Howardena Pindell writes, "I have learned over my 20 years in New York not to 'romanticize' white artists, expecting them to be liberal, open, or necessarily supportive because they are creative people. Pests, a group of nonwhite artists, had hung a poster in Soho on Broome and Broadway last spring which read, 'There are 11,000 artists of color in New York. Why don't you see us?' Someone had written on the poster, 'Because you do poor work' " (Pindell 1988, 161).

3. Not only does Gates tend to use interchangeably the terms signifying, intertextuality, and the dialogic, Stam points out in his essay that the term "intertextuality" was first introduced into critical discourse as Julia Kristeva's translation of Bakhtin's concept of the dialogic. Of course, Gates draws heavily upon Bakhtin's notion of the dialogic in order to describe how critical signification works (Gates and Stam in Kaplan 1988).

4. Of course, there are many other relevant black female figures in black modernism (Bessie Smith and Zora Neale Hurston, for instance), but my attention here is on how a perspective which focuses on the Afro-American "other" of Euro-American modernism and postmodernism must necessarily exclude (black) female subjectivity in some crucial ways.

5. Josephine Baker is on the cover of *Mumbo Jumbo* (Reed 1972).

References

Baldwin, James. 1955. *Notes of a native son*. New York: Beacon Press.

Baraka, Imiri (Leroi Jones). 1963. *Blues people: Negro music in white America*. New York: Grove Press.

Brenson, Michael. 1989. A sculptor's struggle to fuse culture and art. *New York Times* Arts and Leisure Section, October 29.

Brown v. Board of Education, 347 U.S. 483 (1953); 349 U.S. 294 (1955).

Clifford, James. 1988. *The Predicament of culture: Twentieth century ethnography, literature and art*. Cambridge, MA: Harvard University Press.

Ellison, Ralph. 1952. *The invisible man*. New York: Random House.

Foster, Hal. 1985. *Recodings: Art, spectacle, and cultural politics*. Port Townsend, WA: Bay Press.

Gates, Henry Louis Jr. 1988. Figures in black: Words, signs and the "racial" self. In *Postmodernism and its discontents*. E. Ann Kaplan, ed. London and New York: Verso.

Gilman, Sander L. 1986. Black bodies, white bodies: Toward an iconography of female sexuality in late 19th century art, medicine and literature. In *"Race," writing and difference*. Henry Louis Gates, Jr., ed. Chicago: University of Chicago Press.

Hammond, Brian, and Patrick O'Connor. 1988. *Josephine Baker*. London: Jonathan Cape.

Kluger, Richard. 1979. *Simple justice*. Vol. 1. New York: Knopf.

Levine, Lawrence. 1977. *Black culture and black consciousness: Afro-American folk thought from slavery to freedom*. New York: Oxford University Press.

McEvilley, Thomas. 1984. Doctor lawyer Indian chief: " 'Primitivism' in 20th century art" at the Museum of Modern Art. *Artforum* (November).

Minerbrook, Scott. 1989. At ABC: Black journalists make news. In *Emerge* (October).

Minh-ha, Trinh T. 1989. *Woman, native, other*. Bloomington: Indiana University Press.

Morrison, Toni. 1970. *The bluest eye*. New York: Holt, Rinehart and Winston.

Pindell, Howardena. 1988. Art (world) & racism. *Third Text* Vol. 3/4 (Spring/Summer).

Pollock, Griselda. 1990. Differencing the canon. Paper delivered at the College Art Association, February 16.

Reed, Ishmael. 1972. *Mumbo jumbo*. Garden City: Doubleday.

Rose, Phyllis. 1989. *Jazz Cleopatra: Josephine Baker in her time*. New York: Doubleday.

Rubin, William, ed. 1984. *"Primitivism" in 20th century art: Affinity of the tribal and the modern*. 2 vols. New York: Museum of Modern Art.

Schjeldahl, Peter. 1989. Paint the right thing. *Elle* (November).

Spivak, Gayatri. 1989. Who claims alterity? In *Remaking history*. Barbara Kruger and Phil Mariani, eds. Seattle: Bay Press.

Stam, Robert. 1988. Mikhail Bakhtin and left cultural critique. In Kaplan (see Gates 1988).

West, Cornel. 1989. Black culture and postmodernism. In *Remaking history*. Barbara Kruger and Phil Mariani, eds. Seattle: Bay Press.
Williams, Raymond. 1977. *Marxism and literature*. Oxford: Oxford University Press.

SIXTEEN

Analogy as Destiny
Cartesian Man and the Woman Reader

CAROL H. CANTRELL

Feminist studies in the history and philosophy of science have suggested that supposedly neutral and objective discourses are shaped by pairs of dualisms, which though value-laden are assumed to inhere in the order of nature. These hierarchical pairs devalue women, particularly their bodies and their labor, as they sanction the domination of nature. Readers of literature can draw on these studies to address texts and genres which do not thematize gender but rather purport to portray "the human condition." Samuel Beckett's Molloy, *with its clear structure of Cartesian divisions, provides a dramatic example of how an examination of dualisms reveals the presence of a language of gender informing a minimalist literary text.*

In beginning, therefore, to speak from where we are as women, we can begin to make observable at least some of the assumptions built into the sociological discourse. Its own organized practices upon the world have treated these assumptions as features of the world itself. (Smith 1979, 149-50)

To be a woman reader is constantly to test within one's own experience the double assumption that both readers and discourse are gender-neutral. These assumptions are powerful and pervasive: virtually all disciplines presume that gender is as irrelevant to thought as the color of one's hair and as easily dismissed; indeed, in the sciences and social sciences, validity rests on this presumption. When women trained in professional fields learn to transform "the immediate and concrete features of [their] experience . . . into the conceptual mode" (Smith 1974, 8) of their disciplines, gender neutrality seems to be confirmed. But as soon as women readers begin to move back and forth between their experience as women and the assumptions of the discourse they study, the act of reading changes.

For women reading literature, the difference can be a shift of emphasis rather than of strategy, for much literature thematizes sex and/or gender. However, most scientific and philosophical discourse is not "about" gender; indeed these discourses

Hypatia vol. 5, no. 2 (Summer 1990) © by Carol H. Cantrell are governed by rules which exclude gender, for they seek to transcend the particular, the personal, the situational, and the historical, in favor of the general or the universal. Women reading as women in these fields have had to confront directly the gap between the structure of their experience and the structure of the discourse they study. The result has been a number of studies in feminist epistemology which open up not the subject matter but the history and structure of discourse to gender analysis. This body of work has enormous relevance to literary study. It is of particular importance for genres and texts whose surfaces present "the human condition" more or less directly, and which, like philosophical discourse, have strategies for getting beyond the stories of day-to-day life.

Samuel Beckett's *Molloy* is a classic example of such a text: the events in the novel defy location in history or geography; the characters are hard to construe except as operations of the psyche or operations of language. *Molloy* is not about men and women; it is about what is left of humanity when all that can be stripped away has been stripped away.[1] It is thus both resistent to a feminist reading and demanding of one, for it names and defines human reality. In this paper I will gather together materials and methods from feminist epistemology which, like a light held at an oblique angle to a seemingly flat plane, throw into sharp relief the contours of a language of gender informing *Molloy*.

> The trouble is all in the knob at the top of our bodies. I'm not against the body or the head either: only the neck, which creates the illusion that they are separate. (Atwood 1972, 91)

The assumption that readers and texts can be gender-neutral is nested within the long history of the privileging of mind over body in Western culture. In this complex tradition, the division between mind and body is hierarchical, implying that human nature "makes its distinctive character most strongly felt in a certain kind of knowledge . . . which contemplates universals" (Rorty 1979, 43). Reason, the faculty of mind that handles universals, is, according to this tradition, unaffected by the bodily situation of the knower. At the same time, reason is strongly associated with the male and just as strongly dissociated from the female (Harding 1983; Keller 1985; Lloyd 1984). This paradox does not seem paradoxical because the masculine is "unmarked"; that is, it is taken to be the normative or inclusive condition, while the feminine, in contrast, is "marked" as deviant or exceptional (Shapiro 1982). Thus a feminist analysis of the concept of reason suggests that, far from being a privileged human activity free from the taint of gender, reason has served simultaneously to enforce and to deny the reality of gender hierarchy.

Even if reason were gender-neutral, it is defined in relation to pairs of terms that are not. The designation of woman as lesser or partial man (Whitbeck 1986) is reinforced by the analogous valuation of body as inferior to mind. Both pairs are located with a large and interlocking[2] network of polarities articulating a system of values so pervasive they seem to exist within nature itself (Ortner 1974). These numerous pairs, which organize and assign values to perceptions and conceptions, include, for example,

male	female
mind	body
culture	nature
reason	emotion
objectivity	subjectivity
public	private
invention	reproduction
form	matter

This system of polarities is not a group of archetypes; its terms are not eternal and unchanging but rather fluid and at times inconsistent (MacCormack 1980), and each pair has its own complicated history (Jordanova 1980, 1986; Williams 1973; Ellmann 1968). In fact, as a group, these pairs act rather like a language in which gender is a central term. In Iris Young's words, "Gender is not merely a phenomenon of individual psychology and experience. In most cultures it is a basic metaphysical category by which the whole universe is organized. . . . [G]ender differentiation is primarily a phenomenon of symbolic life, in both the individual consciousness and the general metaphysical framework and ideologies of a culture" (1983, 135).

As a governing principle of the symbolic life of a culture, then, gender differentiation and the language of dualisms in which it is embedded leaves its traces within the discourses which participate in that symbolic life. To anticipate my later argument, Beckett's *Molloy* is a particularly clear example of how a language of dualisms functions within a literary text, for *Molloy* embodies Cartesian dualisms with an uncanny clarity and consistency, as I will show. Before turning to Beckett's text, however, I want to sketch out a feminist reading of the Cartesian shift, with special emphasis on its import for the woman reader.

As feminist philosophers and historians of science have shown, the Cartesian shift affected both the context and the content of gender differentiation. While Descartes clearly considered the *cogito* to make human beings equals (Lloyd 1984, 44-50), the effect of his thought was to rigidify and intensify the split between the two sides of the traditional system of polarities by redefining the nature of knowledge and the nature of matter. First, his method, which makes the mind's detachment a precondition for real knowledge, drove a wedge between subject and object, self and other, mind and body, reason and emotion. The historical significance of this wedge can be demonstrated by contrasting Descartes's detachment with Plato's picture of the knower as driven by passion and striving for union with the object of knowledge (Lloyd 1984, 4-41; Keller 1985, 23-32). Moreover, Descartes's reduction of matter to the measurable and the inert intensified the hierarchical relationship between the two sides of the system of polarities. Again, if we contrast Descartes's thought with a prior tradition—in this case, of the long-standing conception of the earth as a living being—we can see the effect of his thought. For after Descartes, veins in human bodies and veins of ore, both living elements in the Renaissance microcosm and macrocosm, are composed of "dead, inert particles moved by external, rather than inherent forces" (Merchant 1980, 193). The "death of nature," as Carolyn Merchant has named this mechanical conception of the world, sanctions its manipulation.

The relationship between subject and object produced by the Cartesian shift affected man's relationship to nature—and man's relationship to woman; in Genevieve Lloyd's words,

> We owe to Descartes an influential and pervasive theory of mind, which provides support for a powerful version of the sexual division of mental labor. Women have been assigned responsibility for that realm of the sensuous which the Cartesian Man of Reason must transcend, if he is to have true knowledge of things. (50)

The "Man of Reason" can live at the necessary remove from the material world in which, after all, his body is embedded, only with substantial support from those who tend to bodily needs and smooth over the difficulties of life outside the circle of reason. This division of responsibilities amounts to a translation of the language of dualisms into private and public social roles. In Dorothy Smith's analysis, "At almost every point women mediate for men the relation between the conceptual mode of action and the actual concrete forms in which it is and must be realized, and the actual material conditions upon which it depends" (1974, 10). The modern sexual division of labor typified by the complementary labors of doctor and nurse has been bolstered by an analogous sexual division of personality, women characterized as naturally more emotional, more passive, more connected to others, men as more analytical, more active, more detached. Man's impartiality has qualified him to be judge, doctor, scientist, administrator; women's partiality has disqualified her. To a great extent her role has been limited to realms where her main labor—care—is all but invisible.

The extent to which the symbolic life of Western culture has absorbed Cartesian dualisms and made self-evident the rightness of Cartesian divisions is registered in its effect on the long-standing cultural codes which associate woman and nature and identify woman with the body. The analogies submerged in these associations (man is to woman as culture is to nature as mind is to body) now sanction various forms of objectification of the inferior terms "woman," "nature," and "body" in activities as different as pornography, factory farming, and modern medicine.

> I am endangered by motherhood. In evacuation from motherhood, I claim my life, body, world as an end in itself. (Allen 1983, 316)

> *We said that to hold back this caring would have been a violence to ourselves.* (Griffin 1980, 198)

Being in a body is not a neutral fact for a woman reader, for the female body and the terms associated with it are not neutral or normative but "marked" in the life she lives, in the discourses she reads. If she chooses to think of herself as a neutral body-less reader, she regards herself differently than a text regards her. If she chooses to be a "marked" or embodied reader, she is proceeding in violation of the text's expectations. Seeing her relationship to a text as a problem forces her to reconsider the question of the relationship between body and mind, as mind is represented by supposedly genderless texts and readers.

Her location is a function of a complex interaction between symbol system and biology, and in this interaction analogy is destiny. Analogy, that is, interprets and valuates anatomy: woman is to nature as man is to culture, or, more complexly, woman is closer to nature than man; her labor mediates nature for culture (Ortner 1974). Her biological rhythms and her capacity to give birth are taken to define her, for they confirm that her alignment with nature is natural. Biology, screened through the grid of her culture's symbolic structures,[3] seems to lock her into her body while loosening the relation of man to his. Thus if woman is defined by her biological rhythms, man in contrast is defined by his disjunction from nature, from natural cycles and processes. Analogy is destiny for him, too. If woman is located on a map of cultural analogies as being close to nature, man must strive to distance himself from nature. Cartesian man, in particular, strives for detachment at both the personal and cultural level in his effort to escape the female/body/nature and to become wholly autonomous; his separation from body, from nature, Susan Bordo argues, "can be seen as a 'father of oneself' fantasy on a highly abstract plane. The sundering of the organic ties between person and nature—originally experienced as . . . a chasm between self and world—is reenacted, this time with the human being as the engineer and architect of the separation" (1986, 452).

This sundering gestures toward what has been torn away, as culture defines itself in opposition to the nature it transcends. For a woman reader, the presence of a language of dualisms within the texts she reads means that she is represented in those texts at critical moments of suppression and valuation. Paradoxically, this language, which has in so many destructive ways shaped her experience and her sense of herself, can be turned inside out, so to speak, and used to track what has been denigrated and what has been lost. Though she cannot jump out of her culture's discourses or her own skin any more than the "man of reason" can, she can use her understanding of the language of gender as a lever to move her self into a new relationship to that language.

Turning a language of dualisms inside out is a critical moment in a woman reader's spiraling movement between experience and language. At one moment in this cycle, binary patterns serve as guides to what is being opposed, to the hidden, the unspoken, the denigrated, in her own life and in lives analogous to her own. Reciprocally, a woman reader's changing sense of her own experience serves as a constantly evolving standpoint from which she reads gendered structures. Such a process of reading, which moves between dominant symbolic structures and the undocumented, devalued, and obscure experience on which these structures depend, can allow a woman reader to read as a woman a novel like Molloy within a framework she shares in common with it; but instead of being swallowed up by it, she can read it for her own needs and uses.

> . . . mostly I stayed in my jar which knew neither seasons nor gardens. And a good thing too. (Beckett 1955, 65)

Samuel Beckett's Molloy is the first novel in a loosely connected trilogy in which "[t]he only fixity is the I alone in a dark, closed place" (Ben-Zvi 1986, 81). Molloy consists of two narratives of exactly equal length, one written by Molloy, the other by Moran, each of whom finds himself alone in a room and bidden to record his story. These stories are quests which mirror one another; Molloy sets off to look for his mother, and Moran is sent off to look for Molloy. While Molloy owns virtually nothing and has only contempt for convention, Moran has a house, garden, and son and tries to keep up appearances. Neither of these quests succeeds in its purported object; Molloy's story ends at the point he manages to wander out of a forest, Moran's when he returns to his desolate house. Both narratives are episodic; indeed they are more recognizable as confused wanderings within a psychic land-scape than as journeys in time and space. Both narratives are emphatically *con-structed*; both narrators refer frequently to the process of writing as they write, and Moran emphasizes the fictional nature of his narrative by denying the truthfulness of his first sentence in his last.

The form of his novel, then, calls attention to itself as an essential part of its meaning. And a reader conscious of the language of dualisms would find in its form an eloquent announcement of the novel's preoccupation with Cartesian divisions.[4] The book is composed of two monologues, that is, two solitary selves, or perhaps one self split in two. And the book is riddled with splits and divisions which seem to proliferate in it like a monomaniacal genealogy. Mind is divided from body, self from world, father from son, head from feet, man from nature, son from mother, action from desire, attribute from object.

In the world of *Molloy* the unity of the self depends on the absorption of or division from all other elements. Thus it is that Molloy's "region is [so] vast [he has] never left it and never shall" (88), and that at the same time "the Molloy country" is a "narrow region whose administrative limits he had never crossed and presum-ably never would" (182-83).

The Molloy country derives both its narrowness and its completeness from its transcendence of the natural world: sense impressions are unreliable; desire for the sensual world is suspect. Moran resents "the spray of phenomena . . . which happily [he] know[s] to be illusory" (151); Molloy has "no reason to be gladdened by the sun and . . . take[s] good care not to be" (39). When Molloy says, "in my region all the plains looked alike, when you knew one you knew them all" (123), he might as well be describing virtually any category of observable phenomena. In his generalizing eyes, gender distinctions collapse, and whether Lousse might be a man, whether Ruth was a man, become problems of logic, not observation. Moran would seem to speak for Molloy too when he praises the delights of total separation of mind from body in a "local and painless paralysis":

> To be literally incapable of motion at last, that must be something! My mind swoons when I think of it. And mute into the bargain! And perhaps deaf as a post! And who knows blind as a bat! And as likely as not your memory a blank! And just enough brain intact to allow you to exult! And to dread death like a regeneration. (192)

This immobilized body is a piece of "a world collapsing endlessly, a frozen world" (53), for the "world dies too, foully named" (41), mind separated from matter rendering lifeless everything that is not mind.

In the context of the narrative's indifference or antipathy to the body, to life itself, our woman reader finds Molloy's description of his own birth especially disturbing:

> Unfortunately it is not of them I have to speak, but of her who brought me into the world, through the hole in her arse if my memory is correct. First taste of the shit. (20)

She experiences this passage as a hostile rewriting of the actuality of her body and her experience. Life as waste, birth as defecation—these devaluations of the whole matter-body-nature side of her culture's dualisms find their focus in a vengeful distortion of the female body, her body. The experience of birth is reduced to entrapment in excrement, in matter, by virtue of Molloy's inaccurate reconstruction of his mother's body.[5] In a parallel act of renaming, Molloy calls his "Ma" "Mag,"

> because for me, without my knowing why, the letter g abolished the syllable Ma, and as it were spat on it, better than any other letter would have done. (21)

From the woman reader's point of view, the movement of the novel compels this hostility toward the female, for it seems to her that a drive for freedom from the body, from nature, sanctions violence against her body, which represents all these things. And a drive toward such freedom governs *Molloy*. Its many separations and divisions assert mind's freedom from and superiority to body, which is mightily present in the narrative as an enemy, an impediment, an aching and defective weight that must be swung around on crutches: the more complete the divorce between mind and body, the better. What is called for is a rebirth into transcendence rather than materiality, and this the woman reader finds in Moran's sly suggestion at the end of his monologue that his story has been a complete fiction: he has made himself his own author. If Descartes may be seen as writing a "father of [him]self fantasy on a highly abstract plane" (Bordo 1986, 452), so may Moran and, even more easily, Molloy. For when Molloy finally emerges from the dark forest through which he has been crawling, the forest ends in a ditch. He opens his eyes and bursts into the light (122); he is virtually reborn. Having had this experience, he too sits down to write and begins by renaming himself and his mother.

> [Woman] became the embodiment of the biological function, the image of nature, the subjugation of which constituted that civilization's title to fame. For millennia men dreamed of acquiring absolute mastery over nature, of converting the cosmos into one immense hunting ground. It was to this that the idea of man was geared in a male-dominated society. This was the significance of reason, his proudest boast. (Horkheimer and Adorno 1972, 248)

Reading these grand words, the woman reader smiles. For do they not show, by contrast, what pathetic and powerless creatures Molloy and Moran are? Molloy controls, dominates nothing; he owns virtually nothing, succeeds at nothing, leaves his imprint nowhere. Similarly, Moran is stripped of property, reputation, even his son. These are heroes shorn of everything—except their detachment. Molloy's achievement is to rise above his desire for his sucking stones; Moran's, to rise above his attachment to his possessions. It is not power but freedom from attachment, from the claims of convention, of family, of the body, of desire, that they seek. Perhaps they are nothing more than the tail-end of a tradition of heroism defined by the domination of nature. Or perhaps this minimalism is after all a guarantee of power—the power to define essential human reality.

For as she reflects on the very minimalism of these claims to the heroic, the woman reader considers that in *Molloy* a substantial portion of her experience has been jettisoned in the name of trimming life down to bare necessity. Just as the novel excised and renamed her reproductive system, so it castigates and then eliminates the work of care which the sexual division of labor has assigned to her—care of the body, of the shelter, of the children. Somewhat to her surprise, she finds that each monologue dwells at length on a rejection or inversion of this kind of care. For Molloy, the middle forty pages of his 120-page monologue are taken up with his resistance to being cared for by the woman he calls Lousse; for Moran, the first two-thirds of his monologue bump repeatedly into the son as obstacle, and child-care shades in and out of neglect and abuse. In both narratives, the labor of human care is devalued as an impediment to freedom.

The preparation of food is an easy example of the mediation of the material world which comprises much of the labor of care, and each monologue registers a protest against it. Molloy feels sure that Lousse is poisoning his food, responding to it by ignoring it or snapping it up like a dog (71-72). Moran, who is the caretaker himself, reverses the activity of nourishing his child with the enema he gives him before their journey. These monologues caricature and invert a more fundamental activity of caretaking—that of attentiveness to another person's needs, which in both narratives becomes a version of voyeurism. Lousse does all that she can to keep Molloy around "just to feel me near her, with her" (63), and spies on him constantly. Even though "with Lousse my health got no worse, or scarcely" (74), he does not need her in any way; on the contrary, her food, shelter, and above all her attention threatens to smother him: "me to she would have buried" (50). Moran, with his desire to maintain unquestioned authority, is as watchful of his son as Lousse is of Molloy; he is wary of his every movement and mood. The result of this spying is to reproduce the value system which creates and fosters separation; the son inevitably leaves his father. Connection with others is as threatening to freedom as is connection with the body.

The essential life of Molloy and Moran, then, cannot be located in the world they share with other people. The essential life is the lonely life of the quest. Both monologues articulate a sharp contrast between the petty comforts of domestic life and the lonely rigors of the quest. There is something a little odd about these rigors, though—they are mainly failures of the body rather than difficulties of terrain or weather. Food and shelter seem to take care of themselves.

> But did I at least eat, from time to time? Perforce, perforce, roots, berries, sometimes a little mulberry, a mushroom from time to time, trembling, knowing nothing about mushrooms. . . . In a word whatever I could find, forests abound in good things. (115)

This is a pretty minimal pastoral scene, but it suffices to eliminate the (woman's) work of gathering food. Safe in the forest, the hero's autonomy is not challenged by any obvious dependency on the material world or those who might mediate it for him by providing food and shelter.

This crabbed pastoral is of central importance to the woman reader in another way as well, which she sees most clearly when she thinks about Lousse's house and Molloy's forest as a dualism. For in this pair of opposites, the forest represents nature and Lousse's house represents culture, thus reversing the more usual association of man with culture, woman with nature. Yet the reversal does not bring about a recognition of her achievement as a maker of culture: it is "chock-full of pouffes and easy chairs, they all thronged about me, in the gloom" (50). Molloy wakes to find himself in a nightdress—"pink and transparent and adorned with ribands and lace" (58). What could be more unnatural? Molloy obviously does not belong here; this world is antithetical to him. He belongs rather out there, in the world of nature away from her artifice and control. He is natural man, and he scratches, farts, and stinks to prove it. And what is the nature of natural man? "It was I who was not natural enough to enter into that order of things" (58). He is separated man, split man, hierarchical man, in a word, Cartesian man.

The woman reader reflects that this implicit claim to the universal and normative has shadowed her reading of *Molloy* from the first. The book's structure is, in Dorothy Smith's words, "determined elsewhere than where she is" (1974, 13). The woman reader is present in the book by negation; its structure of discourse sanctions and perpetuates dualisms which exclude her. If Beckett's narrative implicitly offers a critique of the Cartesian split, it also treats that split as an inescapable condition of human life.

The woman reader, on the other hand, feels a release from this claim. Her developing understanding of the forms of thought underpinning this novel has allowed her to stand apart from them and examine them critically. In fact, she considers that her act of reading has been more than an act of resistance; it has also been an act of recovery. For as she returns to certain marginal passages in the novel that struck her as she read, she feels the force of the voices that have been silenced and the presences that have been excluded. One of these passages reads as follows:

And there was another noise, that of my life become the life of this garden as it rode the earth of deeps and wildernesses. Yes, there were times when I forgot not only who I was, but that I was, forgot to be. Then I was no longer that sealed jar to which I owed my being so well preserved, but a wall gave way and I filled with roots and tame stems. . . . But that did not happen to me often, mostly I stayed in my jar which knew neither seasons nor gardens. (Beckett 1955, 65)

The "sealed jar to which I owed my being so well preserved" is in fact a barrier to contact with the "earth of deeps and wildernesses." It provides an artificial separation from the contexts and consequences of the self so sealed off, from "roots and tame stems." This ahistorical being's loneliness is a cultural construct which actually locates the self it protects within a fairly specific moment in a particular culture and gender. And the effort it has taken for this self to resist definition by history and inclusion within nature, registered in the novel's violence toward the body, is also registered in Moran's physical sensation of loss when he returns from his quest to his un-cared for home and checks to see how his bees have fared:

> I put my hand in the hive, moved it among the empty trays, felt along the bottom. It encountered, in a corner, a dry light ball. It crumbled under my fingers. They had clustered together for a little warmth, to try and sleep. . . . They had been left out all winter, their honey taken away, without sugar. . . . My bees, my hens, I had deserted them. (239)

Notes

An earlier version of this essay appeared in *Women in Beckett: Performance and Critical Perspectives*, ed. Linda Ben-Zvi, and published by the University of Illinois Press, to whom grateful acknowledgment is made for permission to reprint. I am grateful to Linda Ben-Zvi for encouraging me to undertake this project, and thank her and Sue Ellen Charlton for generous and perceptive readings of early drafts. Many thanks also to the students of my spring 1987 women's studies seminar for their spirited discussions of the main issues discussed in this paper.

1. *The Norton Anthology of English Literature: The Major Authors*, a standard classroom text, describes Beckett's heroes: "They take no action, they preach no doctrine, they know nothing save their own ignorance. . . . And yet in some dark way they represent mankind. . . . [T]hey bear witness, as more comfortable folk could not, to the essential holiness of existence" (2543).

2. The history of one of these pairs entails the others; for example, "Public and private are imbedded within a dense web of associational meanings and imitations and linked to other basic notions: nature and culture, male and female. . . . Another scholar might explore the same issues—those having to do with women and politics—by tracing the meaning of nature and culture through the centuries." See Elshtain (1981, 5).

3. Hubbard, et al (1979), note that "we came to understand that women's biology not only is not destiny, but is often not biology" (xviii).

4. Though this paper is not an influence study, it is useful to note that Beckett read Descartes's works in his academic studies and based his poem "Whoroscope" on a biography of Descartes. See Ben-Zvi (1986, 12).

5. What Molloy calls "love" momentarily restores at least the vagina, if not the rest of the female reproductive system: "She had a hole between her legs, oh not the bunghole I had always imagined, but a slit." This recognition of difference, however, is short lived, for Molloy soon speculates about whether his partner didn't really have testicles after all (76).

References

Abrams, M. H., gen. ed. 1986. *The Norton anthology of English literature: The major authors.* New York: Norton.

Allen, Jeffner. 1983. Motherhood: The annihilation of women. In *Mothering: Essays in feminist theory*. Joyce Trebilcot, ed. Totowa, NJ: Rowman and Allenheld.

Atwood, Margaret. 1972. *Surfacing*. Toronto: McClelland and Stewart. New York: Popular Library, 1976.

Beckett, Samuel. 1955. *Molloy*. Patrick Bowles and Samuel Beckett, trans. New York: Grove Press.

Ben-Zvi, Linda. 1986. *Samuel Beckett*. Boston: G.K. Hall.

Bordo, Susan. 1986. The Cartesian masculinization of thought. *Signs* 11(3): 439-56.

Ellmann, Mary. 1968. *Thinking about women*. New York: Harcourt.

Elshtain, Jean Bethke. 1981. *Public man, private woman: Woman in social and political thought*. Princeton, NJ: Princeton University Press.

Griffin, Susan. 1980. *Woman and nature: The roaring inside her*. New York: Harper and Row.

Harding, Sandra. 1983. Is gender a variable in conceptions of rationality? In *Beyond domination: New perspectives on women and philosophy*. Carol Gould, ed. Totowa, NJ: Rowman and Allenheld.

Horkheimer, Max, and Theodor W. Adorno. 1972. *Dialectic of enlightenment*. New York: Seabury Press.

Hubbard, Ruth, Mary Sue Henifen, and Barbara Fried. 1979. *Women look at biology looking at women: A collection of feminist critiques*. Boston: G. K. Hall.

Jordanova, L. J. 1980. Natural facts: A historical perspective on science and sexuality. In *Nature, culture and gender*. See MacCormack (1980).

Jordanova, L. J. 1986. Naturalizing the family: Literature and the biomedical sciences in the late eighteenth century. In *Languages of nature: Critical essays in science and literature*. L. J. Jordanova, ed. New Brunswick, NJ: Rutgers University Press.

Keller, Evelyn Fox. 1985. *Reflections on gender and science*. New Haven, CT: Yale University Press.

Lloyd, Genevieve. 1984. *The man of reason: "Male" and "female" in western philosophy*. Minneapolis: University of Minnesota Press.

MacCormack, Carol P. 1980. Nature, culture, and gender: A critique. In *Nature, culture and gender*. Carol MacCormack and Marilyn Strathern, eds. Cambridge: Cambridge University Press.

Merchant, Carolyn. 1980. *The death of nature: Women, ecology and the scientific revolution*. San Francisco: Harper and Row.

Ortner, Sherry B. 1974. Is female to male as nature is to culture? In *Woman, culture and society*. Michelle Z. Rosaldo and Louise Lamphere, eds. Stanford, CA: Stanford University Press.

Rorty, Richard. 1979. *Philosophy and the mirror of nature*. Princeton, NJ: Princeton University Press.

Shapiro, Judith. 1982. "Women's studies": A note on the perils of markedness. *Signs* 7(3): 717-21.

Smith, Dorothy E. 1974. Women's perspective as a radical critique of sociology. *Sociological Inquiry* 44(1): 7-13.

Smith, Dorothy E. 1979. A sociology for women. In *The prism of sex: Essays in the sociology of knowledge*. J. Sherman and E. T. Beck, eds. Madison: University of Wisconsin Press.

Whitbeck, Caroline. 1986. Theories of sex difference. In *Women and values: Readings in recent feminist philosophy*. Marilyn Pearsall, ed. Sacramento, CA: California University Press.

Williams, Raymond. 1973. *The country and the city*. New York: Oxford University Press.

Young, Iris Marion. 1983. Is male gender identity the cause of male domination? In *Mothering*. See Allen (1983).

SEVENTEEN

Dressing Down Dressing Up
The Philosophic Fear of Fashion

KAREN HANSON

There is, to all appearances, a philosophic hostility to fashionable dress. Studying this contempt, this essay examines likely sources in philosophy's suspicion of change; anxiety about surfaces and the inessential; failures in the face of death; and the philosophic disdain for, denial of, the human body and human passivity. If there are feminist concerns about fashion, they should be radically different from those of traditional philosophy. Whatever our ineluctable worries about desire and death, whatever our appropriate anger and impatience with the merely superficial, whatever our genuine need to mark off the serious from the trivial, feminism may be a corrective therapy for philosophy's bad humor and self-deception, as these manifest themselves when the subject turns to beautiful clothes.

Thoughtful feminists can find themselves concerned about matters of dress and appearance, provoked to attend to and theorize about the causes and consequences of fashion. This reflection may begin with a sunny spirit of analytical confidence and interest, or it may be undertaken with a glum sense of the pressing need to reexamine all aspects of women's lives. Whatever the original mood, however, the enlistment of traditional philosophy as an ally in the exploration of this topic is likely to produce a sour and anxious state.

Feminism may suppose it shares with traditional philosophy an initial distrust of fashion, but this could prove poor ground for fellowship. Philosophy does indeed manifest sustained scorn for attention to personal appearance and fashionable dress, but there is a risk that a sympathetic response to that scorn may simply mean attachment to an unattractive and sometimes abusive partner. What is the character of the philosophic attitude? Whence the philosopher's hostility to fashionable dress?

Beautiful clothes, up to the minute in style, carefully made and proudly worn, do tend more often than not to arouse the philosopher's contempt. But why should this be? Santayana claimed:

Beauty is a value, . . . it is an emotion, an affection of our volitional and appreciative
nature. . . . [And] this value is positive, it is the sense of the presence of something
good, or (in the case of ugliness) of its absence. It is . . . never a negative value. (1961,
43)

And yet the changing modes of dress which *are* a source of pleasure to many, *are*
appreciated and desired by most, are often seen by the philosopher as worse than
worthless: for *this* serious thinker, fashionable beauty—whether of men or of
women—does seem a negative value. Is there any justification for the philosopher's
opposition?

There may be moral, socioeconomic, and political concerns that can be ranged
against the demands and effects of fashion. Some may object to the use of
animals—their pelts in luxurious garments, for example, their oils and their living
tissues in the formulations and the testing of cosmetics. The conditions of clothing
production in the industrial age—the exploitation of workers, the potential for
misallocation of limited agricultural resources, the prospects for economic colonial-
ism—all can contribute to the sense that the beauty of fashion is a false front
covering ugly human misery and economic abuse. Fashion can be seen to mark and
help maintain class differences, to promote and enforce repellent social distinctions
based on wealth, heritage, and gender. New operations of imperialism may be
discerned as the changing standards of Western fashion are disseminated globally,
asserting a peculiar cultural hegemony as they abruptly displace traditional clothing, the indigenous styles presumably better suited to local climate and surely more
expressive of native craft and culture.

But are considerations of these sorts really at the heart of the philosopher's
hostility? The political and social issues connected with textile and apparel manu-
facturing and merchandising can, after all, be directly addressed, addressed *as*
political and economic problems. That there is room for moral improvement in this
area of commerce does not distinguish the fashion business from any other sphere
of human activity, and neither does the fact that individuals, in their concern for
fashionable adornment, can demonstrate a great range of vices and irresponsibilit-
ies. The prospects for profligacy and unfairness are probably no wider in matters of
clothing than they are in matters of food and shelter. Yet some philosophers seem
to reserve a special disapprobation for fashionable dress, even while they enjoy a
well-furnished and spacious dwelling, even while they relish a meal of veal and baby
vegetables, kiwi soufflé and cognac to follow. What could account for this? In
complex and relatively affluent societies, choices among alternative styles and types
of dress become available. Choices are here not only possible but nearly inevitable.
Why should *this* exercise of taste so often provoke disgust?

Fashion is inherently associated with change, and the instability of the fashionable choice may seem to some a proof of the emptiness and confusion of this
sort of discrimination. If there is a philosophic conviction that the desirable cannot
be identified with the desired, it is a conviction perversely supported by adversion
to the vagaries of desire; so that suspicion of fashion is almost immediate: what real
value there possibly be in something virtually defined by *changing* desire? Still,
there is little reason to charge the fashion plate with confusion or ignorance about

the nature of the relevant choices: fashion knows it lives on change. Why must some philosophy—since Plato—deny the propriety of such a life?

The search for lasting truths and enduring values is a noble activity, but it has sometimes engendered a flight from ordinary, common experience, the experience of growth and decay, coming-to-be and passing away. The Platonic version of this flight is both uniquely thrilling and persistently representative. Philosophy again and again finds itself in pursuit of the real truth hidden behind the merely apparent, taking thought to discover what *is* as opposed to what merely *seems* to be the case, and confident that the wisdom worth loving will endure. Philosophy may, then, take itself to have a natural antagonism to fashion, as well as a perfect antipathy to any interest in clothes—those wrappings of the wrappings of the mind—those superficial goods situated at least two removes from reality, from the philosopher's perdurable realm of ideas.

If some notice *must* be made of clothes, however, the attraction to permanence can still be made plain. "The healthy state" that Socrates describes in Book II of the *Republic* has citizens in "summer for the most part unclad and unshod and in the winter clothed and shod sufficiently"; and this community remains content with simple garb, with a simple life, as they "hand on a like life to their offspring" (Plato 618-19). Glaucon's goading of course leads Socrates to consideration of the "luxurious city," the "fevered state," and it is only then that mention must be made of "embroidery" and "the manufacture of all kinds of articles . . . that have to do with women's adornment"; there is suddenly the need for "beauty-shop ladies" and "barbers" (Plato 619).

Utopian visions do typically focus on some version of stable simplicity: Thomas More's good island folk all wear work clothes of durable leather. Most of their public occasions call for a covering cloak, but all citizens wear the same style, the same color ("the color of natural wool") (More 43). Everyone puts on white for church, but with these few outfits every closet is complete, from season to season, year upon year. Temptations to personal adornment are said to have been extinguished long ago by making jewels the playthings of children, gold and silver the material of chamber pots, slaves' chains, and criminals' uniforms.

If there is in such utopian tales a recognition that a wide range of political practices can influence and be influenced by sartorial desires, and that these desires can be socially molded, there is still the assumption that a *right* way of dressing can be found and, once found, sustained. Historical dress reform movements have tended to share this assumption, and have formed themselves around discoveries that prevailing fashions are unhealthy, dysfunctional, unnatural, and irrational. But is there a style of clothing that will promote human health? What functions do we expect our clothes to perform, to assist, to advance? What is natural in the way of dress? And what has reason to do with raiment? If rationality involves appropriate adjustments of means to ends, rational dress will serve the final aims of clothing. But what are those aims? Can we suppose that, behind the flux of time, place, culture, and individual history, clothing has a permanent *point*?

The intuition may prevail that clothing *is* in some way a necessity of life, while the apprehension remains that some forms of attention to this necessity constitute serious mistakes in the conduct of a life worth living. Uneasiness persists on the matters of appearance and change. Thoreau's famous caution— "beware of all enterprises that require new clothes"—may typically be taken as a warning about the vanities of an unperfected society and its distracting demands, and it is true that Thoreau has harsh words to say about fashion and its requirements of novelty. But Thoreau welcomes the new—even, emblematically, new clothes—so long as it is substance—human character—and not just appearance that is transformed:

> I say, beware of all enterprises that require new clothes, and not rather a new wearer of clothes. If there is not a new man, how can the new clothes be made to fit? . . . Perhaps we should never procure a new suit, however ragged and dirty the old, until we have so conducted, so enterprised or sailed in some way, that we feel like new men in the old, and that to retain it would be like keeping new wine in old bottles. Our moulting season, like that of the fowls, must be a crisis in our lives. (15)

Clothing may still seem to figure only the surface, so that change in it, driven only by fashion, is inherently superficial, and on that ground despicable. The change in appearance that is condemned, however, is now a specific type—the merely superficial, the unbecoming illusion of the changed man. And if appearances in general continue to bear deceptive possibilities, and thus remain suspect, appearances can also be celebrated, be themselves celebrations, if the substantial affairs of life are at the same time put right.

If we would follow the spirit of Thoreau's admonition, then, we would not measure our integrity by the shabbiness of our old clothes; we would rather find fitting occasions for the new. If we, too, wish to live deliberately, we, too, might think about clothing; but we might also go on to weigh differently the distinction between personal appearance and reality, judge differently the suitability of a particular desire for change.

Conscientious advocates of superficial change will want to recast the distinction between appearance and substance, and they may make oblique assaults upon the fortress of the functional, the useful, and the natural, as those latter are erected against the artificial, the deceptive, and the irrational forces of culture. Baudelaire is a prime instance of this sort of argumentative championing of the ephemeral surface, the short-lived societal overlay. He insists upon a "historical theory of beauty," a claim that beauty is composed of not only "an eternal, invariable element" but also a "relative, circumstantial" one— "the age, its fashions, its morals, its emotions" (3). "*Particular* beauty, the beauty of circumstance," is a function of its being fugitive, transitory: just as art of the past may have not only a general beauty, but also a specific historical value or interest; so, Baudelaire claims, that which conveys the present can give us pleasure in "its essential quality of being present" (1). Particular beauty throughout the ages has a common source, but its substance is ineluctably indexed by time—it is the "mysterious beauty" contributed "accidently" by *human life* (13). If part of the truth of beauty is a contribution of the momentary, then perhaps fashion, even if—indeed just because—it shadows the ever-changing present, is not to be scorned.

Baudelaire also defends cosmetics, seeing in makeup not the workings of a lie but something more like a poem. According to Baudelaire, our natural state is neither good nor true; he takes seriously the problem of original sin. Moral reformation now positively requires an improvement of our natural condition. (Indeed, we might remember that when Adam and Eve ate the forbidden fruit, and their eyes were opened, the first thing they did was sew fig leaves, to make themselves aprons. God must have approved of this adornment, for even as he curses the couple, he pauses—at Genesis 3: 21—to make them "coats of skins," to clothe them.) Baudelaire claims that if we fairly scrutinize the natural—"all the actions and desires of the purely natural man"—we

> will find nothing but frightfulness. Everything beautiful and noble is the result of reason and calculation. . . . Virtue . . . is artificial, super-natural. . . . Good is always the product of some art. (32)

Good looks are evidently no exception. Baudelaire pleads for the powder that tames the blemishes left by beastly nature, and he praises black eyeliner and bright rouge for their effect of surpassing, not imitating, nature or youth. This artifice can "represent life, a supernatural and excessive life," and it ought to "display itself," not hide, announce its transfiguration of nature "with frankness and honesty" (34).

This way of breaking the tie between the plain and the honest, this mode of opposing the natural and the good, may relieve an ancient philosophic suspicion of change; but it may also breathe new life into a certain Platonic aspiration. A peculiar disdain for the body may paradoxically lie beneath these recommendations for attention to it. Painstaking adornment of the natural figure and face are appropriate not because these features of the human being are worthy of the veneration such a preoccupation might imply. It is rather that the ordinary human body must be overcome—face powder is "to create an abstract unity in the color and texture of the skin," to "[approximate] the human being to the statue, that is to something superior and divine" (Baudelaire 33)—so that the truly worthy element— the soul—may be expressed. Baudelaire's interest in the transformed surface is backed by this conviction about the underlying structure of values, so that he is "led to regard external finery as one of the signs of the primitive nobility of the human soul":

> Fashion should thus be considered as a symptom of the taste for the ideal which floats on the surface of all the crude, terrestrial and loathsome bric-à-brac that natural life accumulates in the human brain: . . . every fashion is . . . a new and more or less happy effort in the direction of Beauty, some kind of approximation to an ideal for which the restless human mind feels a constant titillating hunger. (32)

Thorstein Veblen conveys a very different moral tone in his remarks on clothing, but he, too, aligns an interest in fashion with the strivings of the soul: "It is by no means . . . uncommon . . . , in an inclement climate, for people to go ill clad in order to appear well dressed. . . . The need of dress is eminently a 'higher' or spiritual need" (1899, 1968). And Clive Bell, in endorsing and extending Veblen's view, asks us to verify from our own experience clothing's claim to spirituality, its disdain for the constraints of the material world: "Who does not appreciate the expense, the inconvenience, perhaps even the discomfort of that which they feel themselves compelled to wear?" (1947, 12). This compulsion is really, Bell suggests, "the categorical imperative of fashion," and he hazards a connection between this imperative and another, a tie to our deepest rules of behavior:

[I]t is difficult in praising clothes not to use such adjectives as "right," "good," "correct," "unimpeachable," or "faultless," . . . while in discussing moral shortcomings we tend very naturally to fall into the language of dress and speak of a person's behaviour as being shabby, shoddy, threadbare, down at the heel, botched, or slipshod. (12)

As a straight defense of fashion, this approach is inherently liable to lapse into sarcastic irony. If we would truly seek the spiritual, should we tarry so long getting dressed? How can we take ourselves to be approaching a deeper reality, or higher ideals, by repeatedly changing our clothes and our faces? The bulging closet and the cluttered makeup table seem to instantiate, not to surmount, "the crude, terrestrial and loathsome bric-à-brac" that the sublime soul would prefer to ignore.

And philosophers do tend to cast their lots with the sublime soul and its superior interests. Even Santayana, whose remark about beauty helped to set this puzzle about the philosopher's scorn for beautiful clothes, in fact contrasts merely physical pleasures with the pleasures intrinsic to the sense of beauty, claiming that the "greater dignity and range of aesthetic pleasure" must be attributed to its dissociation from the body (43). All pleasures may require a functioning body, but the pleasures called physical "call attention" to some part of the body, whereas aesthetic pleasures are "transparent." The sense organs that condition aesthetic pleasure do not "intercept our attention," and this is what makes the sense of beauty especially valuable:

The soul is glad, as it were, to forget its connection with the body. . . . [The] illusion of disembodiment is very exhilarating, while immersion in the flesh and confinement to some organ gives a tone of grossness and selfishness to our consciousness. (36)

Fashion, however, calls attention to illusions grounded on embodiment. The last thing it would let the soul forget is its connection to the body, and it is certainly conceivable that these reminders are a source of historic resentment. There is no general philosophic indignation about otherwise comparable cultural artifacts: intricately worked cloth hanging on the wall as a tapestry or lying on the floor as a carpet, metal and stones cast into utilitarian or votive vessels—these can be straightforwardly admired, with no apology. But attention to dress is inseparable from attention to the body—when cloth, metal, and stones are used in clothing, their aesthetic characteristics are at least partly a matter of their relation to the body—and philosophers may begin to feel a kind of rudeness in the appreciative stare.

Some feminists have inflected this stare with gender, complaining of the male gaze.[1] A grievance filed on this score may thus seem to elicit the support of traditional philosophy, but the implications of accepting such chivalrous assistance must be carefully considered. Women may have a keen sense of the threat to identity posed by the gaze that turns its own limitation into the other's liability, but resentment at being regarded as a mere object should not drive the feminist into the comforting arms of traditional philosophy. Philosophy may share certain anxieties about things, may want to insist that we must get beyond the surfaces of things, beyond the merely superficial.[2] But philosophy's drive to get past what it takes to be the inessential has usually been linked with a denial or devaluation of what it has typically associated with the woman. Thus, even when traditional philosophy turns to aesthetics, and, for once, interest can focus unashamedly on appearances, an opportunity is still sought to disparage the body. A tradition that displays this sort of embarrassment about carnality, a repressive tradition, may not be the most agreeable companion on the quest to reassert and revaluate women's lives and feminine experience.

The tradition wants to claim that aesthetic judgments are disinterested. But if, as Kant says, the satisfaction determined by the beautiful is unrelated to inclination, then one who would judge some fashionable dress beautiful will clearly have to cope with some difficult problems of desire. These are general philosophic problems; this uneasiness about desire is not simply a function of trying carefully to follow Kant's aesthetics. Jean-Paul Sartre piously claims that "great beauty in a woman kills the desire for her":

> we cannot simultaneously place ourselves on the plane of the aesthetic and on the realistic plane of physical possession. To desire her we must forget she is beautiful, because desire is a plunge into the heart of existence, into what is most contingent and most absurd. (1972, 225)

Socrates' insistence on the philosopher's distance from physical desire—estrangement from an interest not only in sexual pleasures but also in "other attentions . . . to our bodies," "smart clothes and shoes and other bodily ornaments" (Plato 47)—is a constraining legacy; his deathbed testament that the true philosopher lives for death, practices dying—freeing the soul from the body—constitutes an inheritance philosophers seem to find difficult either to ignore or to accept. They are, after all, only human.

If they were pure mind, spirits, the issue of clothing wouldn't arise. But they are *not* disembodied thinking things, they are in fact neither angels nor brutes, so there is a need for clothes; and that need may stand as irritating proof of some fatal failures. Most obviously, there is the failure to achieve the ideal philosophic death sought from ancient to modern times—the separation of the soul from the body. And as our clothing is testimony to our embodiment, it can whisper of the actual material death that, as humans, we may rather seek, in vain, *to avoid*. The uncanny quality of empty clothes may quietly speak of the intensity of the fact of our embodiment and thus at once murmur the truth of our *real* mortality.

Thoreau says that we may laugh at the clothing of dead kings and queens, but our laughter simply expresses our eerie sense of the mysterious relation between dress and the life of human beings:

All costume off a man is pitiful or grotesque. It is only the serious eye peering from and the sincere life passed within it, which restrain laughter and consecrate the costume of any people. (17)

In his own way, Baudelaire agrees:

If one wants to appreciate them properly, fashions should never be considered as dead things; you might just as well admire the tattered old rags hung up, as slack and lifeless as the skin of St. Bartholomew, in an old-clothes dealer's cupboard. Rather they should be thought of as vitalized and animated by the beautiful women who wore them. (33)

The idea that clothing apart from the animated body is dead is given a more lascivious treatment in a short story by Guy de Maupassant:

O dear friend, do you know more precious moments in life than those in which we watch the woman as she allows each garment in turn to fall with a slight rustle to her feet. . . . And what can be more charming than [women's] movements in removing these soft garments which drop limply as if they had been touched by death . . . (1908, 116-17)

But if clothes detached from a lively human presence seem touched by death, if costumes beheld disconnected from a wearer are pitiful, grotesque, as disturbing as the sight of skin removed from a martyr, then a strong interest in clothes seems once again a sort of perversion of the human mind. Clothes, in their intrinsic and yet always breakable relation to our embodied life, can seem a memento mori. It is then no wonder if some may turn their faces from a notice of dress.

If the thought of clothes can produce this sort of dejection, the appearance of fashionable dress might lead to complete despair. Fashion, defined by changing desire, may cover the changing, always aging human body, but may also—in its very transitoriness—uncover, or underscore, the fact of mortality. Fashions are born and die; they may sometimes be revived, but— just as we feared—the revivals are never quite the same as the originals.

Freud connects a failure to appreciate transient beauty with a revolt against mourning. According to Freud, the mysterious pain of mourning occurs as love clings to objects destroyed or forever lost. Given our instinctive recoil from anything painful, a protective anticipation of the inevitable necessity of mourning may work to block a wholehearted investment of love or admiration when we recognize the fragility, the perishability, of the prospective love object. Freud recounts a desperate walk "through a smiling countryside," in the company of a young poet. The scenery was undeniably beautiful, but the poet

felt no joy in it. He was disturbed by the thought that all this beauty was fated to extinction, that it would vanish when winter came, like all human beauty and all the beauty and splendor that men have created or may create. All that he would otherwise have loved and admired seemed to him to be shorn of its worth by the transience which was its doom. (79)

Freud argued with the unhappy poet. He insisted to the contrary that the transience of the beautiful increases its worth:

> Transience value is scarcity value in time. Limitation in the possibility of an enjoyment raises the value of the enjoyment. . . . The beauty of the human form and face vanish forever in the course of our own lives, but their evanescence only lends them a fresh charm. A flower that blossoms only for a single night does not seem to us on that account less lovely. (80)

Freud found his own considerations "incontestable," but he noticed they "made no impression" upon the poet; so he concluded that "some powerful emotional factor was at work which was disturbing [the poet's] judgment." The problem, again, was the revolt against mourning: the thought that all this beauty would fade had given that sensitive soul "a foretaste of mourning" over the inevitable decease; and an aversion to the pain or grief then interfered with an immersion in the pleasure of beauty.

If this can happen with the beauties of Nature, which, as Freud points out, are so recurrent that "in relation to the length of our lives" they "can in fact be regarded as eternal," how much more likely is despair over clothes, which not only *wear* out but *go* out. The new look becomes old, and what was young and fresh last season may now seem tired and old; by next year it will be dead. Couldn't this trouble the sensitive soul?

Some tough philosophers will declare that this is not their problem. They do not, they are certain, suffer from a sort of fearful love of beautiful new clothes, or hold back their appreciation of fashionable dress because it occasions an unhappy apprehension of human transience. The spiritually hearty assurance returns: if there is a vision of death in the sight of the fashion plate, it is from the appearance that truly vital values have been extinguished, submerged by superficial concerns. Death by this sort of drowning is the fate of fashion-followers, for they are the narcissists: they spend a dangerously inordinate amount of time gazing into their mirrors. And the good life, these philosophers say, is lost.

The story of Narcissus is an appropriate cautionary tale, but its moral may not be fully understood. That beautiful boy is made to fix on his own reflection precisely because of his failure to respond to the glances of others. Narcissus spurns all lovers; he cares not at all about the feelings his appearance seems to inspire. When the gods hear the prayers of one wounded by Narcissus' indifference, and the youth who loved no one is doomed to love himself, it is clear that Narcissus' flaw is not his beauty but his hard heart. Narcissus tells the nymphs who pursue him, who want his love, "You shall have no power over me," and he seems oblivious to the powerful effects of his own good looks on those around him. Unwilling to let others have power over him, uninterested in his power over others, Narcissus is socially disconnected, and it is that disconnection which prefigures his fate. When Narcissus is captivated by his own image in the pool, and he pines away for his own reflection, his problem is not new: he was always too self-absorbed.

The dangers and the appeal of social disconnection are as real as the dangers and the appeal of social conformity. Philosophers may want to view themselves as

critical outsiders, sufficiently alienated to find a perspective on the world and
distanced enough to offer accurate assessments. One who would be fashionable,
however, must attend to the choices of others and let his or her own choices be
somehow, somewhat, influenced by the dynamics of others' desires. William Hazlitt
expresses contempt for such an enterprise by describing fashion as a

> continual struggle between "the great vulgar and the small" to get the start of, or keep
> up with each other in the race of appearances. . . . To look like nobody else is a
> sufficiently mortifying reflection; to be in danger of being mistaken for one of the
> rabble is worse. Fashion constantly begins and ends in the two things it abhors most,
> singularity and vulgarity. (Quoted in Bell 1947, 68)

But if a "race of appearances" seems pointless, and if it seems not only ignoble but
even incoherent to worry about both being odd and being common, the insistence
on a position on the sidelines can also be ill-grounded.

It is not merely that, as Marx almost said, philosophers have tried to interpret
the world, while the point is rather to refashion it. The greater mistake is to suppose
that a place can really be found outside the reach of social judgment and influence.
The philosopher who denies or decries the force of social norms of dress can put
one in mind of Molière's misanthrope, Alceste, that unhappy advocate of plain
speech—"the naked truth"—and plain dress. When Alceste's friend, Philinte,
suggests that politeness, courtesy, decrees a certain outward show, Alceste rails,

> No, no, this formula you'd have me follow,
> However fashionable, is false and hollow.
> (17)

Alceste's rage about a world of false fronts is understandable, and his disgust with
social disguises is not an altogether discreditable reaction. He says he prizes
sincerity, and he presents his bilious mood as a simple result of his devotion to
honesty and truth. His bad temper is also tiresome, however, and requires the
unsolicited indulgence of his friends. Philinte gently combats Alceste's outbursts:

> This philosophic rage is a bit extreme;
> You've no idea how comical you seem. . . .
> (17)

Alceste indeed does not know how he seems. He might want to borrow Hamlet's
line and swear that he is, that he knows not "seems"; but this might not always work
as an oath of authenticity. It could instead attest to failures of tact and self-awareness.

Alceste's resolute refusal to modify his behavior through some anticipatory
thought of how it might be perceived by or affect others, his inability to discern
any but the basest motives in all acts of social courtesy—these suggest a zeal for
incivility that is neither defensible nor uplifting. Alceste does not escape the mores
of this world; he just fails to find or give pleasure. When Thoreau warns us that new

clothes will not fit unless we, too, are new, we might remember that in fitting into society, in taking a proper place and working through the adjustments that may be required on both sides, reciprocally, we may be made new—and so may society—and this is not inevitably for the worse. Alceste's unwillingness to see this leaves him with the option he continually proposes but cannot really achieve—fleeing the world. His demented dream of being honest in isolation, apart from all people, is obviously incoherent; but Alceste's failures extend beneath the logical to the personal.

When he sarcastically derides judgments and affections resting on matters of dress, we may sympathize—

> Because of what high merits do you deem
> Him worthy of the honor of your esteem?
>
> Are you in love with his embroidered hose?
> Do you adore his ribbons and his bows?
> Or is it that this paragon bewitches
> Your tasteful eye with his vast German breeches?
> (50)

But Alceste is the man who wears "green ribbons" (143), and we can see that his grudges against society spring from jealousy as well as from devotion to truth and disgust with superficiality. His failure to acknowledge his own mixed motivations shows he is not wholly honest, even to himself; and thus the problem of not knowing how he "seems" is joined to the problem of not knowing how, what, he *is*.

Self-consciousness, it must be remembered, is generally an epistemological *advance*. One would need a special argument to show that the self-consciousness connected with an awareness of and interest in one's appearance is inherently retrograde. Even the Western myth that most clearly promotes nostalgia for the Eden before self-consciousness deserves a different reading by committed philosophers. When Adam and Eve eat from the tree of knowledge, their eyes *are* opened. They know they are naked, so they sew together the fig leaves and make aprons. When God subsequently adds to their wardrobe, making the coats of skins, his act of clothing them is treated as—it *is*—a ceremony of investiture: accompanying the robing are God's solemn words, "Behold, the man is become as one of us, to know good and evil" (Genesis 3: 22).[3]

Clothing is a part of our difficult, post-Edenic lives; and dress, stationed at a boundary between self and other, marking a distinction between private and public, individual and social, is likely to be vexed by the forces of border wars.[4] Philosophers, those who believe that the life worth living is the examined life, should find that willful ignorance of these matters ill suits them. Could something else be disturbing their thought of fashion?

Philosophers define themselves as the lovers of wisdom, not the beloved. They are the cognizers, and their purest professional aim is to know, not to be known, to think, not to be thought about. A personal interest in dress and open responsiveness to the changing whims of fashion depend upon a recognition that one is *seen*, that one is—among other things—an *object* of others' sight, others' cognition. The activity of philosophy may engender a deep antipathy to the acknowledgment of personal passivity, an acknowledgment required for this recognition.[5] And yet we humans *are* seen—no one is really just a seer. There *is* a passive phase in the human being, and philosophy is wrong to deny or to berate it.

A correction on this point may be classified as a feminine task: the tradition takes the active/passive distinction to sort with the masculine/feminine. And if feminism sometimes wants to break down these distinctions altogether, it also wants to assert the value—the beauty, the truth, the importance—of what has tradition-ally been labeled feminine. Feminists may appropriately offer instruction on the neglected character of passivity in human experience, without thereby contributing to the idea that women alone suffer this fate, that women alone are, in particular, natural objects of sight. Although feminism may have genuine complaints about "the male gaze," an angry refusal to grant the sight of oneself may do little to overcome a world of limited vision. Indeed, there is the worrisome possibility that some feminist refusals of the gaze may not reform but instead simply partake of philosophy's dread of passivity and its devaluation of the body.[6]

But feminism could rather teach philosophy some lessons. Eve helped bring Adam to self-consciousness, to a realization that he was seen, and even God admitted this was an increase in knowledge. So if philosophy—with the help of feminism—could be brought to terms with our embodiment, could work to find an appropriate stance on the relation between the individual and social norms, could come to admit that each of us is, in part, an object to others, then philosophy might just change its attitude toward fashionable dress. Philosophers—wisdom-loving women and men—might then learn how to participate happily, deriving appropri-ate if ephemeral satisfactions, in fashion's fickle embrace.[7]

Notes

1. I thank Hilde Hein for pressing me to be more explicit on this subject and for providing detailed and useful reactions to a number of other points in this paper.

2. I owe this suggestion to Stanley Cavell, who, in a set of helpful comments on a first draft of this paper, asked whether feminism—"or one strand of feminism"—might be understood "to represent or create a new phase in the philosophical rage against the inessential."

3. Genesis 3: 22. This reading of the clothing of Adam and Eve is suggested in a larger reexamination of their story proposed by Dennis M. Senchuk (1985, 6-24).

4. For some discussion of this issue of ambiguous boundaries, see Elizabeth Wilson (1985, ch. 1 & ch. 6).

5. Cf. my "Being Doubted, Being Assured."

6. This formulation and line of thought are also due to Stanley Cavell's generous comments on a first draft.

7. An earlier version of this paper was read in Vancouver, B.C., at the 1988 meeting of the American Society for Aesthetics. I am grateful to Julius Moravscik, and the ASA Program Committee he chaired, for the invitation to give a paper on a topic connected with

fashion and dress, and I profited from the comments of those colleagues and others in attendance at the ASA meeting.

References

Baudelaire, Charles. *The painter of modern life & other essays*. Jonathan Mayne, trans. & ed. London: Phaidon Press, 1964.

Bell, Clive. 1947. *On human finery*. London: The Hogarth Press.

De Maupassant, Guy. 1908. L'Inconnue. *Oevres complètes*. v.mo. Paris: L. Conard. (Also in *The novels and tales of Guy de Maupassant*. 1928. London: Alfred A. Knopf.)

Freud, Sigmund. *On transience*. Vol. 5 of *Collected papers*. James Strachey, ed. New York: Basic Books, 1959.

Hanson, Karen. 1987. Being doubted, being assured. In *Images in our souls*. Vol. 10 of *Psychiatry and the Humanities*. Joseph Smith and William Kerrigan, eds. Baltimore: Johns Hopkins University Press.

Molière, Jean. *The misanthrope*. Richard Wilbur, trans. New York: Harcourt Brace Jovanovich, 1965.

More, Thomas. *Utopia*. Robert M. Adams, trans. New York: Norton, 1975.

Plato. *Phaedo*. In *The collected dialogues*. Hugh Tredennick, trans. Edith Hamilton & Huntington Cairns, eds. New York: Bollingen, 1963.

Plato. *Republic*. In *The collected dialogues*. Paul Shorey, trans. Edith Hamilton and Huntington Cairns, eds. New York: Bollingen, 1963.

Santayana, George. [1896] 1961. *The sense of beauty*. New York: Collier Books.

Sartre, Jean-Paul. 1972. *The psychology of imagination*. London: Methuen.

Senchuk, Dennis M. 1985. Innocence and education. *Philosophical Studies in Education*: 6-24.

Thoreau, Henry David. *Walden and civil disobedience*. Owen Thomas, ed. New York: Norton, 1966.

Veblen, Thorstein. 1899. *The theory of the leisure class*. New York: Macmillan.

Wilson, Elizabeth. 1985. *Adorned in dreams*. Berkeley, CA: University of California Press.

Notes on Contributors

ISMAY BARWELL is currently senior lecturer in the philosophy department at Victoria University, Wellington, New Zealand. She is writing a book about feminine points of view in both narratives and pictures.

CAROL H. CANTRELL is professor of English and chair of women's studies at Colorado State University. She has published work on Ezra Pound and other modern writers and is presently working on a study of image and perception in the work of Marianne Moore and Georgia O'Keeffe.

JOSEPHINE DONOVAN, professor of English at the University of Maine, is the author of several books on feminist theory, feminist criticism, and women's literature, including *Feminist Theory: The Intellectual Traditions of American Feminism* and *After the Fall: The Demeter-Persephone Myth in Wharton, Cather and Glasgow*.

MARILYN FRENCH is the author of numerous books, including the now classic *The Women's Room*. Her most recent book is *The War against Women*.

KAREN HANSON, professor of philosophy and adjunct professor of both women's studies and American studies at Indiana University, is the author of *The Self Imagined: Philosophical Reflections on the Social Character of Psyche* and a co-editor of *Romantic Revolutions: Theory and Practice*.

HILDE HEIN teaches philosophy, feminist theory, and aesthetics at the College of the Holy Cross. Bridging the gap between art world and real world, she is interested in the institutions of culture and has written *The Exploratorium: The Museum as Laboratory*.

MAE GWENDOLYN HENDERSON, associate professor of English and African American studies at the University of Illinois, Chicago, is the author of several articles on black/women's literature and co-editor of the five-volume *Anti-Slavery Newspapers and Periodicals: An Annotated Index of Letters 1817-1871*.

JANE KNELLER is an assistant professor in the philosophy department at Colorado State University and also teaches in the Women's Studies Program at Colorado State. She has published articles on Kant's aesthetic theory and on the role of imagination in the German Enlightenment.

CAROLYN KORSMEYER teaches philosophy at the State University of New York at Buffalo. She is co-author of *Feminist Scholarship: Kindling in the Groves of Academe* and numerous articles in aesthetics.

ESTELLA LAUTER is Frankenthal Professor of Humanistic Studies at the University of Wisconsin—Green Bay. Her books include *Women as Mythmakers: Poetry and Visual Art by Twentieth Century Women*, *Feminist Archetypal Theory* (with Carol Schreier Rupprecht), and *Teaching Literature and Other Arts* (co-edited with Jean-Pierre Barricelli and Joseph Gibaldi).

RENÉE LORRAINE, professor of music at the University of Tennessee at Chattanooga, teaches music history, aesthetics, feminist theory, and double bass. Recent publications include "Recovering Jouissance: Feminist Aesthetics and Music," "A History of Music," and "Pro and Contra 2 Live Crew." She formerly published under the name Renée Cox.

SAN MACCOLL is a lecturer in philosophy at the University of New South Wales in Sydney, Australia. She works on perception, aesthetics, and epistemology and takes part in the graduate program on the teaching of philosophy in schools.

AMY NEWMAN is assistant professor of philosophy at the Philadelphia College of Textiles and Science. She teaches value theory (ethics and aesthetics) and epistemology and is working on a collection of essays exploring constructions of race and gender in nineteenth-century German philosophical theology.

JENEFER ROBINSON is a professor of philosophy at the University of Cincinnati and a member of the editorial board of the *Journal of Aesthetics and Art Criticism*. She has published essays on representation, expression, and style in the arts.

STEPHANIE ROSS is associate professor of philosophy at the University of Missouri—St. Louis. She has written on such topics as caricature, allusion, photography, and modern music and is presently working on a book on the aesthetics of gardens.

ALICE SHEPPARD received her Ph.D. in psychology and has taught at Bloomsburg University in Pennsylvania and at the State University of New York Colleges at Fredonia and at Geneseo. She has published a number of papers on women's humor and social cognition and is completing the book *Cartooning for Suffrage*.

LAURIE SHRAGE teaches philosophy at the California State Polytechnic University, Pomona. She has published articles on the comparable-worth controversy and on feminism and prostitution. She co-edited two issues of the American Philosophical Association's *Newsletter on Feminism and Philosophy* on feminism and aesthetics.

MICHELE WALLACE is associate professor of English and women's studies at the City College of New York and the CUNY Graduate School. She has been a regular contributor to *Zeta*, *The Village Voice*, and *Artforum*. She is the author of *Black Macho and the Myth of Superwoman*.

MARY BITTNER WISEMAN is professor of philosophy at Brooklyn College and the Graduate School of the City University of New York. She is the author of *The Ecstasies of Roland Barthes* and is currently writing *Renaissance Madonnas and the Fantasies of Freud*.

Index

Aborigines: music and dance styles and male dominance, 41

Accessibility: as principle of feminist art, 73-75

Adler, Margot, 39

Adorno, Theodor, 61-63

The Aeneid (Vergil), 69-70

Aestheticism: dynamics of reversal in postmodern, 193-202. *See also* Aesthetics

Aesthetics: doctrine of disinterestedness, vii-viii; basic concepts of and gender bias, viii-ix; feminist philosophical perspectives within theories of, ix; introduction of term, xvn.4; theoretical discipline of and feminist theory, 3-6; theory of as model for feminist theory, 7-14; description of proposed gynecentric, 35-59; basis for development of alternative theory, 53-54; Woolf's theory of, 54-59; nondominative of Cather and Jewett, 59-61; Adorno's dialectical, 61-63; Walker and nondominative, 63-64; women and Kant's theory of taste, 179-89; visual art in Afro-American culture and black, 206-15. *See also* Aestheticism; Art; Feminist aesthetics

Aesthetic Theory (Adorno), 62

African-Americans: women and jazz music tradition, 47; dialogics, dialectics, and literary tradition of women, 119-34; women's expressive culture and literary dialogue among, 135-36.7; black aesthetics and visual art in Afro-American culture, 205-15. *See also* Race

Agriculture: theories on status of women in ancient, preagricultural societies, 40, 49n.1

Allen, Jeffner, 202n.1

Allender, Nina, 82, 83

All the Women Are White, All the Blacks Are Men, But Some of Us Are Brave (Hull, Scott, Smith), 120

Amazons: conventions in suffrage cartoons, 82

Ames, Blanche, 82

Anna Karenina (Tolstoy), 70

Apology (Plato), 176

Aptheker, Bettina, 62-63

Aristotle, 16n.16, 174-76

Art: basic concepts of and gender bias, viii-ix; feminist philosophical perspectives within theories of, ix; doctrine of aesthetic disinterestedness, 11, 12; aesthetic theory and definitions of, 13, 14; institutional theory of, 13, 15n.13; embodiment and disinterestedness, 16n.21; formalist theory of described, 21-22; formalist theory and gender, 22-26; development of feminist theory of, 26-31; formalist and feminist theories compared, 31-32; feminist theory and re-enfranchising of, 33;

gynecentric aesthetics of, 35-48; definition of and existence of feminist aesthetics, 68-76; suffrage campaign and modern feminist, 88-89; contemporary aestheticism and distinction between life and, 193, 201; will to power as and postmodern aestheticism, 196-99; black aesthetic and visual in Afro-American culture, 205-15. *See also* Aesthetics

Art (Bell), 58

Art criticism: sexist and O'Keeffe, 161

Art school movement: women's political art and, 87

Arzner, Dorothy, 145-46, 147

Audience: hypothetical narrator and, 100-101; hypothetical critical point of view, 102-103; contextual film criticism, 142

Austen, Jane, 60, 70, 101

Bachofen, J. J., 38

Bacon, Francis, 10, 16n.19

Baker, Josephine, 211

Bakhtin, Mikhail: notion of dialogism and consciousness, 121, 124; multivocality of black women's writing, 133; processes defining content of psyche, 135n.4

Balbus, Isaac D., 61

Baldwin, James, 209

Barns, Cornelia, 87-88

Bar On, Bat-Ami, 203n.8

Barwell, Ismay, xi-xii

Bataille, Georges, 203n.6

Baudelaire, Charles, 232-33, 236

Baumgarten, Alexander, xvn.4

Beauty: Kant on distinction between masculine and feminine, 170-74; Kant on taste and morality, 181; Kant's aesthetic theory and imagination, 186-89; philosophy's hostility to fashion, 230, 232, 234

Beck, Lewis White, 190n.13

Beckett, Samuel, 219-27

Begler, Elsie B., 41, 49n.4

Bell, Clive, 16n.24, 58, 233-34

Benjamin, Jessica, 200

Berleant, Arnold, 16n.17, 21

Bible: glossolalia and heteroglossia, 124-25, 136n.9; character of Nehemiah, 136n.11

Binary logic: masculinist ideologies and theoretical models of aesthetics, 194; Nietzsche's aestheticism and, 198; deconstruction as methodological approach, 199-200. *See also* Dualisms

Binford, Lewis, 49n.1

Birth control movement: political cartoons and feminist art, 87

The Birth Project (Chicago), 30